UNITED STATES TAXATION OF FOREIGN TRUSTS

UNITED STATES TAXATION OF FOREIGN TRUSTS

by
Charles M. Bruce

KLUWER LAW INTERNATIONAL
The Hague • London • Boston

Published by Kluwer Law International,
P.O. Box 85889, 2508 CN The Hague, The Netherlands.

Sold and distributed in the U.S.A. and Canada
by Kluwer Law International,
675 Massachusetts Avenue, Cambridge, MA 02139, U.S.A.
tel: (617) 354-0140; fax: (617) 354-8595

In all other countries, sold and distributed
by Kluwer Law International,
P.O. Box 85889, 2508 CN The Hague, The Netherlands
tel: 31 70 308 1562; fax: 31 70 308 1555

Library of Congress Cataloging-in-Publication Data

Bruce, Charles M.
United States taxation of foreign trusts / by Charles M. Bruce.
p. cm.
Includes index.
ISBN 9041193820 (alk. paper)
1. Foreign trusts--Taxation--United States. 2. Investments, Foreign--Taxation--Law and legislation--United States. 3. Foreign trusts--Taxation. 4. Investments, Foreign--Taxation. I. Title.

KF6443.B78 2000
336.2'76--dc21

99-086143

ISBN 9041193820

Kluwer Law International incorporates the publishing programs of Graham & Trotman Ltd, Kluwer Law and Taxation Publishers, and Martinus Nijhoff Publishers.

For Dianne, Laura and Mary

"Nobody surely would read a book on trout fishing unless they were either daft about it or wanted to learn about it, or were making a study of this particular abnormality for medical purposes and wanted to be better documented about its symptoms."

J.I. Hall, FISHING A HIGHLAND STREAM (Viking, 1960), p. 86.

ABOUT THE AUTHOR

Charles M. Bruce practices law with the Washington, D.C.-based firm of Moore & Bruce, LLP. His practice is comprised of international tax planning and compliance matters for non-U.S. and U.S. clients, transactions—including equity and debt placements—having international aspects, representation of private clients, and international tax legislative and regulatory projects. At various times he was Adjunct Professor of Law, Graduate Law Program, Georgetown University Law Center; Chairman, Annual Institute on Multinational Taxation, (sponsored by Georgetown University Law Center and the Chamber of Commerce of the U.S.); Visiting Professor, Institut für Ausländisches und Internationales Finanz- und Steuerwesen, Hamburg University, Hamburg, Germany; Attorney-Advisor (Law Clerk), Judge Howard A. Dawson, Jr., United States Tax Court. From 1977 to 1979, he served as Tax Counsel at the United States Senate Finance Committee. Currently he chairs the Subcommittee on Foreign Sales Corporations/Domestic International Sales Corporations of the American Bar Association, Section of Taxation, Committee on Foreign Activities of U.S. Taxpayers; and from 1996-1997, he chaired the Task Force on International Trusts of that Committee.

He has authored or edited a number of books and articles including: "Liquidations and Reorganizations; Madison Square Garden and Kass," 30 TAX LAW REVIEW 303 (1975); "Taxation of the International Seabed," Introductory Notes to IFA Seminar Paper, (Kluwer, 1981); "U.S. Taxation of Foreign Trusts: Post-1976 Act Changes and Continued Uses," 17 TMIJ 192 (1988); "Protection of Assets Trusts," TRUSTS & ESTATES (Nov. & Dec. 1991) (Co-author); Tax Management Portfolio, 264-4th, FOREIGN SALES CORPORATIONS (1988). (Co-author); (U.S. Reporter); "Constraints On Cross Border Takeovers And Mergers," A Report by The Section on Business Law, International Bar Association for International Capital Markets Group, reprinted in INT'L BUS. LAWYER (Feb. 1991). U.S. IRS INTERNATIONAL TAX COMPLIANCE INFORMATION (6 Volume Treatise; Kluwer, 1992) (Editor).

Table of Contents

Preface

This first edition of UNITED STATES TAXATION OF FOREIGN TRUSTS presents the basic rules for taxation of foreign trusts under the U.S. tax system. These materials are intended to be useful for a number of categories of readers including tax practitioners, accountants, tax return preparers, trust officers, investment advisers, private bankers, and students. Some readers, it is assumed, will have had little or no prior exposure to the law of trusts and agency; others will not have had a great deal of experience with U.S. tax principles.

The term "trust" is found in a number of contexts, and it has a number of meanings. A little time is spent describing some of the different situations where trusts appear and giving some background information. This subject is covered more comprehensively in treatises and law review articles dealing only with the origins and workings of trusts. Since the history of the development of trusts in itself is interesting and illuminates some of the uses of trusts today, it is recommended that the reader spend some time with these sources.

As some topics, such as deferred compensation arrangements and charitable—or public—trusts deserve a detailed treatment and yet many readers will not want to spend the time delving into them, they are deliberately set aside for another day.

An attempt is made to step back a few paces from the subject of trust taxation and simply describe a few types of foreign trust. Hopefully this will permit the reader to have some glimmer of the object before heading into the thicket of rules and definitions.

The taxation of foreign trusts under the U.S. Internal Revenue Code has changed radically over the last 25 or so years. With some tax subjects, it is not very useful to look at the now-outdated rules applicable during prior periods. With trusts, however, it is common to find oneself dealing with a trust that has been in existence for many years; and, therefore, one can easily find himself faced with the task of applying one set of rules to one period, another to the next period and still another to the period following that. While it might be cumbersome to say too much about rules that have been amended, it is useful, perhaps, to give a little information.

The "meat and potatoes" of this subject are the rules applicable to regular nongrantor (accumulation) trusts and so-called "grantor trusts." It is curious that, with nongrantor trusts, the most challenging rules—the "throwback rules"—since 1997 only apply to foreign trusts. Almost as curious, as regards grantor trusts, the rules ignoring the trust and treating the grantor as the owner of the trust assets generally apply only to domestic trusts, not to foreign trusts; but there remain several very important exceptions.

There are about a dozen special rules aimed at foreign trusts; and these are explored in some detail. Some of the fallout from these provisions will have to await regulations and case law. Some regulations have been issued in final form, others in temporary or proposed form. This writing was completed after the publication of T.D. 8831, released August 5, 1999 and published in the Federal Register on August 10, 1999.

Certainly it is fair to say that the taxation of foreign trusts is a subject unto itself—for reasons that will unfold.

I suppose many subjects have their tricky side; and with foreign trusts the tricky business comes with the reporting and penalty provisions and the accompanying IRS forms. Since these provisions are quite new, the feeling is generally that of taking the first ride on a recently rebuilt roller coaster. It's not all smooth riding at this point. Nonetheless, my guess is that a significant percentage of the readers will have come to this book looking for help after having taken a quick spin through these forms and the accompanying instructions. Chapters 15 and 16, which deal with the forms, are based on the 1998 Forms 3520 and 3520-A. The 1999 Forms are substantively the same.

Lastly, we turn to the difficult matter of compliance, audits and the like. A word or two are thrown in about large gift reporting and issues surrounding the in-coming immigrant and out-going expatriate.

Examples are used wherever it is thought useful. This is the case especially where the rules get a little thick, and it is helpful, in effect, to paint a picture.

All statutory references are to the Internal Revenue Code of 1986, as amended, unless otherwise noted. Citations in the text and points of limited interest are kept to a minimum; and, therefore, a good deal of information is pushed to the footnotes.

Let me offer this observation: As with much of U.S. tax law, the person struggling to understand it is best advised to start off studying the score—*i.e.*, the text of the statute—very carefully. Even with the "hacking away" that took place in the Small Business Job Protection Act of 1996, the score still has a good deal of consistency and symmetry. The big themes and the artistry of dealing with the provisions only come after developing a familiarity with the text. The early part can be boring for people with high thresholds for entertainment, unlike some of us; but the later stages can be rewarding and a little fun.

Special thanks go to Robert Wade of Jester & Reed, CPAs (Annandale, VA) for help with the description of the forms (Forms 3520, especially Part III, 3520-A, 4970, 1040NR, and 1041, including Schedule J) and the presentation of the examples that appear in Chapter 16. As is explained, when dealing with a foreign nongrantor (accumulation) trust, it is not possible simply to use "off the rack" return preparation software. Also, the forms themselves, should you try to prepare them by hand, are very difficult to follow. In fact, they do not parse well at all. What is necessary, in many instances, is to prepare a spreadsheet that mimics the forms but that modifies them—all in a way that follows the rules in the statute, regulations (though much of this subject has not been addressed in regulations), IRS Notices, etc. These materials would not have been possible without Robert Wade's thoughtful assistance. He helped develop a spreadsheet; and he ran the computations through mock returns.

I am indebted to John Berger at Kluwer Law International for his editorial assistance, to Timothy Hawkins and Fern Inglefield, of Bermuda Trust Company Limited, and my partner Jonathon R. Moore for their many useful thoughts on the subject in general and to Antoinette M. Elgart for her help in preparing the manuscript. Dan

Gray with Crown World Services shared some thoughts about insurance products.

This Guide draws upon materials appearing in articles by the author on the Tax Reform Act of 1976 and the Small Business Job Protection Act of 1996.

Any errors or omissions, of course, are solely the responsibility of the author and should not be attributed to any other person or group.

I would be very grateful if anyone finding a mistake or having a comment on some point were to send me a message at **cbruce@mooreandbruce.com**.

Readers can check for updated information at http://www.lawyers.com/moore&brucellp.

Charles M. Bruce
Washington, D.C.

December 1999

Chapter 1

Introduction

1.1 Introduction

This Guide provides an overview of U.S. tax and reporting rules relating to "foreign"—that is, "non-U.S."—trusts.[1] These rules affect various persons involved in some fashion with a foreign trust, including the settlor (the person who creates the trust by transferring property to the trustee to be held in trust for the benefit of the beneficiaries), the beneficiaries (the persons who are to benefit in one way or the other from the trust) and the trustee (the person—usually a professional trust company—that acts in a fiduciary capacity in holding the trust property and carrying out the terms of the trust).[2]

Not addressed at any length are foreign charitable trusts or trusts having to do with compensation or deferred compensation, such as pension plans.

---

[1] "Foreign" in this context means non-U.S. The definition of "United States person" in section 7701(a)(30) makes clear that any trust is a U.S. trust if a court within the U.S. is able to exercise primary supervision over the administration of the trust and one or more U.S. persons have the authority to control all substantial decisions of the trust.

[2] A detailed discussion of the workings of a trust and the non-tax laws applying to trusts is beyond the scope of this Guide. In the case of a normal trust created under, for example, the laws of Bermuda, there will be Bermuda statutory law that applies to the trust and the trustee and Bermuda and other case law that can apply as well. There are many cases in the various common law jurisdictions around the world that make up the body of precedents defining the workings of a common law trust. *See, e.g.*, Frans Sonneveldt & Harrie L. van Mens, THE TRUST: BRIDGE OR ABYSS BETWEEN COMMON AND CIVIL LAW JURISDICTIONS? (Frans Sonneveldt & Harrie L. van Mens eds., Kluwer 1992). Also, the tax rules of jurisdictions other than the United States are not addressed herein. For a useful introduction to these rules, see IFA CONGRESS SEMINAR SERIES, INTERNATIONAL TAX TREATMENT OF COMMON LAW TRUSTS (Proceedings of a Seminar held in New York in 1986 during the 40th Congress of the International Fiscal Association, Kluwer, 1988).

The substantive U.S. tax rules applicable to the trusts generally appear in Subchapter J, Part I (sections 641-679 of Internal Revenue Code of 1986, as amended ("Code").[3]) The reporting rules, which complement the substantive rules, appear in section 6048 (relating to information with respect to certain foreign trusts; which section appears with other rules relating to information returns) and section 6677 (relating to failure to file information with respect to certain foreign trusts; which section appears with other provisions having to do with assessable penalties).

> ➔ U.S. settlors and beneficiaries will want to pay particular attention to the reporting rules.

The applicable provisions can appear not only in the statute, but also in regulations promulgated under the various statutory provisions, revenue rulings and similar pronouncements by the IRS, and case law. (The statutory provisions are sprinkled throughout the Code. For example, the provisions defining U.S. trust and foreign trust appear in the definitional rules in section 7701.) Unofficial authority, such as IRS Training Materials and treatises, can provide additional insight.

The U.S. has enacted two major amendments to its tax laws applicable to foreign trusts—one in 1976 and the other in 1996.[4] There have also been a number of minor or technical amendments. Regulations explaining the 1996 Act amendments have begun to be promulgated. Also, the Internal Revenue Service, in its 1999 Priority Guidance Plan, has stated that issuing guidance on foreign trusts is a priority task. It can be anticipated that, among other things, the Service may promulgate regulations under new section 642(a)(7) dealing with abusive transactions, which section provides that "[t]he Secretary shall prescribe such regulations as may be necessary or appropriate to carry out the purposes of the part, including regulations to prevent avoidance of such purposes."

U.S. settlors and beneficiaries should be aware that the IRS may audit foreign trusts that were created by or that benefit U.S. persons.

---

[3] All statutory references are to the Internal Revenue Code of 1986, as amended, unless otherwise noted.

[4] Tax Reform Act of 1976 (P.L. 94-455); Small Business Job Protection Act of 1996 (P.L. 104-188).

Also, the IRS has announced that it will scrutinize what is termed "abusive foreign trust arrangements."[5]

In 1997, there were approximately 2,384,000 Forms 1041 and 1041S filed. The government estimates that this figure will slowly drop to around 1,817,000 by 2005.[6] The reason for the reduction is the change in the tax rate structure that is unfavorable for trusts. A very high percentage of these forms undoubtedly relates to domestic trusts. It is not yet known how many Forms 2530 and 2530-A will be filed; and how many of them will include information with respect to distributions from a foreign nongrantor trust.

As will be seen, the basic rules for taxing trusts and beneficiaries are "friendly" toward taxpayers. They are intended, among other things, simply to allocate tax burdens between trusts and beneficiaries, so as to ensure that income is not taxed twice and tax benefits, much as deductions, are not wasted. The special tax rules aimed at foreign trusts and their U.S. beneficiaries are plainly not "friendly" toward taxpayers, and yet they sit on top of the basic rules. This situation results in a number of abnormalities, which will be pointed out along the way.

---

[5] IRS Assistant Commissioner (International) John T. Lyons recently commented on this development. He said that the Service will take a harder stance on what he calls the explosion in the use of trusts, both domestic and foreign, for tax avoidance and evasion, which he called an emerging compliance problem. "The IRS is increasing the amount of resources devoted to this problem, he said, including undertaking education and outreach programs and cultivating relationships with practitioners to identify promoters. Also, the IRS Criminal Investigation Division has a specific initiative in this area, which a national field executive has been named to oversee. Lyons warned that the IRS believes that taxpayers should take responsibility for their own actions and that they may suffer civil and criminal consequences if they become involved in fraudulent activities." Tax Analysts Tax Notes Today, 1999 TNT 10-1. Also, Dale Hart, an IRS Regional Commissioner and the field executive in charge of trusts, has commented that about 150 additional revenue agents will be trained in this subject in 2000. "The IRS intensifies its scrutiny of "abusive" trusts," WSJ Oct. 13, 1999, p. 1.

[6] Zaffino, "Projections of Returns to Be Filed in Cal. Years 1999-2005," <http://www.irs.ustreas.gov/prod/tax_stats/soi/other_nr.html> (visited July 27, 1999). *See also* 1997 Internal Revenue Service Data Book, Publication 55B, Table 7 (Number of Returns Filed).

1.2 How to use this guide

The brief history of trusts (Chapter 2) and discussion of the definitions of trust and foreign trust (Chapter 3) can be viewed as background information. This part is short and should probably be read or "skimmed."

The discussion of different types of trusts (Chapter 4) is intended to introduce some of the terminology and concepts. It also can be "skimmed."

Starting with Chapter 5, the reader is given an overview of the U.S. tax rules applicable to foreign trusts. Much of this information applies to domestic as well as foreign trusts. Some rules, such as the "throwback" rules, as will be seen, no longer apply to domestic trusts; they only apply to foreign trusts. This discussion of the substantive rules—as opposed to reporting and penalty rules—covers Nongrantor Trusts: Simple (Chapter 6), Nongrantor Trusts: Complex; Throwback Rules (Chapter 7), Grantor Trusts (Chapter 8) and Special Rules Applicable To Foreign Trusts (Chapter 9). This part is intended for readers that are interested in a summary of the substantive rules.

In Chapters 10 and 11, the Tax Reform Act of 1976 and the Small Business Job Protection Act of 1996 are discussed in detail. These are the two major pieces of tax legislation affecting foreign trusts. The latter, the 1996 Act, is still being explained in regulations and other Treasury Department and IRS pronouncements. It is possible to learn about the taxation of foreign trusts based simply upon the materials contained in Chapters 5 through 9. However, a careful examination of the 1976 Act and 1996 Act can be very helpful. Also, many trusts in existence today "lived through" these two Acts. Therefore, when deciding how to deal with one of these trusts, it is essential to look at these two prior amendments to the law.[7]

---

[7] Chapter 10 is drawn from the author's 1988 article on the subject. Bruce, "U.S. Taxation of Foreign Trusts: Post-1976 Act Changes and Continued Uses," 17 TMIJ 192 (1988). Chapter 11 is comprised largely of Congressional materials and commentary presented by the author in 1995 at the time the Administration announced proposals that ultimately became the Small Business Job Protection Act of 1996. Remarks by Charles M. Bruce

Chapter 12 highlights some of the effective dates and transition rules that were enacted at the time of the 1996 Act. This part need not be considered if the reader believes that it is not relevant.

Chapter 13 deals with a particular type of foreign trust, called a Protection of Assets trust.

Since foreign trusts frequently own all or some portion of entities, some of the tax consequences of a couple of the more common structures are discussed in Chapter 14. Again, this part is not required if it is not somehow relevant to matters at hand.

One of the most important subjects relating to foreign trusts is reporting. The subject of penalties is tied to the subject of reporting. Chapter 15 is intended to provide a detailed treatment of these subjects.

Chapter 16 discusses the forms that flow from the reporting requirements in the Internal Revenue Code. This part may well be the most important part; and therefore, while a little dry, it is highly recommended.

Chapter 17 discusses the important issue of compliance. In this context, perhaps a better word would be "enforcement." This chapter is intended to explain how the U.S. tax authorities might initiate and conduct an examination of a U.S. taxpayer who is somehow connected with a foreign trust. This part can be read or skipped.

It seems that there are two additional matters that deserve comment. One is the reporting of large gifts by U.S. persons who receive those gifts. The second is the effects of the presence of a foreign trust on individuals immigrating to or expatriating from the U.S., including, as to the latter, long-term U.S. residents. The third is what happens when the grantor of a foreign trust dies. This material can be skipped if it appears unnecessary.

---

to the International Fiscal Association—Bermuda Branch, February 27, 1995, in Hamilton, Bermuda.

Chapter 2

Brief History of Trusts

Before turning to the details of the taxation of foreign trusts under the U.S. Internal Revenue Code and the United States' treaty network and the definitions that necessarily underlie the rules, it may be useful to look briefly at the origins of trusts and some of their early uses.

Few people have a good understanding of trusts, how they work and their uses. Even attorneys—especially those that do not deal with estate planning—may be unfamiliar with the subject. Certainly most settlors and beneficiaries know very little about trusts.

The average person simply does not come in contact with trusts on a regular basis. An individual might encounter them in a pension or other type of deferred compensation plan; but he or she almost certainly has not focused on the workings of the trust that probably embodies the plan. There may be references to different types of trust in an individual's will; but again, that individual probably has not delved into the actual structure and workings of the trust entity. Also, people are generally unclear about the differences between a trust and a bailment, or a trust and an escrow account, or a trust and other arrangements for holding property.

Most people are much more familiar with corporations than they are with trusts.

Also, the fact that there are seemingly so many different trusts in different jurisdictions around a world is confusing. What is the difference between a common law trust and a civil law trust, between a common law trust and a civil law foundation, a regular common law trust and a purpose trust created pursuant to a specific statute, and so forth?

For a variety of reasons, a U.S. person may find him- or herself in contact with a foreign trust; and the pitfall, frequently tripped upon, is assuming that this trust is just like some form of trust that exists in that person's experience in the U.S. There may indeed be many similarities. This is not to say, however, that surprising little differences do not lurk among the pages. Also, the legal system in which the foreign trust sits is undoubtedly different in many subtle and not-so-subtle ways from the American legal system

As will be seen, not all trusts are alike. Also, an entity that is a trust under the laws of one country might be something else—or simply ignored—under the laws of another. For example, a perfectly fine Bermuda trust, which might properly be characterized as a common law trust, might be nothing—that is, it would be ignored—in Switzerland.[8]

The history of trusts shows that some of the uses to which trusts were put eight or nine hundred years ago are not very much different from the uses today. Individuals then were commonly trying to arrange the holding of their property so as to avoid some detriment.

When one looks at the history of trusts and their uses, one is struck by how flexible the concept is.

It is also interesting to note how trusts have evolved over time – reacting to sudden events as well as slow-moving developments in society. As a general matter, whenever arrangements for the holding of property or a particular use of trusts becomes too out of step or too aggressive, there seems always to have been a reaction.

Perhaps some uses of trusts today have become so aggressive and "nonstandard" that the pendulum is beginning to swing back in the other direction. Courts and careful legal advisers might be envisioned as sitting astride that pendulum.

---

[8] *See* International Tax Treatment of Common Law Trusts, proceedings of a seminar held in New York in 1986 during the 40th Congress of the International Fiscal Association, Kluwer. "The concept of trust does not exist under Swiss civil law and no specific tax provision governing trusts is found in the federal and cantonal income and net worth tax laws. . . . Trusts are, therefore, not treated as a separate taxpayer and are not subject to tax *per se*. Trustees are exempt from tax as are nominee owners under Swiss tax laws. Beneficiaries are taxed according to their rights in the trust." Remarks by P. Gillioz at p. 39.

The development of protection of assets trusts, which first saw the light of day in 1979 and then became "popularized" in the mid-1980s, it might be said, is the most significant event in the recent history of trusts. While in principle there is nothing wrong with the use of a trust located outside the settlor's home jurisdiction to provide a measure of protection from a variety of risks, the use obviously can be pushed to an overly aggressive degree. In fact, a large number of things can go awry. The history of trusts shows that whenever a particular use becomes too aggressive or too far afield of normal practices, there is a reaction. This reaction can come in the form of legislation, like the Statute of Uses in 1536[9], or more likely, case law, such as the *Orange Grove* cases.[10] When this happens, settlors and their advisers need to "get back to basics."

It is frequently said that trusts arose when knights rode off on the Crusades and needed a way for their property to be overseen in their absence and perhaps dealt with in the event that they did not return. This is a little simplistic.[11] Also, it might be more accurate to say that religious orders wanted to control land and premises and landowners wanted to dodge onerous feudal burdens.

It is generally accepted that the precursors of trusts are to be found alongside the precursors of bailments, with the development of the concept of "use, trust or confidence." The concept of use is said by some to be traceable to the *Treuhand* or *Salman* in early Continental (German) law, perhaps modified by Roman law notions

---

[9] 27 Hen. VIII, c. 10.

[10] 515 South Orange Grove Owners Association and Others v. Orange Grove Partners and Others (No. 1)(1995) No. 208/94) and 515 South Orange Grove Owners Association and Others v. Orange Prove Partners and Others (No. 2)(1995) No. 1997/98 1 OFLR 3. See also Bruce and Wojewodzki, "Will the Orange Grove Case Have a Long-Term Impact on Cook Islands Asset Protection Trust Law?," Vol. 2, No. 3, JOURNAL OF ASSET PROTECTION (Jan./Feb. 1997).

[11] Maitland does cite one case where "R, who is going to the Holy Land, commits his land to his brother W to keep to the use of his (R's) sons (*commisit terram illam W ad opus puerorum suorum*); on R's death his eldest son demands the land from W, who refuses to surrender it; a suit between them in a seigniorial court is compromised; each of them is to have half the land." Bracton's Note Book, p. 999 (A.D. 1224), cited at Maitland, "The Origins of Uses," VIII HARV. L. REV. (1894), p. 133.

of faith (*fides*). This person acted as an executor who had the obligation to carry out the instructor's directions, as a matter of honor and faith. This obligation might include seeing to it that legacies and the like were paid if the heirs acted contrary to the decedent's instructions. This executor might covenant to do so and might take an oath.

While it is often said that uses were introduced into England shortly after the Norman Conquest (1066 AD), the concept may well predate that event.[12]

Roman law apparently had no equivalent. On occasion a Roman would devise land to a Roman citizen with instructions that the person transfer it to a non-citizen or some other person not competently permitted to inherit the property in order to avoid laws prohibiting such a devise. However, the essence of the use and subsequently the trust—vesting legal ownership in one person while retaining an equitable or beneficial interest in another—was not known in Roman law.[13]

---

[12] The English word use, according to Maitland, is derived from the Latin word *opus*, meaning work, labor, or the product of work or labor, or, in Old French, *os* or *oes*. Thus in ancient times, a person, such as a sheriff, would receive money or goods to the use (*ad opus*) of the King. "Further, long before the Norman Conquest we may find a man saying that he conveys land to a bishop to the use of a church, or conveys land to a church to the use of a dead saint." F. W. Maitland, "The Origin of Uses," 8 HARV. L. REV. 3, p. 128 (1894). Interestingly, the concept of agent did not exist at this early time; an individual received money or other property not as agent for another, such as the King, but to the use of that other person (*ad opus Rex*). *See also*, Bogert, TRUSTS (Sixth Ed.), p. 6.

[13] Advisors in civil law jurisdictions frequently have difficulty dealing with trust issues simply because they are generally unfamiliar with the entity. A number of civil law jurisdictions have adopted statutes that provide for something that looks and behaves very much like a common law trust. For a discussion of civil law concepts, see Lepaulle, "Civil Law Substitutes for Trusts," YALE LAW J., p. 1126-1147 (Convoluted approaches to creating a trust-like entity "need not be used since the civil law affords a technique which achieves the same practical results in a more direct and easy way. We refer to the *fiducia*, which has been considered so much like the trust that it has been used as its French translation in the province of Quebec. Curiously enough, the civil law has not understood all the advantages that could be derived from the use of the *fiducia*. While it is now nearly forgotten by

In its earliest forms, there were two classes of relationship referred to as trusts: active (or special) trusts, and passive (or general, or simple) trusts. The latter category, which was much more common, was originally referred to as a "use." An active trust was generally for a limited duration and required the trustee to perform some actual activities or function with respect to the property. For example, an active trust is: A transfers land to B for B to cultivate and to apply the income for the benefit of C. A use, on the other hand, conferred legal title upon a person without requiring him to perform any activities with respect thereto. For example, a passive trust is: A transfers land to B for B to hold for the benefit of C; C occupies the property, cultivates the land and benefits from the income.

Trusts of all types, but especially passive trusts (uses) evolved as a means of devolving land to younger generations. They also served as a device to avoid a number of burdens and impediments.

It will be recalled that England was a feudal society. The King possessed certain rights, and his lords and vassals bore many duties.

Real property could not be conveyed by will. Therefore, a landowner might convey land to a feoffee, retaining a use for himself, and designating his son as beneficiary.

Ownership of land was subject to many responsibilities and burdens. These feudal burdens included payments exacted on various

---

textwriters and practitioners, it is not dead, and has recently been recognized by courts as perfectly legal. . . . *Fiducia* is the real substitute for a trust; it is its twin institution, since not only are the same functions filled by it, but the same methods are used to achieve them. In both there is a transfer of property to one who has the legal title but derives no personal advantage from it, and who must manage the property for the benefit of someone else, while his own creditors cannot attach it. While, however, the trust is now a thoroughly developed device, and the rights and duties of each party to it are well settled, the *fiducia* has never been of great importance in civil law countries – except in the province of Quebec – and the rights and liabilities arising under it are far from being precisely determined. Hence we conclude that in the *fiducia* the civil law has a legal technique which can easily be developed along the same lines as the trust, if textwriters and practitioners are far-sighted enough to perceive what can be done with it.")

occasions; for example, an "inheritance tax" was imposed when an heir formally inherited the land (when he reached the age of majority if he inherited as a minor). The lord had the right of "wardship" and "marriage" if the heir to property under his control was a minor. The lord frequently required special payments when his eldest son was knighted, when his eldest daughter was married, or—if the lord were captured in battle—when ransom was demanded.[14] Landowners could be required to provide men and arms.

Because these burdens attached to the legal title in the land, they generally could be avoided by transferring to (efeoffing) another of legal title and reserving only the use. "The legal ownership, however, represented by the feoffee to uses, was subject to the incidents of tenure, which could be enforced against the land, but by vesting this seisin in two or more feoffees jointly, whose number was renewed from time to time, and the survivor of whom took the whole legal estate, the burdens incident to the descent of land were generally avoided."[15]

Because during this period the division of legal and beneficial title was not recognized by the common law, there was no recourse for a creditor if the debtor transferred legal title to another, while retaining a beneficial interest.

Likewise, a person who feared that his land would be seized as punishment for a crime against the King could transfer it to a feoffee to uses; the law would not recognize an interest retained by him; and thus he would avoid forfeiture of his land.

Because the marital rights of dower and curtesy only attached to an individual's legal estate, a husband could prevent his wife from attaching a dower interest if before his marriage he conveyed the land to a feoffee.

Without doubt, the development of uses and trusts was spurred by the position of the church and the various religious orders.

---

[14] Ransom was a common form of reparation together with other spoils.

[15] Tiffany, REAL PROPERTY, p. 200.

> In the early years of the thirteenth century the Franciscan friars came hither. The law of their being forbade them to own anything; but they needed at least some poor dormitory, and the faithful were soon offering them houses in abundance. A remarkable plan was adopted. They had come as missionaries to the towns; the benefactor who was minded to give them a house, would convey that house to the borough community "to the use of" or "as an inhabitation for" the friars. Already when Bracton was writing, a considerable number of plots of land in London had been conveyed to the city for the benefit of the Franciscans. The corporation was becoming a trustee. It is an old doctrine that the inventors of "the use" were "the clergy" or "the monks." We should be near the truth if we said that to all seeming the first persons who in England employed "the use" on a large scale were, not the clergy, nor the monks, but the friars of St. Francis.

Maitland, "The Origins of Uses," VIII HARV.L.REV, p. 130.

Finally, it was simply easier to convey a beneficial interest. A legal title could only be conveyed by livery of seisin, fine, or recovery, and was required to be published in one way or another. A use could be created much more quietly and its existence hidden from view.

As regards money and chattels, but not land, the concept of use apparently did not develop with the same particularity as it did with respect to land. Perhaps the fact that money and chattels could easily be reduced to possession was important; or the more rigid customs that attached to the ownership of land may have played a role. In any event, the relationship expressed by the concept of use, or *ad opus*, over time evolved into the form of agency. "In this region the phrase will appear in our own day as expressing rights and duties which the common law can protect and enforce without the help of an 'equity.'

The common law will know the wrong that is committed when a man 'converts to his use' (*ad opus suum proprium*) the goods of another; and in course of time it will know the obligation which arises when money is 'had and received to the use' of some person other than the recipient."[16]

Land, it seems, was generally regarded in a very different light. It was common, apparently, for a person (called a feoffor) to grant land to another (called a feoffee) to the use of the *cestui que use*; and the feoffee was bound in conscience to hold the lands according to the use. He himself could not derive a benefit therefrom. Such arrangements, or feoffments, might benefit a third party or the feoffor. It is generally conceded that "the feoffee to uses, down to the beginning of the fifteenth century, was the German Salman or Treuhand under another name."[17] Bequests of personalty were enforced routinely against executors (feoffees) in the ecclesiastical courts. It would appear, however, that the same types of suits were not prosecuted against executors by devisees of land.[18] Rather it is thought that the King had jurisdiction over such matters; and the ecclesiastical courts were without any power to execute their orders. *Cestuis que use* under a feoffment would pray that the foeffee to a use be summoned to answer in the King's Chancery, which was regarded as the court of conscience since the plaintiff could not have a remedy by the law of the Holy Church nor by the common law.[19] Then, beginning in the reign of Edward I (1272-1307), the devisee could recover land devised to him by a real action in the local common law courts. What apparently did not exist during the period generally

[16] Maitland, "The Origins of Uses," VIII HARV.L. REV., p. 129. 129.

[17] James Barr Ames, "The Origins of Uses and Trusts," Equity p. 740.

[18] On this point there is a disagreement between Justice Holmes and Professor Ames. *See* Holmes, "Early English Equity," Equity, Chapter 41, and James Barr Ames, "The Origins of Uses and Trusts," Equity, Chapter 43. It is possible that in rare instances a feoffor or his heirs pursued before an ecclesiastical court a feoffee to uses on the feoffee's covenant to perform the use; but this probably would not have been an action to enforce the use but to recover the land; it is likely that most feoffors did not extract a form of covenant or oath that could be held up to a court but instead relied upon faithfulness or fidelity of the person making the undertaking.

[19] *Horsmonger v. Pympe*, 10 Seld. Soc., Sel. Cas. Ch. No. 123 (undated but early petition, cited in James Barr Ames, "The Origins of Uses and Trusts," Equity p. 740, footnote 3).

from the latter part of the twelfth century to the early part of the fifteenth century was a right in the *cestui que use* to enforce some form of right against the feoffee and in doing so to enforce the use.

Then in the reign of Henry V (1413-1422) the first decrees issued in favor of the *cestui que use.* These decrees were issued by the Court of Chancery. The Court of Chancery arose over time due to the cumbersome nature and rigidities of the common law courts. Pleadings in the common law courts had become enormously stultified especially as the practice grew of publishing them, as was begun in the reign of Edward I with the dissemination of Year Books; and difficult cases that did not fit within the pleading forms were not being addressed but instead were being referred to Parliament (referred to in early times as the Great Council). This body commonly acted as a judicial body that could itself dispose of the case, or refer it elsewhere, including the Common Law Courts, or enact a new law. Special petitions were being laid before the King and his Council (or Select Council). Some petitions were being referred to the Chancellor, who by 1473, late in the reign of Edward III, was issuing decrees in his own name. In this manner the Court of Chancery came into being as "a distinct court for giving relief in cases which required Extraordinary remedies."[20] These matters were ones where petitioners could not get a remedy in the common law courts although they were entitled to such a remedy; and the Court of Chancery, deriving its authority from the King's royal prerogative, was empowered with a general authority to give relief in all matters of whatsoever nature requiring the exercise of that prerogative.

[20] Spence, "The Court Of Chancery," p. 236.

> In these cases, the Chancellor judged on an ad hoc basis granting specific remedies in the form of decrees. Only the parties involved were bound, or, put otherwise in the words of a famous maxim *equity acts in personam*. Over the years a new system of law developed known as equity—'supplementary law, a sort of appendix added on to our code, or a sort of gloss written round our code, an appendix, a gloss, which used to be administered by courts specially designed for that purpose.' It may be defined as the body of rules developed to mitigate the rigour of the common law.

Frans Sonneveldt & Harrie L. van Mens, THE TRUST BRIDGE OR ABYSS BETWEEN COMMON AND CIVIL LAW JURISDICTIONS?, (1992, Kluwer) at p. 2.

> The King [Edward III, who ruled for 50 years] being, as may well be conceived, looking to the history of his busy reign, unable from his other avocations to attend to the numerous petitions which were presented to him, he, in the twenty-second year of his reign, by a writ or ordinance referred all such matter as were *of Grace*, to be dispatched by the Chancellor or by the Keeper of the privy seal.
>
> The establishment of the Court of Chancery as a regular court for administering extraordinary relief, is generally considered to have been mainly attributable to this or some similar ordinance. It will be observed, that it conferred a general authority to give relief in all matters of what nature soever requiring the exercise of the Prerogative of Grace—differing from the authority on which the jurisdiction of the courts of common law was founded; for there the court held jurisdiction, in each particular case, by virtue of the delegation conferred by the particular writ, and which could only be issued in cases provided for by positive law. This is one of the great and fundamental distinctions

> between the jurisdiction of the courts of common law and that of the Court of Chancery.[21]

Interestingly, only before the Council or the Chancellor, or later, in the Court of Chancery, but not in the Common Law Courts, could the parties be examined under oath.

There was no relief for the *cestui que use* at common law, because it viewed the *feoffee* as the owner of the land. But the Chancellor or the Court of Chancery could not abide the injustice of a feoffee retaining land for himself even though he had received the land upon the faith—the sworn undertaking and pledge—that he would deal with it for the benefit of the *cestui qui use*. "But in the absence of a statute the only remedy for the injustice of disloyal feoffees to uses was to compel them to convey the title to the *cestui que use* or hold it for his benefit. Accordingly the right of the *cestui que trust* was worked out by enforcing the doctrine of personal obedience."[22]

> The first decree for a *cestui que use*, whenever it was given [probably around 1146], was the birth of the equitable use in land. Before that first decree there was and could be no doctrine of uses. . . . But the transformation of the honorary obligation of the feoffee into a legal obligation was purely an English development.

James Barr Ames, "The Origins of Uses and Trusts," Equity p. 742.

Over a period of several hundred years, uses became widespread. Large amounts of land were held in this form. Also, it will be noted, the *cestui que use* ordinarily had possession. "When the use was 'divided' from the seisin the *cestui* usually had possession, that tangible element of property which at that day, even more than now, approximated ownership."[23]

---

[21] Spence, "The Court of Chancery," p. 236.

[22] James Barr Ames, "The Origins of Uses and Trusts," Equity pp. 741-742.

[23] Note, "The Statute of Uses and Active Trusts," 17 MICHIGAN LAW REV. 87, at p. 89.

At first, the fact that trusts were not enforceable in the common law courts caused unjust results and slowed their adoption. With more frequent use for the benefit of the religious orders and recognition before the Chancellor and the Chancery Courts, their popularity grew. The beneficiary's interest began to be recognized as a form of ownership, enforceable against the trustee's heirs, purchasers with notice of the interest, and the recipients of the property as a gift. Only a *bona fide* purchaser without notice of the interest could take the property protected against claims of the beneficiary.

As uses became more prevalent and could be enforced, however, the fact that they were often used to avoid legal duties offended the King (be he King Richard II (1377-1399), Henry V, Henry VI (and his regent), Edward IV, Richard III (1483-1485), Henry VII, or Henry VIII (1509-1547)) and his feudal lords. Also, sentiment against the Church in Rome built steadily. With this tide came an aversion to any references to Roman law; and indeed in the reign of Richard II, the judges prohibited it from being cited in the common law courts. Henry VIII wished to destroy the monasteries and confiscate their property.

Thus, in 1535, the Statute of Uses was enacted with the intent to abolish uses.[24] The Statute[25] abolished the estate of a feoffee to uses,

---

[24] This was the same year that Henry VIII caused his former High Chancellor Sir Thomas More to be beheaded for failing to take the Oath of Supremacy. This was also the time of the systematic plundering of the Catholic monasteries under the hand of Thomas Cromwell and Sir Thomas Pope's Court of Augmentation.

[25] 27 Henry VIII, c. 10. The Statute provides, in pertinent part: "That where any person or persons stand or be seized, or any time hereafter shall happen to be seized, of and in any honours, castles, manors, lands, tenements, rents, services, reversions, remainders or other hereditaments to the use, confidence or trust of any other person or persons, or of any body politick, by reason of any bargain, sale, feoffment, fine, recovery, covenant, contract, agreement, will or otherwise, by any manner means whatsoever it be; that in every such case all and every such person or persons, and bodies politick, that have or hereafter shall have such use, confidence or trust, in fee simple, fee tail, for term of life or for years, or otherwise, or any use, confidence or trust in remainder or reverter, shall from henceforth stand and be seized, deemed and adjudged in lawful seisin, estate and possession of and in the same honours, castles, manors, lands, tenements, rents, services, reversions, remainders and hereditaments, with their appurtenances to all intents,

and ordered that the beneficiary of a use should be given the legal estate, "executing the use." In this manner, Parliament believed it could abolish the use by destroying it at its inception.

The Statute failed remarkably in its intent, primarily due to strict interpretation by the common law courts. The Statute never mentioned personal property, but only interests in real property, when requiring that beneficial title be executed; and then it only spoke of cases where the feoffee to uses was "seized" of the property meaning in possession of a freehold interest as opposed to some other form of interest. Also, the courts interpreted the Statute as only applying to passive trusts, not to active trusts, reasoning that duties of administration required that the trustee have legal title. Thus, a conveyance to a trustee who was required to collect the profits of land and to pay them to the beneficiary would not be executed; legal and beneficial title would remain separate.

Most importantly, the court in *Tyrrel's* case, decided 10 years after Henry VIII's death, determined that the Statute could only operate once on any given conveyance.[26] Therefore, a use upon a use was not affected. In the following case, the Statute worked to execute the use and cause the feoffee to be seized of the land, tenement, etc.: "To A and his heirs, to the use of B and his heirs." But the Statute was not effective in executing the use in the following case: "To A and his heirs, to the use of B and his heirs, to the use of C and his heirs." The use of B was converted to possession and B was given the legal estate, but the use of C remained and was not in turn converted to possession, nor was B's legal estate destroyed. The court reasoned that because a use upon a use was void as a restriction on the fee conveyed, the second use could not be executed. Although it did not happen immediately, in less than a century courts began to

---

constructions and purposes in the law, of and in such like estates as they had or shall have in use, trust or confidence of or in the same; and that the estate, title, right and possession that was in such person or persons that were, or hereafter shall be seized of any lands, tenements or hereditaments, to the use, confidence or trust of any such person or persons, or of any body politick, be from henceforth clearly deemed and adjudged to be in him or them that have, or hereafter shall have, such use, confidence or trust, after such quality, manner, form and condition as they had before, in or to the use, confidence or trust that was in them."

[26] *Tyrrel's Case*, Dyer 155 (1557).

construe "to A and his heirs, to the use of B and his heirs, to the use of C and his heirs" as "to B and his heirs to the use of C and his heirs," creating an obvious means for avoiding the law.

Thus many forms of uses and trusts continued in existence and flourished. The courts of chancery began to refer to all these survivors of the Statute of Uses as trusts, and enforced the equitable interests of the *cestui qui use* or beneficiary. "[T]he interests thus supported by chancery after the Statute of Uses, and called 'trusts,' were composed of the old active or special trusts and that part of the old general trusts or uses which the Statute did not destroy. These interests are the modern trusts which form the basis of the present English and American systems."[27]

In the United States, trust law tends to be state law. There is no federal common law on the subject and no general federal statutes. A few federal statutes do influence trust law, however: the Employee Retirement Income Security Act of 1974 (ERISA) governs trusts established by employers to provide their employees with retirement benefits, federal banking laws govern the conduct of banks acting as trustees, and federal bankruptcy law will in some cases govern the conduct of trustees, trust settlors and trust beneficiaries.

Although the common law is still powerful, several states have begun to enact trust codes. Several Uniform Acts (the Uniform Fiduciaries Act; Uniform Principal and Income Act; Uniform Trustees Accounting Act; Uniform Trust Fund Act; Uniform Testamentary Additions to Trust Act; Model Prudent Man Investment Act; Uniform Trustees Powers Act; Uniform Probate Code) have been adopted to some extent by many states. The American Law Institute's Second Restatement of the Law of Trusts (1957) is often influential in the area.

A few states still have courts of chancery separate from ordinary law courts.

Outside the U.S., there is an enormous body of common law and equitable principles governing trusts. The very great majority of this law appears in the form of case decisions. While a number of

[27] Bogert, TRUSTS (Sixth Ed. 1987), p. 13.

countries have enacted statutes creating trust-like animals, most practitioners, given the choice, are in favour of creating trusts under common law—not civil law. Then if precedent is needed for some obscure reason, it can almost always be found someplace at some date in history.

As will be seen, a number of jurisdictions that have the common law have also enacted new forms of trust—that is, entities that share some trust characteristics but have different features as well.

Chapter 3

Definitions of Trust and Foreign Trust

3.1 In general

The term "trust" can be defined for a number of purposes, including non-tax and tax purposes. Also, different jurisdictions employ different definitions. For example, an entity that is a trust under English law might not be a trust under Canadian or Bermuda law. As a general rule, however, definitions employed in the various common law jurisdictions—such as the United Kingdom, the United States, Canada, Australia, New Zealand, and Bermuda—are quite similar.

In general, a trust is any arrangement whereby beneficial (equitable) title is held by one person or group of persons (the beneficiaries), and a fiduciary responsibility rests upon another (the trustee) to hold legal title and to conserve, protect and manage the property. The beneficiaries do not take part in the management of the assets. Also, the trustee often does not possess the express power to alter the form of investments to take advantage of changes in the marketplace.

The Restatement (Second) of Trusts defines trust as a "fiduciary relationship with respect to property, subjecting the person by whom the title to the property is held to equitable duties to deal with the property for the benefit of another person, which arises as a result of a manifestation of an intention to create it." The Restatement uses the term "express trust" to distinguish the normal trust from a so-called resulting trust or constructive trust. The term "private trust" is used in the Restatement to indicate a trust that is not a charitable or public trust. Speaking of "equitable interest," it is said:

> In a trust there is a separation of interests in the subject matter of the trust, the beneficiary having an equitable interest and the trustee having an interest which is normally a legal interest. An equitable interest is that kind of interest which has its origins in the principles, standards and rules develops by

> courts chancery. A legal interest is that kind of interest which has its origins in the principles, standards and rules developed by courts of common law as distinguished from courts chancery.
>
> The distinction between legal and equitable interests is due to the historical circumstance that these two kinds of interests were originally enforced in different tribunals and by different forms of procedure. The rules governing equitable interests as developed by the courts of chancery were more flexible than the rules governing legal interests. This flexibility was due in part to the conception of the Chancellor—that he was not applying fixed rules but was applying principles of justice based upon his views of the standards of conduct of a conscientious man, and that he was enforcing personal duties rather than securing property interests. It was due in part also to the fact that the procedure in suits in equity was different from the procedure in actions at law. One of the most important differences was that a judgment in an action at law declared unconditionally that the plaintiff was or was not entitled to recover land, chattels, or money, and the judgment, if in favor of the plaintiff, was enforced through execution levied by an officer of the court upon the property or person of the defendant, whereas a decree in a suit in equity was a command addressed to a party to the suit to do or not to do certain acts and this command might be either absolute or conditional.

RESTATEMENT (SECOND) TRUSTS, §2 (1959). The Restatements of law are the products of the American Law Institute. This second edition of the one dealing with trust law, produced in 1959, is a thorough reworking of the first edition, which was published in 1935.

U.S. income tax regulations, defining a "trust" for tax purposes, state as follows:

> In general, the term trust as used in the Internal Revenue Code refers to an arrangement created by will or an *inter vivos* declaration whereby trustees take title to property for the purpose of protecting or conserving it for the beneficiaries under the ordinary rules applicable in chancery or probate courts. Usually the beneficiaries of such a trust do no more than accept the benefits thereof and are not the voluntary planners or creators of the trust arrangement. However, the beneficiaries of such a trust may be the persons who create it and it will be recognized as a trust under the Internal Revenue Code if it was created for the purpose of protecting or conserving the trust property for beneficiaries who stand in the same relation to the trust as they would if the trust had been created by others for them. Generally speaking, an arrangement will be treated as a trust under the Internal Revenue Code if it can be shown that the purpose of the arrangement is to vest in the trustees responsibility for the protection and conservation of property for beneficiaries who cannot share in the discharge of this responsibility and, therefore, are not associates in a joint enterprise for the conduct of business for profit.

Regs. §301.7701-4(a), Income Tax Regulations.

The definition of a "trust" in the Hague Convention on the Law Applicable to Trusts and on Their Recognition is also helpful:

> Article 2. For the purposes of this Convention, the term "trust" refers to the legal relationships created—inter vivos or on death—by a person, the settlor, when assets have been placed under the control of a trustee for the benefit of a beneficiary or for a specified purpose.
>
> A trust has the following characteristics—

> The assets constitute a separate fund and are not a part of the trustee's own estate;
>
> Title to the trust assets stands in the name of the trustee or in the name of another person on behalf of the trustee;
>
> The trustee has the power and the duty, in respect of which he is accountable, to manage, employ or dispose of the assets in accordance with the terms of the trust and the special duties imposed upon him by law.
>
> The reservation by the settlor of certain rights and powers, and the fact that the trustee may himself have rights as a beneficiary, are not necessarily inconsistent with the existence of a trust.[28]

---

[28] The Hague Convention was adopted by the Hague Conference on October 20, 1984, and technically came into force on January 1, 1992. The United Kingdom, Italy, Luxembourg, Malta, The Netherlands, United States, Canada, Australia, and France have signed the treaty. Italy, the United Kingdom, The Netherlands, Malta, Australia, Canada (in respect of Alberta, New Brunswick, British Columbia, Newfoundland, Manitoba, Saskatchewan, and Prince Edward Island) have ratified it and implemented it within their jurisdictions. Under the United Kingdom's ratification are included Bermuda, British Antarctic Territory, Falkland Islands, Turks and Caicos Islands, St. Helena and dependencies, South Georgia and the South Sandwich Islands, Sovereign base areas of Akrotiri and Dhekelia, British Virgin Islands, Hong Kong, Isle of Man, Jersey, and Gibraltar. The Convention has no effect for fiscal purposes. "The purpose of the Convention was partly educational: it was intended to familiarize people brought up in the civil law tradition with the concept of trusts, and in this connection the Convention served as a model for judicial decisions. The subject of the Convention was the treatment in civil law countries of trusts established in common law countries. . . . The Convention was limited to trust problems and did not extend to preliminary issues (such as the validity of a will or deed, the rule against perpetuities, and so on). . . . [It provides] that countries might go beyond the Convention in recognizing the institution of the trust. The choice-of-law rules were similar to the rules for contracts. The settlor was free to choose the law governing the trust, subject to conditions. Any trust which complied with the rules for [sic] applicable law must be recognized." Proceedings of a Seminar held in New York in 1986

Trust documents, sometimes referred to as a "trust indenture," "trust agreement," or "trust deed," typically identify the settlor and the beneficiaries, as well as the trustee. However, it is not uncommon for the trustee simply to accept the property being transferred in trust under an instrument sometimes called a "declaration of trust." The beneficiaries may be named in this document, or they may simply be described as a class of beneficiaries. It may then be left to the trustee's discretion to make distributions among members of this class.

As will be seen, trusts can be revocable or irrevocable. They can be created for a stated term. The trustee or trustees can operate in isolation, or they can be advised—but not directed—by a committee of advisors or a protector. A trust can be created under the laws of one jurisdiction and administered in another. The *situs* (or location) of the trust can be changed from one jurisdiction to another.

A trust, as a general matter, can own or operate anything, just as an individual can. Various powers can be retained by the settlor, such as the power to substitute a new trustee. In the U.S., any one of a number of powers will cause the trust to be ignored for tax purposes, and the settlor to be taxed on any income accruing to the trust as if he were the owner of the trust's assets. Trusts can also migrate relatively simply from one jurisdiction to another. In fact, one reason for using a foreign trust is the ease and speed with which it can be related.

Where the arrangement is created under foreign law, the laws of the foreign jurisdiction will be applied to determine the nature of the parties' relationships. Then U.S. tax rules will be applied to determine whether the arrangement in fact is a trust or something else. The fact that the arrangement is called a trust or is treated under foreign law as a trust is not determinative.

---

during the 40th Congress of the International Fiscal Association, Kluwer, 1988, remarks of Professor Trautman summarized at p. 54. For a more comprehensive explanation of the treaty, see Alfred E. von Overbeck, Report on the Hague Convention, reproduced as Appendix 51, Vol. 1, "International Trust Laws" (Glasson, Ed.).

Courts will apply U.S. tax precedents to determine who is the true settlor of the trust. The fact that a person is named as the settlor will not determine the outcome. Transactions may be recast and interim steps can be collapsed.[29]

A foundation created under civil law rules, it might be noted, may or may not be characterized as a trust for U.S. tax purposes.

Not all entities labeled a "trust" will be treated as a trust for U.S. tax purposes. For example, a business trust might be treated as an association taxable as a corporation. Also, some forms of investment trust can fall outside the definition of "trust" for tax purposes.

If the entity is not a trust, it is necessary to determine what it is. It might be, for example, a foreign corporation that is a controlled foreign corporation for U.S. tax purposes; in which case, the "beneficiaries" might in fact be treated as shareholders of the company.

Under the definitional framework of U.S. tax law, an entity generally is either going to be a business entity (that is, an association taxable as a corporation or a partnership) or a trust.[30]

3.2 Incomplete transfers; "sham" trusts

It is obviously quite important to know the character of the entity in order to apply the correct tax rules. If the entity is a valid foreign

---

[29] *See, e.g., Bixby v. Commissioner*, 58 T.C. 757; *Haeri v. Commissioner*, T.C. Memo 1989-20. The *Haeri* case is interesting for a number of reasons. It arose out of an investigation of Ashland Oil, Inc., since Mr. Haeri performed consulting services for Ashland in connection with its business in Iran.

[30] As has been noted, trusts are creatures of the English common law and are generally unknown in most civil code jurisdictions. Over the years, however, a number of civil law countries have enacted statutes that create a legal framework for trust relationships. *See* MODERN INTERNATIONAL DEVELOPMENTS IN TRUST LAW, Hayton (Editor), (Kluwer, 1999). There has also been a movement toward the adoption of trust statutes by developing civil law countries. *See* Gordon & Summers, "Trusts and Taxes in Civil Law Emerging Economies: Issues, Problems, and Proposed Solutions," TAX NOTES INT'L, July 20, 1992.

trust, this is one thing; if it is not a valid trust and falls in the category, say, of property being held by a nominee on behalf of the transferor, it is something quite different. For example, an individual cannot enter into a contractual arrangement, such as a private annuity, with himself. Also, it may make a difference in the application of various reporting rules. In fact, there are few things worse in tax practice than thinking the taxpayer is one thing and finding out subsequently that he is another.

Cases challenging the validity of a trust are relatively infrequent in U.S. tax law. When they crop up, it is often in the context of some type of enforcement or collection action. In years gone by it could be said that cases of "sham" trust were rare. It is relatively easy to create a trust; all that is required is property, a transfer of the property, a trustee receiving the property and holding it for the benefit of someone, and beneficiaries. In fact, when an arrangement falls through for some reason, a court will often construct a trust out of the pieces. However, over the last decade and half, there has been a significant increase in the number of trusts attacked as nonexistent or a "sham." A number of these trusts were created by settlors—often with the help of U.S. advisers—trying to avoid creditors. In various ways, some, but not all, of these arrangements failed to meet the criteria of a trust.[31]

The trust or some of its workings can be invalidated in a number of ways. One way is for the initial transfer in trust to be found not to have achieved its end. Another can arise where the trust, while having been created nominally, is operating not as a trust but as something else—as the settlor's *alter ego*. Also, the formalities can be ignored by the settlor and the trustee to the extent that a court will simply ignore—or look through—the trust as a mere form, without the substance of a trust. The case law jumps around between these

[31] *See generally*, Bruce, Gray & Luria, "Exploring The Protection Of Assets Trusts," TRUST & ESTATES (Nov. & Dec. 1991). Some protection of assets trusts are in reality not trusts because the "grantor" has not let go of the property (*i.e.*, there has not been a completed transfer in trust) or the "trustee" has not behaved like a trustee (*i.e.*, it has not taken control over the trust property and administered the trust for the benefit of the beneficiaries).

lines of precedents; but usually, upon close inspection, a given factual situation falls in one place or another.[32]

There are a few cases on point. Most of them deal with domestic trusts; only a few with foreign trusts. The leading decision dealing with domestic trusts—so-called "family trusts"—is *Markosian v. Commissioner*, decided by Judge Drennan in 1980.[33] The petitioners, husband and wife, transferred all of their business and personal assets, including the husband's dental equipment, his lifetime services and all remuneration therefrom, to a family trust as to which they were the only trustees. Petitioners continued to use their home and personal assets, and the husband continued to use his office and dental equipment in his practice. The husband, however, received all of the gross income from his dental practice and deposited it in his personal account. Petitioners then paid 80 percent of the gross income from the dental practice to the trust as a "fee." The Tax Court held that the trust was devoid of economic reality and should be treated as a nullity for federal income tax purposes. The Court began by stating that it would focus on the economic reality of the matter, not the technical considerations and legal niceties or the law of trusts. "When the form of the transaction has not, in fact, altered any cognizable economic relationships, we will look through that form and apply the tax law according to the substance of the transaction." [34] It went on to say that the trust, in form, might be valid under a strained interpretation of the facts; but, even if in form the trust was valid, it was not administered like a trust. For example, the terms of the trust and supporting documents were not adhered to. It was also apparent that taxpayers did not exercise the ordinary duties of trustees in accordance with the strict principles of a fiduciary. Most importantly, however, the Court said, there was no economic reality or substance to the transaction. It laid out a four-part analysis. First, the relationship of the grantors to the property transferred did not differ in any material aspect before and after the creation of the trust. Second,

---

[32] For an excellent and entertaining discussion of this subject, see Willoughby, MISPLACED TRUST (Gostick Hall Publications, 1999). *See also*, *Mark Bixby*, 58 T.C. 757 (1972) (involving trusts created prior to the enactment of section 679 with Bank of N.T. Butterfield in Bermuda) and *Rahman v. Chase Bank Trust Company (CI) Ltd and Others* (1991) JLR 103.

[33] *Markosian v. Commissioner*, 73 T.C. 1235 (1980).

[34] *Id.* at 1241.

petitioners, as equal grantors, were also co-trustees, with no independent person empowered to prevent them from acting in derogation of the interests of the other beneficiaries. Third, there was no perceived economic interest that passed to other beneficiaries under the trust arrangement. Fourth, petitioners did not feel bound by any restrictions imposed by this trust or the law of trusts. "In our opinion, the above factors, together with the lack of any valid purpose other than the avoidance of tax, are enough to deprive the trust of all trappings of economic reality and mandate that we disregard this attempt to shift income by creation of this paper entity."[35] Interestingly, realizing that a precedent for ignoring a trust could have enormous implications, the Court added the following: "This is not to say, as a general rule, that income from a trust legally created and administered may be lightly attributed to the settlor outside of the statutory provisions provided by Congress in sections 671 through 677 [the grantor trust provisions]."[36] The *Markosian* case has been followed in a number of cases including, most recently, the case of *Muhich v. Commissioner*.[37] It will be noted that these cases involve very raw facts and often result from the promotion of trust schemes in one form or another.

A case dealing with foreign trusts is *Zmuda v. Commissioner*, decided by Judge Drennan two years after the *Markosian* case. In that case, the taxpayers cause to be created in Turks and Caicos three purported "all business trusts." They used a stranger—the brother of a local notary—to act as the settlor of the trusts. Certificates of beneficial interests were issued for nominal amounts but by their terms gave holders no interest in the income, management, or corpus of the trusts except in the event of termination. The trustees were given fee simple interests in the corpus and complete power to manage the trusts and distribute the income and corpus to whomever they chose. The taxpayers were appointed the trustees of Trust No. 1, which had no assets or business activities. Trust No. 1, in turn, was appointed trustee of both Trusts No. 2 and No. 3. Trust No. 2 was

[35] *Id.* at 1244-1245. During the years at issue, because of the rates applicable to trusts as opposed to individuals, there was an advantage in directing income to a trust. This is no longer the case. This change in the rate structure effectively ended the use of family trusts.
[36] *Id.* at 1245.
[37] *Muhich v. Commissioner*, T.C. Memo 199-172 (June 14, 1999).

inactive except as a conduit of funds. Taxpayers transferred real-estate contracts and deeds of trust on real estate formerly owned by them to Trust No. 3 in exchange for 100 units of beneficial interests in Trust No. 3, which they subsequently sold to Trust No. 2 for $50. All payments on the contracts and deeds of trust were deposited in bank accounts in the U.S. opened in the name of Trust No. 3 by petitioners as agents of the trust. The income received by Trust No. 3 was funneled to petitioners in the year at issue (1978). This arrangement, using preprinted forms, was acquired by the taxpayers as part of a package from a promoter in the U.S.

The IRS argued, first, that the creation of the trusts was a sham since the transactions had no substance or utility apart from tax considerations; and therefore taxpayers remained the owners of the income-producing property and were taxable on the income therefrom. Alternatively, the Service contended that the taxpayer should be treated as the owner of the trust assets under the grantor trust rules. The taxpayers said that the trusts have been validly created. Also, in response to the IRS's grantor trust argument, they said that the entities should not be considered as trusts for federal income tax purposes. Presumably they were arguing that they were some form of association taxable as a corporation; but it is not clear who, under their approach, were the shareholders.

The court said that it would look to the realities of the situation, citing its earlier decision in *Markosian*. It found that although in form the transferor of property to Trust No. 3 allegedly altered the economic relationship of the taxpayers to the property transferred, in substance he did not do so.

> This is because . . . [Trust No. 3], itself, cannot be recognized as a viable entity for tax purposes. In form, . . . [Trust No. 3] has a foreign creator . . . and a foreign trustee . . . to administer the business trust. However, in substance is clear that petitioners were not only the creators and grantors of [Trust No. 3] but also were the trustees of [Trust No. 3]. In determining the settlors of a trust, we look beyond the named grantors to the economic realities to determine the true grantor.

The court cited *Stern v. Commissioner*[38] and *Bixby v. Commissioner.*[39] This rule applies, the Court said, whether the "trusts" are viewed as regular trusts or so-called "common law business trusts." Furthermore, it was noted that the nominal settlor had nothing to do with the management or operation of the trust. The taxpayers adopted the "off the rack" terms of the trusts and documentation thereof which provided the plans to implement the trusts, and transferred to the trusts the only assets that were ever contributed. The taxpayers were the only trustees of the trusts and they acted as the trust's agents—apparently without disclosing the agency relationship to anyone. "Thus, as trustees . . . and agents . . ., petitioners stood in exactly the same position with respect to the properties transferred . . . as they did before the transfer." They had complete control and they had the ability to distribute the income and corpus to whomever they chose, including themselves; and, in fact, they transferred a portion of the trusts' funds to themselves after first "funneling" it through one of the trusts. The transfer of property to the trust did not create rights in anyone else in the transferred assets. "In summary, we find that ... [the three trusts] are paper entities structured solely to avoid taxes."

The IRS has issued a number of revenue rulings on "sham" trusts. A 1980 Revenue Ruling analyzes a "foreign tax haven double trust." An agent in a foreign country, who was labeled as the "creator," created a trust in that country, naming the taxpayer as trustee. The trust received income-producing property from the taxpayer. The "creator" then created a second trust in the same country naming the first trust as trustee. The Service determined that the purported creation of the two trusts was a sham and the form of the transaction had no tax effect. (Oddly, the Service went on in the Ruling to note the existence of the grantor trust provisions in the Code—in particular section 679—and the excise tax in section 1491 (which was in existence at that time). Once there is a determination that the trust is a sham, there is nothing more to say other than that the taxpayer remains the owner of the assets.)[40]

---

[38] *Stern v. Commissioner*, 77 T.C. 614 (1981).
[39] *Bixby v. Commissioner*, 58 T.C. 757 (1972).
[40] Rev. Rul. 80-74, 1980-1 C.B. 137.

A second ruling, issued in 1990, dealt with a foreign trust created as part of an attempt to avoid U.S. taxes on recording rights that had been licensed. The taxpayer was a resident alien entertainer.[41]

The Ruling is odd for a number of reasons, as will be seen.

T, the resident alien entertainer, organized a domestic personal service corporation (PSC) and transferred to it the rights to his recordings in return for all the stock. At about the same time, T created a foreign trust, the beneficiaries of which were the individual members at any given time of a national association of entertainers of which T was a member. The trustee, a nonadverse party, had absolute discretion to manage and deal with the trust property and distribute income and corpus to any of the individual trust beneficiaries as it saw fit. T retained the unrestricted power to remove the trustee and replace it with whomever he chose. No distributions were ever made from the trust. (The character of the trustee is not disclosed; therefore, it is not known whether the trustee was a well-reputed international trust company or an individual who was not a professional fiduciary. Nor is it known whether the association, whose members were named as beneficiaries, or the members themselves, were ever informed of the existence of the trust.) T then transferred to the foreign trust all the stock of a foreign corporation (FC), which was licensed by PSC under a royalty agreement to reproduce T's recordings. FC, it was said, performed no significant services with respect to the recording rights. It re-licensed the recording rights to an unrelated company in an arm's-length transaction for royalties that exceeded the royalty that FC was obligated to pay to PSC. FC derived all of its income in this manner. A portion of the royalties earned by FC, in turn, was paid to PSC; the remainder of FC's earnings were distributed annually to the trust as dividends. There had been no distributions from the trust. The 255-word description of the facts is surprisingly brief and "broad-brushed." The Service simply concludes as follows:

> The facts and circumstances of this case indicate that . . . T controls the foreign trust. The economic substance, therefore, is the same as if PSC had directly licensed recording rights to the unrelated

---

[41] Rev. Rul. 90-106, 1990-2 C.B. 162.

> company. Through . . . T's control of PSC and the trust and his indirect control of FC (through the trust), . . . T, it is concluded, retains effective control over the entire royalty income. The trust has no substance, utility, or purpose apart from tax considerations, so the income of the trust will be included in . . . T's gross income. <u>The fact pattern set forth in this ruling is one of many where a trust may be disregarded. Whenever the facts and circumstances indicate that the grantor controls the trust, the same analysis will apply</u>. [Emphasis added.]

The ruling goes on to comment that even if the trust were valid, the grantor trust provisions in general and section 679 in particular would apply. Therefore, T would be treated as the owner of all the assets of FC under section 671. Also, the ruling notes that section 482 (relating to the Secretary's power to allocate income and deductions among taxpayers) could be applied to allocate the income and expenses of FC to PSC.

The ruling is strange in that it is not well drafted and, based on the information presented, it would have been preferable to rely on the grantor trust provisions as opposed to the sham trust doctrine. The exercise of "shamming" must be based on a very detailed examination of the facts; and this ruling is simply too breezy. It is especially important to carefully examine the facts when dealing with a trust because trusts, unlike business entities, have no ingrained logic based on concepts such as business purpose. They deal with individual and family issues. Also, fiduciaries, by their very nature, serve the purposes of the beneficiaries; and it is common for one of the beneficiaries to be the settlor. Understandably, trusts should be ignored when there has not really been a transfer to the trust or the trust has not been operated, in reality, as a trust; that is, no real fiduciary relationship was created, the settlor was not placed in any different position with respect to the property, the beneficiaries' interests never came into being, and so forth. However, it must be recalled that with the typical living trust, taxable as a grantor trust, the settlor creates a trust, the family's local banker serves as trustee, and the settlor, as beneficiary, is treated preferentially during his or her lifetime. It certainly is the case that the trustee is going to act to the benefit of the settlor-beneficiary; under the circumstances, that is its duty. The settlor-beneficiary might in fact be named as an adviser—as opposed to co-trustee. As Judge Drennan acknowledged in the *Markosian* case, tax authorities should be slow to set aside trusts because there are so many and such a variety of trusts.[42]

The grantor trust provisions are the mechanism enacted by Congress to address these issues. Section 671 clearly states that "No items of trust shall be included in computing the taxable income and credits of the grantor or any other person solely on the grounds of his dominion and control over the trust under section 61 (relating to definition of gross income) or any other provision of this title, except as specified in this subpart." The regulations adopted in 1956 and amended in 1971 and again in 1980 reiterate this position. Except as provided in the subpart containing the grantor trust rules, "income of the trust is not included in computing the taxable income and credits of a grantor or another person solely on the grounds of his dominion and control over the trust."[43]

One might also wonder how the Revenue Ruling 90-106 came about. Certainly no one was foolish enough to file for a ruling on these facts. The Service must have felt the need to publish in effect a warning; this would explain the extraordinarily gratuitous statement—"the fact pattern set forth in this ruling is one of many where trusts may be disregarded." Suffice it to say that this rock star might have been better dealt with in an audit and then a court case.[44]

It should not be concluded that the IRS can easily succeed simply by asserting that a trust was a "sham." In fact, the litigation arm of the IRS (Chief Counsel's office) probably puts too much stock

---

[42] In fact, the Tax Court has been careful not to ignore the legal position of a trustee as fiduciary. In *Estate of Hilton W. Goodwyn v. Commissioner*, T.C. Memo. 73-153, the Court refused to treat the taxpayer as co-trustee where as advisor to the trust he repeatedly advised the trustee to take a particular action and the trustee invariably complied.

[43] Treas. Reg. § 1.671-1(c).

[44] *See* VanderWolk, "Substance-Over-Form Attack on Grantor Trust Misses the Mark," TNI (April 1991), pp. 385-387.

in the argument. Courts are generally mindful that there are millions of trusts in existence; most of these were created for entirely valid individual and family reasons; and a court should be wary of creating precedents in this area.

A good example is the case of *In Re Eugene V. Richards Jr., et ux.*[45] The U.S. Bankruptcy Court for the Eastern District of Pennsylvania denied the IRS's motion for summary judgment concluding that the Richardses, who had filed for voluntary bankruptcy, had not fraudulently conveyed property in a trust, the trust in question was not a sham, and their bankruptcy petition should not be dismissed as in bad faith. Mr. and Mrs. Richards had purchased a residence in 1983. They owned it as joint tenants with rights of survivorship. A year later they transferred it to a trust for the benefit of their son. (They created a deed for the property that identified them as trustees for the benefit of the son. A trust document, as such, was not executed until around 1996.) They did so, they said, so as to ensure that the son would eventually have the family home. At the time of the transfer, the Richardses jointly were liable for federal income taxes in the amount of $2,700. The husband separately owed $25,000 for unpaid employment taxes. The couple paid the taxes for which they were jointly liable; but the employment taxes remained unpaid. (They said that they stopped receiving bills from the IRS for the employment taxes in 1991.) In 1996, the government brought action against the taxpayers to reduce to judgment tax assessments for 1987-89 and 1994 totaling $50,000. About six months later, the Richardses filed for bankruptcy; and the IRS moved for summary judgment contending that its claim was secured by the residence that the Richardses allegedly transferred to the trust. They IRS argued that the taxpayers failed to create a valid trust under applicable state law, the 1984 transfer to the trust was a fraudulent conveyance that should be set aside, the trust was a sham, and the trust was the Richardses alter ego. In a lengthy and carefully reasoned decision, the bankruptcy judge ruled against the Service—refuting all its arguments. The court found that the making of the deed satisfied the Pennsylvania statute of frauds applying to trusts involving real property. The transfer was not a fraudulent conveyance because, among other things, the joint liability had been

[45] 81 AFTR2d Para. 98-644 No. 97-14798 DWS (reprinted in 98 TNT 82-13).

satisfied. Also, the IRS could not use the existence of the tax debt owed by one spouse to set aside the transfer of property owned in the entireties. The trust was not a sham. It was not created to avoid the payment of taxes. Unlike cases such as *Markosian*, an economic interest passed to the son, and the trustees (the parents) were bound by restrictions imposed on them. As trustees, they had imposed on them a duty to administer the trust solely in the interest of the beneficiary. "Whereas they could have done as they pleased with the property before the trust, that changed with the trust's creation." As to the IRS's alter ego argument, in the context of a motion for summary judgment, the Court commented that the facts were too unclear to grant the government's motion.

The case demonstrates that it really does not take a great deal to create a trust; and once found to exist, a trust cannot be lightly set aside. The case for the validity of a trust can be greatly enhanced by one or two simple things evidenced in the file—such as, a showing that the settlors were actually prevented from doing something because they no longer owned the property out right.

3.3 Definition of foreign trust

Before the changes made by the Small Business Tax Act of 1996, the definitions of a trust that would be treated as a "United States person" (*i.e.*, a "domestic trust") and a "foreign trust" were circular and depended upon an analysis of a number of factors; in other words, it was a "wavering line" test.[46] The definition of a "foreign trust" was replaced with a "bright line" test by the 1996 Act. Regulations were promulgated under the new provisions in final form on February 1, 1999.

---

[46] Under prior law, the statutory definition consisted only of a statement that a foreign trust is a trust "the income of which, from sources without the United States which is not effectively connected with the conduct of a trade or business within the United States, is not includible in gross income under Subtitle A." The test looking to various factors grew out of court cases and one or two rulings. *See, e.g., B.W. Jones Trust v. Commissioner*, 132 F. 2d 914 (4th Cir., 1943); *First National City Bank v. Internal Revenue Service*, 271 F. 2d 616 (2d Cir., 1959), *cert. denied*, 361 U.S. 948 (1960); Rev. Rul. 60-181, 1960-1 C.B. 257.

In addition to clarifying the rule, the Treasury Department, in proposing the change, said it wanted to "increase the flexibility of settlors and trust administrators to decide where to locate and in what assets to invest. For example, if the location of the administration of the trust were no longer a relevant criterion, settlors of foreign trusts would be able to choose whether to administer the trusts in the United States or abroad based on non-tax consequences."[47] Treasury Department officials, at the time, commented that the new definition was intended to level the competitive playing field for trust business between U.S. and foreign institutions. Under the prior definition, a foreign person who preferred to use a U.S. financial institution as trustee might have decided not to do so because of the likelihood that the trust would have been taxed as a U.S. trust. Under the new law, a foreign person can use a U.S. financial institution without creating a taxable U.S. trust.[48]

The statute, as amended, defines United States person to include a trust if (a) a court within the U.S. is able to exercise primary supervision over the administration of the trust (the court test) and (b) one or more U.S. persons have the authority to control all substantial decisions of the trust (the control test). Both tests must be met in order to pass muster. A "foreign trust," it follows, means any trust other than one that fits this description.

The regulations, in nine pages, spell out the details and provide useful examples. Unless specifically provided, the taxable income of a foreign trust is computed in the same manner as the taxable income of a nonresident alien individual who is not present in the U.S. at any time. The rules in section 7701(b) defining resident alien and nonresident alien, and including so-called "day-counting" rules, do not apply to trusts. Also, significantly, the regulations provide that a foreign trust is not considered present in the U.S. at any time for purposes of the rules taxing the capital gains of nonresident aliens

[47] Treasury Department, "General Explanation of the Administration's Revenue Proposals," p. 25 (Feb. 7, 1995).

[48] There is no evidence that non-U.S. settlors and beneficiaries are clamoring to use U.S. financial institutions as trustees of non-U.S. (foreign) trusts. With respect to a related subject, it is evident that non-U.S. persons frequently avoid U.S. banks—including the foreign branches of U.S. banks—because of concerns over regulatory burdens, loss of privacy, etc.

present in the U.S. for 183 days or more. (This result was made even plainer by the subsequent enactment of section 641(b) as part of the Taxpayer Relief Act of 1997.[49] That section provides that in determining the income of a foreign trust, the trust shall be treated as a nonresident alien individual who is not present in United States at any time. Therefore, a foreign trust cannot claim to be engaged in a U.S. trade or business in a given year so as to try to avoid the consequences of an accumulation distribution.)

The terms of the trust instrument, assuming it is in writing, and applicable—often foreign—law must be applied to determine whether the court test and control test are met.

> ➔ The regulations seem to indicate that certain things must appear in the trust instrument. Practitioners will want to revisit their "form" trust indentures so as to avoid embarrassing and possibly expensive gaffes.

With regard to the court test, the regulations provide a so-called "safe harbor" rule for determining whether this test is met. A trust satisfies the court test if the trust instrument does not direct that the trust be administered outside the U.S., the trust in fact is administered exclusively in the U.S., and the trust is not subject to an automatic migration provision. An automatic migration provision is described as one providing that a U.S. court's attempt to assert jurisdiction or otherwise supervise administration of the trust, directly or indirectly, causes the trust to migrate from the U.S. Not included in the description is a provision that the trust will migrate from the U.S. only in the case of foreign invasion or widespread confiscation or nationalization of property.

> ➔ A trust does not qualify as a domestic trust if it meets the "safe harbor" test. It merely passes the first test, that is, the court test. It still has to deal with the control test.

The term "court" includes any federal, state or local court. The phrase "is able to exercise" means the court has or would have the

---

[49] Taxpayer Relief Act of 1997 (P.L. 105-34).

authority under applicable law to render orders or judgments resolving issues concerning administration of the trust. The term "primary supervision" means that a court has or would have the authority to determine substantially all issues regarding the administration of the entire trust. The term "administration of the trust" means the carrying out of the duties imposed by the terms of the trust instrument and applicable law, including maintaining the books and records of the trust, filing trust returns, managing and investing the assets in the trust, defending the trust in suits by creditors, and determining the amount and timing of distributions.

Four types of trusts will be viewed as meeting the court test. They are: (a) Trusts that are registered in a court within the U.S. by an authorized fiduciary under a state statute substantially similar to the Uniform Probate Code, Article VII, Trust Administration.[50] (b) Testamentary trusts if all fiduciaries of the trust have been qualified as trustees by a court within the U.S. (c) *Inter vivos* trusts if the fiduciaries and/or beneficiaries take steps with a court in the U.S. to cause the administration of the trust to be subject to the primary supervision of such court. (d) Trusts that are subject to primary supervision with respect to their administration by both a U.S. Court and foreign court.

With regard to the control test, "U.S. person" means any U.S. individual, corporation, partnership, trust, estate, or the like. A domestic corporation is a U.S. person regardless of whether its shareholders are U.S. persons. The regulations take some trouble to explain the meaning of "substantial decisions." Such decisions are those that persons are authorized or required to make under the terms of the trust instrument and applicable law and that are not ministerial. Ministerial decisions include decisions regarding details, such as the bookkeeping, the collection of rents, and the execution of investment decisions. Substantial decisions include decisions concerning

[50] Section 7-201 of the Uniform Probate Code gives exclusive jurisdiction over the internal affairs of a trust to the courts of the state in which a trust is registered. The following sixteen states have adopted the Uniform Probate Code: Alaska, Arizona, Colorado, Florida, Hawaii, Idaho, Maine, Michigan, Minnesota, Montana, Nebraska, New Mexico, North Dakota, South Carolina, South Dakota, and Utah. 8 Uniform Laws Annotated 1 (West Supp. 1996).

whether and when to distribute income or corpus, the amount of any distributions, the selection of a beneficiary, whether a receipt is allocable to income or principal, whether to terminate the trust, whether to compromise, arbitrate or abandon claims of the trust, whether to sue on behalf of the trust or defend suits against the trust, whether to remove, add or replace a trustee, whether to appoint a successor trustee to succeed a trustee who died, resigned or otherwise ceased to act as a trustee, even if the power to make such a decision is not accompanied by an unrestricted power to remove the trustee, unless the power to make such a decision is limited such that it cannot be exercised in a manner that would change the trust's residency from foreign to domestic, or vice versa, and investment decisions (however, if the U.S. person hires an investment advisor to make decisions for the trust, the investment decisions made by the advisor will be considered substantial decisions controlled by the U.S. person if the U.S. person can terminate at will the investment adviser's power to make decisions).

"Control" is obviously a key concept. "Control" means "having the power, by vote or otherwise, to make all of the substantial decisions of the trust, with no other person having the power to veto any of the substantial decisions. To determine whether United States persons have control, it is necessary to consider all persons who have authority to make a substantial decision of the trust, not only the trust fiduciaries."[51]

> ➔ Thus, a decision that can be made by a grantor or, in the case of a decision that affects the portion of a trust in which a beneficiary has an interest, by that beneficiary, can be viewed as a substantial decision, regardless whether the grantor or the beneficiary is acting as a fiduciary. For example, if a trust contains a provision permitting a foreign grantor to revoke the trust, the trust will fail the control test and will not be characterized as a U.S. trust. Likewise, if a trust contains a provision permitting a foreign beneficiary to appoint all or a portion of the income to herself, the trust will fail the test and will not be a U.S. trust. This approach seems to create a bias in

[51] Treas. Reg. § 301.7701-7(d)(1)(iii).

> favor of foreign trusts. It has been suggested that a trust should be able to elect to be taxed as a U.S. trust, but this election has not been enacted or put in place administratively.

For certain, any automatic migration provision to the effect, for example, that an attempt by any governmental agency or creditor to collect information from or assert a claim against the trust will cause one or more substantial decisions of the trust to no longer be controlled by U.S. persons, will cause the trust to flunk the control test.

The regulations provide for a number of special rules, including rules relating to the replacement of any person who has authority to make a substantial decision of the trust (for example, that person dies or becomes incapacitated), effective dates, grandfather rules, and a special election to remain a domestic trust.[52]

The foreign trust definitional rules are intended to support the United States' strong efforts to tax most foreign trusts—one way or the other. However, because the definitions are unique among tax systems throughout the world, there is a danger that anomalies will pop up. Also, it seems likely that they will operate as an invitation to create hybrid entities, that is, ones that are, say, U.S. trusts for U.S. purposes and foreign trusts for other purposes under foreign law.

It will be noted that there might be a New York trust, created under New York law, with New York trustees, and with administration in New York; and this trust would be treated as foreign if, for example, the settlor had a power to revoke. The trust, because foreign, would not be subject to tax in the U.S. It would not be surprising if the settlor's "home country" viewed this as a U.S. trust

---

[52] The IRS has published guidance granting certain trusts additional time to comply with these rules. Notice 96-65, 1996-2 C.B. 232. Also, the IRS has provided guidance explaining how trusts meeting certain conditions may elect continued treatment as a U.S. person. This Notice prescribes the time and manner for filing a statement of election with the IRS. Notice 98-25, I.R.B. 1998-18. This Notice was made obsolete by the Treasury Decision (T.D. 8813) adopting the domestic and foreign trust definitional rules effective February 2, 1999.

and did not tax it. Taking a slightly different example, assume all the same facts except instead of the settlor having a power to revoke, an entity, say a charitable foundation resident in Bermuda, had a power to appoint the income of the trust to itself, whether or not exercised. The trust would be treated as foreign and would not be subject to U.S. tax; it would not be subject to tax in Bermuda; and it might well not be subject to tax in the settlor's home jurisdiction. This result obviously is the one that the Treasury Department wanted; but it does look odd in some respects.

Undoubtedly this type of trust, which is treated as "foreign" for U.S. tax purposes, will be treated as U.S. for other purposes, such as rules governing foreign ownership.

It should be noted that the criteria for determining whether a trust is foreign, such as the control test, is different from the section 872(f) rules, discussed below. Therefore, a trust can be "foreign" but not a "grantor" trust.

Lastly, a foreign trust can appoint a U.S. agent to perform parts of the administration of the trust, such as the fiduciary and tax accounting and return preparation, without worrying that doing so will subject the trust to U.S. tax. It will not. The key administrative chores could be left outside the U.S. and, of course, the assets could be kept outside the U.S.

Chapter 4

Different Types of Trusts for Tax Purposes; Some Common Types of Foreign Trust; Examples of Uses

4.1 Some different types of trusts (domestic and foreign) for tax purposes

It is helpful to become conversant with the terminology used in U.S. tax law when referring to trusts.

4.1.1 "Ordinary trusts"

U.S. tax rules, in general, recognize two types of "ordinary trust."[53]

4.1.1.1 "Simple trust"

The first, called a "simple" trust, is any trust the terms of which provide that all of its income is required to be distributed currently and do not provide that any amounts are to be used for charitable purposes.[54]

4.1.1.2 "Accumulation trust"

All other trusts are called "accumulation" trusts because these trusts can accumulate income for subsequent distribution.[55]

By its terms (normally embodied in a written trust indenture), a trust—"simple" or "accumulation"—can be revocable or irrevocable.[56]

---

[53] An "ordinary" trust is sometimes referred to as a "pure" trust. Since this term is not defined in the Code, use of this term is avoided. *See*, Significant Service Center Advice 1998-006, 98 TNT 234-26 (Doc 98-34325).
[54] Section 651.
[55] Section 661.

Trusts can be domestic (U.S.) or foreign; that is, a trust can be a "simple" foreign trust, or an "accumulation" foreign trust, or a revocable "simple" foreign trust, or a revocable "accumulation" foreign trust, and so forth.

As will be seen, a number of special rules apply to "foreign trusts" as opposed to domestic trusts. For example, loans of cash or marketable securities directly or indirectly from a foreign trust to a U.S. grantor or beneficiary (or a person who is related to a U.S. grantor or beneficiary) are treated as distributions; and the trust making the loan cannot be categorized as a "simple" trust.[57] Section 643(i). There are also special rules that apply when a domestic trust becomes—by migration or otherwise—a foreign trust, and *vice versa*.

Of course, when discussing "ordinary" trusts we are not addressing charitable (or public) trusts or trusts somehow associated with deferred compensation arrangements.

Categories Of Trusts For U.S. Tax Purposes

Domestic	Grantor trusts where the grantor is taxed as the owner of the assets under section 671.
	Nongrantor trusts. • "Simple" trusts that distribute income currently. • "Accumulation" trusts—all trusts other than "simple" trusts.
Foreign trusts	Grantor trusts where the grantor is treated as the owner of the assets under section 671 but presumably is not subject to U.S. taxation.

[56] Whether the trust is "revocable" or "irrevocable" should not be confused with the nature of the transfer in trust by the Settlor at the time of creation of the trust. This transfer is almost always irrevocable. If it is not irrevocable but is contingent or can somehow be voided or reversed, there probably is no transfer and a trust has not been created.

[57] An earlier version of the 1996 legislation would have treated the use of trust property, such as an apartment or a boat, as a constructive distribution. H.R. 981 § 207.

	Nongrantor trusts. • "Simple" trusts that distribute income currently and therefore distributions are not subject to the "throwback" rules. "Accumulation" trusts—all trusts other than "simple" trusts; distributions to U.S. beneficiaries are subject to the "throwback" rules.

4.2 Some common types of foreign trusts

While foreign trusts appear in a wide variety of situations, there are a number of common uses. These include: foreign protection of assets trusts created typically but not always by U.S. individuals, foreign grantor and nongrantor trusts (or "ordinary" trusts) benefiting U.S. beneficiaries, pre-immigration trusts settled by individuals before immigrating to the U.S. (which can be foreign nongrantor trusts if they somehow avoid new amendments to section 679), and foreign pension and similar employment-related trusts.

Common Types of Foreign Trust

Description of trust	Character under U.S. tax rules
International family trust to hold assets and make distributions to members of the family disbursed in several jurisdictions including the U.S.	Might be a foreign grantor trust if created by a non-U.S. individual who is still alive and the trust is revocable. Otherwise, a foreign nongrantor trust taxed as an accumulation trust.
Pre-immigration trust created by a settlor prior to immigrating to the U.S.	Might be a foreign nongrantor trust if created more than 5 years before coming to the U.S. Otherwise, a section 679 grantor trust all the income of which is taxable to the settlor.
Foreign protection of assets trust created by a U.S. individual	Taxed as a grantor trust under section 679.
Foreign trust created by U.S. individual to make gifts to non-U.S. persons.	Foreign nongrantor trust not subject to U.S. tax.

4.3 Examples of uses

The following examples will illustrate some of the types of trusts that exist. The descriptions are brief; and therefore there may be questions that arise as to unstated facts. The U.S. tax treatment is noted. However, the taxation of these types of trusts is discussed at greater length below. No mention is made of the reporting requirements. (See below.) Issues of taxation in the country of the situs of the trust and taxation of non-U.S. beneficiaries are not addressed.

Example 1. F, a French national, transfers property to T, a Bermuda trust company, for the benefit of his daughter, who, while French, is a U.S. resident alien living in New York City. The trust is irrevocable.

The trust is a foreign accumulation trust that, as will be seen, will be treated as a nongrantor trust. [The father is not taxed in the U.S. on the creation of the trust. The trust itself is not subject to U.S. tax. The daughter is taxable on distributions made to her under the rules, including the "throwback" rules, applicable to accumulation distributions.]

Example 2. The facts are the same as in Example 1, except the trust is revocable.

The trust is a foreign trust that, as will be seen, will be treated as a grantor trust. The French father will be treated as the owner of the assets under section 671. [The father is not taxed in the U.S. on the creation of the trust. The trust itself is not subject to U.S. tax. Since the father is viewed as the owner of the assets and thus the prospective taxpayer (but as a nonresident alien individual he does not pay U.S. tax), the daughter is not taxable on distributions; rather, it is as if the father were making gifts—which are not included in income for tax purposes—to his daughter.]

Example 3. The facts are the same as in Example 1, except the father as well as the daughter is a beneficiary of the trust. Less than 5 years after creating the trust, the father immigrates to the United States and obtains permanent residence ("green card") status.

The trust, as will be seen, will be treated as a foreign grantor trust; it will be viewed the same as it would be if the father were a U.S. resident at the time he created the trust. [The father will be treated as the owner of the assets and taxed on income earned by the trust.]

Example 4. A, a U.S. citizen, transfers cash to T, a Bermuda trust company, for the benefit of his grandchildren, who are Swedish. The trust is irrevocable and contains no provisions falling within the grantor trust rules in sections 672-678 of the Code. The settlor retains the power to expand and contract the class of beneficiaries, but in no event can he or any other U.S. person be a beneficiary. The trust accumulates income in some years and distributens income and principal in other years to the grandchildren.

The trust is a foreign nongrantor trust. [A is not subject to gift taxation at the time of creation of the trust; because he has not made a completed gift, the transfer does not occasion a gift tax. The trust is not subject to U.S. tax. Nor are the beneficiaries subject to U.S. tax.]

Example 5. B, a U.S. citizen, transfers property to T, a Bermuda trust company, for the benefit of a class of beneficiaries including his spouse and children. B has a remainder interest in the trust. The trust has a stated term of 20 years. The settlor retains the power to expand and contract the class of beneficiaries. The trust indenture contains a number of provisions intended to provide a measure of protection from future litigants and creditors. The settlor is solvent at the time of creation of the trust; and he has reserved sufficient assets to maintain his standard of living at the current level. In the third year of the trust a distribution is made to one of the children.

The trust is a foreign grantor trust. [The initial transfer in trust is not subject to gift tax. The later distribution to one of the children is subject to gift tax at that time. The trust, in essence, is ignored; and the settlor is treated as the owner of the assets. He is taxed on the income of the trust.]

Example 6. X, an Argentine national, transfers property to T, a Bermuda trust company, for the benefit of members of his family living in Brazil and Europe. The trust is irrevocable.

The trust is a foreign nongrantor trust. [The settlor, the trust and the beneficiaries are not subject to U.S. income or gift tax.]

Example 7. The facts are the same as in Example 6, except one of the beneficiaries spends a good deal of time in the U.S. Sometimes distributions are made to this beneficiary when she is present in the U.S. This beneficiary does not have permanent residence status in the U.S.; she is not present in U.S. more than 121 days per year on a running average; nor does she "flunk" any other test under section 7701(b) of the Code.

The trust is a foreign nongrantor trust. [The results under U.S. tax rules are the same as they are in Example 6. It makes no difference that the beneficiary is a nonresident alien individual present the U.S. at the time of the distribution. U.S. gift tax rules should not apply to the distribution.]

Chapter 5

Taxation of Trusts: Overview; Distributable Net Income

Before reviewing the rules as they evolved through several legislative amendments and focusing on the recent 1996 Act, an overview of the subject of U.S. taxation of trusts, and, in particular, so-called "foreign trusts," may be appropriate.[58] The first part of this chapter gives that overview, including a brief description of a few typical types of foreign trust. The second part introduces the reader to the concept of distributable net income (DNI), which is a keystone of the taxation of trusts and beneficiaries.

The next several chapters deal in greater detail with "simple" nongrantor trusts, "complex" nongrantor trusts, including the "throwback" rules and the special interest charge in section 668, and, lastly, grantor trusts.

➔ These tax rules are generally applicable to both trusts and estates; but the focus here is on trusts.

5.1 General

The general rules applicable to the taxation of trusts are contained in Subpart A of this Subchapter (sections 641-645). Trusts compute their tax as individuals, unless otherwise provided. The tax is computed on taxable income and is paid by the fiduciary. The tax is imposed at rates that increase steeply from 15% on amounts of taxable income not in excess of $1,500 to 39.6% on amounts in excess of $7,500.[59] "Simple" trusts—those that distribute current

---

[58] For a comprehensive introduction to the trusts and estates tax rules, see Ferguson, Freeland & Ascher, FEDERAL INCOME TAXATION OF ESTATES, TRUSTS, AND BENEFICIARIES (3rd Ed., 1998) and Zaritsky & Lane, FEDERAL INCOME TAXATION OF ESTATES AND TRUSTS (2nd Ed., 1993).

[59] Section 1(e).

income only—are allowed a $300 deduction; "complex" or "accumulation" trusts are allowed a $100 deduction.

Administration expenses and the distribution deduction (section 651 for "simple trusts" and section 661 for "complex trusts") are deductible in arriving at adjusted gross income.

While it is true as a general matter that trusts can deduct fees paid the trustees and investment advisory fees,[60] problems can arise where the trust earns tax-exempt income or capital gains. The Code disallows income tax deductions on indebtedness incurred "to purchase or carry obligations" the interest on which is tax-exempt.[61] Where there is both taxable income and tax-exempt income in the trust, the question is how to allocate the deduction between these two categories. The regulations are not very helpful, suggesting that a reasonable proportion of the deduction determined in light of all the facts and circumstances should be allocated to each.[62] Several different formulae have been bandied about by the Service and the courts. A popular one is based on the ratio of exempt income to total "ordinary income" of the trust for the year in question. Also, there is the suggestion in IRS revenue rulings that capital gains not includable in DNI as well as other items not includable in DNI may not appear in the denominator of the allocation formula.[63]

Trusts are permitted to take the deduction for net operating losses provided by section 172.[64] A net operating loss arises when the expenses and other deductions incurred in the operation of a trade or business exceed the sum of the gross income from that business plus the taxable income earned from all other sources. Nonbusiness deductions are deductible only to the extent of nonbusiness income in computing the amount of the net operating loss. Since most trusts are not operating a business, net operating losses usually are not an

[60] Section 212 (relating to expenses for production of income).

[61] Section 265(a)(2). Since as a general matter capital gains are excluded from DNI in the case of a domestic trust but included in the case of a foreign trust, this may be one point where foreign trusts come out ahead.

[62] Reg. § 1.265-1(c).

[63] Rev. Rul. 77-355, 1977-2 C.B. 82.

[64] Section 642(d).

issue—except where the trust owns and operates income-producing real estate that constitutes a trade or business.

A conduit principle generally applies. Trusts are regarded as separate taxpayers and as conduits through which income flows to the beneficiaries. Income distributed on a current basis is taxed to the beneficiary that receives it. Income accumulated for future distribution is taxed to the estate or trust. Income taxable to a beneficiary generally has the same character that it had in the hands of the fiduciary. The measure for determining the taxability of beneficiaries and the deductibility of distributions by a trust is "distributable net income" (DNI). (This concept is discussed at greater length below.) Amounts that are required to be distributed currently are deductible by the trust, to the extent of DNI, regardless of the source of the distribution.

Most trusts are required to report income and loss on the calendar year basis. A foreign trust, which by statute is treated as a nonresident alien individual who is not present in the U.S. at any time, can have a taxable year that is not a calendar year.[65]

In the case of a "simple" trust that distributes all of its income currently, the trust is allowed to deduct the amount of income that is required to be distributed currently, limited only by the DNI for the taxable year. The beneficiaries must include the income required to be distributed regardless whether such income is actually distributed, up to the amount of DNI. If the income required to be distributed exceeds the DNI of the trust, only a proportionate part of each item is includible in the beneficiaries' income. In apportioning this income, each item retains the same character it had in the hands of the trust.

DNI limits the amount deductible by a trust and the amount taxable to the beneficiaries. Essentially DNI is the taxable income of the trust modified slightly. The concept of DNI also is used to determine the character of amounts distributed to beneficiaries. Taxable income is adjusted by adding to it items that are not includible in the gross income of the trust but which may nevertheless be available for distribution to the beneficiaries, such as tax-exempt interest and excluded dividends. The deductions for personal

[65] Section 641(b).

exemptions and for amounts paid, credited or required to be distributed to beneficiaries are not taken into account, thus restricting the benefit of these deductions to the trust.

The tax rules applicable to accumulation distributions, including "throwback" rules, appear in sections 665-668 and are intended to prevent a trust from accumulating income for distribution to beneficiaries at some later date, when the beneficiaries will pay little or no tax on the distribution. However, since the income tax rates for fiduciaries were "compressed" beginning in 1988, the accumulation of trust income has become less advantageous and the "throwback" rules have become less of a concern. The Taxpayer Relief Act of 1997[66] repealed these rules, generally speaking, for domestic trusts. Today the "throwback" rules only apply to foreign trusts and a very limited number of domestic trusts—including domestic trusts that at one time were foreign trusts.

It will be noted that, as a general matter, distributions of income required to be distributed on a current basis from a complex trust will be taxed to that trust and its beneficiaries in the same manner as the same kind of distributions from a simple trust are taxed to it and its beneficiaries. In other words, current income of a trust, whether a simple trust or a complex trusts, will be treated the same. The Code is drafted in such a way as to permit persons concerned only with a simple trust to avoid having to wrestle with the very complicated rules concerning complex (accumulation) trusts.

In addition, with respect to accumulation distributions from foreign trusts, an interest charge applies.[67] The purpose for this charge is to eliminate the benefit of not having paid the tax at an earlier date—the date when the income was earned by the trust. In other words, it offsets the time value of money enjoyed by the trust and the beneficiary because they had the use of the government's funds.

As will be discussed in greater detail in Chapter 9, there are a number of special rules applicable only to foreign trusts.

---

[66] Taxpayer Relief Act of 1997 (P.L. 105-34).

[67] Section 668.

5.2 Foreign trust definition

New rules for determining the residence of a trust were enacted as part of the 1996 Act changes. The new rules provide greater clarity but at the cost of a strong bias in favor of "foreignness." Under the Code, a trust is a foreign trust unless both of the following conditions are met: (1) A court or courts within the U.S. must be able to exercise primary supervision over administration of the trust; and (2) one or more U.S. fiduciaries have the authority to control all substantial decisions of the trust.[68] For a detailed discussion of these rules, see Chapter 3.

5.3 Foreign grantor trusts

If a trust is a foreign trust under the residence rules described above, and it is a grantor trust under the rules in sections 641-679 of the Code, it is a foreign grantor trust. It must be recalled, however, that many trusts are removed from the category of grantor trust by section 672(f) because the grantor is not subject to U.S. tax. Two types of foreign grantor trust that continue to exist after the enactment of the 1996 Act rules are foreign protection of assets trusts and certain foreign trusts—mainly a revocable foreign trust with an individual, living grantor.

5.3.1 Protection of assets trusts

A so-called foreign "protection of assets trust" typically is created by a U.S. individual. It is a grantor trust because—among other reasons—it ordinarily falls within the rules in section 679, described elsewhere. The grantor is treated as the owner of all of the trust's assets, and all the income earned by the trust is taxed to her. In the usual case, the transfer to the trust will not be a completed gift; therefore, no gift tax will be triggered and the assets will remain in the settlor's estate for estate tax purposes. Nor will a section 684 tax be incurred on the transfer of appreciated property to the trust. As can be seen, this type of trust, if properly drafted and executed, will have no tax consequences at the time of creation. However, for non-tax purposes—*i.e.*, creditors' rights, bankruptcy and other

[68] Sections 7701(a)(30)(E) & (31)(B).

purposes—the settlor will be viewed as having divested herself of the assets.

> ➔ The settlement of a protection of assets trust can feature a completed gift or not. In theory, it could be a grantor trust not under 679—because, for example, it has no U.S. beneficiaries—but under one of the other grantor trust provisions in sections 671-678; it might not even be revocable. Also, a protection of assets trust can be created by a nonresident alien settlor. Therefore, the term "asset protection trust," in fact, can cover a greater variety of trusts than might at first appear.

Protection of assets trusts were made possible because the tax law, in the Tax Reform Act of 1976, diverged strongly from non-tax laws. Section 679, enacted at that time, provides that for tax purposes a U.S. settlor can transfer property to a foreign trust that has, or has the possibility of having, U.S. beneficiaries, and the settlor—if he has not triggered the gift tax—will be treated as having done nothing. The trust will be ignored for tax purposes, even though, in reality, the settlor has made a "no-strings-attached" transfer, such that for all other purposes he will be treated as merely the former owner of the assets.

A foreign jurisdiction is chosen because U.S. judgments cannot simply be enrolled and enforced through the mechanism of another country's court system. Also, other legal systems often take a more conservative view of the issues surrounding fraudulent transfers, punitive damages and the like. In a sense the legal system of a jurisdiction, such as Bermuda or the Isle of Man, functions more like the U.S. legal system at the turn of the century than the U.S. system today. For example, it is unlikely that a Judge (called a "Deemster") and jury in the Isle of Man would award plaintiffs billions of dollars in punitive damages in an automobile product liability suit.

A well-conceived protection of assets trust can provide a valuable measure of protection against future liabilities of all sorts. It is not, however, a product—like a bar of deodorant soap. It must first and foremost be a trust. It can have a number of special features.

The first protection of assets trust with a U.S. settlor was settled in Bermuda in 1979.[69] A large, well-known trust company, owned by one of the banks, acted as the trustee. The choice was made in that situation to trigger the gift tax so as to "soak up" some of the gift tax unified credit amount.[70] The U.S. tax consequences were fully opined upon by U.S. counsel; and local Bermuda counsel, with the assistance of English counsel, issued an opinion on all the Bermuda tax and legal issues including the validity of the trust. There was no underlying corporate or limited partnership structure. For the next five or six years, several dozen trusts like this one were created in Bermuda and the Isle of Man. They did not rely upon special statutes overriding fraudulent conveyance rules (so-called "Statute of Elizabeth Override Statutes"), but rather existed comfortably in the body of normal trust rules. Beginning around 1983 or 1984, protection of assets trusts became more widely known and were "discovered" by aggressive U.S. lawyers looking for something new to promote. Since then, in effect, there have been two strata of this type of trust: at the low end of the market, packaged protection of assets trusts (often referred to as "Asset Protection Trusts" or a "APT Trusts"); and at the high-end, trusts that look very much like the first protection of assets trusts. The APT trusts commonly have a structure underlying the trust. For example, the foreign trust might be a 99% limited partner in a U.S. limited partnership. The settlor or a U.S. company might serve as the general partner in the limited partnership. The assets remain in the limited partnership on the theory that if trouble develops, the assets will be transferred to the foreign trust. At the same time, beginning in the mid-1980s, a number of jurisdictions—eventually more than a dozen—enacted Statute of Elizabeth Override Statutes to facilitate this type of trust by making clear that the fraudulent conveyance rules traceable to the 1570 Statute of Elizabeth would be overridden in certain clearly defined circumstances.[71] One jurisdiction, the Cook Islands, went "hog wild" in an effort to attract this segment of the business.[72] These trusts are

[69] These trusts are quite similar to trusts created for non-U.S. individuals wishing to safeguard assets from political risks in their home country. In this respect, they are not novel or new.

[70] Section 2010.

[71] Statute of Elizabeth (13 Eliz 1 C5) (an Act of Parliament in 1570).

[72] In view of some practitioners, the Cook Islands and perhaps one or two other jurisdictions have gone way overboard in pandering to the low-end of the protection of assets trusts market. Also, many of the trusts and

being attacked—sometimes successfully—on a number of theories. Also, the settlors occasionally find themselves in a very uncomfortable position—that is, in contempt of court and in jail—essentially because they have tried to have the best of both worlds. They maintain control over the assets and continue to deal with the assets as if they owned them; and they rely upon the existence of the trust when confronted by unhappy creditors.[73] In the

---

underlying structures being promoted are flawed in one way or another. *See* Willoughby, MISPLACED TRUST (Gostick Hall Publications, 1999). In order to understand how bad the situation has become, the reader might look at the notorious *Orange Grove* cases. *515 Sourth Orange Grove Owners Association and Others v. Orange Grove Partners and Others* (No. 1) (1995) No. 208/94) and *515 South Orange Grove Owners Association and Others v. Orange Grove Partners and Others* (No. 2)(1995) No. 1997/98 1 OFLR 3. "It is doubtful whether the highest domestic court of any jurisdiction has ever delivered more scathingly critical judgments of the jurisdiction's own legislation and it is much to the credit of the Cook Islands judiciary that such unfortunate legislation has been so sweepingly discredited." *Id.* at p. 38. *See also* Bruce & Wojewodzki, "Will The *Orange Grove* Case Have A Long-Term Impact On Cook Islands Asset Protection Trust Law?," Vol. 2, No. 3, Journal Of Asset Protection (Jan./Feb. 1997). "This decision [referring to the first *Orange Grove* case] illustrates that a jurisdiction can go overboard in trying to attract business and cater to a trade—especially the low end of the trade. . . . Many reputable advisers now agree that settlors should avoid the Cook Islands." *Id.* at p. 44.

[73] The recent case of *FTC v. Affordable Media, LLC, Denyse Anderson and Michael Anderson,* illustrates how settlors can find themselves first in a bind and then in jail. The Andersons, through their company, engaged in a telemarketing business that amounted to a ponzi scheme. The Federal Trade Commission stepped in to stop the business and obtained a preliminary injunction ordering, among other things, repatriation of assets, *i.e.,* the proceeds from the illegal scheme. The defendants did not comply; they were held in contempt; and they appealed to the United States Court of Appeals for the Ninth Circuit. The defendants had created an APT Trust in the Cook Islands. They claimed that it was impossible for them to cause the assets to be repatriated. The District Court found as a matter of fact that they controlled the trust; and the appellate court was unwilling to say that this finding was erroneous. "With foreign laws designed to frustrate the operation of domestic courts and foreign trustees acting in concert with domestic persons to thwart the United States courts, the domestic courts will have to be especially chary of accepting a defendant's assertions that repatriation or other compliance with a court's order concerning a foreign trust is impossible. Consequently, the burden on the defendant of proving

meantime, at the high-end of the market, careful settlors continue to enjoy the protection that a classic common law trust provides.

Chapter 13 deals at greater length with this subject.

5.3.2 Certain revocable and irrevocable foreign trusts

Exceptions to the rules of section 672(f), which negate the grantor trust rules where they result in foreign ownership, are revocable trusts and trusts the income of which during the grantor's lifetime are distributable to the grantor or his/her spouse. Here the grantor again is treated as the owner of the assets and the person who earns the income. If the grantor is not a U.S. citizen or resident and, therefore, does not pay U.S. taxes, U.S. taxes are properly avoided, as was the case under the pre-1996 Act rules. Of course, these exceptions fall away when the grantor dies.[74] This subject is also discussed in Section 9.2.

5.3.3 Specific gifts through a foreign nongrantor trust (Pecuniary Dynastic Offshore Trusts)

A Pecuniary Dynastic Offshore Trust is a foreign nongrantor trust created to take advantage of the provision in section 663(a)(1) that

---

impossibility as a defense to a contempt charge will be especially high. Given these considerations, we cannot find that the District Court clearly erred in finding that the Andersons compliance with the repatriation order was not impossible because the Andersons remain in control of their Cook Islands trust." It will be noted that the Andersons were co-trustees of the trust at the outset and tried to hide the fact that they were also "protectors" of the trust. They previously had been able to obtain in excess of $1 million from the trust in order to pay their taxes. When trouble arose, the Andersons attempted to resign as protectors. "This attempted resignation indicates that the Andersons knew that, as protectors of the trust, they remained in control of the trust and could force the foreign trustee to repatriate the assets. . . . Given the nature of the Andersons so-called 'asset protection' trust, which was designed to frustrate the power of United States' courts to enforce judgments, there may be little else that a district court judge can do besides exercise its contempt powers to coerce people like the Andersons into removing the obstacles they placed in the way of the court."

[74] The author has suggested to one or two good-humored clients that upon the grantor's death, he should be stuffed by a taxidermist and stood in a corner. This tax plan generally has not been well-received by grantors; and almost certainly it would not be smiled upon by the IRS.

excludes from a complex trust's deductible distributions and from a beneficiary's includible amount an amount that, under the terms of the trust's governing instrument, is paid as a gift of a specific sum of money or specific property and that is payable in not more than three installments. Thus, an amount coming out of the trust as a section 663(a)(1) gift will not be subject to the onerous throwback rule and interest charge in Subpart D of Subchapter J.

Tax planners are suggesting that the settlor can create a foreign trust with U.S. beneficiaries, suffer the consequences of the trust being treated as a grantor trust until he dies; benefit—through the foreign trust—from deferral of U.S. taxes on income earned by the trust after his death until such time as a gift is made to U.S. beneficiaries, and avoid the throwback rule and interest charge on a large specific gift subsequently made to U.S. beneficiaries in three installments. The benefit is the tax-free accumulation of income and the tax-free gift payments to the U.S. beneficiaries. The large size of the gifts usually assumes that there will be considerable appreciation on top of the amount initially contributed. There are additional fillips to address the Generation Skipping Tax and the possibility that some U.S. beneficiaries may cease to be U.S. citizens sometime down the road, but this is the basic idea.[75]

It is pointed out that the IRS might argue that the gift is not specific under the meaning of the statute. Or it might argue that the gift is residuary in character. Or it might say that the gift is conditional. And it is pointed out that Congress might act to close this opportunity at some point in the future.

Two additional points might be considered. First, the last sentence of section 663 states: "For this purpose an amount which can be paid or credited only from the income of the estate or trust shall not be considered as a gift or bequest of a specific sum of money." The IRS might point to this language and argue that the gift is not a gift of a specific sum of money.

Secondly, the fact that specific gifts were not addressed in the Small Business Job Protection Act of 1996, which enacted the many

---

[75] Kurlander & Delgass, "Pecuniary Dynastic Offshore Trusts: New Opportunities for U.S. Citizens," TRUSTS & ESTATES, July 1999.

changes in the foreign trust tax and reporting area, was recognized as work on the legislation was being completed. Some believe that the Congressional and Treasury Department staffs felt at the time that Treasury Department and the IRS could address this issue in the "abusive transactions" legislative regulations to be written under section 643(a)(7). If we were to place a bet, we would not bet against this happening. Then the question becomes what will be the effective date of the regulations, if promulgated. The answer is nobody knows; but this type of anti-abuse regulation frequently carries an effective date retroactive to the date of enactment.[76] Lastly, we note that it may be cumbersome to reverse out of a trust containing specific gift language that, by its nature, cannot be conditional.

5.4 Distributable net income

It is often said that distributable net income is the "measuring rod" for the taxation of trusts and beneficiaries. The DNI of a trust limits the amount of a deduction that a trust can deduct under sections 651 and 661 (applicable to simple and complex trusts, respectively) and as to which the beneficiaries can be taxed under sections 652 and 662 (applicable again to simple and complex trusts, respectively). DNI establishes and helps retain the character of different items of income passing from the trust to its beneficiaries. It is used to determine how income distributed by a trust is allocated among the beneficiaries. Also, DNI limits the amount of undistributed net income (UNI) that can be retained by a trust without causing the application of the difficult "throwback" rules on the receipt of distributions by beneficiaries.

Section 643 (definitions applicable to Subpart A, B, C, and D) provides rules for the computation of distributable net income (DNI). DNI, with respect to any taxable year, is the taxable income of the trust computed with a number of modifications.

1. No deduction is taken for distributions.

2. No deduction is taken for the applicable personal exemption under section 642(b).

---

[76] The most famous case of retroactive legislation occurred in the foreign trusts (section 679) area in the Tax Reform Act of 1976.

3. Capital gains are excluded from DNI to the extent such gains are allocated to corpus and are not either paid, credited, or required to be distributed to any beneficiary during the taxable year or paid, currently set aside, or used for a charitable purpose. Capital losses also are excluded except to the extent they are taken into account in determining the amount of gains that are paid, credited, or required to be distributed to any beneficiary during the taxable year. The 50% exclusion for gain from certain small business stock, under section 1202, is not taken into account. (The reference to section 1202 formerly referred to the regular capital gains deduction; but the capital gains tax rules have been reworked in recent years. Beginning after May 6, 1997, the maximum capital gains rate, in general, is 20%. The lower capital gains rate applies not only to individuals, but also to trusts and estates. The lower rate also applies under the alternative minimum tax.) (It will be noted that this portion of the rule only applies to domestic trusts and will be overriden so far as foreign trusts are concerned. See below.) The regulations reiterate that gains are ordinarily excluded from DNI and are not ordinarily considered as paid, credited, or required to be distributed to any beneficiary unless they are allocated to income under the terms of the governing instrument or local law by the fiduciary on its books or by notice to the beneficiary, or are allocated to corpus and actually distributed to beneficiaries during the taxable year, or are utilized—pursuant to the terms of a governing instrument or the practice follow by the fiduciary—in determining the amount which is distributed or required to be distributed. There are special rules for charitable payments.

> ➔ The handling of capital gains and losses for domestic trusts can be beneficial when applying the tax rules applicable to a domestic simple trust that earns income, including capital gains, and distributes it on a current basis to foreign beneficiaries. The domestic trust will be taxable as any other U.S. taxpayer—that is, it will be subject to the progressive rate schedule applicable to the trust's net income; and the trust will be entitled to the trust-level deduction for distributions made to beneficiaries including capital gains that are included in DNI. If, for example, gains are allocated to corpus and are actually distributed to beneficiaries

> during the taxable year, gains should be included in DNI and should, in effect, lift the limitation on the amount of the deduction. Distributions from the trust to the foreign beneficiaries will be subject to withholding tax, if any, at the Code or reduced treaty rate.[77]

4. As regards simple trusts, extraordinary dividends or taxable stock dividends which the fiduciary, acting in good faith, does not pay or credit to any beneficiary on the ground that they are properly allocable to corpus under the terms of the governing instrument and applicable local law, are excluded.

5. Tax-exempt interest generally is included in DNI; however the amount included must be reduced to reflect the disallowance of expenses and interest relating to tax-exempt income.[78]

6. Special rules are provided for foreign trusts. Foreign source gross income is included in DNI, but it is reduced by amounts that would be deductible but for the disallowance of expenses and interest related to tax-exempt income. Foreign source income is determined without regard to the rules relating to income exempt under treaties.[79] Most importantly, with respect to foreign trusts, the general capital gains rule described above will not apply. "In case of such a [foreign] trust, there shall be included gains from the sale or exchange of capital assets, reduced by losses from such sales or exchanges to the extent such losses do not exceed gain from such sales or exchanges."[80] The regulations that should elaborate upon these particular rules have not been promulgated.[81]

---

[77] *See Wittschen v. Commissioner*, 5 T.C. (1945), *acq*., 1945 C.B. 7; *Isidro Martin-Montis Trust v. Commissioner*, 75 T.C. 381 (1980), *acq*., 1981-2 C.B. 2. *See also* Zaritsky, Foreign Trusts, Estates and Beneficiaries, BNA Tax Management Portfolio 911-1st and Roberts & Warren, U.S. INCOME TAXATION OF FOREIGN CORPORATIONS AND NONRESIDENT ALIENS, 11-75 (PLI 1971).

[78] Section 265.

[79] Section 894.

[80] Section 643(a)(6)(C).

[81] It should be noted that a trust can realize a gain on the distribution of appreciated assets. This gain is recognized if the distribution is made in satisfaction of a pecuniary sum, and the trustee may elect to recognize the

A common misunderstanding is the thought that DNI is essentially the same as fiduciary accounting income under U.S. accounting rules. It is not. DNI can be greater or less than fiduciary accounting income. When it is greater, current distributions charged to principal for accounting purposes may nevertheless be taxable as income to beneficiaries that receive distributions. If current distributions are not made, beneficiaries may be subject to tax under the "throwback" rules in later years. When DNI is less than fiduciary accounting income, some distributions to current income beneficiaries are tax-free even though any economic burden of the tax deductions falls on other beneficiaries (generally the recipients of principal distributed in the future). Also, non-U.S. fiduciary accounting income may differ from U.S. fiduciary accounting income. (In a number of popular non-U.S. jurisdictions, the accounting rules are drawn from Canadian and U.K. accounting rules.)

Some of the workings of the rules relating to DNI can be illustrated as follows. Assume that the trust incurs a trustee's fee that according to local law must be charged to trust income or corpus. If the fee is chargeable to trust income, then it will reduce the amount distributable to the beneficiaries. The trustee's fee is also a deductible expense for federal income tax purposes; and therefore it will offset the trust's gross income in the computation of taxable income. However, if on the other hand the trustee's fee is charged against corpus, it will not reduce trust income and the beneficiaries' distribution. It will be deducted for tax purposes and thus taxable income will be less than trust income. If Trust A has $100,000 of taxable income and has paid a trustee's fee of $10,000, which is chargeable to corpus, then the beneficiaries will receive $100,000 of trust income. Since the taxable income of the trust and, it follows, its DNI, is only $90,000, the beneficiary will be taxed on only $90,000. If the beneficiary were taxed on $100,000 and the trust, with $90,000 of taxable income, were given a special deduction of ten thousand dollars, the $10,000 would have been lost or wasted in the

---

gain on any other distribution of appreciated assets. Treas. Reg. § 1.661(a)-2(f).

computation of tax income. In order to prevent this result, the Code gives the beneficiaries the benefit of the deduction.[82]

Questions frequently arise as to the tax consequences of an assignment of income relating in some fashion to a trust. According to a line of Supreme Court and Courts of Appeals cases, if a beneficiary who is entitled to income from a trust makes an absolute assignment of all or part of his interest to another person for the remainder of his (the assignor's) life, the assignor will not be taxable upon the income subsequently distributed to the assignee.[83] If, however, such a beneficiary makes an assignment of all or part of his interest to another person for a relatively short period of time—say, eight years—or simply from time to time, then the assignor will be treated as the taxpayer with respect to the income distributed. For example, in Harrison v. Schaffner, the taxpayer, who was a life beneficiary of a testamentary trust, in December 1929 assigned to her children specified amounts from the income of the trust for the year following the assignment. She repeated this process the next year. The Supreme Court decided that she, not the children, was responsible for the tax. "We think that the gift by a beneficiary of a trust of some part of the income derived from the trust property for the period of a day, a month or a year involves no such substantial disposition of the trust property as to camouflage the reality that he is enjoying the benefit of the income from the trust of which he continues to be the beneficiary . . ." [84]

The IRS set forth the rules for the taxation of assignments of trust income in Rev. Rul. 55-38, as follows:

---

[82] McDaniel, Ault, McMahon, & Simmons, FEDERAL INCOME TAXATION (4th Ed. 1998), p. 1,248.

[83] *Blair v. Commissioner*, 300 U.S. 5 (1937).

[84] *Harrison v. Schaffner*, 312 U.S. 579 (1941) (assignor treated as the taxpayer); *Blair v. Commissioner*, 300 U.S. 5 (1937) (assignee treated as the taxpayer). Sometimes the reasoning of the "assignment of income" line of cases is difficult to reconcile. As has been suggested, it may be that the right to receive income for short periods, such as the assignment in *Schaffner*, takes on a stronger resemblance to the receipt by the assignor followed by a gift of the income, than to the transfer of appreciated property. In any event, it will be noted that the tax result in a *Schaffner*-like case flows from general tax principles, not the trust provisions in Subchapter J.

> Where the lifetime income beneficiary of a testamentary trust from time to time gives his written consent, pursuant to the terms of the will, to pay a certain portion of the trust income to another individual, the amounts so paid will be taxable as income to the beneficiary inasmuch as he, in point of substance, has parted with no substantial interest in property other than the specified payments of income. See Harrison v. Sarah H. Schaffner, 312 U.S. 579, Ct. D. 1503, C.B. 1941-1, 321. However, in the case of an irrevocable assignment, valid under local law, of trust income for a period of not less than 10 years, such income will be taxable to the assignee, provided the facts are not such as would subject the lifetime income beneficiary (the assignor) to the tax on the income under the principles of section 39.22(a)-21 of Regulations 118, section 167 of the Internal Revenue Code of 1939, Edward B. Douglas v. Willcuts, 296 U.S. 1, Ct. D. 1041, C.B. XIV-2, 250 (1936), or I. T. 4007, C.B. 1950-1, 11. In such a case the position of the assignor is analogous to that of the grantor of a trust. Under such circumstances, because of the period and character of the assignment, the lifetime income beneficiary will be considered to have made a disposition of a substantial interest in the trust property. See Edward T. Blair v. Commissioner, 300 U.S. 5, Ct. D. 1205, C.B. 1937-1, 175.

Rev. Rul. 55-38, 1955-1 C.B. 389.

The regulations under section 102 contain additional information. Section 102 provides that gross income does not include the value of property acquired by gift, bequest, devise, or inheritance. However, it is further provided that the income from any property acquired by gift, etc. will not be excluded; and where the gift, etc. is of income from property, the amount of such income will not be excluded. "Any amount included in the gross income of a beneficiary under subchapter J shall be treated for purposes of . . . [section 102] as a gift, bequest, devise, or inheritance of income from property."[85] The regulations make clear that any amount (i.e., distribution) required to be included in gross income of a beneficiary (the recipient of the distribution) will not be excluded from gross income since it will be viewed as a gift, etc. of income from property. An exception is provided for any amount excluded from the gross income of a beneficiary under section 663(a)(1) (the provision dealing with a gift or bequest of a specific sum of money or a specific property payable all at once or in not more than three installments). The regulations go on to provide: "Section 102 is not intended to tax a donee upon the same income which is taxed to the grantor of a trust or assignor of income under section 61 or sections 671 through 677, inclusive."[86]

> ➔ If a foreign nongrantor trust was established to distribute income to Beneficiary A, a nonresident alien individual, during his life with the remainder to Beneficiary B, and Beneficiary A periodically assigns his distributions to C, a U.S. taxpayer, Beneficiary A would be viewed as the taxpayer and C would not be subject to tax. This result flows from the general assignment of income principles, not any particular provision of tax law applicable to trusts or gifts. For purposes of Section 6039F (Noticc Of Large Gifts Received From Foreign Persons) and Form 3520, it is unclear whether C need treat these facts as amounting to a gift. The better view, it is suggested, is that the recipient should do so and should report the receipt on Form 3520. It would be helpful if the instructions to Form 3520 were changed to address this point.

> ➔ The rule in section 663(a)(1) (relating to specific gifts, bequests, etc.) that specific gifts are not included in the amount deductible by the trust and

[85] Section 102(b).

[86] Treas. Reg. § 1.102-1(e), Income Tax Regs. (emphasis added). This regulation was adopted December 28, 1956, shortly after Rev. Rul. 55-38 was published.

includable by the beneficiaries may be viewed by some as an oversight in that such an amount paid by a foreign trust to U.S. beneficiary will not be taxed but will be treated in essence as a gift. It is suggested that this is not an unwarranted result. As discussed above at paragraph 5.3.3, such gifts—sometimes made through so-called "Pecuniary Dynastic Offshore Trusts"—have a number of cumbersome features. Also, it should be appreciated that the abusive transactions regulations, to be issued under section 643(a)(7g), may rectify this oversight; and it is highly unlikely that Congress will spring to its feet to defend the taxpayers' position.

Chapter 6

Nongrantor Trusts: Simple

Simple, nongrantor trusts are what might be thought of as regular trusts all the income of which is required to be distributed on a current basis. Such trusts are not taxed on income earned; but instead they deduct when computing taxable income as the amount of income that is required to be distributed currently. It follows that the beneficiaries are required to include in income the amount required to be distributed currently, whether in fact distributed or not. Normal tax rules will apply to determine whether income is earned.

The rules governing the taxation of simple trusts are contained in Subpart B of Chapter J (sections 651 and 652). The Code does not use the term "simple," but it appears in the regulations. A simple trust, as defined in section 651 (deduction for trusts distributing current income only), is a trust the terms of which provide that all of its income is required to be distributed currently and which does not provide that any amounts are to be paid, permanently set aside, or used for charitable purposes. The trust will not be a simple trust in any taxable year in which the trust actually distributes amounts other than current income. Section 651 also provides that a simple trust will be allowed a deduction in the amount of the income which is required to be distributed currently. It goes on to limit this deduction to the amount of the trust's DNI. "For this purpose, the computation of distributable net income shall not include items of income which are not included in the gross income of the trust and the deductions allocable thereto."[87]

Section 652 (inclusion of amounts in gross income of beneficiaries of trusts distributing current income only) deals with the taxation of the beneficiaries of a simple trust. The amount of income for the taxable year required to be distributed currently by a simple trust will be included in the gross income of the beneficiaries to whom the income is required to be distributed, whether or not

[87] Section 651(b).

distributed. If the amount distributed exceeds the trust's DNI, there will be included in the gross income of each beneficiary an amount that bears the same ratio to DNI as the amount of income required to be distributed to such beneficiary bears to the amount of income required to be distributed to all beneficiaries.[88]

The amounts included in income will have the same character in the hands of the beneficiary as in the hands of the trust. "For this purpose, the amounts shall be treated as consisting of the same proportion of each class of items entering into the computation of distributable net income of the trust as the total of each class bears to the total distributable net income of the trust, unless the terms of the trust specifically allocate different classes of income to different beneficiaries."[89]

For example, where the trust indenture provides that all the income is payable on a current basis to Beneficiary A and the remainder, upon Beneficiary A's death, is payable to Beneficiary B, the trust is a simple trust.

Where the trust indenture provides that all the income is payable on a current basis to Beneficiaries A, B, C, and D, and it is left to the trustee, in the exercise of its discretion, to "sprinkle" the income among the beneficiaries, giving some more than others or not giving some anything, the trust is still a simple trust.

If the trustee has discretion to distribute corpus during the taxable year but does not do so, the trust is still a simple trust.

A trust can be treated as a simple trust in one year and a complex trust in another.

If the trust instrument does not allocate different classes of income to different beneficiaries and local law does not require such an allocation, each beneficiary will be deemed to receive some of a portion of each class of items entering into distributable net income in proportion to the beneficiary's share of trust income. This "proration rule" prevents a trustee from allocating tax exempt income to high-

[88] Section 552(a).
[89] Section 652(b).

bracket beneficiaries and taxable income to lower-bracket beneficiaries. If different classes of income are specifically allocated to different beneficiaries under the trust instrument, each beneficiary will be deemed to receive the items of income specifically allocated to her. However, the regulations provide that any special allocation must have an economic effect independent of tax consequences. An allocation pursuant to a provision of a trust instrument granting the trustee discretion to allocate different classes of income to different beneficiaries is not a specific allocation by the terms of trust.

For example, if a trust indenture provided that all U.S. source income should be distributed to Beneficiary A, a U.S. taxpayer, and all non-U.S. source income to Beneficiary B, a nonresident alien, this specific allocation might be ignored as not having an economic effect independent of income tax consequences. Arguably the result might be different if a trust indenture provided that all dollar denominated income from "dollar" investments would be distributed to Beneficiary A, and all British pounds sterling denominated income from "sterling" investments would be distributed to Beneficiary B.[90]

[90] *Muir v. Commissioner*, 10 TC293 (1948).

Chapter 7

Nongrantor Trusts: Complex; "Throwback" Rules; Interest Charge

7.1 General

Subpart C of Subchapter J deals with trusts that may accumulate income or that distribute corpus. Subpart D (Treatment Of Excess Distributions By Trusts) provides definitions and rules relating to "throwbacks" and the imposition of an interest charge on accumulation distributions from foreign trusts. Until 1997, domestic trusts and their beneficiaries, as well as foreign trusts and their beneficiaries, had to worry about the "throwback" rules in Subpart D. Since 1997, these rules, in general, only apply to foreign trusts and their beneficiaries. Also, the 1996 Act made significant changes in the rules governing the computation of tax on accumulation distributions from a foreign trust and the interest rate charged. The regulations under the relevant Code provisions have not yet been amended to reflect these changes; but proposed regulations may be forthcoming in the near future.

Subpart C contains special rules relating to charitable remainder trusts.[91] These rules will not being reviewed here.

7.2 Rules relating to complex (accumulation) trusts

It should be recalled when dealing with a complex (accumulation) trust, that some of the rules – those for the deduction by the trust of income required to be distributed currently and for inclusion in income by the beneficiaries of such income – are the same as they are for a simple trust. Income required to distribute currently flowing through a complex trust should be treated the same as that income traveling through a simple trust.

---

[91] Section 664.

The income of the trust is going to be taxed either to the beneficiaries or the trust because the gift exemption applies only to the amount placed in trust. The tax provisions, especially those applicable to complex trusts, are intended to ensure that a gift (or an inheritance, the case of an estate) will be excluded from gross income; income on trust property will be taxed, but only once; rules for the allocation of income that is taxed and allocation of different types of income, such as tax-exempt income, will be applied; there will be no need for tracing amounts through the hands of the trust into the hands of beneficiaries; the federal income tax rules will accommodate the local law pattern governing fiduciary accounting and administration rules and will utilize fiduciary accounting concepts for determining the relevant potential tax exposure of various beneficiaries; and deductions will not be wasted.

In order to do all this, the Code, where necessary, applies a so-called "tier system."

Where all the trust's income must be distributed currently and no corpus is distributed, the results are the same as they are with a simple trust. That is, the beneficiaries as a group are taxed to the extent of DNI. If the total distribution exceeds DNI because, for example, trustees' fees or other items are charged to corpus, then each beneficiary's taxable amount is that proportion of DNI which the amount of the distribution the beneficiary receives bears to the total distribution to all beneficiaries, unless the trust instrument provides otherwise. If DNI includes items of income that have a special tax status, such as tax-exempt interest, each beneficiary will be considered as receiving a proportionate share of each class of item, unless the trust instrument has provided that a particular class of income will be distributed to certain beneficiaries.

Where the trust distributes not only income but also corpus, matters become considerably more complicated. For example, a domestic trust has gross income of $15,000, consisting of $5,000 of capital gains, allocable to corpus by the trust instrument, and $10,000 of interest income. It has no expenses. Its DNI is $10,000 (recalling that with respect to domestic trusts capital gains allocable to corpus are excluded from DNI). The trust is required to distribute the $7,500 to Beneficiary A, which it does, and it exercises its discretion to distribute $3,500 to Beneficiary B. Since the amount to be deducted by the trust and included in income by the beneficiaries is limited by the amount of DNI, how will DNI be allocated between the two beneficiaries?

Section 662(a) provides ordering and allocation rules. Included in the gross income of the beneficiary to whom an amount that is deductible by the trust is paid, credited or required to be distributed, is the sum of the following: (1) The amount of income for the taxable year required to be distributed currently to such beneficiary, whether or not actually distributed. What happens if this figure exceeds DNI? If the amount of income required to be distributed currently to all beneficiaries exceeds the distributable net income (computed without any charitable deduction) of the trust, then there will be included in the gross income of the beneficiary an amount that bears the same ratio to DNI as the amount of income required to be distributed currently to such beneficiary bears to the amount required to be distributed currently to all beneficiaries. In other words, there is a straight-forward *pro rata* allocation. (This is Tier 1.) (2) All other amounts properly paid, credited or required to be distributed to the beneficiary. If the sum of the amount described in (1) and the amount described in (2) exceeds the DNI of the trust, then there will be included in the gross income of the beneficiary an amount which bears the same ratio to the DNI (reduced by the amounts described in (1)) as the other amounts properly paid, etc. to the beneficiary bear to the other amounts properly paid, etc. to all beneficiaries. (This is Tier 2.) In other words, the Code allocates DNI first among all beneficiaries to whom the trustee is required to distribute income currently. These distributions "soak up" DNI to the extent it is available. If there is any DNI remaining, it is allocated among the recipients of any other distributions.

The Tier 1 beneficiaries typically receive taxable distributions because there is sufficient DNI to cause their distributions to be taxable (*i.e.,* to "cover" their distributions). Tier 2 beneficiaries typically are taxed on their distributions only to the extent of the balance of DNI remaining after allocation to the Tier 1 beneficiaries. "Thus it is generally the tier two beneficiaries who reap the benefit of the DNI ceiling limitation. The statute treats second-tier distributions as inheritances of income only to the extent DNI is available; distributions in excess of DNI are excludible from gross income. If tier two distributions exceed the DNI that remains after tier one allocations, the statute allocates the remaining DNI ratably among the tier two beneficiaries." It should be noted that a beneficiary can appear in both Tier 1 and Tier 2 because, for example, she is receiving income required to be distributed currently and other income. Also, DNI can be carried out not only by an actual distribution of income required to be distributed currently, but also by an amount required to be paid out currently that for whatever reason was not so distributed.

As regards both tiers, the conduit principle applies; the amounts distributed will have the same character in the hands of the beneficiary as in the hands of the trust. Where there are a number of beneficiaries, unless the terms of governing instrument specifically provide otherwise, the distributions will be treated as consisting of the same proportion of each class of items entering into the computation of DNI as the total of each class bears to the total DNI of the trust. (There are special rules in the case of charitable deductions.)

Since it may be difficult to figure out who gets what, the trustee of a complex trust is permitted to elect to treat any distribution made within 65 days after the end of a taxable year as if the distribution had been paid earlier, on the last in the taxable year ending just before the distribution.[92] The election is made by completing the appropriate line on Form 1041 (U.S. Fiduciary Income Tax Return). The election is irrevocable for the taxable year and is effective only for the year of the election. Where the trustee wishes to avoid a build-up of undistributed net income, he can do so more easily with a little time to make the computations.

If the trust distributes property, sections 643(e) requires that the amount taken into account under sections 661 (for simple trusts) and 662 (for complex trusts) is the lesser of the basis of the property or its fair market value. If appreciated property is distributed, therefore, the trust's deduction and the beneficiary's income exclusion will be limited to the basis of the property in the hands of the trust. The beneficiary will have a transferred basis for the property, *i.e.*, the same basis as existed for the trust. In this event, the appreciation will be taxed to the beneficiary at the time of a subsequent sale or other disposition of the property. Section 643(e)(3) allows the trustee to

[92] Section 663(b).

elect to recognize gain or loss on the distribution, in which case the trust's deduction and beneficiary's income inclusion will be determined with reference to the fair market value of property. The beneficiary will have a basis that is increased by the amount of gain or decreased by the amount of loss recognized by the trust. The pre-distribution appreciation will not be taxed beneficiary.

> ➔ The trustee of a foreign trust will want to consider making the election to have the trust taxed on the gain even though capital gains are included in DNI because other factors may cause U.S. Tier 2 beneficiaries to receive nontaxable income.

As a separate matter, a distribution of appreciated property in satisfaction of a monetary request will be treated as resulting in the recognition of gain

Section 663(c) provides for the treatment of separate shares as separate trusts. This treatment is mandatory—not elective. A trustee can be required to apply the separate share rule even though separate and independent accounts are not maintained for each share and there is no physical segregation of assets. The rule states that for the sole purpose of determining the amount of DNI in the application of the deduction and inclusion rules in sections 661 and 662, substantially separate and independent shares of different beneficiaries in a trust "shall" be treated as separate trusts; and this treatment will be carried over into the application of the "throwback" rules. The rule is intended to prevent a beneficiary from being taxed on a distribution that represents a corpus distribution as to that beneficiary, but which—absent this rule—would be treated as a taxable distribution because trust income is accumulated for the benefit of another beneficiary. The regulations under section 663(c) are helpful in explaining the rule. They state that the applicability of the rule will generally depend upon whether distributions of the trust are to be made in substantially the same manner as if separate trusts had been created. The rule will not be applied to a trust or a portion of a trust that is subject to a power to distribute, apportion or accumulate income or distribute corpus to or for one or more beneficiaries within a class of beneficiaries, unless payment of income, accumulated income or corpus of a share of one beneficiary cannot affect the proportionate share of income, accumulated income or corpus of any shares of the other beneficiaries, or "unless substantially proper adjustment must thereafter be made (under the governing instrument) so that substantially separate and independent shares exist."[93]

7.3 "Throwback" rules and interest charge on accumulation distributions from a foreign trust

7.3.1 General

Subpart D of Subchapter J deals with the taxation of accumulation distributions. These distributions sometimes are referred to as "excess distributions." Of course, by definition, they will always be coming from a complex trust—since simple trusts distribute current income only.

These rules appear in four sections of the Code (sections 665-668). Since enactment of the Taxpayer Relief Act of 1997, the complicated "throwback" rules no longer apply to most domestic trust.[94] They only apply to foreign trusts and domestic trusts created before March 1, 1984, unless it is shown that the pre-March 1, 1984 trust would not be aggregated with one or more other trusts under the rules for the treatment of multiple trusts in section 643(f).

The general idea, as will be seen, is that distributions from income that has been accumulated will be thrown back into the recipient's prior taxable years and taxed almost as if the recipient had received and paid tax on this income in those prior years. However, the approach used by the Code is far from exact. If one went back and re-computed the taxes of the beneficiary assuming distributions in prior years, the result would be different from the result arrived at by applying the throwback rule. The throwback rule, as will be seen, is essentially a formula that contains a provision for averaging certain figures. Also, in order to eliminate the advantage of deferring the tax until the year of the subsequent distribution, an interest charge is applied to the postponed tax amounts.

---

[93] Reg. § 1.663(c)-3, Income Tax Regs. The regulations are quite detailed.

[94] P.L. 105-34, effective with respect to distributions in taxable years beginning after August 5, 1997 (*i.e.*, generally 1998).

In order to follow the workings of these provisions, it is necessary to understand several definitions. These definitions form the working parts of the puzzle. "Part of the complexity of the throwback rules is due to the statute's reliance on terminology unfamiliar even to most tax lawyers."[95] One definition—that of distributable net income (DNI) —has already been addressed.

Unfortunately, the regulations under these definitional provisions have not been amended to reflect any of the statutory changes over the last 23 or so years. Obviously, this area of the law has not captured the Service's attention. Much of what is contained in the regulations is simply no longer relevant.

7.3.2 Definitions applicable to Subpart D

Section 665 provides the definitions that are referred to the remainder of Subpart D.

Undistributed net income (UNI) means the amount by which the DNI of the trust for the taxable year exceeds the sum of all current and other distributions from the trust plus the amount of taxes imposed on the trust attributable to such DNI.[96] Put differently, UNI is DNI, less the trust's distribution deduction under sections 651 and 661 and the trust's taxes on DNI.[97]

As a general matter, the phrase "taxes imposed on the trust" means the amount of the taxes that are imposed for a taxable year of the trust that are allocable to the undistributed portions of DNI and gains in excess of losses from sales or exchanges of capital assets.

---

[95] Ferguson Freeland & Asher, FEDERAL INCOME TAXATION OF ESTATES, TRUSTS, AND BENEFICIARIES (3rd ed., 1998) p. 9-5.

[96] Section 665(a). It will be recalled that current distributions include income that is required by the trust document to be distributed currently whether or not distributions of current income in fact are made. Reg. § 1.651(a)-1(b). Also, a trust can be a simple trust for one year and a complex trust for another year.

[97] The references and mechanical workings of the "throwback" rules apply to complex trusts—not to simple trusts. Simple trusts, by definition, do not accumulate income.

With respect to foreign trusts, this term includes the amount of any allocated foreign taxes.[98]

When calculating the UNI available in a given year, accumulation distributions in intervening years—years between the year of accumulation and the current year—must be taken into account. UNI, however, will not be reduced by distributions in intervening years that are excluded as specific gifts, etc., under section 663(a)(1).[99]

Accumulation distributions in those situations where the "throwback" rules will continue to apply means the amount by which so-called other distributions (*i.e.*, distributions that are not current distributions) exceed DNI less the amount of current distributions. "In other words, an accumulation distribution occurs when tier two distributions exceed the DNI remaining after tier one distributions."[100] The DNI figure cannot be reduced below zero for this purpose.

The regulations provide that a distribution from one trust to another trust will generally be treated as an accumulation distribution. This rule applies regardless whether the distribution is to an existing trust or to a newly created trust, and regardless whether the trust to which the distribution was made was created by the same person who created the trust from which the distribution was made or by a different person. (It would seem that this regulatory rule would apply only to a distribution, not a contribution to the corpus of a trust.) (At one time there was a special capital gains throwback rule. This rule was repealed by the Tax Reform Act of 1976. (*See* Chapter 10, below.) In light of this capital gains throwback rule, the regulations provided that a distribution made from one trust to a second trust will be deemed an accumulation distribution by the first trust to the ultimate beneficiary of the second trust if the primary purpose of the distribution to the second trust was to avoid the capital gains distribution provisions.)[101]

---

[98] Section 665(d).

[99] Reg. § 1.665(a)-1A(d).

[100] Ferguson, Freeland & Ascher, FEDERAL INCOME TAXATION OF ESTATES, TRUSTS, AND BENEFICIARIES (3rd Ed.) (Aspen Law & Business 1998), p. 9-7.

[101] Reg. § 1.665(b)-1A(b)(1), Income Tax Regulations.

The regulations further provide that if amounts forming all or part of an accumulation distribution are used for the support of a dependent or are used in satisfaction of a person's legal obligations, then such amounts will be treated as a distribution directly to the person whose obligations are being satisfied.[102]

> ➔ In order for a reduction in DNI/UNI to be affected, it is not necessary that the recipient beneficiary be a U.S. taxpayer. For example, if income were accumulated by a foreign complex trust in Year 1 and an accumulation distribution were made in Year 2 to a nonresident alien individual, this distribution would have the effect of carrying out (reducing) UNI.

For purposes of calculating the additional taxes and interest charge on amounts thrown-back into prior years, "other amounts properly paid or credited or required to be distributed" (*i.e.*, amounts other than current distributions) will not include amounts properly paid, credited or required to be distributed to a beneficiary from a trust as income accumulated before the birth of such beneficiary or before such beneficiary attained age 21; provided, however, this beneficial rule will not apply in the case of a foreign trust.[103] Also, if the amounts properly paid, credited or required to be distributed by the trust do not exceed the income of the trust for that year, there will be deemed to have been no accumulation distribution. This provision is designed to prevent distributions of a current year's trust income to a beneficiary from being treated as an accumulation distribution where the trust's financial accounting income is greater than its DNI.

The term "preceding taxable year" can be important because it determines the "reach" of the "throwback" rule. With respect to a foreign trust created by a U.S. person, the term will not include a taxable year of a trust to which these rules do not apply. Due to the effective dates of the Internal Revenue Code of 1954, the provisions of Subpart D will not, in the case of a foreign trust created by a U.S. person, be applied to a taxable year that begins before 1954 or ends

[102] Reg. § 1.665(b)-1A(b)(3), Income Tax Regulations.
[103] Section 665(b).

before August 17, 1954. (This rule is one of the few remnants of the distinction between a foreign trust created by a U.S. person and other foreign trusts remaining after the Tax Reform Act of 1976.)

7.3.3 The "throwback" rules (sections 666 and 667)

The basic workings of the "throwback" rules are set forth in section 667 (treatment of amounts deemed distributed by trust in preceding years). However, in order to make these rules work, it is necessary to allocate the amount of any accumulation distribution during the taxable year to preceding years; and rules for doing this are contained in section 666 (accumulation distribution allocated to preceding years).

Section 667 (a) states the general rule. The tax imposed by the Code on a beneficiary for a taxable year in which an accumulation distribution is included in his income shall be determined only as provided in section 667; in other words, these rules apply notwithstanding and override any other provisions in the Code. Such tax consists of the sum of

(1) a "partial tax" computed on the beneficiary's taxable income, reduced by amounts thrown back to the beneficiary during the taxable year,

(2) a "partial tax" on the amounts thrown back computed in accordance with section 667(b), and

(3) in the case of a foreign trust, the interest charge determined as provided in section 668.

Section 667(b) provides detailed rules for determining the "partial tax" on the amounts thrown back. There are six steps to be followed.

1. It is necessary to determine the number of preceding taxable years of the trust to which amounts have been thrown back. This determination is made in accordance with the rules set forth in section 666, discussed below.

2. Focusing on the beneficiary's five taxable years immediately preceding the year of the accumulation distribution, exclude ("kick out") the one taxable year for which the beneficiary's

taxable income was the highest and the one taxable year for which his taxable income was the lowest.

3. To the beneficiary's taxable income for each of the remaining three years, add the amount thrown back (including taxes deemed distributed), divided by the number of preceding taxable years as previously determined.

4. Determine the average increase in tax for the subject three taxable years attributable to the average amount thrown back.

5. Multiply the average increase in tax determined under Step 4 by the number of preceding taxable years as previously determined.

6. Determine the excess of the amount determined under Step 5 over the amount of taxes deemed distributed to the beneficiary under sections 666(b) and (c).

In order to take the first step, it is necessary to determine the number of preceding taxable years to which amounts have been thrown. This determination is accomplished by making the allocation of the accumulation distribution to preceding years set forth in section 666. That section provides that the amount of the accumulation distribution shall be deemed to be an amount of other income (that is, income that is not required to be distributed currently) distributed on the last day of the preceding taxable years commencing with the earliest of such years to the extent that such amount exceeds the total of any undistributed net income for all earlier preceding taxable years. This approach can be likened to the old trick where champagne glasses are stacked on top of one another and filled by pouring champagne in the glass at the top of the stack. Here, the champagne is the amount of the accumulation distribution; the champagne glasses are the preceding taxable years in which there was some amount of UNI; the size of the glasses vary in accordance with the amount of UNI; and glasses are stacked in accordance with their age—the oldest glass (earliest preceding taxable year) at the top. The accumulation distribution will be allocated to the first preceding taxable year of the trust in which there was UNI, to the extent of that UNI. If the accumulation distribution exceeds the trust UNI for that year, the excess will then be allocated to the next year of the trust in which there was UNI, to the extent of that UNI, and so forth, until the accumulation distribution is entirely accounted for (the champagne runs out).[104]

Section 667(b)(3) slips in a special rule (a form of a *de minimis* rule) that can affect the calculation of the number of preceding taxable years. It states that if the UNI deemed distributed in any preceding taxable year is less than 25 percent of the amount of the accumulation distribution divided by the number preceding taxable years to which the accumulation distribution is allocated (think of this as an average figure), the number of preceding taxable years with respect to which an amount is deemed distributed shall be determined without regard to such year.

Also, for purposes of calculating the "partial tax" on the accumulation distribution, the taxable income of the beneficiary for the taxable year will not be deemed to be less than zero. In other words, the beneficiary cannot benefit from a loss year.[105]

It is clear that for purposes of allocating to preceding taxable years an accumulation distribution of the current year, the UNI of the preceding taxable years is reduced by the amount from such prior years deemed distributed in any accumulation distribution of UNI made in any taxable year intervening between the preceding taxable years and the current taxable year. This rule is necessary to avoid double counting. There is no requirement that the prior accumulation distributions that carried out amounts of UNI occasioned a payment of U.S. tax.

If adequate information is not available to determine the proper application of the "throwback" rules, then the amount distributed to the beneficiary during the current year will be deemed to be an accumulation distribution consisting of UNI earned during the earliest

---

[104] This stacking rule is different if an accumulation distribution is made before January 1, 1970. Section 1.666(a)-1A (a), Income Tax Regulations. The current regulations contain a number of special provisions relating to foreign trusts. These regulations were adopted in 1972, before the changes enacted as part of the Tax Reform Act of 1976. These regulations need to be withdrawn and new regulations put in their place.

[105] Section 667(b)(2).

preceding taxable year of the trust in which it can be established that the trust was in existence. Obviously, among other things, this rule will work strongly against the taxpayer when it comes time to apply the interest charge.

The best way to learn the operations of the "throwback" rule is probably to work through an example.

Example. ABC Trust is a foreign nongrantor accumulation trust created under the laws of Bermuda. The trust is not subject to tax in Bermuda; however, it does incur some taxes in other non-U.S. countries.[106] It was created in Year 1 with a transfer in trust of $100,000. In Year 11, the trust distributes $85,000 to Beneficiary A, a U.S. citizen. In prior years, it had the following record of earnings and taxes.

Year	DNI	Taxes	UNI
1	$10,000	$1,500	$8,500
2	$15,000	$2,250	$12,750
3	$8,000	$1,200	$6,800
4	$7,500	$1,125	$6,375
5	$8,500	$1,275	$7,225
6	$2,000	$300	$1,700
7	$500	$75	$425
8	$6,500	$975	$5,525
9	$8,000	$1,200	$6,800
10	$10,000	$0	$10,000
Totals	$76,000	$9,900	$66,100

[106] Under section 665(d)(2), taxes imposed on the trust includes the amount of any income, war profits and excess profits taxes (reduced by any amount of such taxes deemed distributed to any beneficiary under sections 666(b) and (c)), imposed by any foreign country or possession of the U.S. on the foreign trust which, under regulations, are so properly allocable. Presumably "taxes" also includes U.S. taxes. However, the question of how to treat U.S. taxes paid by a foreign trust generally does not arise since a foreign trust is treated as a nonresident alien not present in the U.S. and, therefore, is not subject to U.S. taxes. U.S. taxes withheld on interest, dividends and the like paid to the foreign trust are not taken into account; this income is earned by the foreign trust net of withholding taxes.

The distribution of $85,000 creates an accumulation distribution of $75,000.

Beneficiary A's taxable income for these years is as follows.

Year	Taxable Income	
1	$180,000	
2	$182,000	
3	$175,000	
4	$175,000	
5	$165,000	
6	$200,000	
7	$155,000	
8	$165,000	
9	$130,000	
10	$125,000	

Step 1. Pursuant to the allocation rules in section 666, the accumulation distribution is allocated to the first year in which the trust has UNI, that is, Year 1. Year 1 absorbs $8,500 of the accumulation distribution. Next, the accumulation distribution is allocated to the next year in which the trust has UNI, that is, Year 2. Year 2 absorbs $12,750 of the accumulation distribution. This allocation process is continued until the entire accumulation distribution is absorbed; and in this case, this does not occur since the amount of the accumulation distribution ($75,000) exceeds the total amount of UNI ($66,100).

The resulting allocation of the $75,000 accumulation distribution looks like this.

Year	DNI	Taxes	UNI	Accumulation Distribution Allocable To Year
1	$10,000	$1,500	$8,500	$8,500
2	$15,000	$2,250	$12,750	$12,750
3	$8,000	$1,200	$6,800	$6,800
4	$7,500	$1,125	$6,375	$6,375
5	$8,500	$1,275	$7,225	$7,225
6	$2,000	$300	$1,700	$1,700
7	$500	$75	$425	$425
8	$6,500	$975	$5,525	$5,525
9	$8,000	$1,200	$6,800	$6,800
10	$10,000	$0	$10,000	$10,000
Totals	$76,000	$9,900	$66,100	$66,100

It will be noted that $8,900 of the $75,000 ($75,000 - $66,100) is not absorbed and should be viewed as a distribution of corpus.

The *de minimis* rule of section 667(b)(3) must then be applied. Twenty-five percent (25%) of the amount of the accumulation distribution divided by the total number of preceding taxable years to which the accumulation distribution relates is $1,875. There are two years with UNI of less than $1,875, that is, Years 6 and 7. These two years are "kicked out;" and therefore, for purposes of section 667(b)(1)(A), there are 8, not 10, years to which amounts will be thrown back.

Step 2. Looking at the five taxable years immediately preceding the year of the distribution, that is, Years 6 through 10, the year with the highest taxable income and the year with the lowest taxable income are "kicked out" of the calculation. Therefore, we "kick out" Year 6 and Year 10.[107]

Step 3. Now dealing only with Years 7, 8 and 9, it is necessary to add to each the amount thrown back. For these purposes, the amount thrown back is increased by the amount of taxes imposed on the trust

[107] It will be noted that a beneficiary's taxable income can include an amount thrown back to that taxable year on account of a prior accumulation distribution from the same or a different trust. Thus, this picture of the beneficiary's history of taxable income can change over time; and it is not enough simply to look at his old tax returns.

for such preceding taxable year attributable to the UNI. "Taxes" does not include the alternative minimum tax. Also, this approach applies so long as the amount thrown back to the year in question equals or is greater than the UNI for that taxable year; if it is less, it will be necessary to perform a *pro rata* apportionment under section 666(c).

The amount thrown back is derived first by dividing the amount of the accumulation distribution ($75,000) by the number of preceding taxable years (8) ($75,000 / 8 = $9,375).

To the amount thrown back it is necessary to add the amounts of tax imposed on the trust in the preceding years. Since the amounts of accumulation distribution attributable to each of Years 1 through 10 (see Step 1) is not less than UNI, the entire amount of the trust's taxes constitutes an additional amount thrown back to each of these years. Therefore, by adding for each preceding year the amount of taxes imposed on the trust to the accumulation distribution allocable to the year, we arrive at the following:

Year	Accumulation Distribution Allocable To Year (Sec. 666(a))	Taxes Deemed Distributed (Sec. 666(b) &(c))	Amount Thrown Back
1	$8,500	$1,500	$10,000
2	$12,750	$2,250	$15,000
3	$6,800	$1,200	$8,000
4	$6,375	$1,125	$7,500
5	$7,225	$1,275	$8,500
6	$1,700	$300	$2,000
7	$425	$75	$500
8	$5,525	$975	$6,500
9	$6,800	$1,200	$8,000
10	$10,000	$0	$100
Totals	$66,100	$9,900	$66,100

It will be noted that only $100—not $10,000—is thrown back in Year 10; this is because the total amount of UNI is $66,100. Sixty-six thousand dollars worth of UNI was distributed in Years 1-9.

The total amount thrown back is $66,100. This figure, then, must be divided by the number of preceding taxable years as previously determined—that is 8; and the result is $8,262.50 ($66,100 / 8 = $8,262.50). This average figure ($8,262.50) is added to the beneficiary's taxable income for each of the three remaining years:

Year 7	$155,000	$8,262.50	$163,262.50
Year 8	$165,000	$8,262.50	$173,262.50
Year 9	$130,000	$8,262.50	$138,262.50

Step 4. Next, focusing on the three taxable years resulting from the winnowing process in *Step 2* (Years 7, 8 and 9), it is necessary to compute the average increase in tax of the beneficiary for each of these three years.[108]

Year	Actual Taxable Income	Actual Tax	Increased Taxable Income	Tax On Increased Income	Increase In Tax
Year 7	$155,000.00	$44,257.50	$163,262.50	$47,232.00	$2,974.50
Year 8	$165,000.00	$47,857.50	$173,262.50	$50,832.00	$2,974.50
Year 9	$130,000.00	$35,257.50	$138,262.50	$38,232.00	$2,974.50

Under these circumstances, the average increase in tax is obviously $2,974.50 (($2,974.50 + $2,974.50 + $2,974.50) / 3 = $2,974.50).

➔ The tax rates being used are those actually applicable in the prior years. The fact that the calculation is dealing with three out of the most recent five years means that the taxpayer will not have to go too far back into history. However, it will be noted that these rates can jump around if Congress changes the rates or the taxpayer moves from one category to another—say, from married filing jointly to single.

[108] Here, for ease, the rate applied in the prior years is 36% on amounts over $128,100 but not over $278,450—which is the next to highest rate applicable for 1998 for single individuals.

Step 5. The next step is to multiply the average increase in tax as determined above by the number of preceding taxable years; that is, $2,974.50 times 8 equals $23,796.00.

Step 6. Lastly, the excess of the amount arrived at in *Step 5* ($23,796.00) over the total amount of taxes deemed distributed under section 666(b) and (c) ($9,900, which is the total for all the years, as shown in column 3 in the schedule in *Step 3*, above) is determined: $23,796 less $9,900 equals $13,896.

This amount, $13,896, is the partial tax on the $75,000 accumulation distribution. It is this figure that will be added to the partial tax computed on the beneficiary's taxable income absent the amounts deemed distributed by the trust in preceding years and the section 668 interest charge.

> ➔ This example understates the amount of the partial tax commonly due to the throwback. This is because the example assumes that there are significant taxes imposed on the trust. These taxes reduce the amount thrown back and taxed to the recipient. With the typical foreign trust, however, there would be little or no taxes imposed on the trust.

Section 667(c)(1) provides a special rule where a beneficiary has received distributions from more than two trusts. The rule states that if as to a preceding taxable year there have been amounts thrown back from two other trusts, then as to amounts thrown back from a third trust (or fourth trust, or fifth trust, etc.), taxes imposed on the trust will not be subtracted. It is not clear why this rule was put in place; it may be a legislative example of "enough is enough."

> ➔ Form 3520 provides that the beneficiary should use Form 4970 as a worksheet to calculate the tax on an accumulation distribution. Form 3520, p. 8.

1. Interest charge on accumulation distributions

Section 668 imposes an interest charge on accumulation distributions from a foreign trust. The interest rate is the floating rate applied under section 6621 to underpayments of tax, instead of 6% as under prior law. Interest is compounded daily. (Simple interest accrues through 1995.) Interest charges are computed over a specially calculated number of years rather than with reference to the length of time between the year of the earliest undistributed accumulations and the year of distribution, as under previous law.

The number of years over which interest is calculated is determined by the following method intended to produce a "dollar-weighted" number of years:

1. The undistributed net income for each year is multiplied by the number of years between such year and the year of the distribution (counting the year of the accumulation but not the year of distribution);

2. All products computed in the first step are added together;

3. The sum of such products calculated in the second step is divided by the aggregate amount of the trust's undistributed income.

For purposes of this computation, an accumulation distribution will be treated as having come proportionately from each year with respect to which there is undistributed net income (other than a year during which the beneficiary was not a U.S. person) rather than from the earliest accumulation years.[109]

Example: Assume that the facts are the same as in the example set forth in paragraph 7.3.2, above. The period for which interest is charged is determined as follows:

[109] In other words, this is not the "old champagne trick" approach to throwing amounts back, as used in section 666.

A	B	C	D
Year	UNI	Number of Intervening Years	B X C
1	$8,500	10	$85,000
2	$12,750	9	$114,750
3	$6,800	8	$54,400
4	$6,375	7	$44,625
5	$7,225	6	$43,350
6	$1,700	5	$8,500
7	$425	4	$1,700
8	$5,525	3	$16,575
9	$6,800	2	$13,600
10	$10,000	1	$10,000
Totals	$66,100		$392,500

Divide the sum of Column D ($392,500) by the aggregate of UNI ($66,100) ($392,500 / $66,100 = 5.9380). The quotient is rounded in accordance with regulations to be promulgated; but the regulations have not been issued. The instructions to Form 3520 and line 56 of that Form provide that this figure should be rounded to the nearest half-year. Thus, 5.9380 would be rounded to 6.

Next, it is necessary to compute the actual amount of the section 668 interest charge. Interest accumulates on the amount of the partial tax on the accumulation distribution (the section 667(a)(2) figure) for the period beginning on the date that is the applicable number of years prior to the applicable date and ending on the applicable date. For example, in the example just given, if Year 11 is 1999 and the beneficiary is a calendar-year taxpayer, the applicable date would be June 30, 1999. If the taxpayer receives only a single accumulation distribution during the taxable year, he or she can use the actual date of the distribution—say, September 1, 1999—as the applicable date.

→ It will be noted, however, that if the mid-year date convention is not used, the taxpayer will not be able to rely upon Table B in Form 3520, which provides the combined interest rate imposed on the total accumulation distribution (that is, the IRS has done the calculation based on various "applicable number of years of the trust" and provided the "combined

> interest rate"). Instead, the taxpayer will have to calculate the combined interest rate. There are ways to access information about the floating section 6621(a)(2) rate; but after obtaining the information about the rate, performing this calculation is difficult. The IRS should consider making available the formulae that underlie Table B or referencing a website.

With respect that part of the applicable period that falls prior to 1996 but after 1976 (*i.e.*, between the 1996 Act and the 1976 Act), interest accumulates at a simple rate of 6% per annum. It is only for those portions of the applicable period that fall after 1995 that interest is compounded daily at the rate imposed on an underpayment of tax under section 6621(a)(2).

> ➔ This compounded interest rate is imposed not only on the partial tax but also on the total simple interest attributable to pre-1996 periods. Therefore, where pre-1966 years are involved, a separate calculation of this amount of interest must be made. This figure is then added to the amount of partial tax on the accumulation distribution; and the compounded interest rate is applied to this total figure. Since it is common for trusts to have been in existence for a relatively long period of time, the problem of having to deal with at least two interest calculations will be frequently encountered.

Assuming for simplicity's sake that the facts are as stated in the example above, none of the years are pre-1996 years, the taxpayer is a calendar-year taxpayer, and the mid-year convention described in the instructions to Form 3520 is used, the combined interest rate will be 0.6618. Therefore, the section 668 interest charge will be $9,196 ($13,896 X 0.6618 = $9,196).

Looking back at section 667, using this example, the total of the section 667(a)(2) partial tax and the section 668 interest charge is $23,092.

Section 668(b) provides a limitation on the total amount of the interest charge. The total amount of the interest charge when added to the section 667(a)(2) partial tax cannot exceed the amount of the accumulation distribution exclusive of tax treated as being distributed under section 666(b) or (c).

> → As noted above, the example used understates the amount of the section 667(a)(2) partial tax and therefore the amount of the interest charge and the total of these two amounts. If more than ten years are involved, the interest charge can double the partial tax. Also, it is easy to conceive of a situation where the section 668(b) limitation would apply.

Chapter 8

Grantor Trusts

This chapter discusses grantor trusts. Those topics that are most relevant to the taxation of foreign grantor trusts are highlighted. Since the taxation of grantor trusts alone can be the subject of a fairly lengthy treatise, some aspects will be touched upon lightly rather than examined exhaustively.

A few of the important provisions relating to foreign grantor trusts are discussed not in this chapter but in the next—the one dealing with special rules applicable to foreign trusts.

The grantor trust rules are fairly strong medicine; that is, they dictate that a certain person—almost always the grantor—will be treated as the taxpayer with respect to income earned by the trust. It follows, therefore, "as night follows day," that other persons (the trust itself and the beneficiaries of the trust) will not be taxed. Thus, while the result can be bad for the person that is marked as the taxpayer, it can be very favorable for the other involved parties. This fact makes these provisions a form of attractive nuisance. Taxpayers seek to find ways to use them to their advantage; and Congress and the tax authorities try to combat this.

8.1 General

In some cases, the grantor of a trust retains such extensive controls or powers over the trust that he or she is considered to remain the owner of the trust property for income tax purposes. Under the "grantor trust" rules of the Code, the settlor of the trust is treated as the owner of the trust assets and must include in income all items of income, deduction, credit, etc. related to such property. This result obtains even if none of the trust income is paid or otherwise made available to the settlor. It follows that the trust and the beneficiaries are relieved of any tax obligation. When the trust makes a distribution, it is treated as, in effect, a gift by the grantor to the beneficiary. Sections 641 through 679 spell out in great detail what results in imposition of the grantor trust rules.

A grantor trust can be a domestic trust or a foreign trust, except that, as will be seen, the 1996 Act changes go a long way towards eliminating foreign grantor trusts. Prior to these changes, a non-U.S. grantor could create a domestic or foreign trust.[110] He or she could keep sufficient control over the trust to cause it to be a grantor trust. The grantor, therefore, would be treated as the owner of the trust assets, but the grantor would not pay any U.S. tax because not resident for tax purposes. And the beneficiary, even though perhaps a U.S. citizen or resident, would not pay any tax on distributions. The 1996 Act added a rule preventing the application of the grantor trust rules where they would result in the owner of the trust assets being someone other than a U.S. citizen or resident or a domestic corporation, *i.e.*, the grantor trust rules can only apply to make someone who is subject to the U.S. tax jurisdiction taxable, not to make someone who is not subject to U.S. tax, and therefore will not pay the tax, taxable.[111] This rule applies whether the trust is a domestic trust or a foreign trust.

> ➔ It should be noted that section 6048© provides that domestic trusts with foreign activities, to the extent Treasury Department regulations provide, can be treated as foreign trusts. "To the extent provided in regulations, a trust which is a United States person shall be treated as a foreign trust for purposes of this section and section 6677 if such trust has substantial activities, or holds substantial property, outside the United States." However, Notice 97-34, 1997-1 CB 422 states that the Treasury Department and the IRS are studying the approporate scope of this particular provision; and until further guidance is issued, all domestic trusts will be treated as domestic trusts, not foreign trusts, pursuant to this provision.

Subpart E of Subchapter J (relating to grantors and others treated as substantial owners) deals with grantor trusts. Section 671 provides the punch line; that is, what are the consequences if the trust is a

[110] The usual practice was to create a foreign grantor trust.
[111] Section 672(f).

grantor trust. Section 672 provides a number of definitions and special rules. Five sections—sections 673 through 677—provide rules that if triggered will cause the trust to be treated as a grantor trust. Section 678 is a special rule that can cause someone other than the grantor to be treated as the owner of the assets—that is, the taxpayer—under section 671. (This is the so-called *Mallinckrodt* rule, named after a famous case.)

Section 679 is a truly unique provision. In effect, it provides that a grantor can relinquish all practical control over the trust property and still be treated as the owner of such property simply because he or she is a U.S. person, the trust is a foreign trust and there is a U.S. beneficiary with respect to any portion of the trust. It follows that while for tax purposes the settlor remains the owner of the assets in question, for other purposes (such as creditors' rights), the settlor will be treated as not owning the assets. It is this diversion of tax law and other law that led to the creation of "Protection of Assets Trusts" and the growth of a multi-billion dollar protection of assets business.

> ➔ The question whether a settlor making a transfer in trust is making a taxable gift and therefore must pay the gift tax is separate from the issues surrounding characterization of the trust. For example, a settlor can make a completed gift or not when he/she makes a transfer to a nongrantor or grantor trust. Just because the grantor is treated as owner of the assets under the grantor trust rules does not mean that he/she has not made a completed gift.[112] Moreover, the new definition of "grantor" contained in proposed regulations New Reg. § 1.671-2T turns in part upon whether there has been a gratuitous transfer. Reg. § 1.671-2T(e)(2) states that "[a] transfer of property to a trust may be considered a gratuitous transfer without regard to whether the transfer is treated as a gift for gift tax purposes."

Years ago, taxpayers commonly sought to push income into trusts, where the income would be taxed at a lower rate. This splintering of income was intended, in effect, to offset the effects of

[112] Reg. §25.2511-2(d).

the progressive rate structure. However, in recent years, the Code has been amended to provide generally reduced rates (for example, with the Tax Reform Act of 1986) and a compression of the structure of rate brackets for trusts (Tax Reform Act of 1986).[113] Now the trend is more toward creating "defective" trusts—ones that will be treated as grantor trusts—so as to choose who will be the taxpayer; and it will be recalled that the distributions can actually go to the beneficiaries without tax. For example, a parent might establish a trust for a child so as to have income accumulated in the trust. But in order to avoid having the income taxed at the high rate applicable to the trust, the trust will be drafted to "flunk" one of the grantor trust rules; but ordinarily the provision will not be one that would cause the trust property to be included in the grantor's estate.

The history of the grantor trust provisions is an interesting one.[114] Predecessor provisions of the ones in the Code today were enacted in 1924, but they were quite limited in scope. The IRS first sought to have Congress expand them and then, this failing, began aggressively litigating in the area. In 1940, the Service won the landmark case of *Helvering v. Clifford*,[115] which held that the settlor's dominion and control over the trust property was such that even though he did not violate the statutory provisions then in effect, he should be treated as the owner of the assets. But the case did not establish a clear set of rules for dealing with the many factual situations that can present themselves; and a large number of cases arose at the lower court and courts of appeals levels. In 1945, the Treasury Department issued the so-called "Clifford regulations" in an attempt to lay down comprehensive rules. These were criticized as a usurpation of the Congress' legislative power. Then, with enactment of the Internal Revenue Code of 1954, Congress formulated a complete set of rules applicable to trusts. It adopted many provisions from the Treasury Department's regulations. Also, importantly, it provided that the rules in Subpart E should trump the judicial concept of "dominion and

---

[113] This compression means that the tax rates applicable to trusts "zip" up from 15% on the first $1,700, through 3 skinny brackets, to 39.6% on amounts over $8,350.

[114] *See* Ferguson, Freeland & Ascher, FEDERAL INCOME TAXATION OF ESTATES, TRUSTS, AND BENEFICIARIES (3rd Ed.) (Aspen Law & Business 1998), §10.02.

[115] *Helvering v. Clifford*, 309 U.S. 331 (1940).

control." "No items of a trust shall be included in computing the taxable income and credits of the grantor or of any other person solely on the grounds of dominion and control over the trust under section 61 ... or any other provision of this title, except as specified in this subpart."[116] The rules in subpart E seem to have been successful in settling this area of the law; and they have gone relatively untouched since enactment. The one big exception is section 679 (relating to foreign trusts having one or more U.S. beneficiaries), which was enacted in 1976 and has been fiddled with on a couple of occasions.

8.2 Transactions between the grantor trust and the settlor

As section 671 in effect treats the grantor as the owner of the assets legally belonging to a grantor trust, it is difficult to envision in all cases how a transaction between the trust and the grantor (settlor) should be viewed. On the one hand, it would appear that were a grantor to enter into a sales transaction with a grantor trust as to which he is grantor, he is dealing with himself. On the other hand, the trust will have a trustee, and that trustee may be entirely independent from the grantor. In this light it appears that the grantor is dealing with a separate party.

This situation was analyzed in the case of *Rothstein v. United States.*[117] There the taxpayer created an irrevocable trust for his children. His wife was the trustee. Subsequently he purchased from the trust its sole asset, which was shares in a closely held corporation. He paid for the shares with an unsecured promissory note. The corporation was then liquidated. The taxpayer claimed a short-term capital loss because he received an amount in liquidation that was less than his basis in the stock, that is, the amount he paid the trust for the shares. The IRS redetermined his tax and assessed a deficiency on the ground that since the taxpayer was the grantor, the trust with which he dealt should be disregarded and the taxpayer should not treat the cost of the shares as his adjusted basis for purposes of computing gain. The Second Circuit (Judge Friendly) determined that the taxpayer should not be viewed as dealing with himself but rather as dealing with a separate person – that is, the trustee of the

[116] Section 671. *See Estate of Hilton W. Goodwyn*, 35 T.C.M. 1026 (1976).
[117] 574 F. Supp. 19 (D. Conn. 1983), *rev'd*, 735 F.2d 704 (2d Cir. 1984).

trust. Section 671, it was said, simply attributes items of income, deductions and credits from a grantor trust to its grantor.

> Section 671 makes it plain that it was not Congress's intention that the taxation of grantor/owners be governed by what might otherwise seem the sensible general principle that a taxpayer may not have meaningful dealings with himself. . . . Nowhere does § 671 direct that the grantor's basis in property purchased from the trust be deemed any different from what it would otherwise be, namely, his cost of acquiring it. . . . [Section] 671 dictates that, when the grantor is regarded as "owner," the trust income shall be attributed to him – this and nothing more.

The IRS, in Revenue Ruling 85-13,[118] has announced that it will not follow the decision in *Rothstein*.

> In Rothstein v. United States, 735 F.2d 704 (2d Cir. 1984), the court considered a transaction that is in substance identical to the facts described in this ruling. The court held that the grantor was the owner of a trust under section 675(3) of the Code because by exchanging an unsecured note for the entire trust corpus, the grantor had indirectly borrowed the trust corpus. The court held further, however, that although the grantor must be treated as the owner of the trust, this means only that the grantor must include items of income, deduction, and credit attributable to the trust in computing the grantor's taxable income and credits, and that the trust must continue to be viewed as a separate taxpayer. The court held, therefore, that the transfer of trust corpus to the grantor in exchange for an unsecured promissory note was a sale and that the taxpayer acquired a cost basis in the assets.

---

[118] Rev. Rul. 85-13, 1985-1 C.B. 184.

> In Rothstein, as in this case, section 671 of the Code requires that the grantor includes in computing the grantor's tax liability all items of income, deduction, and credit of the trust as though the trust were not in existence during the period the grantor is treated as the owner. Section 1.671-3(a)(1) of the regulations. It is anomalous to suggest that Congress, in enacting the grantor trust provisions of the Code, intended that the existence of a trust would be ignored for purposes of attribution of income, deduction, and credit, and yet, retain its vitality as a separate entity capable of entering into a sales transaction with the grantor. The reason for attributing items of income, deduction, and credit to the grantor under section 671 is that, by exercising dominion and control over a trust, either by retaining a power over or an interest in the trust, or, as in this case, by dealing with the trust property for the grantor's benefit, the grantor has treated the trust property as though it were the grantor's property. The Service position of treating the owner of an entire trust as the owner of the trust's assets is, therefore, consistent with and supported by the rationale for attributing items of income, deduction, and credit to the grantor.
>
> The court's decision in Rothstein, insofar as it holds that a trust owned by a grantor must be regarded as a separate taxpayer capable of engaging in sales transactions with the grantor, is not in accord with the views of the Service. Accordingly, the Service will not follow Rothstein.

Revenue Ruling 85-13, 1985-1 C.B. 184.

The *Rothstein* decision has been criticized in a number of quarters. Also, in 1996, in a set of proposed regulations, the Service rewrote the rule by stating "For purposes of subtitle A of the Internal Revenue Code, a person that is treated as the owner of any portion of a trust under subpart E is considered to own the trust assets attributable to that portion of the trust."[119] Yet when Congress has wanted to provide that the treatment in section 671 should not be available, it has not been shy about making its point. Section 672(f) is a perfect example. Therefore, it seems that all parties – the courts, the IRS, others – should be slow to import a different meaning into the statute.

8.3 Definition of grantor

The consequence of a trust being characterized as a grantor trust is that the burden of taxation is shifted from one person—the trust—to another—the settlor or, in the case of section 678, some other person. Therefore, identifying who is the grantor can be quite important. Until recently, there was no definition of the term "grantor" in either the Code or the regulations. The term generally was considered to mean "settlor" or the person who creates a trust.

On June 5, 1997, the Service published proposed regulations under section 671 defining grantor. There were a large number of critical comments on these proposed regulations. On August 10, 1999, the Service published T.D. 8831 replacing these proposed regulations with temporary regulations effective as of that date.

The new temporary regulations (Section 1.671-2T) provide as follows.

> For purposes of part I of subchapter J, chapter 1 of the Internal Revenue Code, a grantor includes any person to the extent such person either creates a trust, or directly or indirectly makes a gratuitous transfer (within the meaning of paragraph (e)(2) of this section) of property to a trust. For purposes of this section, the term property includes cash. If a person creates or funds a trust on behalf of another person, both persons are treated as grantors of the trust. (See section 6048 for reporting requirements that apply to grantors of foreign trusts.) However, a person who creates a trust but makes no gratuitous

[119] Reg. §1.671-2(f), Proposed Income Tax Regs., REG-209826-96, 9/27/96. These regulations have not been finalized.

> transfers to the trust is not treated as an owner of any portion of the trust under sections 671 through 677 or 679. Also, a person who funds a trust with an amount that is directly reimbursed to such person within a reasonable period of time and who makes no other transfers to the trust that constitute gratuitous transfers is not treated as an owner of any portion of the trust under sections 671 through 677 or 679. See also section 1.672(f)- 5(a).
>
> ...
>
> A grantor includes any person who acquires an interest in a trust from a grantor of the trust if the interest acquired is an interest in certain investment trusts described in section 301.7701- 4(c) of this chapter, liquidating trusts described in section 301.7701-4(d) of this chapter, or environmental remediation trusts described in section 301.7701-4(e) of this chapter.

Reg. §1.671-2T, Temporary Regulations (Aug. 10, 1999).[120]

The Temporary Regulations go on to describe the treatment of transfers by a corporation, partnership or trust. If a gratuitous transfer is made by a corporation or a partnership to a trust and is for a business purpose, the corporation or partnership will be treated as the grantor of the trust. For example, if a corporation makes a gratuitous transfer to a trust in order to secure a legal obligation of the corporation to a third party unrelated to the corporation, the corporation will be treated as the grantor. However, if a corporation

[120] The idea that someone could create a trust but not make a gratuitous transfer to the trust is a little hard to fathom, since a trust must be funded to come into existence. Treasury and the IRS want to treat a nominal creator as a grantor so as to ensure that someone will be responsible for reporting the creation of a foreign trust by a U.S. person even if the trust is not immediately funded. "At the same time, Treasury and the IRS believe that an accommodation grantor, such as an attorney who creates a trust on behalf of a client, (although a grantor) should not be treated as an owner of the trust." T.D. 8831, Explanation of Provisions and Revisions, 2 (Comments and Changes to Section 1.671-2(e): Definition of Grantor).

or a partnership makes a gratuitous transfer to a trust that is not for a business purpose but, for example, is for a personal purpose of the shareholders or partners, the gratuitous transfer will be treated as a constructive distribution to the shareholders or partners and the shareholders or partners will be treated as the grantors of the trust. For example, if a corporation makes a gratuitous transfer to a trust that is for the benefit of a child of a shareholder, the gratuitous transfer will be treated as a distribution to the shareholder and a subsequent gratuitous transfer by the shareholder to the trust.[121]

Concerning transfers by trusts, if a trust—any trust, not just a grantor trust—makes a gratuitous transfer of property to another trust, the grantor of the transferor trust generally will be treated as the grantor of the transferee trust. While one might think that this rule no longer applies when the grantor is dead, an example in the Temporary Regulations makes clear that the rule still applies.[122] The rules pull up short of treating the creation of the trust by a trust as a constructive distribution to the grantor of the trust that creates the new trust. T.D. 8831 states parenthetically: "These rules do not affect the determination of whether or not the gratuitous transfer from the

[121] T.D. 8831 cites *Epstein v. Commissioner*, 53 T.C. 459 (1969), *acq. on another issue*, 1970-2 C.B. xix. This type of novel "recasting" rule can cut a number of different ways. Obviously, it is intended to "catch" a variety of cases. However, it will also apply where the corporation is a foreign corporation and the shareholder of the corporation is a nonresident alien. The nonresident alien will be the constructive grantor of the trust for U.S. tax purposes but almost certainly not the grantor for purposes of his or her home country rules. What happens if the foreign corporation has the right to revoke the trust? Is this also treated as constructively belonging to the shareholder? And what happens if the shareholder is simply given the power to revoke the trust?

[122] G creates and funds a trust, T1, for the benefit of G's children and grandchildren. After G's death, under authority granted to the trustees in the trust instrument, the trustees of T1 transfer a portion of the assets of T1 to another trust, T2, and retain a power to revoke T2 and revest the assets of T2 in T1. Under paragraphs (e)(1) and (5) of this section, G is the grantor of T1 and T2. In addition, because the trustees of T1 have retained a power to revest the assets of T2 in T1, T1 is treated as the owner of T2 under section 678(a). Reg. §1.671-2T (Example 8), Temporary Regulations (Aug. 10, 1999)

transferor trust is a distribution subject to sections 651 or 661."[123] However, if a person with a general power of appointment over the transferor trust exercises that power in favor of another trust, then such person will be treated as the grantor of the transferee trust, regardless of the fact that the grantor of the transferor trust is treated as the owner of the transferor trust under the grantor trust rules.

8.4 Attribution of trust income, deductions, etc. to grantors and other substantial owners

Section 671 provides that where the rules of sections 672-679 (*i.e.*, Subpart E) specify that the grantor or another person will be treated as the owner of any portion of a trust, the consequence is there will be included in computing the taxable income and credits of that person those items of income, deductions and credits against tax of the trust that are attributable to that portion of the trust. Any remaining portion of the trust will be taxed under the other Subparts of Subchapter J. Also, "[n]o items of a trust shall be included in computing the taxable income and credits of the grantor or of any other person solely on the grounds of his dominion and control over the trust under section 61 . . . or any other provision of this title, except as specified in this subpart."[124]

The concept that the taxation of a trust can be split up into pieces or portions is an interesting one. Neither the Code nor the regulations defines "portion" as such, but the regulations under section 671 discuss the concept and give a number of examples. Apparently there can be an almost endless number of ways to split up the trust; the regulations merely illustrate some of the ways. As shown, the grantor or another person can be treated as owning (a) the entire trust (corpus

[123] If there is a constructive distribution from the first trust and re-contribution to the new trust, then it should follow that the distribution can carry out UNI, which affects the taxation of any subsequent accumulation distribution. Once the statute or the regulations sets up a constructive transaction, it is difficult to see how some consequences should pertain and others not.

[124] It is tempting to say that Subpart E completely occupies the field when considering taxing a grantor or other person on income nominally belonging to a trust. However, rules relating to assignments of income, family partnerships, gift-leasebacks, and "sham" are kept alive by the regulations and an occasional court case.

as well as ordinary income), (b) specific property and its income, (c) an undivided fractional interest in the trust, (d) a specific "dollar amount," (e) ordinary income, (f) income allocable to corpus. When reading the examples in the regulations, it should be kept in mind that the trust's governing instrument can specify that such-and-such portion of the trust will be subject, for example, to a power to revoke.

Most retained interests and powers, such as a right to revoke or appoint in favor of the grantor or another person, take the form of financial accounting income; for example, a transfer in trust with a retained right to all the income—which is commonly viewed as the ordinary income portion of the trust, not income allocable to corpus. However, there is nothing to prevent the governing document from "cutting the pieces" differently. "For example, a grantor might retain an income interest labeled in any of the following ways: 'income subject to the Federal income tax,' 'gross income,' 'taxable income,' 'DNI,' or 'tax-exempt income.'"[125]

When determining how to handle items of income, deduction, etc. where the grantor or another person is treated as the owner of only ordinary income or only income allocable to corpus, the regulations fall back on concepts used in Subparts A-D. For example, if such person is treated as an owner of the ordinary income earned by the trust, because of an interest in or power over such income, he or she will take into account for purposes of computing tax liability those items which would be included in computing the tax liability of a current income beneficiary, including expenses allocable to corpus that enter into the computation of DNI.[126]

➔ A foreign trust might be a grantor trust as to a portion of the trust and a nongrantor trust as to the remainder. Also, by using the term "portion," section 672(f) adopts the various ramifications of this term. For example, A, a nonresident alien, settles ABC Trust. The indenture provides that A retains the power to revoke the trust to the extent of all income (ordinary income and income allocable to

[125] Ferguson, Freeland & Ascher, FEDERAL INCOME TAXATION OF ESTATES, TRUSTS, AND BENEFICIARIES (3rd Ed., 1998), p. 10-24.
[126] Reg. § 1.671-3(c), Income Tax Regs.

corpus). As to that portion of the trust allocable to ordinary income and income allocable to corpus, it will be treated as a grantor trust, and the grantor, A, will treated as the owner. Section 672(f)(2)(A)(i) should apply to the effect that the grantor trust rules are not withdrawn; and distributions to a U.S. beneficiary are not taxable.[127] The remainder of the trust (in reality, the corpus) is treated as a non-grantor trust. Distributions to a U.S. beneficiary from this portion of the trust are subject to the rules applicable to distributions from a foreign accumulation trust; but there will be no "throwback" of income since there is no DNI/UNI account. This result should not be viewed as especially surprising.

8.5 Definitions and special rules

Section 672 contains definitions and special rules pertaining to grantor trusts and one or two other subjects that are further afield—such as the possible recharacterization of any gift from a foreign corporation or partnership.

"Adverse party" is defined as any person having a substantial beneficial interest in the trust that would be adversely affected by the exercise or non-exercise of the power that he possesses respecting the trust. A person having a general power of appointment over the trust property is deemed to have a beneficial interest in the trust.[128]

"Nonadverse party" means any person who is not an adverse party.[129]

"Related or subordinate party" means any nonadverse party who is the grantor's spouse (if the spouse is living with the grantor) and any one of the following: the grantor's father, mother, issue, brother or sister, an employee of the grantor, a corporation or any employee of a corporation in which the grantor's stock holdings are "significant from the viewpoint of voting control," a subordinate employee of a

[127] Rev. Rul. 69-70, 1969-1 C.B. 182.
[128] Section 672(a).
[129] Section 672(b).

corporation in which the grantor is an executive. For purposes of section 672(f) (Subpart E not to result in foreign ownership), section 674 (power to control beneficial enjoyment) and section 675 (administrative powers), a related or subordinate party will be presumed to be subservient to the grantor unless such party is shown not to be subservient by a preponderance of the evidence.[130]

If a person holds a power exercisable subject to a precedent giving of notice or taking effect only after the passage of time, the power will nonetheless be taken into account.[131]

With regard to powers held by a spouse, a grantor is treated as holding any power or interest held by any individual who was the spouse of the grantor at the time of the creation of the power or interest or any individual who became the spouse of the grantor after the creation of such power or interest (with respect to periods after the spouse became a spouse). An individual who is legally separated from his or her spouse under a decree of divorce or of separate maintenance is not considered as married.[132]

Section 672(f) is a subject unto itself; and it is discussed at length in Chapter 9.

Tucked within section 672(f)—at section 672(f)(4)—is a rule that applies to any gift (or bequest) from a foreign corporation or partnership. The rule gives the Secretary the ability to recharacterize the gift or bequest for U.S. tax purposes as something else "as the Secretary determines to be appropriate to prevent the avoidance of the purposes of . . . [section 672(f)]." This provision also is discussed in Chapter 9.

Also tucked within section 672(f)—at section 672(f)(5)—is an anti-avoidance rule aimed at situations where a foreign person has

[130] Section 672(c).
[131] Section 672(d).
[132] Section 672(e). While these rules reflect a somewhat dated view of life, they probably do as good a job as any similar set of rules. They assume that spouses are subservient, spouses that have obtained a court decree of separate maintenance are not, different sex or same sex partners that live together are not, employees are (including an employee in a corporation in which the grantor is an "executive"), and independent contractors are not.

transferred property to a trust that would be a "good" foreign grantor trust even after the application of the new section 672(f) rules and a U.S. beneficiary of the trust transferred directly or indirectly property to the nominal grantor. This is the so-called "anti-give-and-go rule;" but it can apply in a number of situations. This rule too is discussed in Chapter 9.

With respect to the section 672(f) provisions, the Secretary is given specific authority to prescribe regulations necessary or appropriate to carry out the purposes of the subsection.[133]

8.6 Powers and interests that will cause a trust to be treated as a grantor trust

These provisions are summarized below.

8.6.1 Reversionary interests (Section 673)

The grantor will be treated as the owner of any portion of a trust as to which he has a reversionary interest in either the corpus or the income if, as of the inception of that portion of the trust, the value of such interest exceeds 5% of the value of such portion.

With respect to a reversionary interest taking effect at death of a minor who is a lineal descendant beneficiary, the grantor will not be treated as the owner of such portion solely by reason of a reversionary interest in such portion that takes effect upon the death of a beneficiary before the beneficiary reaches age 21.

8.6.2 Power to control beneficial enjoyment (section 674)

As a general rule, a grantor will be treated as the owner of any portion of a trust as to which the beneficial enjoyment of the corpus or the income is subject to a power of disposition, exercisable by the grantor or a nonadverse party, or both, without the approval or consent of any adverse party.

There are a number of exceptions. These are listed below.

[133] Section 672(f)(6).

1. Power to apply income to support of a dependent. A power described in section 677(b) (relating to obligations of support) to the extent that the grantor would not be subject to tax under that section.

2. Power affecting beneficial enjoyment only after occurrence of event. A power, the exercise of which can only affect the beneficial enjoyment of the income for a period commencing after the occurrence of an event such that a grantor would not be treated as the owner under section 673 if the power were a reversionary interest; but the grantor may be treated as the owner after the occurrence of the event unless the power is relinquished.

3. Power exercisable only by will. A power exercisable only by will, other than a power residing with the grantor to appoint by will the income of the trust where the income is accumulated for such disposition by the grantor or may be so accumulated in the discretion of the grantor or a nonadverse party, or both, without the approval or consent of any adverse party.

4. Power to allocate among charitable beneficiaries. A power to determine the beneficial enjoyment of the corpus or the income therefrom if the corpus or income is irrevocably payable for a purpose specified in section 170(c) (relating to definition of charitable contributions) or to an employee stock ownership plan (as defined in section 4975(e)(7)) in a qualified gratuitous transfer (as defined in section 664(g)(1)).

5. Power to distribute corpus. A power to distribute corpus either (a) to or for a beneficiary or beneficiaries or to or for a class of beneficiaries (whether or not income beneficiaries) provided that the power is limited by a reasonably definite standard which is set forth in the trust instrument; or (b) to or for any current income beneficiary, provided that the distribution of corpus must be chargeable against the proportionate share of corpus held in trust for the payment of income to the beneficiary as if the corpus constituted a separate trust. A power does not fall within the powers described in this provision if any person has a power to add to

the beneficiary or beneficiaries or to a class of beneficiaries designated to receive the income or corpus, except where such action is to provide for after-born or after-adopted children.

6. Power to withhold income temporarily. A power to distribute or apply income to or for any current income beneficiary or to accumulate the income for him or her, provided that any accumulated income must ultimately be payable (a) to the beneficiary from whom distribution or application is withheld, to his/her estate, or to his/her appointees (or persons named as alternate takers in default of appointment) provided that such beneficiary possesses a power of appointment which does not exclude from the class of possible appointees any person other than the beneficiary, his/her estate, his/her creditors, or the creditors of his/her estate, or (b) on termination of the trust, or in conjunction with a distribution of corpus which is augmented by such accumulated income, to the current income beneficiaries in shares which have been irrevocably specified in the trust's governing instrument. Accumulated income will be considered so payable although the trust documents provide that if any beneficiary does not survive a date of distribution that could reasonably have been expected to occur within the beneficiary's lifetime, the share of the deceased beneficiary is to be paid to his or her appointees or to one or more designated alternate takers (other than the grantor or the grantor's estate) whose shares have been irrevocably specified. A power does not fall within the subject powers if any person has a power to add to the beneficiary or beneficiaries or to a class of beneficiaries designated to receive the income or corpus except where such action is to provide for after-born or after-adopted children.

7. Power to withhold income during disability of a beneficiary. A power exercisable only during the existence of a legal disability of any current income beneficiary, or the period during which any income beneficiary shall be less than 21 years of age, to distribute or apply income to or for such beneficiary or to accumulate and add the income to corpus. A power will not fall within the subject powers if any person has a power to add to the beneficiary or beneficiaries or to a

class of beneficiaries designated to receive the income or corpus, except where such action is to provide for after-born or after-adopted children.

8. Power to allocate between corpus and income. A power to allocate receipts and disbursements as between corpus and income, even though expressed in broad language.

There is an exception for certain powers of an independent trustee. The general rule providing for grantor trust treatment will not apply to a power solely exercisable (without the approval or consent of any other person) by a trustee or trustees, none of whom is the grantor, and no more than half of whom are related or subordinate parties who are subservient to the wishes of the grantor (*i.e.*, an independent trustee) (a) to distribute, apportion, or accumulate income to or for a beneficiary or beneficiaries, or to, for, or within a class of beneficiaries; or (b) to pay out corpus to or for a beneficiary or beneficiaries or to or for a class of beneficiaries (whether or not income beneficiaries). However, a power does not fall within this exception if any person has a power to add to the beneficiary or beneficiaries or to a class of beneficiaries designated to receive the income or corpus, except where such action is to provide for after-born or after-adopted children. For periods during which an individual is the spouse of the grantor (within the meaning of section 672(e)(2)), any reference in this subsection to the grantor will be treated as including a reference to such individual.

In addition, the general rule providing for grantor trust treatment will not apply to a power solely exercisable (without the approval or consent of any other person) by a trustee or trustees, none of whom is the grantor or spouse living with the grantor, to distribute, apportion, or accumulate income to or for a beneficiary or beneficiaries, or to, for, or within a class of beneficiaries, whether or not the conditions of section 674(b)(6) or (7) are satisfied, if such power is limited by a reasonably definite external standard which is set forth in the trust's governing instrument. A power does not fall within the powers described in this provision if any person has a power to add to the beneficiary or beneficiaries or to a class of beneficiaries designated to receive the income or corpus except where such action is to provide for after-born or after-adopted children.

8.6.3 Administrative powers *(Section 675)*

The grantor will be treated as the owner of any portion of a trust as to which he or she holds certain administrative powers. These powers are listed below.

1. A power to deal for less than adequate and full consideration. This is a power exercisable by the grantor or a nonadverse party, or both, without the approval or consent of any adverse party, that enables the grantor or any person to purchase, exchange or otherwise deal with or dispose of the corpus or income for less than an adequate consideration.

2. A power to borrow without adequate interest or security. This is a power exercisable by the grantor or a nonadverse party, or both, that enables the grantor to borrow the corpus or income, directly or indirectly, without adequate interest or without adequate security except where a trustee (other than the grantor) is authorized under a general lending power to make loans to any person without regard to interest or security.

3. Borrowing of the trust funds. This provision is triggered where the grantor has directly or indirectly borrowed the corpus or income and has not completely repaid the loan, including interest, before the beginning of the taxable year. This rule will not apply to a loan that provides for adequate interest and adequate security, if such loan is made by a trustee other than the grantor and other than a related or subordinate trustee subservient to the grantor. For periods during which an individual is the spouse of the grantor, any reference in this paragraph to the grantor will be treated as including a reference to such spouse.

4. General powers of administration. A power of administration is exercisable in a nonfiduciary capacity by any person without the approval or consent of any person in a fiduciary capacity. For these purposes, the term "power of administration" means any one or more of the following

powers: (a) a power to vote or direct the voting of stock or other securities of a corporation in which the holdings of the grantor and the trust are significant from the viewpoint of voting control; (b) a power to control the investment of the trust funds either by directing investments or reinvestments, or by vetoing proposed investments or reinvestments, to the extent that the trust funds consist of stocks or securities of corporations in which the holdings of the grantor and the trust are significant from the viewpoint of voting control; or (c) a power to reacquire the trust corpus by substituting other property of an equivalent value.

8.6.4 Power to revoke (Section 676)

The grantor will be treated as the owner of any portion of a trust, whether or not he is treated as such owner under any other provision of Subpart E, where at any time the power to revest in the grantor title to such portion is exercisable by the grantor or a non-adverse party, or both. The regulations point out that if the title to a portion of the trust will revest in the grantor upon the exercise of a power by the grantor or a nonadverse party, or both, the grantor is treated as the owner of that portion regardless of whether the power is a power to revoke, to terminate, to alter or amend, or to appoint.[134]

The general rule stated above will not apply to a power the exercise of which can only affect the beneficial enjoyment of the income for a period commencing after the occurrence of an event such that a grantor would not be treated as the owner under section 673 (relating to reversionary interests) if the power were a reversionary interest. The grantor, however, may be treated as the owner after the occurrence of such event unless the power is relinquished.

8.6.5. Income for the benefit of the grantor (Section 677)

Section 677 provides that a grantor will be treated as the owner of any portion of a trust, whether or not he is treated as the owner under section 674 (relating to the power to control beneficial enjoyment),

[134] Reg. § 1.676(a)-1, Income Tax Regs.

whose income without the approval or consent of any adverse party is, or, in the discretion of the grantor or a nonadverse party, or both, may be:

1. distributed to the grantor or the grantor's spouse;

2. held or accumulated for future distribution to the grantor or the grantor's spouse; or

3. applied to the payment of premiums on policies of insurance on the life of the grantor or the grantor's spouse (except policies payable for charitable purposes).

This provision will not apply to a power the exercise of which can only affect the beneficial enjoyment of the income for a period commencing after the occurrence of an event described in section 673 (relating to reversionary interets); but the grantor may be treated as the owner after the occurrence of the event unless the power is relinquished.

Section 677(b) deals specifically with obligations of support. It provides that the income of a trust will not be considered taxable to the grantor under the general rule of section 677 or any other provision merely because such income in the discretion of another person, the trustee or the grantor acting as trustee or co-trustee, may be applied or distributed for the support or maintenance of a beneficiary (other than the grantor's spouse) whom the grantor is legally obligated to support or maintain, except to the extent that such income is actually so applied or distributed. In cases where amounts applied or distributed for this purpose are paid out of corpus or out of income other than income for the taxable year, such amounts will be treated as an amount paid or credited within the meaning of section 661(a)(2) and will be taxed to the grantor under section 662.

8.6.6 Person other than grantor treated as substantial owner (Section 678)

The grantor trust rules generally result in the grantor being treated as the owner of the trust's assets and taxable on the income earned on those assets. The exception is stated in section 678.[135]

Section 678 provides that a person other than the grantor will be treated as the owner of any portion of a trust with respect to which such person has a power exercisable solely by himself to vest the corpus or the income therefrom in himself.[136]

The fact that a power to appoint income exists is sufficient to cause the holder to be taxed. The rule applies regardless of the fact that the power is unexercisable because, for example, the holder is a minor and no guardian has been appointed.[137]

How should powers to appoint income to someone other than the holder be treated? Revenue Ruling 67-268[138] held that where a trustee had a discretionary power to distribute income to the trustee's wife, section 678 did not apply to make the trustee the taxpayer. The power was not a power to appoint income in himself. Section 672(e) apparently does not bear on this result, because that section deals with grantors' spouses, not holders-of-a-power-to-appoint spouses.

Section 679(b) creates a form of "trumping." It provides that the general rule of section 678 will not apply with respect to a power over

---

[135] The rule in section 678 is based on the Eighth Circuit's decision in *Mallinckrodt v. Nunan*, 146 F.2d 1 (8th Cir.), *cert. denied*, 342 U.S. 871 (1945). Practitioners frequently refer to trusts falling within this provision as *Mallinckrodt* trusts.

[136] In addition to the general rule, this section provides that the same result will pertain if such person has previously partially released or otherwise modified such a power and after the release or modification retains such control as would, applying the rules of sections 671 to 677 as if the person in question were the grantor, subject the grantor of the trust to treatment as the owner of the trust's assets.

[137] *Trust No. 3 v. Comissioner*, 285 F.2d 102 (7th Cir. 1960); Rev. Rul. 81-6, 1981-1 C.B. 385.

[138] Rev. Rul. 67-268, 1967-2 C.B. 226.

income, if the grantor of the trust or a transferor (to whom section 679 applies) is otherwise treated as the owner under the provisions of this subpart other than this section.[139] This rule seems oddly worded since it refers only to a "power over income" and makes no mention of a power over corpus. It has been suggested by some that this wording must be a drafting error, pure and simple.[140] The IRS seems to take this view. However, the regulations repeat the wording of the statute; and there has been no effort to correct the "error" by way of a technical corrections provision in one of the many tax bills that have been enacted since enactment of this provision in 1954.[141]

Another exception applies with respect to obligations of support. The general rule will not apply to a power that enables a person, in the capacity of trustee or co-trustee, merely to apply the income of the trust to the support or maintenance of a person whom the holder of the power is obligated to support or maintain except to the extent the income is in fact so applied. In cases where the amounts so applied or distributed are paid out of corpus or out of "other than income of the taxable year," such amounts shall be considered to be an amount paid or credited within the meaning of section 661(a)(2) and shall be taxed to the holder of the power under section 662.[142]

---

[139] This special rule applies whether the grantor is treated as the owner under section 679 or some other section in the section 673-677 series—lest the reader have problems deciding what is the object of the parenthetical referring to section 679.

[140] Ferguson, Freeland & Ascher, FEDERAL INCOME TAXATION OF ESTATES, TRUSTS, AND BENEFICIARIES (3rd Ed., 1998), p. 10-116 and authorities cited at footnote 23 therein.

[141] Sec. 1.678(b)-1, Income Tax Regs. reads: "Section 678(a) does not apply <u>with respect to a power over income</u>, as originally granted or thereafter modified, if the grantor of the trust is treated as the owner under sections 671 to 677, inclusive." [Emphasis added.] This language was first enacted as part of the Internal Revenue Code of 1954. (Aug. 16, 1954, ch. 736, 68A Stat. 231.) This particular subsection was amended at the time of the 1976 Act. It is not as if the Legislative Counsel's Offices on the House and Senate sides and the Joint Committee on Taxation and Treasury Department drafters were not looking at this language. (Oct. 4, 1976, Pub. L. 94-455, title X, 1013(b), 90 Stat. 1615.)

[142] Again, this rule seems to apply with respect only to income. Here, however, the regulations seem to disregard this point and refer to corpus as well as income. "Section 678(a) treats a person as an owner of a trust if he has a power exercisable solely by himself to apply the income <u>or corpus</u> for

Section 678 does not apply with respect to a power that has been renounced or disclaimed within a reasonable time after the holder first becomes aware of its existence. Also, assuming the disclaimer is valid under applicable local law, section 678 should not have any effect even if the holder is slow to disclaim since the holder should be viewed as no longer possessing the offending power.

> ➔ Section 678 generally does not apply where there is a foreign trust since the trust will either be a foreign nongrantor trust by virtue of section 672(f), discussed below, or, if the trust is a grantor trust because one of the exceptions to section 672(f) apply, the grantor will be treated as the taxpayer under sections 678(b) and 679.

8.6.7 Foreign trusts having one or more U.S. beneficiaries (Section 679)

The workings of this provision that applies only to foreign trusts are discussed in Chapter 9 at paragraph 9.13.

---

the satisfaction of his legal obligations, other than an obligation to support a dependent . . . " Reg. § 1.678(a)-1(b), Income Tax Regs.

Chapter 9

Special Rules Applicable to Foreign Trusts

1. General

A large number of special rules apply to foreign trusts and beneficiaries of foreign trusts. Most of these rules came into the Code during the 1976 and 1996 Acts. As will be appreciated, the rules are intended to "catch" tax avoidance practices and to close perceived "loopholes."

In a few instances, the rules may lead to unintended results.

At the time of the consideration of the 1996 Act, the Administration considered, but decided against, treating the use of trust property as a constructive distribution. For example, if a beneficiary of a trust were permitted to use an apartment owned by the trust, that rent-free use would be treated as a distribution. It would be necessary to value the use. When the proposal arose, many people commented that it was a bad idea because it would affect many trusts, it would be difficult to justify applying the rule only to foreign trusts, valuation would be difficult to enforce, and so forth. The proposal was dropped from the final version of the statute.

> ➔ This episode, it would seem, clearly establishes that use of trust property is in no form a distribution from the trust. With this in mind, trustees and beneficiaries might wish to lean away from making distributions and, instead, maintain value within the trust. With a little thought, a great deal can be accomplished following this strategy.

This chapter will focus on the tax rules specially designed for foreign trusts and their beneficiaries. These are presented in no particular order.

9.2 Grantor trust rules generally cannot apply in the case of foreign trusts (Section 672(f))

9.2.1 General (Section 672(f)(1))

Section 672(f) provides that the rules generally applicable in the case of a grantor trust will not apply where they will result in foreign ownership. "This subpart shall apply only to the extent such application results in an amount (if any) being currently taken into account (directly or through 1 or more entities) under this chapter in computing the income of a citizen or resident of the United States or a domestic corporation." In other words, the idea is that the grantor trust rules when viewed in the context of foreign trusts and beneficiaries can only hurt taxpayers, not help them.

This rule came into the statute as part of the 1996 Act. (*See* the discussion at Chapter 11, below.)

The exceptions are some of the most important ones applicable to foreign trusts. The general rule barring the application of the grantor trust rules will not apply to any trust, or portion of a trust, if the power to revest absolutely in the grantor title of the trust property is exercisable solely by the grantor without the approval or consent of any other person or with the consent of a related or subordinate party who is subservient to the grantor (*i.e.*, the trust is revocable) or the only amounts distributable from the trust (whether the amounts are income or corpus) during the lifetime of the grantor are amounts distributable to the grantor or the spouse of the grantor. A third exception is compensatory trusts. The general rule will not apply to any trust distributions that are taxable as compensation for services rendered. (The provisions of the final regulations explaining the workings of these exceptions to the general rule are discussed below at paragraph 9.2.2.)

These rules were the subject of proposed regulations published on June 5, 1997. [143] There were a number of problems with the proposed

[143] For comments on the regulations, see "N.Y. State Bar Association Urges Revision Of Inbound Grantor Trust Regs," 97 TNT 239-22 (Dec. 4, 1997) (hereinafter "NYSBA Comments"). *See also* "Bruce Seeks to Clear Up Confusion in Grantor Trust Regs," 97 TNT 162-48 (Aug. 8, 1999)

regulations. A number of these were corrected in the final regulations published in August 1999.[144] The final regulations are also simpler.

One of the things made clear by the regulations is that the regular rules of section 671 concerning the meaning of the term "portion" will apply in this context. "The determination of the portion of a trust treated as owned by the grantor or other person is to be made based on the terms of the trust and the application of the grantor trust rules and Section 671 and the regulations thereunder."[145]

This section of the regulations contains the following useful example.

> Example. (i) A, a nonresident alien, funds an irrevocable domestic trust, DT, for the benefit of his son, B, who is a United States citizen, with stock of Corporation X. A's brother, C, who also is a United States citizen, contributes stock of Corporation Y to the trust for the benefit of B. A has a reversionary interest within the meaning of section 673 in the X stock that would cause A to be treated as the owner of the X stock upon application of the grantor trust rules without regard to section 672(f). C has a reversionary interest within the meaning of section 673 in the Y stock that would cause C to be treated as the owner of the Y stock upon application of the grantor trust rules without regard to section 672(f). The trustee has discretion to accumulate or currently distribute income of DT to B.
>
> (ii) Because A is a nonresident alien, application of the grantor trust rules without regard to section 672(f) would not result in the portion of the trust consisting of the X stock being treated as owned by

---

(hereinafter "Bruce Comments"); "Bruce Requests to Testify on Grantor Trust Regs, 97 TNT 181-96 (Aug. 6, 1997); Full Text: Unofficial Transcript of IRS Hearing On Application Of Grantor Trust Rules To Trusts Established By Foreigners," 97 TNT 169-67 (Aug. 27, 1997).

144 T.D. 8831, REG252487-96.

145 Regulations § 1.672(f)-1(a)(2), Income Tax Regs.

> a United States citizen or resident. None of the exceptions in section 1.672(f)-3 applies because A cannot revest the X stock in A, amounts may be distributed during A's lifetime to B, who is neither a grantor nor a spouse of a grantor, and the trust is not a compensatory trust. Therefore, pursuant to paragraph (a)(1) of this section, A is not treated as an owner under subpart E of part I, subchapter J, chapter 1 of the Internal Revenue Code, of the portion of the trust consisting of the X stock. Any distributions from such portion of the trust are subject to the rules of subparts A through D (641 and following), part I, subchapter J, chapter 1 of the Internal Revenue Code.
>
> (iii) Because C is a United States citizen, paragraph (a)(1) of this section does not prevent C from being treated under section 673 as the owner of the portion of the trust consisting of the Y stock.

Regulations § 1.672(f)-1(b), Income Tax Regs.

Section 672(f)(3) contains special rules for certain foreign corporations. This provision provides:

> Except as otherwise provided in regulations prescribed by the Secretary –
>
> (A) a controlled foreign corporation (as defined in section 957) shall be treated as a domestic corporation for purposes of paragraph (1), and
>
> (B) paragraph (1) shall not apply for purposes of applying section 1297.

Section 672(f)(3).

The final regulations—narrowing somewhat the approach taken in the proposed regulations—are targeted on potentially abusive situations. If the owner of a trust upon application of the grantor trust rules without regard to section 672(f) is a CFC, PFIC or FPHC, the

CFC, PFIC or FPHC, as the case may be, will be treated as a domestic corporation for purposes of applying the general rule of section 1.672(f)-1. Therefore, a CFC, PFIC or FPHC generally will be treated as the owner of a trust if it would be so treated under sections 671 through 678 without regard to section 672(f). A CFC, PFIC or FPHC will be treated as a domestic corporation solely for purposes of applying the general rule of section 672(f). Thus, a CFC, PFIC or FPHC will be treated as a foreign corporation for purposes of section 1.672(f)(4) (relating to recharacterization of purported gifts).

If a trust to which a CFC, PFIC or FPHC has made a gratuitous transfer makes a gratuitous transfer to a U.S. person, the CFC, PFIC or FPHC, as the case may be, will be treated as a foreign corporation for purposes of determining how the transfer will be treated in the hands of the U.S. person, and the rules of section 672(f)(4) will apply. If a trust that a CFC, PFIC or FPHC is treated as owning under section 678 (the *Mallinckrodt* trust rule) makes a gratuitous transfer to a U.S. person, the rules of section 672(f)(4) will apply as if the CFC, PFIC or FPHC had made a gratuitous transfer to the trust.[146]

It may be worthwhile to note the Treasury Department and the IRS proposed regulations in September 1996—after the 1996 Act was enacted but before any of the regulations projects under that Act got underway—under sections 671 (relating to trust income, deductions, and credits attributable to grantors and others as substantial owners) and under section 1297 (relating to passive foreign investment company).[147] One of the objects of the proposed regulations is to prevent foreign corporations that are not CFCs from avoiding PFIC status by contributing "passive assets" to a foreign nonexempt employees' trust and, since the foreign corporation-employer is not treated as the owner of the trust assets, avoiding classification as a PFIC. If a principal purpose for the transfer of property is to avoid classification of the foreign corporation as a PFIC, the following rule applies: if the foreign employer has a power or interest described in sections 673 through 677 over the trust, then the grantor trust rules will apply for purposes only of the PFIC provisions and only as regards the amount in the trust that is equal to the fair market value of

[146] *See* T.D. 8831, Explanation of Provisions and Revisions, para. 4.

[147] Prop. Regulations § 1.671-1 & 1.1297-4, REG-209826, 61 F.R. 50778-50787 (Sept. 27, 1996).

the property that is transferred for the purpose of avoiding classification as a PFIC.

Whether a principal purpose for a transfer is the avoidance of classification as a PFIC will be determined on the basis of all of the facts and circumstances, including whether the amount of assets held by the foreign employees' trust is reasonably related to the plan's anticipated liabilities, taking into account any local law and practice relating to proper funding levels.[148]

> → These proposed rules show how complicated things can get. First, there are grantor trust rules. Secondly, these rules are made inapplicable if they do not result in a tax to a citizen or resident of the U.S. or a domestic U.S. corporation. Thirdly, the grantor trust rules are made applicable again but only for a limited purpose (the application of the PFIC rules) and only to the extent transfers have as a principal purpose the avoidance of the PFIC rules. Also, determining the line over which transfers should not go, which can be tied to reasonably anticipated liabilities, will be more fun than most taxpayers will be able to stand.

9.2.2 Exceptions to the general rule (Section 672(f)(2))

The exceptions to section 672(f) fall in three categories: revocable trusts, trusts that can distribute only to the grantor or the grantor's spouse and compensatory trusts. The rationale for the first two exceptions is that the ownership arrangement is such that it is the economic equivalent of the grantor owning the assets of the trust and making a gift directly to the recipient. If these were not exceptions, grantors would cause partial revocations or distributions to them; and then they would make gifts. U.S. tax law for a very long time—since the Revenue Act of 1924[149]—has treated these situations as being the equivalent of ownership of the assets by the grantor. There is little doubt that the grantor would be treated in effect as the owner of the

[148] Prop. Regulations § 1.671-1 & 1.1297-4, REG-209826, 61 F.R. 50778-50787 (Sept. 27, 1996).

[149] Revenue Act of 1924, § 219(g), 43 Stat. 253, 277.

trust assets even before the Clifford regulations and the Code sections codifying those regulations.

The Treasury Department and the IRS proposed regulations on this subject as part of a larger package of proposed regulations in June 1997. After considering written and oral comments, they published final regulations in August 1999. They made some changes and "stuck to their guns" with respect to some points. The regulations in this area reserve one subject—that is, the treatment of reinsurance trusts.[150]

One thing that emerges from the final regulations is the message that the regulations-writers feel that any exceptions to the rule of section 672(f) must be narrowly drawn, and they will not be caught up in a desire for consistency.

> Treasury and the IRS believe it is neither necessary nor appropriate for the regulations promulgated under the statutory exceptions to section 672(f) to be consistent with the regulations promulgated under other provisions of part I of subchapter J, chapter 1 of the Code. Section 672(f) reflects a policy determination that foreign persons should not be allowed "to affirmatively [sic] use the domestic anti-abuse rules concerning grantor trusts" to avoid U.S. tax on trust income distributed to U.S. beneficiaries. Dept. of the Treasury, General Explanations of the Administration's Revenue Proposals, at 12 (1995). Section 672(f) operates to implement that policy determination by providing that the grantor trust rules generally do not apply where their effect would be to treat a foreign person as the owner of any portion of a trust. S. Rep. No. 35, 104th Cong., 1st Sess. 161 (1995). The exceptions in section 672(f)(2) must be interpreted narrowly to preserve the primary operation of the general rule. See, for example, Commissioner v. Clark, 489 U.S. 726, 739 (1989) ("In construing provisions . . . in which a general statement of policy is qualified by an

[150] T.D. 8831.

> exception, we usually read the exception narrowly in order to preserve the primary operation of the provision.").

T.D. 8831, Explanation of Provisions and Revisions, Para. 5 (Comments and Changes to section 1.672(f)-3: Exceptions To General Rule).

> ➔ Grantors and their advisors can plan trust structures that clearly qualify under one of the exceptions. The regulations provide detailed guidelines. Taxpayers should opt for simplicity; and they should make the trust fall squarely within one of the exceptions. An audit should be anticipated; and the documents should be such that the revenue agent can easily determine that the trust qualifies as a foreign grantor trust and, therefore, the U.S. beneficiary is not taxable.

9.2.2.1 Certain revocable trusts

The general rule of section 672(f) barring the application of the grantor trust rules where they result in foreign ownership does not apply to any portion of a trust if the power to revest absolutely in the grantor title to such portion is exercisable solely by the grantor (or, according to the regulations, in the event of the grantor's incapacity, by a guardian or other person who has unrestricted authority to exercise such power on the grantor's behalf) without the approval or consent of any other person. Also, if the grantor can exercise such power only with the approval of a related or subordinate party who is subservient to the grantor, such power is nonetheless treated as exercisable solely by the grantor.[151]

If a trust (or portion of a trust) fails to qualify for this exception in a particular taxable year, it will be subject to the general rule of section 672(f) not only for that taxable year but also for all

[151] A portion of the trust can be protected from the workings of section 672(f) (*i.e.*, can be a valid foreign grantor trust distributions from which will not be at the mercy of the accumulation distribution rules) and part not. The portion that is protected might be the DNI of the trust.

subsequent taxable years of the trust. A trust cannot "jump around" from one year to the next.[152]

The regulations provide a "183-day rule" that gives some relief should the power to revest not be in place every day of the year. Under the regulations, the grantor is treated as having a power to revest for a taxable year of the trust if he or she has such power for a total of 183 or more days during the taxable year of the trust. However, if the first or last taxable year of the trust (including the year of the grantor's death) is less than 183 days, the grantor is treated as having a power to revest for purposes of this exception only if the grantor has such power for each day of that taxable year.

The regulations also spell out the grandfather rule contained in the 1996 Act. (This rule did not go into the Code, just the Act). The general rule of section 672(f) will not apply to any portion of a trust that was treated as owned by the grantor under section 676 (relating to power to revoke) on September 19, 1995, as long as the trust would continue to be so treated thereafter. This treatment will not apply to any portion of the trust attributable to gratuitous transfers to the trust after September 19, 1995. Also, if in the trust are both amounts held in the trust on September 19, 1995, and amounts that were gratuitously transferred to the trust after September 19, 1995, then the trust must comply with certain "separate accounting rules" set forth in the regulations. Essentially the amounts that were gratuitously transferred to the trust after September 19, 1995, must be treated as a separate portion of the trust. The assets need not, however, be physically segregated.

> ➔ It seems that the importance of this grandfather rule is not great. It merely "grandfathers" revocable trusts that qualified under section 676 but not under the slightly tighter framework of new section 672(f)(2)(A)(i). It would have been a different matter if the statute said any trust in existence on or before September 19, 1995 is not effected by the new rules; but this is not the case.

[152] There is no particular reason for a rule of this type, other than that the authorities want to take a tough approach. Tests under the grantor trust rules are generally on a year-by-year basis.

The examples in the final regulations are quite instructive and give a "feel" for some of the issues as seen through the Service's eyes.

> Example 1. Grantor is owner. FP1, a foreign person, creates and funds a revocable trust, T, for the benefit of FP1's children, who are resident aliens. The trustee is a foreign bank, FB, that is owned and controlled by FP1 and FP2, who is FP1's brother. The power to revoke T and revest absolutely in FP1 title to the trust property is exercisable by FP1, but only with the approval or consent of FB. The trust instrument contains no standard that FB must apply in determining whether to approve or consent to the revocation of T. There are no facts that would suggest that FB is not subservient to FP1. Therefore, the exception in paragraph (a)(1) of this section is applicable.
>
> Example 2. Death of grantor. Assume the same facts as in Example 1, except that FP1 dies. After FP1's death, FP2 has the power to withdraw the assets of T, but only with the approval of FB. There are no facts that would suggest that FB is not subservient to FP2. However, the exception in paragraph (a)(1) of this section is no longer applicable, because FP2 is not a grantor of T within the meaning of section 1.671-2T(e).
>
> Example 3. Trustee is not related or subordinate party. Assume the same facts as in Example 1, except that neither FP1 nor any member of FP1's family has any substantial ownership interest or other connection with FB. FP1 can remove and replace FB at any time for any reason. Although FP1 can replace FB with a related or subordinate party if FB refuses to approve or consent to FP1's decision to revest the trust property in himself, FB is not a related or subordinate party. Therefore, the

> exception in paragraph (a)(1) of this section is not applicable.
>
> Example 4. Unrelated trustee will consent to revocation. FP, a foreign person, creates and funds an irrevocable trust, T. The trustee is a foreign bank, FB, that is not a related or subordinate party within the meaning of section 1.672(c)-1. FB has the discretion to distribute trust income or corpus to beneficiaries of T, including FP. Even if FB would in fact distribute all the trust property to FP if requested to do so by FP, the exception in paragraph (a)(1) of this section is not applicable, because FP does not have the power to revoke T.

Treas. Reg. § 1.672(f)-3(a)(4), Income Tax Regs.

Example 3 caused a stir among a number of commentators, but it seems correct. The power to "hire-and-fire" the trustee should not be viewed as a power to control absolutely or tantamount to a power to revoke or revest assets.

9.2.2.2 Certain trusts that can distribute only to the grantor or the grantor's spouse

Section 672(f) will not apply to any trust (or portion of a trust) if at all times during the lifetime of the grantor the only amounts distributable (whether income or corpus) from such trust (or portion thereof) are amounts distributable to the grantor or the grantor's spouse. Payments of amounts that are not gratuitous transfers, according to the regulations, are not amounts distributable.

Specific rules apply with respect to amounts distributable in discharge of legal obligations. A trust (or portion of a trust) does not fail to qualify under this exception solely because amounts are distributable in discharge of a legal obligation of the grantor or the spouse. An obligation is considered, as a general matter, a legal obligation if it is enforceable under the local law of the jurisdiction in which the grantor (or the spouse of the grantor) resides. However, with respect to obligations running to related parties (under the related party rules in section 643(h) (having to do with distributions through nominees)), an obligation to such a person—other than an individual who is legally separated from the grantor under a decree of divorce or of separate maintenance—will not be viewed as a legal obligation for purposes of this special rule unless it was contracted *bona fide* and for adequate and full consideration in money or money's worth.

Notwithstanding the last "related party" rule, amounts distributable in support of dependents who are less than 19 years old or permanently and totally disabled can qualify.[153]

A grandfather rule similar to the one discussed above generally applies for foreign grantor trusts falling within section 677 (person other than grantor treated as substantial owner); and the same separate accounting proviso goes along with this.

Here again useful examples appear in the regulations.

> Example 1. Amounts distributable only to grantor or grantor's spouse. H and his wife, W, are both nonresident aliens. H is 70 years old, and W is 65. H and W have a 30-year-old child, C, a resident alien. There is no reasonable expectation that H or W will ever have an obligation under local law to support C or any other individual. H creates and funds an irrevocable trust, FT, using only his separate property. H is the grantor of FT within the meaning of section 1.671-2T(e). Under the terms of FT, the only amounts distributable (whether income or corpus) from FT as long as either H or W is alive are amounts distributable to H or W. Upon the death of both H and W, C may receive distributions from FT. During H's lifetime, the exception in paragraph (b)(1) of this section is applicable.
>
> Example 2. Effect of grantor's death. Assume the same facts as in Example 1. H predeceases W. Assume that W would be treated as owning FT

[153] The regulations writers had a hard time deciding what to do about reinsurance trusts. This subject was "reserved" for later action.

under section 678 if the grantor trust rules were applied without regard to section 672(f). The exception in paragraph (b)(1) of this section is no longer applicable, because W is not a grantor of FT within the meaning of section 1.671-2T(e).

Example 3. Amounts temporarily distributable to person other than grantor or grantor's spouse. Assume the same facts as in Example 1, except that C (age 30) is a law student at the time FT is created and the trust instrument provides that, as long as C is in law school, amounts may be distributed from FT to pay C’s expenses. Thereafter, the only amounts distributable from FT as long as either H or W is alive will be amounts distributable to H or W. Even assuming there is an enforceable obligation under local law for H and W to support C while he is in school, distributions from FT in payment of C's expenses cannot qualify as distributions in discharge of a legal obligation under paragraph (b)(2) of this section, because C is neither permanently and totally disabled nor less than 19 years old. The exception in paragraph (b)(1) of this section is not applicable. After C graduates from law school, the exception in paragraph (b)(1) still will not be applicable, because amounts were distributable to C during the lifetime of H.

Example 4. Fixed investment trust. FC, a foreign corporation, invests in a domestic fixed investment trust, DT, that is classified as a trust under section 301.7701-4(c)(1) of this chapter. Under the terms of DT, the only amounts that are distributable from FC's portion of DT are amounts distributable to FC. The exception in paragraph (b)(1) of this section is applicable to FC’s portion of DT.

Example 5. Reinsurance trust. A domestic insurance company, DI, reinsures a portion of its business with an unrelated foreign, insurance company, FI. To satisfy state regulatory requirements, FI places the premiums in an irrevocable domestic trust, DT. The trust funds are held by a United States bank and may be used only to pay claims arising out of the reinsurance policies, which are legally enforceable under the local law of the jurisdiction in which FI resides. On the termination of DT, any assets remaining will revert to FI. Because the only amounts that are distributable from DT are distributable either to FI or in discharge of FI's legal obligations within the meaning of paragraph (b)(2)(i) of this section, the exception in paragraph (b)(1) of this section is applicable.

Example 6. Trust that provides security for loan. FC, a foreign corporation, borrows money from B, an unrelated bank, to finance the purchase of an airplane. FC creates a foreign trust, FT, to hold the airplane as security for the loan from B. The only amounts that are distributable from FT while the loan is outstanding are amounts distributable to B in the event that FC defaults on its loan from B. When FC repays the loan, the trust assets will revert to FC. The loan is a legal obligation of FC within the meaning of paragraph (b)(2)(i) of this section, because it is enforceable under the local law of the country in which FC is incorporated. Paragraph (b)(2)(ii) of this section is not applicable, because B is not a related person for purposes of section 1.643(h)-1(e). The exception in paragraph (b)(1) of this section is applicable.

Treas. Reg. § 1.672(f)-3(b)(4), Income Tax Regs.

9.2.2.3 Compensatory trusts

The third exception from the section 672(f) rule barring foreign grantors, their trusts and the U.S. beneficiaries of those trusts from availing themselves of the grantor trust rules, deals with compensatory trusts. The final regulations provide that section 672(f) will not apply to any portion of (a) a nonexempt employees' trust described in section 402(b) (relating to the taxation of beneficiaries of nonexempt employees' trusts), including a trust created on behalf of a self-employed individual; (b) a trust, including a trust created on behalf of a self-employed individual, that would be a nonexempt employees' trust described in section 402(b) but for the fact that the trust's assets are not set aside from the claims of creditors of the actual or deemed transferor (*i.e.*, a so-called "rabbi trust"[154]); and (c) any additional category of trust that the Commissioner may designate.

Whether tax-exempt compensatory trusts can be treated as owned by a foreign person, according to the Treasury and the IRS, is moot because there are special statutory rules that govern those trusts.

---

[154] A "rabbi trust"—named this because the arrangement was first used by a congregation to provide for the retirement of its rabbi—is a form of non-qualified deferred compensation. It is used to provide employees with some assurance that retirement or termination benefits will be paid to them. It is structured as a grantor trust, with the employer-company taxable on the income earned on the funds and the employees not taxable (and the employer-company not entitled to a deduction) until payments are made to the employees. The trust can be revocable or irrevocable by the employer, but it is usually irrevocable. It is normally funded. The employer retains certain administrative powers over the trust. The assets can be used only to pay promised benefits to employees, usually upon retirement, death or termination of employment without cause, but the assets also remain available to creditors upon the bankruptcy or insolvency of the employer. The IRS has provided guidance regarding advance rulings to the effect that the employees are not in constructive receipt of income when made the beneficiaries of this type of trust. Rev. Proc. 71-19- 1971- 698, amplified by Rev. Proc. 92-65, 1992-2 C.B. 428. It has also issued a model grantor trust for use in "rabbi trust" arrangements. Rev. Proc. 92-64, 1992-2 C.B. 422. The author commented in response to the proposed regulations that there should be no change in existing law with respect to trusts used for business purposes. It appears correct not to change the result of existing law with respect to rabbi trusts. Provided the trust's assets are exposed to general creditors of the company in the event of insolvency, a company, including a non-U.S. company, in connection with a funded deferred compensation plan, should be able to establish a trust, which might be a foreign trust under the new residency rules because, for example, there is no U.S. fiduciary. The trust could be a grantor trust. The employees would not be in constructive receipt of income or incur an economic benefit as a result of the creation or maintenance of the trust. The employees would be taxed upon receipt of payments of compensation from the trust. Bruce Comments.

> Treasury and the IRS contemplate that a nonexempt employees' trust described in section 402(b) will be treated as owned by a beneficiary of the trust only to the extent provided in regulations section 1.402(b)-1(b)(6). See also proposed regulations section 1.671-1(g) and section 1.671-1(h), which were published in the Federal Register (61 FR 50778) on September 27, 1996, for proposed rules describing when an employer will be treated as an owner of any portion of a nonexempt employees' trust described in section 402(b) that is part of a deferred compensation plan.

T.D. 8831, Explanation of Provisions and Revisions, Para. 5.C.

The Treasury Department and the IRS, in the final regulations, reserved the right to designate additional categories of trusts to which the compensatory trust exception applies. "The Commissioner may, in revenue rulings, notices, or other guidance published in the Internal Revenue Bulletin . . . , designate categories of compensatory trusts to which the. . . [exception for compensatory trusts] does not apply."[155]

9.3 Purported gifts from corporations and partnerships recharacterized as distributions (Section 672(f)(4))

Section 672(f)(4) contains a rule for the recharacterization of certain purported gifts. It provides that in the case of a transfer, directly or indirectly, from a partnership (domestic or foreign) or a foreign corporation which the recipient treats as a gift or bequest, the IRS may recharacterized the transfer "in such circumstances as ...[it] determines to be appropriate to prevent the avoidance . . . [of section 672(f)]."

Proposed regulations were announced; and these were changed somewhat in the final regulations issued on August 5, 1999 (published in the Federal Register on August 10, 1999).

[155] Treas. Reg. § 1.672(f)-3(c)(2), Income Tax Regs.

In general, the final regulations recharacterize all distributions from any partnership (domestic or foreign), or from any foreign corporation, regardless of whether there is a foreign trust in the picture.[156]

The rules set forth in the regulations are generally applicable to any transfer after August 10, 1999, by a partnership or foreign corporation, or by a trust to which a partnership or foreign corporation makes a gratuitous transfer after August 10, 1999.

With respect to purported gifts from partnerships, if a U.S. person (U.S. donee) directly or indirectly receives a purported gift or bequest from a partnership (domestic or foreign), the purported gift or bequest must be included in the U.S. donee's gross income as ordinary income. This result follows regardless of whether in any trust exists. (As can be seen, this provision can have effects far beyond the confines of sections 672(f) or, for that matter, the income tax provisions relating to trusts.)

As to purported gifts from foreign corporations, if a U.S. donee directly or indirectly receives a purported gift or bequest from any foreign corporation (but not a domestic corporation), the purported gift or bequest must be included in the U.S. donee's gross income as if it were a distribution from the foreign corporation. Again, this rule applies regardless of the fact that there is no trust in sight.[157]

---

[156] Gifts from trusts to which a partnership or foreign corporation has made a gratuitous transfer will generally be treated as a distribution from the partnership or the foreign corporation. This point holds regardless of who is treated as the grantor of the trust (or portion thereof) under section 671. Reg. § 1.672(f)-4(c), Income Tax Regs.

[157] If the foreign corporation is a passive foreign investment company (within the meaning of section 1297), the rules of section 1291 apply. For purposes of section 1012 [(basis of property—cost)], the United States donee is not treated as having basis in the stock of the foreign corporation. However, for purposes of section 1223 [(holding period of property)], the United States donee is treated as having a holding period in the stock of the foreign corporation on the date of the deemed distribution equal to the weighted average of the holding periods of the actual interest holders (other than any interest holders who treat the portion of the purported gift attributable to their interest in the foreign corporation in the manner described in paragraph (b)(1) of this section). For purposes of section 902, a

Normal corporate tax rules are overridden to a degree that seems remarkable and perhaps unnecessary. For example, if a U.S. donee receives a purported gift from a foreign corporation, the purported gift generally must be included in the U.S. donee's gross income as a distribution from the foreign corporation. Does it make a difference if the corporation has no earnings and profits? Does the purported gift, which is taxed as ordinary income to the recipient, carry out any earnings and profits? If not, it appears that the same amount—first as a gift and then as a dividend—might be taxed twice.[158]

While the Code and the regulations speak in terms of purported gifts, it should be recalled that so far as most of the world is concerned, the transaction is legally a gift. For example, under the laws of many countries, an agreement to transfer money to another person that is not supported by consideration formalized in some fashion – for example, made under seal – is a gift; and such agreement is not enforceable. Also, another jurisdiction might impose some form of gift or capital transfer tax; while, as to the same transaction, the U.S. will treat it, for example, as a distribution.

There are some limited exceptions to these general rules. First, they will not apply if the U.S. donee can prove to the IRS that either (a) a U.S. taxpayer who holds an interest in the partnership or foreign corporation reported the purported gift or bequest for U.S. tax purposes as a distribution and a subsequent gift or bequest or (b) a nonresident alien individual who holds directly or indirectly an interest in the partnership or foreign corporation reported the purported gift or bequest for purposes of the tax laws of the nonresident alien individual's country of residence as a distribution and a subsequent gift or bequest to the United States donee, and the United States donee timely complied with the reporting requirements of section 6039F, if applicable. This exception, as it applies to the nonresident alien individual, is an interesting one. Many jurisdictions do not have an income tax; and most of those jurisdictions that have an income tax will not view these facts as tantamount to a distribution

---

United States donee that is a domestic corporation is not treated as owning any voting stock of the foreign corporation.
Reg. § 1.672(f)-4(a)(2), Income Tax Regs.
[158] Bruce Comments.

followed by a gift. What happens if the foreign jurisdiction does not have an income tax? Does the exception not apply? What happens if the foreign jurisdiction has an income tax but it does not apply under these circumstances? In either case, can the parties bring themselves within the exception by writing a letter to the government ministry in charge of fiscal matters, disclosing all the facts and concluding that no tax or other fiscal imposition is required?

Second, the recharacterization rule will not apply to the extent a U.S. donee that is a corporation can establish that the purported gift or bequest was treated for U.S. tax purposes as a contribution to the capital of the U.S. donee to which section 118 (contributions to the capital of corporation) applies. It will be recalled that in some limited circumstances there can be such a thing as contributions to capital by nonshareholders. Section 118(a).

Third, an exception applies where all the beneficial owners of the domestic partnership are U.S. citizens or residents or domestic corporations.

Fourth, the recharacterization rule will not apply if either (a) the U. S. donee is a nonprofit organization described in section 170(c) (charitable contribution defined); or (b) the transferor has received an IRS ruling or determination letter, which has been neither revoked nor modified, recognizing its exempt status, and the transferor made the transfer pursuant to an exempt purpose for which the transferor was created or organized. "For purposes of the preceding sentence, a ruling or determination letter recognizing exemption may not be relied upon if there is a material change, inconsistent with exemption, in the character, the purpose, or the method of operation of the organization."[159] This last requirement is a little unusual since the U.S. donee ordinarily would not know whether there has been a change in the method of operation of a foreign nonprofit organization that has received a U.S. tax-exempt determination letter. It seems that this person should be entitled to rely upon the fact that the donor has received a determination letter that has not been revoked.

Where a trust is in the picture, a special set of rules apply. Gifts from trusts to which a partnership or foreign corporation has made a

[159] Reg. § 1.672(f)-4(b)(4), Income Tax Regs.

gratuitous transfer will generally be treated as a distribution from the partnership or the foreign corporation. This point holds regardless who is treated as the grantor of the trust (or portion thereof) under section 671. Reg. § 1.672(f)-4(c), Income Tax Regs. However, if taking this tack, the U.S. tax does not exceed the U.S. tax that would be due if the U.S. donee treated the transfer as a distribution from the trust (or portion thereof), then the U.S. donee must treat the transfer as a distribution from the trust (or portion thereof) that is subject to the Subpart F rules applicable to nongrantor trusts. (The $10,000 *de minimis* rule, discussed below, will still apply.) This additional "wrinkle" will only apply where the partnership or foreign corporation has made a gratuitous transfer to the trust. Also, this "wrinkle" will not apply to the extent the U.S. donee can prove to the IRS that the transfer represents an amount that is, or has been, taken into account for U.S. tax purposes by a U.S. citizen or resident or a domestic corporation. "A transfer will be deemed to be made first out of amounts that have not been taken into account for United States tax purposes by a United States citizen or resident or a domestic corporation, unless the United States donee can demonstrate to the satisfaction of the Commissioner that another ordering rule is more appropriate."[160] For example, if a taxpayer can show that he has properly taken into account a distribution from a foreign trust—which distribution was, in fact, a nontaxable distribution of corpus, then he should not be taxed under this regulation on a "gift" from the foreign corporation.

The regulations contain a detailed definition of "purported gift or bequest." In general, a purported gift or bequest is any transfer of property by a partnership or foreign corporation other than a transfer for fair market value to a person who is not a partner in the partnership or a shareholder of the foreign corporation (or to a person who is a partner in the partnership or a shareholder of a foreign corporation, if the amount transferred is inconsistent with the partner's interest in the partnership or the shareholder's interest in the corporation, as the case may be). For purposes of this section, the term property includes cash.

[160] Reg. § 1.672(f)-4(c)(3), Income Tax Regs.

There is an important exception for transfers to unrelated parties. No portion of a transfer will be treated as a purported gift or bequest if the U.S. donee can demonstrate to the satisfaction of the Commissioner that she is not related to a partner or shareholder of the transferor[161] or does not have "another relationship with a partner or shareholder of the transferor that establishes a reasonable basis for concluding that the transferor would make a gratuitous transfer to the United States donee."[162] Apparently this means, among other things, as a practical matter, that a large, publicly-held foreign corporation can make a *bona fide* gift to a U.S. person, whereas the recipient of a "gift" from a small foreign corporation will have a difficult time demonstrating that there is no friendly relationship with one or more of the shareholders. It will be noted that friendly relationships with the management of the large corporation do not work against the recipient.

Lest the taxpayer figure out how to use the recharacterization rules to his advantage, the regulations contain a prohibition on the affirmative use of "recharacterization". A taxpayer is prohibited from using the rules of section 672(f)(4) if a principal purpose for using such rules is the avoidance of any tax imposed by the Internal Revenue Code. Accordingly, the IRS can depart from the section 672(f)(4) rules and recharacterize the transfer in accordance with its form or its economic substance.

Section 672(f)(4) (f) will not apply if, during the taxable year of the U.S. donee, the aggregate amount of purported gifts or bequests that is transferred to such donee, directly or indirectly, from all partnerships or foreign corporations that are related does not exceed $10,000.

The following examples illustrate the workings of these provisions in the Code and regulations.

> Example 1. Distribution from foreign corporation. FC is a foreign corporation that is wholly owned by A, a nonresident alien who is resident in Country C.

[161] Here the regulations refer to the related party rules in section 643(h).
[162] Reg. § 1.672(f)-4(c)(3), Income Tax Regs.

FC makes a gratuitous transfer of property directly to A's daughter, B, who is a resident alien. Under paragraph (a)(2) of this section, B generally must treat the transfer as a dividend from FC to the extent of FC's earnings and profits and as an amount received in excess of basis thereafter. If FC is a passive foreign investment company, B must treat the amount received as a distribution under section 1291. B will be treated as having the same holding period as A. However, under paragraph (b)(1)(ii) of this section, if B can establish to the satisfaction of the Commissioner that, for purposes of the tax laws of Country C, A treated (and reported, if applicable) the transfer as a distribution to himself and a subsequent gift to B, B may treat the transfer as a gift (provided B timely complied with the reporting requirements of section 6039F, if applicable). [This example indicates that if Country C does not have an income tax, the requirement that the distribution be reported is not applicable.]

Example 2. Distribution of corpus from trust to which foreign corporation made gratuitous transfer. FC is a foreign corporation that is wholly owned by A, a nonresident alien who is resident in Country C. FC makes a gratuitous transfer to a foreign trust, FT, that has no other assets. FT immediately makes a gratuitous transfer in the same amount to A's daughter, B, who is a resident alien. Under paragraph (c)(1) of this section, B must treat the transfer as a transfer from FC that is subject to the rules of paragraph (a)(2) of this section. Under paragraph (a)(2) of this section, B must treat the transfer as a dividend from FC unless she can establish to the satisfaction of the Commissioner that, for purposes of the tax laws of Country C, A treated (and reported, if applicable) the transfer as a distribution to himself and a subsequent gift to B and that B timely complied with the reporting requirements of section 6039F, if applicable. The alternative rule in paragraph (c)(2) of this section would not apply as long as the United States tax computed under the rules of paragraph (a)(2) of this section is equal to or greater than the United States tax that would be due if the transfer were treated as a distribution from FT.

Example 3. Accumulation distribution from trust to which foreign corporation made gratuitous transfer. FC is a foreign corporation that is wholly owned by A, a nonresident alien. FC is not a passive foreign investment company (as defined in section 1297). FC makes a gratuitous transfer of 100X to a foreign trust, FT, on January 1, 2001. FT has no other assets on January 1, 2001. Several years later, FT makes a gratuitous transfer of 1000X to A's daughter, B, who is a United States resident. Assume that the section 668 interest charge on accumulation distributions will apply if the transfer is treated as a distribution from FT. Under the alternative rule of paragraph (c)(2) of this section, B must treat the transfer as an accumulation distribution from FT, because the resulting United States tax liability is greater than the United States tax that would be due if the transfer were treated as a transfer from FC that is subject to the rules of paragraph (a) of this section.

Example 4. Transfer from trust that is treated as owned by United States citizen. Assume the same facts as in Example 3, except that A is a United States citizen. Assume that A treats and reports the transfer to FT as a constructive distribution to himself, followed by a gratuitous transfer to FT, and that A is properly treated as the grantor of FT within the meaning of section 1.671-2T(e). A is treated as the owner of FT under section 679 and, as required by section 671 and the regulations thereunder, A includes all of FT's items of income, deductions, and credit in computing his taxable income and credits. Neither paragraph (c)(1) nor paragraph (c)(2) of this section is applicable, because the exception in paragraph (c)(3) of this section applies.

> Example 5. Transfer for less than fair market value. FC is a foreign corporation that is wholly owned by A, a nonresident alien. On January 15, 2001, FC transfers property directly to A's daughter, B, a resident alien, in exchange for 90X. The Commissioner later determines that the fair market value of the property at the time of the transfer was 100X. Under paragraph (d)(2)(i) of this section, 10X will be treated as a purported gift to B on January 15, 2001.

9.4 Expanded anti-conduit rule (Section 643(h))

Prior to the 1996 Act and beginning in 1962, the Code contained a special rule, in section 665(c), applicable to distributions by foreign trusts created by a U.S. person.[163] The amount paid to a U.S. person by a payor who is not U.S. person and which was derived, directly or indirectly, from a foreign trust created by a U.S. person, was deemed by virtue of this provision to been paid directly by the foreign trust. The provision obviously was intended to catch distributions from a foreign trust created by a U.S. person, which were "routed" through some intermediary. This provision pre-dated the enactment of section 679 as part of the Tax Reform Act of 1976, which section makes the U.S. grantor taxable on the income earned by the foreign trust as if he were the owner of the assets. With section 679 in place, there is no need to worry about "catching" disguised distributions from the trust.

The language of this provision, as can be seen, is quite broad. The Treasury Department, in its regulations, limited its reach somewhat. The limitation states that in the case of a distribution to a beneficiary who is a U.S. person, the general rule will not apply if the distribution is received by such beneficiary under circumstances indicating lack of intent on the part of the parties to circumvent the rules generally applicable to distributions from a foreign trust.[164]

---

[163] Section 665(c), Internal Revenue Code of 1986 (prior to amendment by the Small Business Job Protection Act (P.L. 104-188)).
[164] Treas. Regs. § 1.665(c)-1A, Income Tax Regs.

The 1996 Act moved this provision for where it was (section 665(c)) to new section 643(h). That provision now reads: "Any amount paid to a United States person which is derived directly or indirectly from a foreign trust of which the payor is not the grantor shall be deemed in the year of payment to have been directly paid by the foreign trust to such United States person."[165] It will be noted that the trust no longer need be created by a U.S. person and the payor can be a U.S. payor as well as a foreign payor, for the rule to apply.

This is obviously a very broad provision and the Treasury Department and the IRS have properly acted to define better its reach. The Treasury Department proposed regulations under section 643(h). Comments were received and a public hearing was held on August 27, 1997. After consideration of the comments, the proposed regulations were revised and final revised regulations were published on August 5, 1999 (published in the Federal Register on August 10, 1999).[166] These final regulations are effective with respect to transfers made to U.S. persons after August 10, 1999.

The regulations institute a "principal purpose of tax avoidance" test. For purposes of the taxing and reporting provisions, any property that is transferred to a U.S. person by another person (a so-called "intermediary", who can be domestic or foreign) who has received property from a foreign trust will be treated as property transferred directly by the foreign trust to the U.S. person if the intermediary received the property from the foreign trust pursuant to a plan one of the principal purposes of which was the avoidance of United States tax.[167]

---

[165] Section 643(h). "Property" includes cash. Treas. Regs. § 1.643(h)-1(f).

[166] The wording of the proposed regulations was frankly too broad in a number of respects. NYSBA Comments.

[167] Treas. Regs. § 1.643(h)-1(a)(1), Income Tax Regs. In an area such as this one, some form of "catch all" language such as that which appears in the regulations may be necessary, but its application, it is submitted, should have been limited to instances where the recipient of the distribution, on whom the tax liability is imposed, knows or has reason to know of the tax avoidance purpose. This type of limitation appears in Proposed Reg. Sec. 1.672(f)-4 (relating to recharacterization of purported gifts from partnerships and corporations).

A transfer will be deemed to have been made pursuant to a tax avoidance plan if the U.S. person falls within the following description.

1. The U.S. person is related (as defined below) to the grantor of the foreign trust, or has another relationship with the grantor of the foreign trust that establishes a reasonable basis for concluding that the grantor of the foreign trust would make a gratuitous transfer to the U.S. person;

2. The U.S. person receives from the intermediary, within the period beginning 24 months before and ending 24 months after the intermediary's receipt of property from the foreign trust, either the property the intermediary received from the foreign trust, proceeds from such property or property in substitution for such property; and

3. The U.S. person cannot demonstrate to the satisfaction of the IRS that (a) the intermediary has a relationship with the U.S. person that establishes a reasonable basis for concluding that the intermediary would make a gratuitous transfer to the United States person, (b) the intermediary acted independently of the grantor and the trustee of the foreign trust, (c) the intermediary is not an agent of the U.S. person under generally applicable U.S. agency principles, and (d) the U.S. person timely complied with the reporting requirements of section 6039F (relating to giving notice of large gifts and bequests received from foreign persons), if the intermediary is a foreign person.[168]

The notion of a relationship described as "another relationship with the grantor of the foreign trust that establishes a reasonable basis for concluding that the grantor of the foreign trust would make a gratuitous transfer to the U.S. person" appears to be a ground-breaking one. The Code and regulations ordinarily speak in terms of blood or marital or employment relations.

The regulations make clear that nongratuitous transfers are not affected. Section 643(h) is not intended to apply to the extent that

[168] Treas. Regs. § 1.643(h)-1(a)(2), Income Tax Regs.

either the transfer from the foreign trust to the intermediary or the transfer from the intermediary to the U.S. person is a transfer that is not a gratuitous transfer. Gratuitous transfer is defined in the section 671 regulations.

Also, the regulations clearly state that the distributions-through-nominees rule does not apply if the intermediary is the grantor of the portion of the trust from which the property that is transferred is derived.

➔ Thus, a nonresident alien grantor who causes a partial revocation of the trust and turns around and immediately makes a transfer of the funds to a U.S. beneficiary, need not worry about section 678(h) causing the transfer to be treated as an accumulation distribution from the trust.

The regulations also contain specific rules as to the effect of disregarding an intermediary. These rules determine when the U.S. person will be treated as having received the property in question.[169]

[169] Treas. Regs. § 1.643(h)-1(c), Income Tax Regs. The intermediary generally is treated as an agent of the foreign trust, and the property is treated as transferred to the U.S. person in the year the property is transferred, or made available, by the intermediary to the U.S. person. Also, the fair market value of the property transferred is determined as of the date of the transfer by the intermediary to the U.S. person. For purposes of section 665(d)(2), the term taxes imposed on the trust includes any income, war profits, and excess profits taxes imposed by any foreign country or possession of the U.S. on the intermediary with respect to the property transferred. However, if the IRS determines, or if the taxpayer can demonstrate to the IRS's satisfaction, that the intermediary is an agent of the U.S. person, the property will be treated as transferred to the U.S. person in the year the intermediary receives the property from the foreign trust. The fair market value of the property transferred will be determined as of the date of the transfer by the foreign trust to the intermediary. For purposes of section 901(b), any income, war profits, and excess profits taxes imposed by any foreign country or possession of the U.S. on the intermediary with respect to the property transferred will be treated as having been imposed on the U.S. person.

It follows that if section 643(h) applies, the intermediary should be excused from taxation. Thus, the fair market value of the property received by the intermediary and transferred to the U.S. person is not taken into account in computing the intermediary's gross income.

The final regulations contain a *de minimis* rule. Transfers not in excess of $10,000 will not be subjected to section 643(h). "This section does not apply if, during the taxable year of the United States person, the aggregate fair market value of all property transferred to such person from all foreign trusts either directly or through one or more intermediaries does not exceed $10,000."[170]

The final regulations contain 11 examples, which are reproduced here in their entirety.

> (g) Examples. The following examples illustrate the rules of this section. In each example, FT is an irrevocable foreign trust that is not treated as owned by any other person and the fair market value of the property that is transferred exceeds $10,000. The examples are as follows:
>
> Example 1. Principal purpose of tax avoidance. FT was created in 1980 by A, a nonresident alien, for the benefit of his children and their descendants. FT's trustee, T, determines that 1000X of accumulated income should be distributed to A's granddaughter, B, who is a resident alien. Pursuant to a plan with a principal purpose of avoiding the interest charge that would be imposed by section 668, T causes FT to make a gratuitous transfer (within the meaning of section 1.671-2T(e)(2)) of 1000X to I, a foreign person. I subsequently makes a gratuitous transfer of 1000X to B. Under paragraph (a)(1) of this section, FT is deemed to have made an accumulation distribution of 1000X directly to B.
>
> Example 2. United States person unable to demonstrate that intermediary acted independently.

[170] Treas. Regs. § 1.643(h)-1(d), Income Tax Regs.

GM and her daughter, M, are both nonresident aliens. M's daughter, D, is a resident alien. GM creates and funds FT for the benefit of her children. On July 1, 2001, FT makes a gratuitous transfer of XYZ stock to M. M immediately sells the XYZ stock and uses the proceeds to purchase ABC stock. On January 1, 2002, M makes a gratuitous transfer of the ABC stock to D. D is unable to demonstrate that M acted independently of GM and the trustee of FT in making the transfer to D. Under paragraph (a)(2) of this section, FT is deemed to have distributed the ABC stock to D. Under paragraph (c)(1) of this section, M is treated as an agent of FT, and the distribution is deemed to have been made on January 1, 2002.

Example 3. United States person demonstrates that specified conditions are satisfied. Assume the same facts as in Example 2, except that M receives 1000X cash from FT instead of XYZ stock. M gives 1000X cash to D on January 1, 2002. Also assume that M receives annual income of 5000X from her own investments and that M has given D 1000X at the beginning of each year for the past ten years. Based on this and additional information provided by D, D demonstrates to the satisfaction of the Commissioner that M has a relationship with D that establishes a reasonable basis for concluding that M would make a gratuitous transfer to D, that M acted independently of GM and the trustee of FT, that M is not an agent of D under generally applicable United States agency principles, and that D timely complied with the reporting requirements of section 6039F. FT will not be deemed under paragraph (a)(2) of this section to have made a distribution to D.

Example 4. Transfer to United States person less than 24 months before transfer to intermediary. Several years ago, A, a nonresident alien, created and funded FT for the benefit of his children and their descendants. A has a close friend, C, who also is a nonresident alien. A's granddaughter, B, is a resident alien. On December 31, 2001, C makes a gratuitous transfer of 1000X to B. On January 15, 2002, FT makes a gratuitous transfer of 1000X to C. B is unable to demonstrate that C has a relationship with B that would establish a reasonable basis for concluding that C would make a gratuitous transfer to B or that C acted independently of A and the trustee of FT in making the transfer to B. Under paragraph (a)(2) of this section, FT is deemed to have distributed 1000X directly to B. Under paragraph(c)(1) of this section, C is treated as an agent of FT, and the distribution is deemed to have been made on December 31, 2001.

Example 5. United States person receives property in substitution for property transferred to intermediary. GM and her son, S, are both nonresident aliens. S's daughter, GD, is a resident alien. GM creates and funds FT for the benefit of her children and their descendants. On July 1, 2001, FT makes a gratuitous transfer of ABC stock with a fair market value of approximately 1000X to S. On January 1, 2002, S makes a gratuitous transfer of DEF stock with a fair market value of approximately 1000X to GD. GD is unable to demonstrate that S acted independently of GM and the trustee of FT in transferring the DEF stock to GD. Under paragraph (a)(2) of this section, FT is deemed to have distributed the DEF stock to GD. Under paragraph (c)(1) of this section, S is treated as an agent of FT, and the distribution is deemed to have been made on January 1, 2002.

Example 6. United States person receives indirect loan from foreign trust. Several years ago, A, a nonresident alien, created and funded FT for the benefit of her children and their descendants. A's daughter, B, is a resident alien. B needs funds temporarily while she is starting up her own business. If FT were to loan money directly to B, section 643(i) would apply. FT deposits 500X with

FB, a foreign bank, on June 30, 2001. On July 1, 2001, FB loans 400X to B. Repayment of the loan is guaranteed by FT's 500X deposit. B is unable to demonstrate to the satisfaction of the Commissioner that FB has a relationship with B that establishes a reasonable basis for concluding that FB would make a loan to B or that FB acted independently of A and the trustee of FT in making the loan. Under paragraph (a)(2) of this section, FT is deemed to have loaned 400X directly to B on July 1, 2001. Under paragraph (c)(1) of this section, FB is treated as an agent of FT. For the treatment of loans from foreign trusts, see section 643(i).

Example 7. United States person demonstrates that specified conditions are satisfied. GM, a nonresident alien, created and funded FT for the benefit of her children and their descendants. One of GM's children is M, who is a resident alien. During the year 2001, FT makes a gratuitous transfer of 500X to M. M reports the 500X on Form 3520 as a distribution received from a foreign trust. During the year 2002, M makes a gratuitous transfer of 400X to her son, S, who also is a resident alien. M files a Form 709 treating the gratuitous transfer to S as a gift. Based on this and additional information provided by S, S demonstrates to the satisfaction of the Commissioner that M has a relationship with S that establishes a reasonable basis for concluding that M would make a gratuitous transfer to S, that M acted independently of GM and the trustee of FT, and that M is not an agent of S under generally applicable United States agency principles. FT will not be deemed under paragraph (a)(2) of this section to have made a distribution to S.

Example 8. Intermediary as agent of trust; increase in FMV. A, a nonresident alien, created and funded FT for the benefit of his children and their descendants. On December 1, 2001, FT makes a gratuitous transfer of XYZ stock with a fair market value of 85X to B, a nonresident alien. On November 1, 2002, B sells the XYZ stock to a third party in an arm's length transaction for 100X in cash. On November 1, 2002, B makes a gratuitous transfer of 98X to A's grandson, C, a resident alien. C is unable to demonstrate to the satisfaction of the Commissioner that B acted independently of A and the trustee of FT in making the transfer. Under paragraph (a)(2) of this section, FT is deemed to have made a distribution directly to C. Under paragraph (c)(1) of this section, B is treated as an agent of FT, and FT is deemed to have distributed 98X to C on November 1, 2002.

Example 9. Intermediary as agent of United States person; increase in FMV. Assume the same facts as in Example 8, except that the Commissioner determines that B is an agent of C under generally applicable United States agency principles. Under paragraph (c)(2) of this section, FT is deemed to have distributed 85X to C on December 1, 2001. C must take the gain of 15X into account in the year 2002.

Example 10. Intermediary as agent of trust; decrease in FMV. Assume the same facts as in Example 8, except that the value of the XYZ stock on November 1, 2002, is only 8OX. Instead of selling the XYZ stock to a third party and transferring cash to C, B transfers the XYZ stock to C in a gratuitous transfer. Under paragraph (c)(1) of this section, FT is deemed to have distributed XYZ stock with a value of 80X to C on November 1, 2002.

Example 11. Intermediary as agent of United States person; decrease in FMV. Assume the same facts as in Example 10, except that the Commissioner determines that B is an agent of C under generally applicable United States agency principles. Under paragraph (c)(2) of this section, FT is deemed to have distributed XYZ stock with a value of 85X to C on December 1, 2001.

Treas. Regs. § 1.643(h)-1(g), Income Tax Regs.

9.5 Anti-"give-and-go" rule (Section 672(f)(5)); definition of "grantor" in final regulations

9.5.1 Anti-"give-and-go" rule (Section 672(f)(5))

Section 672(f)(5) creates a special rule where the grantor of the trust (either a U.S. or foreign trust) is a foreign person. The rule provides that if, absent this rule, a foreign person would be treated as the owner of the trust assets (in other words, it is a domestic or foreign grantor trust with a foreign grantor) and such trust has as one of its beneficiaries a U.S. person, the U.S. beneficiary will be treated as the grantor (the true grantor) to the extent that she has made, directly or in directly, transfers to the foreign person (that is, to the nominal grantor). Any gift from the U.S. beneficiary to the foreign person will not be taken into account if that gift would be excludable from gift taxes under section 2503(b). Section 2503(b), in general, excludes from gift tax the first $10,000 of gifts made to any person by the donor during the calendar year.

This rule is aimed at situations where a non-U.S. person transfers property to another non-U.S. person before, for example, immigrating to the U.S. The recipient non-U.S. person then transfers the property to a foreign or domestic grantor trust, leaving the non-U.S. person, arguably, as the grantor of the trust and, under section 671, the owner of the assets, who would be treated as the taxpayer.

In effect, this is a codification of the constructive settlor rule found in the case law and rulings.

It will be noted that there is no time period for testing this rule. The first transfer might have taken place in Year 1, the transfer to the trust might have taken place in Year 10, and the first distribution from the trust to the U.S. beneficiary might have taken place in Year 15. The rule is very broad, and, since it calls for an endless tracing of assets, may be difficult for the IRS to assert and for the taxpayer to defend.

This provision is sometimes referred to as the anti-“give-and-go” rule.

The final regulations with respect to this provision state that if, but for section 672(f)(5), a foreign person would be treated as the owner of any portion of a trust, any U.S. beneficiary of the trust will be treated as the grantor of a portion of the trust to the extent the U.S. beneficiary, directly or indirectly, made transfers of property to such foreign person (without regard to whether the U.S. beneficiary was a U.S. beneficiary at the time of any transfer) in excess of transfers to the U.S. beneficiary from the foreign person. The rule, however, will not apply to the extent the U.S. beneficiary can prove to the IRS that the transfer by the U.S. beneficiary to the foreign person was wholly unrelated to any transaction involving the trust.

The regulations include the following examples. The interaction with section 679—in particular the rule in section 679(a)(4) (special rule applicable to foreign grantor who within 5 years becomes a U.S. person)—should be noted.

> Example 1. A, a nonresident alien, contributes property to FC, a foreign corporation that is wholly owned by A. FC creates a foreign trust, FT, for the benefit of A and A’s children. FT is revocable by FC without the approval or consent of any other person. FC funds FT with the property received from A. A and A’s family move to the United States. Under paragraph (a)(1) of this section, A is treated as a grantor of FT. (A may also be treated as an owner of FT under section 679(a)(4).)
>
> Example 2. B, a United States citizen, makes a gratuitous transfer of $1 million to B’s uncle, C, a nonresident alien. C creates a foreign trust, FT, for the benefit of B and B’s children. FT is revocable by C without the approval or consent of any other person. C funds FT with the property received from B. Under paragraph (a)(1) of this section, B is treated as a grantor of FT. (B also would be treated as an owner of FT as a result of section 679.)

Treas. Reg. Sec. 1.672(f)-5, Income Tax Regs.

9.5.2 Definition of "grantor" in final regulations

Somewhat related to this rule is a definition that was inserted in the proposed regulations under 671 and revised somewhat in the temporary regulations that replaced the proposed regulations.[171]

Nothing new was added to the statute as part of 1996 Act on this point, but temporary regulations section 1.671-2(e) add a definition of the term "grantor." This term appears throughout the Code, but heretofore it has never been defined in the regulations. The definition clearly applies not only for purposes of foreign trusts but also for purposes of all the grantor trust provisions of Subpart E of Subchapter J of the Code. The temporary definition defines "grantor" as:

> any person to the extent such person either creates a trust, or directly or indirectly makes a gratuitous transfer . . . of property to a trust. . . . [T]he term property includes cash. If a person creates or funds a trust on behalf of another person, both persons are treated as grantors of the trust. (See section 6048 for reporting requirements that apply to grantors of foreign trusts.) However, a person who creates a trust but makes no gratuitous transfers to the trust is not treated as an owner of any portion of the trust under sections 671 through 677 or 679. Also, a person who funds a trust with an amount that is directly reimbursed to such person within a reasonable period of time and who makes no other transfers to the trust that constitute gratuitous

[171] On June 5, 1997 Treasury and the IRS published a notice of proposed rulemaking (REG-252487-96) under section 671, among other sections. 62 FR 37819. Comments were received and a public hearing was held on August 27, 1997. After consideration of the comments, the proposed regulations under section 671 were revised and issued as temporary regulations.

> transfers is not treated as an owner of any portion of the trust under sections 671 through 677 or 679.

Temp. Reg. § 1.671-2T(e)(1), Income Tax Regs.[172]

A gratuitous transfer is defined as any transfer other than a transfer for fair market value; and the temporary regulations plainly state that a transfer of property to a trust may be considered a gratuitous transfer without regard to whether the transfer is treated as a gift for gift tax purposes.

A transfer will be viewed as "for fair market value" only to the extent of the value of property received from the trust, services rendered by the trust or the right to use property of the trust. For example, rents, royalties, interest, and compensation paid to a trust are transfers for fair market value only to the extent that the payments reflect an arm's length price for the use of the property of, or for the services rendered by, the trust. "[A] person will not be treated as making a transfer for fair market value merely because the transferor recognizes gain on the transaction."[173]

A grantor, the temporary regulations provide, includes any person who acquires an interest in a trust from a grantor of the trust if the interest acquired is an interest in certain investment trusts, liquidating trusts, or environmental remediation trusts.

The temporary regulations explore the consequences of transfers made by corporations, partnerships and trusts. If a gratuitous transfer

---

[172] The Temporary Regulations dropped a provision in the proposed regulations that granted very broad authority to the IRS District Counsel. Proposed Regulation 1.671-2(e)(4)(i)(C) stated: "Notwithstanding any other provision of this paragraph (e), the district director may determine, based upon the facts and circumstances, that a direct or indirect transfer to a trust is more properly characterized as a gratuitous transfer if the transfer was structured with a principal purposes of avoiding U.S. tax. See, e.g., sections 643(a)(7) and 679(d)." There are too many issues arising in connection with the creation of or transfer to trusts, and they are too varied, for this specific grant of authority to be appropriate. The Treasury Department and the Service wisely omitted this provision from the final regulations. *See* Bruce Comments.

[173] Temp. Reg. § 1.671-2T(e)(2)(ii), Income Tax Regs.

is made by a corporation or partnership to a trust and is for a business purpose of the corporation or partnership, the corporation or partnership will generally be treated as the grantor of the trust. For example, if a corporation makes a gratuitous transfer to a trust in order to secure a legal obligation of the corporation to a third party unrelated to the corporation (as with some form of arrangement intended to secure an indebtedness), the corporation will be treated as the grantor of the trust. However, if a corporation or partnership makes a gratuitous transfer to a trust that is not for a business purpose of the transferor but, for example, is, for a personal purpose of one or more of the shareholders or partners, the gratuitous transfer will be treated as a constructive distribution to the shareholders or partners and the shareholders or partners will be treated as the grantors of the trust. "For example, if a partnership makes a gratuitous transfer to a trust that is for the benefit of a child of a partner, the gratuitous transfer will be treated as a distribution to the partner under section 731 and a subsequent gratuitous transfer by the partner to the trust."[174] In the same vein, if a trust makes a gratuitous transfer of property to another trust, the grantor of the transferor trust generally will be treated as the grantor of the transferee trust.[175] However, if a person with a general power of appointment over the transferor trust exercises that power so as to cause a transfer to another trust, then such person will be treated as the grantor of the transferee trust; and this rule will pertain even if the grantor of the transferor trust is treated as the owner of the transferor trust under subpart E of part I, subchapter J, chapter 1 of the Internal Revenue Code.[176]

---

[174] Temp. Reg. § 1.671-2T(e)(4), Income Tax Regs.

[175] If the grantor, who was an individual, is no longer alive, it seems that the transferor trust should be viewed as the grantor, since it is difficult to envision a dead individual as the grantor of a trust. The temporary regulations appear to reach a different conclusion. *See* Example 8, Temp. Reg. § 1.671-2T(e)(6), Income Tax Regs.

[176] The commentary at the beginning of T.D. 8831, which promulgates the temporary regulations under 671, as well as other regulations, states parenthetically that "These rules do not affect the determination of whether or not the gratuitous transfer from the transferor trust is a distribution subject to sections 651 or 661." Following the pattern set with corporations and partnerships—and there is no reason not to follow this pattern—a gratuitous transfer from a transferor trust to another trust should be treated as a constructive distribution to the grantor of the transferor trust under sections 651 and 661 and a subsequent gratuitous transfer by the grantor to the trust.

The temporary regulations contain a number of useful examples. These are set forth below.

> (6) The following examples illustrate the rules of this paragraph (e). Unless otherwise indicated, all trusts are domestic trusts and all other persons are United States persons. The examples are as follows:
>
> Example 1. A creates and funds a trust, T, for the benefit of her children. B, subsequently makes a gratuitous transfer to T. Under paragraph (e)(1) of this section, both A and B are grantors of T.
>
> Example 2. A makes an investment in a fixed investment trust, T, that is classified as a trust under section 301.7701-4(c)(1) of this chapter. A is a grantor of T. B subsequently acquires A's entire interest in T. Under paragraph (e)(3) of this section, B is a grantor of T with respect to such interest.
>
> Example 3. A, an attorney, creates a foreign trust, FT, on behalf of A's client, B, and transfers $100 to FT out of A's funds. A is reimbursed by B for the $100 transferred to FT. The trust instrument states that the trustee has discretion to distribute the income or corpus of FT to B, and B's children. Both A and B are treated as grantors of FT under paragraph (e)(1) of this section. In addition, B is treated as the owner of the entire trust under section 677. Because A is reimbursed for the $100 transferred to FT on behalf of B, A is not treated as transferring any property to FT. Therefore, A is not an owner of any portion of T under sections 671 through 677 regardless of whether A retained any power over or interest in T described in sections 673

This action will or will not carry out DNI/UNI, as the facts may be. The drafters of the regulations may have realized that a constructive distribution-gratuitous transfer might lead to unfortunate, from the Treasury Department's and IRS's standpoint, consequences.

through 677. A also is not treated as an owner of any portion of T under section 679. Both A and B are responsible parties for purposes of the reporting requirements in section 6048.

Example 4. A creates and funds a trust, T. A is not treated as an owner of any portion of the trust under subpart E. B holds an unrestricted power, exercisable solely by B, to withdraw certain amounts contributed to the trust before the end of the calendar year and to vest those amounts in B. B is treated as an owner of the portion of T that is subject to the withdrawal power under section 678(a)(1). However, B is not a grantor of T under paragraph (e)(1) of this section because B neither created T nor made a gratuitous transfer to T.

Example 5. A transfers cash to a trust, T, through a broker, in exchange for units in T. The units in T are not property for purposes of determining whether A has received fair market value under paragraph (e)(2)(ii) of this section. Therefore, A has made a gratuitous transfer to T, and, under paragraph (e)(1) of this section, A is a grantor of T.

Example 6. A borrows cash from T, a trust. A has not made any gratuitous transfers to T. Arm's length interest payments by A to T will not be treated as gratuitous transfers under paragraph (e)(2)(ii) of this section. Therefore, under paragraph (e)(1) of this section, A is not a grantor of T with respect to the interest payments.

Example 7. A, B's brother, creates a trust, T, for B's benefit and contributes $50,000 to T. The trustee invests the $50,000 in stock of Company X. C, B's uncle, sells property with a fair market value of $1,000,000 to T in exchange for the stock when it has appreciated to a fair market value of $100,000. Under paragraph (e)(2)(ii) of this section, the $900,000 excess value is a gratuitous transfer by C.

> Therefore, under paragraph (e)(1) of this section, A is a grantor with respect to the portion of the trust valued at $100,000, and C is a grantor of T with respect to the portion of the trust valued at $900,000. In addition, A or C or both will be treated as the owners of the respective portions of the trust of which each person is a grantor if A or C or both retain powers over or interests in such portions under sections 673 through 677.
>
> Example 8. G creates and funds a trust, T1, for the benefit of G's children and grandchildren. After G's death, under authority granted to the trustees in the trust instrument, the trustees of T1 transfer a portion of the assets of T1 to another trust, T2, and retain a power to revoke T2 and revest the assets of T2 in T1. Under paragraphs (e)(1) and (5) of this section, G is the grantor of T1 and T2. In addition, because the trustees of T1 have retained a power to revest the assets of T2 in T1, T1 is treated as the owner of T2 under section 678(a).
>
> Example 9. G creates and funds a trust, T1, for the benefit of B. G retains a power to revest the assets of T1 in G within the meaning of section 676. Under the trust agreement, B is given a general power of appointment over the assets of T1. B exercises the general power of appointment with respect to one-half of the corpus of T1 in favor of a trust, T2, that is for the benefit of C, B's child. Under paragraph (e)(1) of this section, G is the grantor of T1, and under paragraphs (e)(1) and (5) of this section, B is the grantor of T2.

Temp. Reg. § 1.671-2T(e)(6), Income Tax Regs.

Referring to Example 3, attorneys will need to be mindful of their reporting responsibilities under this rule.

Referring to Example 8, it appears that while the trust document contained authority for the trustees to settle T2, G did not know and could not have known that the trustees would take this step. It is difficult to conclude that a dead individual should be treated as the grantor of a trust, T2, based on the actions of his trustees after his death.

9.6 Foreign trust treated as nonresident alien who is not present in the U.S. (section 642(b))

Section 641(b) contains a last sentence added by the Taxpayer Relief Act of 1997 (P.L.105-34) enacted on August 5, 1997. The sentence reads "For purposes of this subsection [which provides the general rules for the computation and payment of tax by trusts and estates], a foreign trust or foreign estate shall not be treated as a nonresident alien individual who is present in the United States at anytime." As a result, a foreign trust will not be able to mitigate the effects of the rules applicable to foreign trusts by subjecting itself to U.S. tax by obtaining a taxable presence of the U.S. If the trust is a foreign nongrantor trust, for example, it will have to deal with the sections 665-668 rules applicable to the treatment of excess distributions by trusts, *i.e.*, the accumulation distribution, "throwback" and interest charge rules.

This provision is effective as if included in the provisions of the 1996 Act—generally effective for years beginning after December 31, 1996.

9.7 Gains accumulated and distributed lose their character as capital gains and are taxed as ordinary income (Sections 643(a)(6) & 667(a))

As discussed in the Chapter 10 which deal with the Tax Reform Act of 1976, Congress, with some subtle legislative drafting, removed the capital gains character of gains earned by a foreign trust, accumulated and distributed. This was achieved, simply put, by including capital gains in distributable net income and then not retaining its capital gains character for any purpose. This approach can be contrasted with the approach for tax-exempt income, which is included in DNI and whose character as tax-exempt is specifically retained.

Later, in connection with the Revenue Act of 1978 (P.L. 95-600), it was recognized that this obliteration of character wrongly applied to distributions to nonresident aliens and foreign corporations as well as U.S. beneficiaries. Section 667(e) was enacted to build back into the construction of distributable net income capital gains character—but only in the case of a distribution from a trust to a nonresident alien individual or foreign corporation. In fact, all aspects of character—not just the capital gains aspect—were restored.

It should be noted that the obliteration of character when income is run through a particular entity, here, a foreign accumulation trust, can be what is referred to in tort law as an "attractive nuisance." Some of the anomalous results are noted in chapter 10. The ability to "launder out" unfavorable tax characteristics may, in certain circumstances, lead to the erasure of the passive investment income taint and avoidance of source rules where these are undesirable. The subpart F provisions aimed at terrorist countries arguably could be avoided by passing income through a foreign accumulation trust.[177]

9.8 Provisions calling for regulations regarding "abusive" transactions (section 643(a)(7))

In a number of places in the provisions on foreign trusts, the statute calls for regulations to be written by the Treasury Department. The most noteworthy of these provisions appears in section 643(a)(7). "The Secretary shall prescribe such regulations as may be necessary or appropriate to carry out the purposes of this part, including regulations to prevent avoidance of such purposes."

The Treasury Department and the IRS, understandably, are waiting to see how taxpayers and their advisors react to the many provisions enacted in the 1996 Act. Three years have now passed since enactment of these provisions. A great deal has been written and said on the subject. It can now be anticipated that the Service

---

[177] Section 901(j) (relating to the denial of foreign tax credit, etc., with respect to certain foreign countries), added by the Budget Reconciliation Act of 1986 (P.L. No. 99-509). *See* Bruce & Gray, "U.S. Taxation Of Foreign Trusts: Post-1976 Act Changes And Continued Uses," Vol. 17 Tax Management Int'l Journal No. 5 (May 13, 1988), at footnote 10.

will promulgate regulations addressing a number of the practices that have cropped up.

One of the areas that may be addressed is arrangements intended to avoid categorization as a trust. Almost all the new rules apply only where there is a trust. If an entity or contractual arrangement can be formulated which falls outside the definition of a trust, these rules might be avoided. For example, will a usufruct avoid the trust definition?

> A usufruct is the property right given from one to another to enjoy the use of property, typically but not necessarily real property, without altering it or diminishing it. A usufruct can be conditional or unconditional, and can be made *inter vivos* or via testament. The holder of the usufruct, the usufructor, manages the property. Usufruct was originally a Roman law concept, and derives from the Latin *ususfructus*, "to use the fruit." Usufructs exist in civil, but generally not common, law systems, and are specifically provided for in civil codes.[178]

The IRS will want to apply the rules broadly; but it might be constrained by the fact that any changes that it proposed could affect not just foreign trusts but all types of trusts. There are probably millions of trusts in existence today; and there are many types of trusts that are used in connection with financial transactions—such as the securitization of assets. The IRS will want to tread carefully with respect to this subject.

It also will be interesting to see if, and if so how, the IRS approaches the many types of insurance products that are used essentially as trust substitutes.

---

[178] Gordon & Summers, "Trusts and Taxes in Civil Law Emerging Economies: Issues, Problems, and Proposed Solutions," Tax Notes Int'l, July 20, 1992.

9.10 Loans from foreign trust to U.S. grantor or beneficiary taxable as ordinary income (Section 643 (i))

In the past, and with respect to a domestic trust, a trust could make a loan to the grantor or a beneficiary, and it would not be treated as a distribution. In fact, this is a common practice.

Section 643(i) provides that if the foreign trust makes a loan of cash or marketable securities, directly or indirectly, to a U.S. grantor or beneficiary, or to any other person who is related to the grantor or beneficiary, the amount of the loan will be treated as a distribution. Also, in such a case, the trust will be treated as a complex trust—as opposed to a simple trust.

One of the consequences of this last rule is that the distribution will not carry out any capital gains. Capital gains coming out of a trust in the form of an accumulation distribution are added to DNI and lose their character as capital gains—that is, are converted into ordinary income.

The Treasury Department, in the House Committee Report on the Small Business Job Protection Act of 1996, was directed to provide a regulatory exception to this rule where the loan is structured with arm's-length terms. "Congress expected that Treasury regulations will provide an exception from this treatment for loans with arm's-length terms. In applying this exception, the Congress further expected consideration be given to whether there is a reasonable expectation the loan will be repaid."[179]

Regulations have not been promulgated under this provision.

9.11 "Throwback" rules made inapplicable for domestic trusts, but not foreign trusts (Section 665(c))

Section 665(c) provides an exception for accumulation distributions for most domestic trusts. Any distribution from a domestic trust after the effective date of this change (August 5, 1997)

---

[179] Staff of the Joint Committee On Taxation, 104th Cong., 2d Sess., General Explanation Of Tax Legislation Enacted In The 104th Congress, (Comm. Print 1996).

will not be subjected to the complex "throwback" rules. This exception, however, will not apply to a foreign trust, including—unless excused by regulations—a domestic trust that was formerly a foreign trust and a trust created before March 1, 1984, unless it is established that the trust would not be aggregated with other trusts under section 643(f) (which provides special rules for the treatment of multiple trusts) were that section to be applied to such trust.

At the same time the exemption from the "throwback" rules was enacted, Congress provided that pre-contribution gain on property sold by a domestic trust would no longer be taxed at the contributor's marginal tax rates (old section 644).

The "throwback" rules and "pre-contribution" rule in section 644 were intended to combat the practice of saving taxes by directing income to a trust which, as a separate taxpayer, might pay tax at a lower rate. When these rules were first put into the Code, a taxpayer could reduce his tax liability by transferring property to one or more trusts, so the income from the property would be taxed at lower rates. Congress, in the Tax Reform Act of 1984, curtailed the use of multiple trusts. Then, in the Tax Reform Act of 1986, it provided a new rate schedule for trusts (and estates) and thereby practically eliminated the possible tax benefit attaching to the use of a trust.

Accordingly, all the complexities associated with the "throwback" rules fall only on foreign trusts. Also, the matrix of forms and instructions relating to this subject are only relevant for trustees of foreign trusts and the beneficiaries of these trusts. It might be assumed that there is not a great deal of impetus for dealing administratively with these topics. However, it must be said that the IRS and Treasury Department are attempting to provide explanations and up-dated forms.

The workings of the "throwback" rules are explained in Chapter 7.

9.12 Interest charge on accumulation distributions (section 668)

Starting with the Tax Reform Act of 1976, and as modified by the 1996 Act, there have been provisions applying an interest charge on top of the additional tax imposed by the "throwback" rules. The interest charge is designed to offset the "time benefit of money" inherent in not paying tax on an accumulation distribution until the year of distribution.

Prior to the 1996 Act changes, effective January 1, 1996, interest on accumulation distributions was computed at 6 percent simple interest per year. Beginning on January 1, 1996, however, the interest charge has been changed to the same compounded rate that applies to an underpayment of tax under section 6621(a)(2) (the "underpayment rate").

Under the new interest charge rules, the interest charge is compounded, based on the underpayment rate. Simple interest is accrued through 1995. However, starting on January 1, 1996, compound interest rates based on the underpayment rate is imposed on (a) tax amounts determined under the accumulation distribution rules and (2) the total accrued simple interest for pre-1996 periods. In computing the interest charge, the accumulation distribution is allocated proportionately to prior trust years in which there is undistributed net income (provided that the distributions were made to U.S. citizens or resident beneficiaries), rather than to the earliest year that the trust had undistributed net income.

Section 668 sets forth a formula to determine the period for which interest is charged using the underpayment rate. The House Committee Report on the legislation provides as follows:

> Under the formula, for example, if a foreign grantor trust had $100 of undistributed net income each year in years 1 through 3 and the trust distributes $100 of accumulated income to its U.S. beneficiary in year 4, the taxpayer has to pay interest using the . . . [underpayment rate] as if the income accrued for 2 years. /4/ In addition, the $100 accumulation distribution reduces the trust's undistributed at income by $33 each year for years 1 through 3. /5/
>
> ---
>
> 4. The number of years is determined as a weighted average as follows: ($100 X 3 years) + ($100 X 2 years) + ($100 X 1 year) / $300 + 2.

5. That is, one-third of the $100 of distribution reduces the $100 of undisputed net income for each of years one, 23.

As seen in Chapter 7, the actual reporting and calculation of the interest charge can be very difficult.

9.13 The special grantor trust rules, including the 5-year "clawback" rule (section 679)

Section 679 (foreign trusts having one or more United States beneficiaries), in a nutshell, provides that if (a) a trust is a foreign trust, (b) it is created by a U.S. person and (c) it has—or has the possibility of having—a U.S. beneficiary, then for tax purposes the trust will be ignored and the grantor (settlor) will be treated as the owner of the assets. This is one of the most remarkable provisions in the Code. It is rare for taxpayers to be able to the decide who will be treated as the taxpayer (that is, who will be responsible for paying taxes) on the basis of "formalities." Intent plays no role in the workings of these provisions.

It will be noted that the grantor can have absolutely no relationship with the property after the transfer in trust, *i.e.*, he can merely be the former owner of the assets. Under this rule, however, he will remain until his death or the termination of the trust the owner of the assets and the person responsible for reporting on his return all the income and losses. This follows even if the grantor under applicable legal principles is not entitled to any information about the trust. As grantor, he is a "responsible party" under section 6048. Form 3520 (Annual Return To Report Transactions With Foreign Trusts And Receipt Of Certain Foreign Gifts) must be filed by him because during the tax year he is treated as the owner of the assets of the trust. It makes no difference that he did not receive any type of real economic benefit.

The rationale for the provision seemed like a good one at the time. U.S. individuals were using foreign trusts essentially to defer taxes. One popular device of the day was the creation of a foreign trust followed by the transfer of assets in return for a private annuity. Some other practices were obviously very aggressive. Congress wanted to eliminate some of the anomalies in this area of the law and in the use of foreign trusts as a means of achieving tax deferral.[180] In order to achieve this end, it decided to drop a large bomb (in the form of section 679) on the area.

As with many strong provisions in the Code, the realization that the provision is a two-edged sword slowly came to the fore. The most remarkable outgrowth of this provision is protection of assets trusts. Under section 679, the individual grantor is doing nothing for tax purposes; but for other legal purposes, including creditors' rights, bankruptcy, and the like, he has removed the assets from his personal estate (balance sheet).

Embedded in section 679 is a special rule applicable to a foreign grantor who later becomes a U.S. person. It provides that if a nonresident alien individual becomes a resident alien, that is, becomes a U.S. taxpayer, within five years after directly or indirectly transferring property to a foreign trust, section 679 and the reporting rules in sections 6048 will apply as if the individual made the transfer in trust immediately upon coming to the U.S. The amount of the transfer is equal to the amount in the trust attributable to the property transferred by him. Undistributed net income for years prior to the time the individual came to the U.S. are taken into account in determining the amount in the trust attributable to property transferred by him. The determination of the date when the individual becomes a resident alien is tied to the "starting date" rules under section 7701(b).

Also embedded in this section is a rule for taxing the grantor should the trust at some later date acquire a U.S. beneficiary. If a foreign trust is not a section 679 grantor trust because it does not have a U.S. beneficiary, but in a subsequent year it somehow acquires such a beneficiary, then the grantor is treated as having income for the taxable year equal to the undistributed net income of the trust at the

---

[180] Based on the colloquies occurring at a markup on Oct. 1, 1975, the House Ways and Means Committee may have thought that it had created a new tool to be used against organized crime. The suggestion was made during the Committee's markup that some of the money being transferred by U.S. persons to foreign trusts was "dirty money." Although the staff backed away from the suggestion in the ensuing discussion, the mention of "dirty money" may have poisoned the deliberations. *See* Bruce, "U.S. Taxation of Foreign Trusts: Post-1976 Act Changes and Continued Uses," Tax Management International Journal, Vol. 17, No. 5 (May 13, 1988).

close of the immediately preceding taxable year. (Again this is a rather remarkable provision. A beneficiary who at the outset of the trust was not a U.S. resident alien might decide to immigrate to the U.S. By doing so, she would cause the grantor suddenly to become taxable on all the income earned in the trust. The grantor, however, might have derived absolutely no benefit from that income in the past and have no chance of benefiting in the future.)

While the bulk of this section was enacted in 1976 with some retroactive effective dates reaching back to May 21, 1974, regulations have never been promulgated. This provision is viewed as an anti-tax avoidance provision; and it was probably thought best not to provide information that might be taken by some as a "roadmap" around the rules. Also, other regulations projects undoubtedly were viewed as more important.

Not covered by section 679 are transfers by reason of death and transfers at fair market value. For example, a bequest (death-time gift) to a foreign trust will not cause the trust be treated as a grantor trust under this provision. By way of further example, a transfer of cash or property to a foreign trust in exchange for consideration equal to or greater than the fair market value of the cash or property transferred will not cause the trust to be so treated. Consideration other than cash will be taken into account at its fair market value. On this point, certain obligations will not be taken into account under the so-called "fair market value exception." When judging the adequacy of the consideration coming back to the transferor from the trust, not taken into account is any obligation of certain persons and the any obligation that is guaranteed by such persons. The "certain persons" are the trust, any grantor, owner or beneficiary of the trust, and any person who is related to any of these persons. The rules for determining who is "related" are the same as those applicable to loans from foreign trusts, which rules appear in section 643(i). A technical correction added as part of the Taxpayer Relief Act of 1997 makes clear that for purposes of determining whether U.S. person's transfer to a trust is for fair market value consideration, the related persons whose obligations are disregarded include the owner of the trust and certain persons who are related to such owner.

9.14 Transfers of appreciated property to a foreign trust are taxed as a sale. (Section 684)

Section 684 provides that any transfer of property by a U.S. person to a foreign trust or estate is taxable as a sale or exchange of the property for its fair market value. The U.S. transferor recognizes gain equal to the excess of the property's fair market value over its adjusted basis in the hands of the transferor.

Section 684(b), however, makes clear that this general rule will not apply to a transfer to a foreign trust by a U.S. person to the extent that any person is treated as the owner of the foreign trust under section 671. Thus, a U.S. grantor will not be subject to this provision if he transfers appreciated property to a foreign grantor trust.[181]

There is also a special rule applicable to domestic trusts that migrate outside the US. Where a domestic trust becomes a foreign trust, all the trust assets are considered to have been transferred to the foreign trust. Therefore, appreciated property owned by the domestic trust will be deemed to have been sold on the day that the domestic trust is converted into a foreign trust; and gain will be recognized by the domestic trust on that date.[182]

The section 684 rules are effective August 5, 1997.

---

[181] This outcome coincides with the result arrived out under old section 1491, which was repealed effective August 5, 1997. The IRS for many years asserted the applicability of the section 1491 35% excise tax on a transfer to a foreign trust, even if that trust was taxed as a "grantor trust" with the U.S. person being taxed as the grantor. Rev. Rul. 69-450, 1969-2 C.B. 168; Rev. Rul. 80-318, 1980-2 C.B. 245. The IRS, in 1987, reversed its position and announced that no section 1491 excise tax would apply on a transfer of appreciated assets to a foreign trust so long as that trust is a "grantor trust" and the grantor is a U.S. person. Rev. Rul. 87-61, 1987-2 C.B. 219.

[182] On its face, this very clear rule would seem to take precedence over the theory that where a person makes a transfer to a domestic trust and the domestic trust then migrates outside the U.S., the original transferor will be treated as the transferor to the foreign trust. It makes a difference as to who will be responsible for paying the tax. On the other hand, it would seem that the Service is always free to argue the "step transaction" theory or one of the several variations of that theory.

This set of rules replaces the excise tax rules in old section 1491. Old section 1491 sat by itself in Chapter 5 of Subtitle A of the Code (Tax On Transfers To Avoid Income Tax). It came into existence in 1932. It imposed on the transfer of appreciated property by a U.S. citizen or resident, or by a domestic corporation or partnership, or by a domestic trust or estate, to a foreign corporation as paid-in surplus or as contribution to capital, or to a foreign trust or estate, or to a foreign partnership, a 35% excise tax on the excess of the fair market value of the property transferred over the total of the adjusted basis of the property in the hands of the transferor and the amount of gain recognized on the transfer. Similar to new section 684, old section 1491 contained a rule to the effect that if a domestic trust became a foreign trust (*i.e.*, migrated outside the U.S.), the domestic trust would be treated as having transferred all its assets to the foreign trust immediately before becoming a foreign trust.

As can be seen, this excise tax was an ersatz capital gains tax on the transfer of appreciated property outside the US. In fact, perhaps because it was worded as an excise tax, it looked somewhat like a form of currency control.

While transfers from the U.S. settlor to a foreign grantor trust are made an exception to the section 684 rule, the question arises what happens when the grantor dies, if there is appreciated property in the foreign trust at that time? This question is discussed in Chapter 18.

9.15 Distributions of the income accumulated before the birth of the beneficiary or before the beneficiary attains age 21

Pursuant to the "throwback" rules, section 665(b) provides, in general, that the term "accumulation distribution" means, for a taxable year, the amount by which the amounts specified in section 661(a)(2) (any other amounts—other than income required to distributed currently—properly paid or credited or required to be distributed) exceed DNI for such year reduced, but not below zero, by the amount specified in section 661(a)(1) (income required to be distributed currently). However, for purposes of section 667 (which determines the treatment of amounts accrued by the trust in preceding years) the amounts specified in paragraph 661(a)(2) shall not include amounts properly paid, credited or required to be distributed to a beneficiary from a trust as income accumulated before the birth of the beneficiary or before the beneficiary attains the age of 21. If the amounts properly paid, etc. by the trust do not exceed the income of the trust for the year, there will be no accumulation distribution for the year. However, this rule is specifically made inapplicable to a foreign trust.[183]

[183] Section 665(b).

Chapter 10

Tax Reform Act of 1976

10.1 Introduction

One of the characteristics of trusts is that they tend to stay in existence for a very long time. Therefore, it is not unusual for there to be in existence today a trust that was created and began earning income prior to the effective dates of the 1976 Act. Therefore, it would have "cruised" through the changes made by the two "Big" Acts, the 1976 Act and the 1996 Act, and a number of lesser Acts, including the 1986 Act and the 1997 Act. Also, other changes, such as, changes affecting the taxation of capital gains, the alternative minimum tax and passive foreign investment companies, to name just a few, were coming into the law at the same time.

Thus, the rules governing the U.S. taxation of trusts that have some history to them vary over time; and, importantly, the accounting for trusts' "taxable income", "distributable net income", "undistributed net income", and the like, has changed with the enactment of the various statutes. Obviously, this has created a good deal of complexity and a number of problems. For example, a trust in existence today, which was created prior to the 1976 Act, may need accounting records that can be recast for U.S. tax purposes beginning with the creation of the trust; or it may like to have some information permitting the computation of distributable net income as of January 1, 1977.

It is therefore useful to look at the rules as they existed before the 1976 Act, between the 1976 Act and the 1996 Act, and today. A prior rule may affect an existing trust. Also, an understanding of the evolution of the rules helps one better understand the current provisions.

As will become obvious, underlying the enactment of all the U.S. tax rules since 1962 is a deep-seated suspicion of the use of foreign trusts. Initially this was directed at U.S. settlors; but more recently the suspicion has spread to non-U.S. settlors and trustees.

This discussion of the 1976 Act is based on an article published in 1988.[184]

10.2 Taxation of Trusts: Pre-1976 Act

Prior to the 1976 Act, foreign trusts were taxed in the same manner as a nonresident alien individual. The income of a foreign trust belonged to it; and, so long as the trust was not engaged in a U.S. trade or business, its income was taxed in the U.S. only to the extent that the income of any nonresident alien not engaged in a trade or business in the United States was taxed. Thus, in such cases, U.S.-source capital gains were generally not taxed; U.S.-source dividends, interest, rents, and other so-called periodic payments were subject to withholding at the flat statutory rate of 30%, and foreign source income was not taxed at all.

Grantors, beneficiaries, and both foreign and domestic trusts were subject to the complex rules of the Code, including the grantor trust rules. In general, both U.S. grantors and U.S. beneficiaries of a foreign trust were taxed in essentially the same manner as they would have been with respect to a domestic trust. Under the grantor trust rules, grantors (and others considered substantial owners) are treated for tax purposes as the owners of that portion of a trust with respect to which they have retained or acquired certain significant powers or interests in the trust. Such powers and interests include a power of revocation, a reversionary interest and certain powers to determine who will enjoy trust property or income. If a U.S. grantor created a foreign trust and retained a prescribed power or interest, he would have been taxed on the trust's income as if he owned the trust property directly; and the trust and its beneficiaries, so far as the U.S. was concerned, would have been relieved of taxation. Similarly, if a non-U.S. grantor established a grantor trust, the U.S. beneficiaries would not have been taxable on income distributed to them, even though the grantor might not be subject to U.S. tax.

Trusts other than grantor trusts are generally taxed as separate taxable entities in the same manner as individuals. To the extent the trust distributes income to beneficiaries, it is entitled to a deduction.

---

[184] Bruce, U.S. Taxation of Foreign Trusts: Post-1976 Act Changes and Continued Uses, 17 TMIJ 192 (1988).

As a result, the trust is treated as a conduit and taxed only on income accumulated but not distributed to the trust's beneficiaries. The amount of the distribution includible in the beneficiaries' income and the corresponding amount deductible by the trust are measured by the trust's "distributable net income" or "DNI."[185]

Where a trust accumulated income, beneficiaries were taxed on accumulation distributions as if they had received the distributions in the year the trust had received the income with respect to which the distribution was made. This "throwback" rule was intended to dissuade trusts from accumulating income during years in which the beneficiaries had for one reason or another fallen into lower tax brackets. The "throwback" rule employed an "exact" method or a "shortcut" method to calculate the beneficiary's income taxes with respect to a distribution of accumulated income. A corollary to the "throwback" rule for accumulated trust income was an unlimited "throwback" rule for capital gains allocated to the corpus of a trust. Normally, an accumulation distribution of capital gains would not be deemed to be made until all of a trust's "undistributed net income"[186] had been distributed.

The ordinary income of a foreign trust required by its terms to distribute income currently (*i.e.*, a "simple trust") would be taxed to its U.S. beneficiaries, whether or not in fact distributed, in generally the same manner as a domestic simple trust. There were certain minor differences. In the case of domestic trusts and foreign trusts created by non-U.S. persons (hereinafter called an "FFT"), capital gains property allocable to corpus would belong to the foreign trust and would not be taxed to the beneficiary (which is to say that DNI of these trusts generally did not include capital gains). In the case of a foreign trust created by the United States persons (a "USFT"), capital gains would be included in DNI, which meant that capital gains, like items of ordinary income, would be taxed currently to the U.S. beneficiaries. In calculating DNI in the case of USFT, only net capital gains (that is, capital gains reduces by capital losses, but not below zero) would be included. Further, the capital gains deduction would not be taken into the account in calculating DNI. Nevertheless,

---

[185] "Distributable net income" is defined in section 643(a). It is similar to taxable income, with a number of important modifications.

[186] "Undistributed net income" is defined in section 665(a).

the capital gains deduction was not lost because the character of the capital gains carried over to the beneficiaries so as to permit use of that deduction at the beneficiary level. By its terms, the capital gains "throwback" rule did not apply to any simple trust, whether a domestic trust or a foreign trust (a FFT or a USFT). Thus, where capital gains, created and accumulated in years while a foreign trust was a simple trust, were distributed (for example, upon termination), the beneficiaries would not be taxed under the capital gains "throwback" rules.

Distributions from a foreign trust that could accumulate trust income for future distribution (*i.e.*, a "complex trust") were subject to different rules. To the extent made out of DNI, distributions of a complex FFT would be taxed to United States beneficiaries in the same manner as the DNI of a simple FFT. Similarly, distributions to the extent of the DNI of a complex USFT would be taxed to the United States beneficiaries in the same manner as the DNI of a simple UFST, keeping in mind that, for these purposes, DNI included net capital gains without allowance of the section 1202 deductions.[187]

As noted above, distributions by a trust of accumulated income would be thrown back to the beneficiaries' taxable years corresponding to the year in which the trust earned the income. Under a separate "throwback" rule, capital gain accumulation distributions were not deemed to be made until all undistributed net income had been absorbed by distributions of accumulated income, and then only to the extent of "undistributed capital gain." As a practical matter, the capital gain "throwback" rule was not applicable to the USFT because the DNI of a USFT included capital gains. To the extent the USFT's capital gains were not distributed currently, they were therefore included in undistributed net income and did not enter into the calculation of undistributed capital gain.

A U.S. beneficiary of either an FFT or USFT was obliged to take into account the components of DNI as if he had received them directly. The character and source of those components, as a general rule, were established at the trust level and carried over to the beneficiaries. For example, the beneficiary had to take into account

[187] The 50% capital gains deduction formerly in section 1202 was repealed in 1978. Today, capital gains, in general, are taxed at a 20% rate. Section 1(h).

items of tax preference generated by the trust. By statutory exception, however, gross income from sources within the U.S. was determined without regard to treaty exemptions. As a result, a beneficiary might lose the benefit of the favorable source rules of a treaty. If a foreign trust received income upon which the U.S. imposed the 30% withholding tax, the U.S. beneficiaries would be entitled to a credit for the taxes withheld when the income component to which the taxes were attributable was deemed distributed as DNI to the trust's beneficiaries. Further, the amount of any accumulation distribution to a U.S. beneficiary was increased (or "grossed up") by the amount of federal income taxes paid by the foreign trust with respect to that distribution. In the case of foreign income taxes paid with respect to an accumulation distribution, a foreign tax credit should have been allowable to the beneficiary subject to the various limitations imposed by former sections 901-907. To be contrasted with the requirement that federal income taxes be "grossed up," the beneficiary did not also have to include foreign income taxes allowable as a credit in his income as part of the accumulation distribution.

A transfer of appreciated stock or securities by a U.S. person to a foreign trust, foreign partnership or foreign corporation was generally subjected under former section 1491 to a 27.5% excise tax on the amount of any unrealized gain (fair market value over the adjusted basis of the transferor) unless the transferor could show to the IRS prior to the transfer that it was not in pursuance of a plan having as one of its principal purposes the avoidance of federal income taxes. The purpose of this tax was to levy a surrogate capital gains tax on such transfers, which were thought to be means of avoiding a tax on the appreciation. By its terms, former section 1491 did not apply to transfers of other appreciated property, such as real estate. Nor should the tax have applied to transfers of stock and securities in a taxable exchange, since the provision dealt with transfers to avoid income tax, although technically a prior ruling would have been in order.

Under former section 6048, a U.S. person creating or transferring property to a foreign trust was required to file an information return on Form 3520. Form 3520 had to be filed by: (a) the grantor, in the case of creation of an *inter vivos* trust; (b) the fiduciary of an estate, in the case of a testamentary trust; or (c) the transferor, in the case of a simple transfer. The U.S. beneficiary would generally not be liable for the filing of a return or the reporting of information until he received a distribution that would have to be included in his gross income. In the case of a distribution that was not includible in gross income, there was no duty to report the distribution.

Under the Bank Secrecy Act of 1970[188] and the implementing regulations, any person, including a resident alien, who has a financial interest in, or signature authority or other authority over, a foreign bank account was required to file an information return on Form 4683. This requirement applied where legal title to the account was in a trust in which a U.S. person had a present beneficial interest in more than 50% of the assets or from which that person received more than 50% of the current income.

Prior to the 1976 Act, foreign trusts were commonly, and properly, used in estate plans to get property out of the estate and accumulate income abroad for the beneficiaries. Sometimes, a foreign trust would be the recipient of property transferred in exchange for a private annuity (though for this to be effective, the transferor-annuitant would have to die prematurely; otherwise the property would come back to him in the form of annuity payments). Many foreign trusts were created to avoid the rule against perpetuities applicable to most domestic trusts. Foreign trusts were also created for convenience's sake by U.S. citizens residing abroad and for the circumvention of forced heirship laws.

Undoubtedly, some foreign trusts were used improperly. One scheme was simply to create a foreign trust and then take back the income earned by it in the form of "loans," which no one ever intended be repaid.

10.3 Taxation of trusts: between 1976 Act and 1996 Act

This section will discuss the Tax Reform Act of 1976, probably the most important set of amendments to the foreign trusts tax law. In other words, the focus in this section is on the taxation of foreign trusts between the effective dates of the 1976 Act and those of the 1996 Act. In general—but with several exceptions, the effective date of the 1996 Act is August 20, 1996.

---

[188] P.L. No. 91-508.

Several goals in the foreign trust area were announced in connection with the Tax Reform Act of 1976. First, what was perceived as a tax-free accumulation of income, while the income remained in the foreign trust, was to be ended by having the grantor taxed on the income of the foreign trust. Second, an interest charge was imposed on taxes paid by a U.S. beneficiary in those situations where the grantor trust rules did not apply. Third, the "throwback" rules applicable to accumulation distributions from domestic and foreign trusts (USFTs and FFTs) were simplified and put on an equal footing. Also, the excise tax on transfers to foreign entities was increased and broadened. A fourth goal was to tighten the reporting requirements.[189]

10.3.1. Ending the tax-free accumulation of income; the grantor trust rule

Section 1013(a) of the Tax Reform Act of 1976 added to the grantor trust area of the Code section 679, under which any U.S. person transferring property directly or indirectly to a foreign trust that has a U.S. beneficiary, is treated as the owner of that portion of such trust attributable to the property transferred. The transferor can be any individual U.S. citizen, resident or domestic partnership, corporation, estate, or trust. Testamentary transfers are, notably, not affected. Nor are sales or exchanges for fair market value affected so long as the transferor's gain is realized currently and either recognized currently or returned on the installment method. So-called "open transactions" fell outside this last exception, as did transfers of property to a foreign trust in exchange for a private annuity. Transfers producing no gain or a loss also fell outside the exception, if construed literally. An election under section 1057, also added in 1976, to treat a transfer to a foreign trust as a taxable sale or exchange, prevented a transfer from triggering section 679.

---

[189] In the House Ways and Means Committee mark-up session on HR 10612 (which became the Tax Reform Act of 1976), the staff asked for and received permission to explore ways of tightening the reporting requirements in this area with the staffs at the Treasury Department. This effort was never undertaken. As a practical matter, the 1996 Act is the outcome of this desire to tighten the reporting rules.

Section 679 only applies for income tax purposes; it has no bearing on gift or estate taxation. Also, the provision does not apply to qualified stock bonus, pension, or profit-sharing trusts "created or organized outside the United States" to which contributions are made by a U.S. employer.

It should be noted that a transferor might pay a gift tax on a transfer which, for income tax purposes, could be viewed as a transfer to himself (in other words, there can be a completed gift on a transfer in trust to a grantor trust). There is no provision for a refund of the gift tax paid. Under section 679, gains and losses are treated as belonging to the grantor, whether the foreign trust accumulates trust income or distributes it to the beneficiaries or whether the grantor actually ever receives any of the income. A U.S. grantor can be taxed under this provision at the same time that a foreign beneficiary is taxed by a foreign country on the same amount of income and the U.S. grantor is not allowed a foreign tax credit as a result. Also, the provision applies irrespective of whether the grantor retains any interest in, or power over, the trust income or principal, or whether the grantor is related to any beneficiary.

A U.S. grantor is taxable as owner of the trust property only if, at any time during the grantor's taxable year, the trust has a U.S. beneficiary. A foreign trust is assumed to have a U.S. beneficiary (section 679(c)(1)) unless "(A) under the terms of the trust (to include any written or oral agreements), no part of the income or corpus of the trust may be paid or accumulated during the taxable year to or for the benefit of a United States person, and (B) if the trust were terminated at any time during the taxable year, no part of the income or corpus of such trust could be paid to or for the benefit of a United States person." All the income of the trust is taxable to the grantor even though U.S. beneficiaries have only a very small beneficial interest in the trust.

A grantor of a foreign trust not taxable in the year of creation of the trust because there was no U.S. beneficiary at that time can become taxable in a later year when a U.S. beneficiary springs up. For example, one of the beneficiaries might move to the U.S. and become a U.S. resident or citizen, in which case the grantor would be taxable in the later year not only on the trust's income during that year, but also to the extent of the undistributed net income of the trust on hand at the close of its immediately preceding taxable year and attributable to the property originally transferred. Thus, all the accumulated and current income of a foreign trust could be taxed to the grantor in one year if one of its beneficiaries intentionally or unintentionally becomes a resident or citizen of the U.S.

To determine whether a foreign trust has a U.S. beneficiary, a new set of attribution rules was added to the Code. A trust having a foreign partnership as a beneficiary is treated as having a U.S. beneficiary if a single U.S. person is a partner. A foreign trust having as a beneficiary a foreign trust or estate is treated as having a U.S. beneficiary if such foreign trust or estate has a single U.S. beneficiary (in the sense described above). Surprisingly, the rule for corporate beneficiaries is not so all-encompassing: if a foreign trust has, as a beneficiary, a foreign corporation, the foreign trust will be treated as having a U.S. beneficiary (section 679(c)(2)) only if "more than 50 percent of the total combined voting power of all classes of stock entitled to vote of such corporation is owned (within the meaning of section 958(a)) or is considered to be owned (within the meaning of section 958(b)) by United States shareholders (as defined in section 951(b))." It follows that the section 679 grantor trust provision in its entirety can be avoided by "decontrolling" the beneficiary(ies) of the subject foreign trust.

Example. By way of illustration, A, a U.S. person, transfers property to a foreign accumulation trust, the sole beneficiary of which is a corporation owned 50% by U.S. persons and 50% by non-U.S. persons. The foreign trust does not have a U.S. beneficiary, and, therefore, the grantor is not taxable under section 679. Alternatively, the foreign trust has as its sole beneficiary a foreign corporation owned 100% by twelve U.S. beneficiaries. Under section 951(b), a shareholder, though a U.S. resident or citizen, is not categorized as a "U.S. shareholder" unless he or she owns or is considered as owning 10% or more of the total combined voting power of all classes of stock entitled to vote of such foreign corporation. Thus, the provision can be avoided by interposing a corporate beneficiary and either putting U.S. shareholders together with foreign shareholders, or by gathering a large number of unrelated U.S. shareholders. Of course, it might be argued that such a corporation, if it performs no other function, should be ignored.

A foreign trust that was created at a time when the grantor was a nonresident alien apparently will not be subjected to these provisions should the grantor subsequently become a resident alien since section 679 speaks in terms of a transfer by a U.S. person. When determining who the grantor is, it should be recalled that the named grantor may be viewed as a "nominal" grantor, and another who transferred most of the corpus to the trust, as the "true" grantor.

One of the most troublesome aspects of section 679 is its possible interaction with the controlled foreign corporation and foreign personal holding company provisions (and, since 1986, the passive foreign investment company provisions).[190] If the U.S. grantor is to be treated as the owner of the foreign trust property, he may find himself taxable as a shareholder in a CFC or FPHC and subject to the attendant reporting requirements.

10.3.2. Changes of general application.

Section 701 of the 1976 Act revised the method of taxing accumulation distributions from a trust. The "exact method" and the "shortcut method" of computing the tax throwbacks were abolished, and a shortcut method only was installed. Under this method, the partial tax on an accumulation distribution, incurred in the year of distribution, is computed by throwing a part of the distribution back to three of the preceding five years, as explained below, computing the additional tax that would have been due if that additional income had been included in income, averaging the additional tax, and assuming that that amount of additional tax would have been incurred in each prior year during the period of accumulation. This approach obviously is imperfect; but it was hoped that it would eliminate the necessity of both the trust and all its beneficiaries keeping records *ad infinitum.*

---

[190] Sections 1291-1298 (relating treatment of certain passive foreign investment companies), added Pub. L. 99-514, title XII, 1235(a), Oct. 22, 1986, 100 Stat. 2566, and amended Pub. L. 100-647, title I, 1012(p)(1), (3), (6), (7), (9), (12)-(14), (28), (31), (33), title VI, 6127(b), Nov. 10, 1988, 102 Stat. 3515-3517, 3520, 3521, 3715.

This method, however, works to the disadvantage of trusts and beneficiaries that have a history of increasing amounts of income.

Example. A trust accumulates all its income in years 1977 through 1986; each year's income exceeds the preceding year's income. In 1987, it distributes that income to its sole beneficiary, A. Under the shortcut method, a *pro rata* portion of the income distributed (1/10th, since the income was accumulated over a period of 10 years) is thrown back into each of three of five years immediately preceding the year of distribution. The three years are chosen in this way: the five preceding taxable years of the taxpayer are looked at; the years with the highest and lowest taxable income are thrown out ("high-low kick-out rule"), leaving three years. Accordingly, 1/10th of the income distributed is thrown back to 1982, 1/10th to 1983, and so forth. An additional tax, which would have been due had the income actually been distributed in those years, is computed for each of the three years (for example, $200 for 1983, $300 for 1984, and $400 for 1985), and these are averaged (equaling $300). This average yearly additional tax is then multiplied by the number of years involved (10). The result is $3,000 of partial tax under the "throwback" rule.

It is to this amount ($3,000, in the example), basically, that the interest charge is applied. It should be noted that this approach inflates the amount of interest due by applying the interest charge, which itself is the result of a rough estimation, to a total figure, $3,000, representing the total of yearly additional taxes that would have been incurred in years 1977 through 1986. Theoretically, interest would be running for 10 years only on 1/10th of the $3,000, for nine years on another 1/10th, and so forth.

Section 701 of the 1976 Act also added a rule to deal with the problem of multiple trusts, foreign or domestic. Where a beneficiary receives accumulation distributions from more than two trusts with respect to the same year, the beneficiary must compute his tax under the shortcut method as described above, except, as to distributions from a third trust and all subsequent-in-time distributions from additional trusts, the distribution is not to be grossed up by the amount of foreign and U.S. taxes paid by the trust and no credit for payment of such taxes is to be given. Accumulation distributions of less than $1,000 are ignored for purposes of this rule.

In the case of domestic trusts, the revised "throwback rule" was not applied to distributions of income accumulated before the birth of the recipient beneficiary or before he becomes 21 years old. This relief is lost, however, where the multiple trust rule applies to any distribution received by the beneficiary. More importantly, this relief is not available to U.S. beneficiaries of foreign trusts.

The capital gains throwback rule (former section 669) was repealed and, at least for domestic trusts, a special rule was added by section 701 of the 1976 Act to attack the problem of persons transferring appreciated property to a trust and letting the trust sell the property and recognize the taxable gain, the gain thereby being taxed to the trust at a lower rate, the trust having less other income. Under the rule, embodied in section 644, if the trust sells the property within two years of receipt, the trust's tax on the gain will be equal to the additional tax that the transferor would have paid had the gain been taxed to him in the year of sale. It is as if the trust were the transferor's agent.

While there is nothing to prevent this provision being employed where a U.S. person transfers appreciated property to a foreign trust, the committee reports make no mention of this provision in the foreign trust area. Presumably, if a U.S. grantor came within the province of the section 679 grantor trust rule, he would be taxed on the gain upon resale of the appreciated property, rather than the trust (since sections 671 and 679 apparently override section 644). What if a U.S. grantor transferred appreciated property to a foreign trust having no U.S. beneficiary (and therefore was outside section 679), and the transfer was taxable under section 1491?[191] The resale of the property not more than two years after its initial transfer to the trust would not be taxable under section 644 because the trust is the taxpayer, and, under these facts, the trust is a foreign trust whose capital gains generally are not taxed.

[191] Section 1491 was repealed in 1997. P.L. 105-34, title XI, subtitle D, 1131(a), Aug. 5, 1997.

10.3.2.1 Changes affecting only U.S. beneficiaries of foreign trusts

Under prior law, as previously noted, capital gains of USFTs were, in effect, allocated to income and included in DNI. Therefore, capital gains, if accumulated, were accumulated as DNI, and subsequent accumulation distributions always included some capital gains (a *pro rata* portion), just as they included some of every other item of DNI, such as tax-exempt interest, rents, etc. Capital gains of FFTs could be accumulated as capital gains, separate and apart from items of DNI. In order to make a distribution of accumulated capital gains, an FFT had to first distribute all DN I items—normally ordinary income items—before it could distribute capital gains, which would be subject to the capital gains throwback rule. As noted, the capital gains throwback rule was eliminated by section 701(c) of the 1976 Act. The rule was no longer needed for any type of foreign trust because section 1013(c) of the Act dictated that FFTs, like USFTs, would include capital gains in DNI.

In addition, by virtue of some subtle drafting, all capital gains of all foreign trusts are not only included in DNI but are converted into ordinary income. Capital gains are added to DNI net of capital losses but undiminished by any capital gains deduction. Then, under the workings of section 667(a), all items comprising an accumulation distribution are included in the income of the beneficiary under section 662(a)(2), which simply puts them in the beneficiary's gross income but does not provide for the retention of their character as capital gains, rents, interest, etc. Only tax-exempt interest is both put into the beneficiary's gross income and made to retain its character as tax-exempt interest. All capital gains, unaffected by any capital gains deduction, go into DNI and are distributed as such, and the beneficiary is not entitled to any deduction.

Thus, the beneficiary of a foreign trust is placed in a worse situation than the beneficiary of a domestic trust or one who receives capital gains directly. Since the DNI of a domestic trust does not include capital gains, its capital gains are taxable as such at the trust level, and the beneficiary is not taxed on that income upon subsequent distribution. The capital gains of the foreign trust, whether created by a U.S. person or a nonresident alien, are taxed as ordinary income to the beneficiary when distributed. Also, since most foreign countries tax capital gains at favorable rates, any foreign tax credit available to the beneficiary will be too little.

Several things might be noted concerning the obliteration of the character of income items. First, it applies to all items of distributable net income distributed in an accumulation distribution by any trust wherever located. Not only do capital gains distributed by a foreign trust cease to be capital gains (a result that had less "sting" after the 1986 Act elimination of the capital gains deduction, but more "sting" since the 20% capital gains maximum rate was instituted in 1998),[192] but also rents distributed by a domestic trust cease to be rents; both are transformed into amorphous ordinary income. Second, the ability to "launder out" unfavorable tax characteristics may lead to unintended results. Third, the destruction of the capital gains character will occur only where capital gains are includible in DNI, *i.e.,* where foreign trusts accumulate income and where any type of trust, foreign or domestic, allocates capital gains to income and accumulates it. Fourth, income entitled to special treatment under a treaty may lose its character and any treaty benefits attached thereto (although this result remains to be determined). Fifth, the obliteration of character of items of income can be avoided by distributing income currently.[193]

At first, it was unclear whether 667(a) obliterated "source" as well as "character," since it was then unclear whether "source" was in fact an attribute of character, in the same way that "passive income" or "business income" is an attribute of character. However, the Technical Corrections Act of 1978 verified that "source" is indeed subsumed within "character" and therefore that it, too, is affected by the statutory obliteration. Section 2(r) of that Act acknowledged this fact and called for the retention of character (including source) for the

---

[192] Section 5001(a)(1) of the Internal Revenue Service Restructuring and Reform Act of 1998 (P.L. 105-206).

[193] Certain Subpart F provisions added by section 8041 of the Budget Reconciliation Act of 1986 (P.L. 99-509) perhaps can be avoided by running income through such an accumulation trust. For instance, the workings of sections 901(j) (relating to denial of foreign tax credit, etc., with respect to certain foreign countries) and 952(a)(5) (relating to the inclusion in Subpart F income of amounts derived from any foreign country during any period during which section 901 (j) applies to such country) depend upon the source of the income.

limited purpose of determining when U.S. withholding tax should be imposed on distributions from domestic trusts to nonresident aliens and foreign corporations, but for no other purposes.

In the Technical Corrections Act of 1978, Congress clarified the workings of the foreign tax credit and the "throwback" rule as modified by the 1976 Act. Domestic trusts and foreign trusts were again treated differently. With respect to domestic trusts, the foreign tax credit, as well as other credits claimed by the trust (including the now-repealed investment tax credit), were made available in the distribution year to the beneficiary by allowing the amounts of the credits as offsets against the partial tax on the distribution. No attempt was made to flow through identifiable credits to specific computation years of the beneficiary. The beneficiary's foreign tax credit position in the computation year, and whether he elected the credit either then or in the year of distribution, are irrelevant. Since the domestic trust is subject to the foreign tax credit limitation, there was thought to be no need to apply those limitations at the beneficiary level. As for foreign trusts, the rules are considerably more complicated. Since foreign trusts generally are not taxable and thus are not subject to all U.S. tax rules, such as the foreign tax credit limitation, the credit and accompanying limitations and recapture rules are applied in the computation year on the basis of facts then in existence. Numerous special provisions are made applicable.

10.3.2.2 Changes in the section 1491 excise tax

Section 1015 of the Tax Reform Act of 1976 increased the tax rate under old section 1491 from 27.5% to 35%. It also significantly broadened that section's impact by making it applicable not just to transfers of stock or securities but to transfers of all types of property and by making clear that section 1491 taxes any gain not recognized by the transferor at the time of the transfer. Section 1491 provides that the 35% excise tax shall apply where there is a transfer by a U.S. citizen or resident or by a domestic corporation, partnership, trust, or (as amended by the 1978 Technical Corrections Act) estate "to a foreign corporation as paid-in surplus or as a contribution to capital, or to a foreign estate or trust, or to a foreign partnership . . ." Transfers to a foreign capital stock account are not affected. Resident aliens were affected under prior law, and they remain affected under this provision. There is no requirement that the transferor and the transferee be related.

The excise tax amounts to 35% of the excess of the fair market value of the property transferred over the sum of the transferor's adjusted basis for the property plus the amount of gain recognized, if any, to the transferor at the time of the transfer. Thus, as the legislative history reflects, the provision is intended to tax transferors as if they had sold the property at the time of the transfer and recognized all the gain in one year.

> [A]ll sales and exchanges (including tax free exchanges, installment sales, and private annuity transactions), regardless of how any gain on these transactions is reported, are within the scope of the excise tax provision. But to the extent the transferor immediately recognizes gain on the transfer, the amount against which the tax is applied is reduced.

Staff of the Joint Committee on Taxation, 94th Cong., 2d Sess., General Explanation of the Tax Reform Act of 1976, 225 (Jt. Comm. Print 1976) ("JCT 1976 Act Explanation").

This taxing provision does not parallel the triggering provision under section 679; that is, a transfer by U.S. person to a foreign trust will not trigger application of section 679 if all gain is realized immediately and recognized immediately or under the installment method. If reported on the installment method, however, such transfer will be subject to the section 1491 excise tax, assuming gain is realized. (In such a case, the taxpayer may choose to make the section 1057 election, noted below.)

Section 1491 did not apply if, before the transfer, it had been established to the satisfaction of the Secretary that the transfer is not in pursuance of a plan having as one of its principal purposes the avoidance of U.S. income tax. The transferor had to submit a sworn statement of facts and, in effect, obtain a ruling from the Service. The legislative history provided guidance on the tax avoidance issue.

> It is contemplated that ordinary business sales or exchanges involving an unrelated foreign trust [or

> any other foreign entity for that matter] would normally be determined not to be in pursuance of a plan of tax avoidance. However, where the transferor of the property is directly or indirectly related in some way to the foreign entity receiving the property, then under normal circumstances, the transfer could be one in pursuance of a plan having as its principal purpose the avoidance of federal income taxes. Such a transfer would thus normally be subject to the excise tax.

Ibid. at 226.

(The Tax Reform Act of 1984, P.L. No. 98-369, in section 131, eliminated the advance ruling and tax avoidance purpose standard for transfers of property abroad.)

Section 1491 also did not apply to a transfer described in section 367, which concerns the tax treatment of exchanges relating to the organization, reorganization, and liquidation of corporations where a foreign corporation is involved in the transaction. The 1976 Act made some procedural and substantive changes in this area. One decision was to give section 367 sway over section 1491. Historically, neither provision might have governed an exchange involving a foreign corporation. For example, if a transfer were in exchange for stock possessing at least 80% of the total combined voting power of all classes of stock entitled to vote and at least 80% of the total number of shares of all other classes of stock of the foreign corporation, the transfer would be one to which section 367 applied (since section 351 would apply to the transfer), and, therefore, it would fall outside the ambit of section 1491. If. however, sections 351 and 367 did not apply, the transfer would be a taxable sale or exchange, but gain might not have to be recognized all in one year. Gain might be reported on the installment method. Again, the Tax Reform Act of 1984 made changes to better harmonize sections 1491, 1057 and 367.

Section 1491 also does not apply where the transferor has elected to treat the transfer as a taxable sale or exchange and to recognize all gains in the year of transfer. Section 1057 was added in 1976 to provide such an election. It reads:

> In lieu of payment of the tax imposed by Section 1491, the taxpayer may elect (for purposes of this subtitle), at such time and in such manner as the Secretary may prescribe, to treat a transfer described in Section 1491 as a sale or exchange of property for an amount equal in value to the fair market value of the property transferred and to recognize as gain the excess of—
>
> (1) the fair market value of the property so transferred, over
>
> (2) the adjusted basis (for determining gain) of such property in the hands of the transferor.

The election is to be afforded on a transfer-by-transfer basis. The election apparently will not permit the recognition of losses, as the legislative history states: "[T]o the extent that gain is recognized pursuant to the election, the transfer is not subject to the excise tax, and normal rules will apply to increase the basis to the transferee by the amount of the gain recognized."[194] This language calls attention to an important point. There is no step-up in the basis of property transferred to a foreign entity on account of the section 1491 excise tax.

Section 1491 does not apply if the transferee is an organization exempt under part I of subchapter F of chapter 1, other than a 401(a) qualified pension, profit sharing, etc. trust. Charitable organizations, business leagues, social clubs, and small mutual casualty companies are among those organizations that are exempt; groups such as farmers' cooperatives and political organizations are not.

The principal feature of section 1491 was the absence of a step-up in basis as a result of the excise tax. If a taxpayer were not allowed to elect retroactively as to open years, section 1491 could have become more widely used by international examiners than section 482 (relating to the allocation of income and deductions among taxpayers), since agents would have been able to gain a double tax for

[194] JCT 1976 Act Explanation.

the government and avoid the cumbersome collateral adjustments under section 482. Section 1491 has not, however, been used in this way.

Section 1491 was repealed in 1997.[195] It was replaced, in effect, by section 684 (relating to recognition of gain on certain transfers to certain foreign trusts and estates).

10.3.2.3 Changes in reporting requirements

A U.S. settlor of a foreign trust or a U.S. transferor of money or property to a foreign trust is required to report these transfers on his or her individual income tax return. In addition, he or she must file an information form (Form 3520) within 90 days of the creation of, or transfer to, the foreign trust. The form calls for the disclosure of the name, address, and identification number of the transferor, the trust, the fiduciary, and the beneficiaries, as well as the interests of the various beneficiaries. The location of the trust records and books of account must also be disclosed. In addition, if a U.S. person is taxable as the owner of the trust's assets under section 679, that person must file an annual return (Form 3520-A). Special penalties are provided for failure to file these returns. If the transfer of property to the foreign trust was subject to the excise tax in section 1491. the transferor must also file an additional form (Form 926).

A U.S. or non-U.S. trustee of a trust can voluntarily notify the IRS of the fiduciary relationship using Form 56.

A grantor of a foreign trust taxable under section 679 may be required to file a "Report of Foreign Bank and Financial Accounts" with the Treasury Department (Form 90-22.1). Likewise, a beneficiary who has a present beneficial interest in more than 50% of the assets or current income of any type of foreign trust must file this form.

[195] Taxpayer Relief Act of 1997, P.L. 105-34, title XI, subtitle D, 1131(a), Aug. 5, 1997.

Obviously, twenty years later, with the Small Business Job Protection Act of 1996, Congress decided that greatly increased reporting was necessary in the case of foreign trusts, with accompanying stringent penalties. What happened in the interim is that taxpayers began creating Protection of Assets Trusts, which the Tax Reform Act of 1976 ironically engendered. As this type of trust became popularized by promoters, the use of them moved "down market" to less well advised and more aggressive individuals. It followed that some of these taxpayers failed to file the required returns—sometimes with the help of the promoters.

10.4 Changes made by the Tax Reform Act of 1986

The Tax Reform Act of 1986 made some significant changes in trust taxation. The accumulation distribution ("throwback") rules were supplemented by removing the incentive for a trust to accumulate income. This was accomplished by imposing substantially higher tax rates on trusts than on individuals. Also, the ability to avoid grantor trust status was limited by deleting the "10-year rule" and by taxing the grantor on any portion of a trust in which he or she has a reversionary interest if, as of the creation of that portion, the value of such an interest exceeds 5% of the value of that portion. Interests and powers of the grantor's spouse are considered interests and powers of the grantor as far as these rules are applied. All trusts must also use a tax year that more closely matches that of the grantor and all trusts must now make estimated tax payments.

10.5 Interest charge

Section 1014 of the Tax Reform Act of 1976 added section 668 of the Code, which was aimed at ending the tax-free accumulation of income in foreign trusts not affected by the section 679 rule, which category may include a large number of trusts. The provision provided for a 6% per annum interest charge to be paid by a U.S. beneficiary receiving an accumulation distribution from a foreign trust. Under the amended throwback rules, discussed below, the recipient beneficiary in the year of the distribution pays a tax composed of three parts: (1) a partial tax on his gross income exclusive of the amount of the accumulation distribution; (2) a partial tax on the amount of the accumulation distribution computed according to the amended "throwback" rules; and (3) the new interest charge. In no event is the amount of the partial tax on the accumulation distribution plus the interest charge thereon to exceed the actual amount of the accumulation distribution.

The interest charge is 6% of the partial tax on the accumulation distribution times the number of years the tax has been deferred (counting the year the income was earned by the trust, but not counting the year of the distribution). The interest is not compounded. If income, all of which had been earned in 1984, were distributed in 1987, the interest charge would be 6% of the partial tax times three. Where the accumulation distribution consists of income earned in more than one year, the numbers of years of tax deferral are averaged, and the interest charge computed on that average figure.

Example. If income earned in 1984, 1985 and 1986 were distributed in 1987, the interest charge would be computed by first averaging the number of years of deferral (three years for "1984 income," two years for "1985 income," one year for "1986 income," or an average of two years) and then multiplying the average number of years (two) by the 6% rate to get the total interest charge (12%).

The interest charge paid, it is provided, shall not be deductible, though interest on late payment of tax is generally allowed as a deduction (although that was phased out in the period following the 1976 Act).

The interest charge applied to distributions made in taxable years beginning after December 31, 1976. For purposes of this provision only, any undistributed net income existing in a trust as of January 1, 1977, is to be treated as having been earned in the trust's first taxable year beginning after December 31, 1977. This effective date, beginning for calendar-year taxpayers in 1977, contrasted with the effective dates of the other provisions affecting foreign trusts, generally 1976, or, in the case of the changes in the excise tax on transfers, late in 1975. The interest charge applied against accumulation distributions made from trusts, which could have included ironclad, irrevocable trusts created long before May 21, 1974, the applicable effective date.

As a practical matter, foreign trusts not subject to the grantor trust rules that have, or may have in the future, U.S. beneficiaries, should have recomputed undistributed net income as of January 1, 1977, before the facts and figures grew stale, rather than waiting until the year of an accumulation distribution to the U.S. beneficiary.

10.6 Changes in taxation of beneficiaries of accumulation trusts.

The 1976 Act contained amendments affecting beneficiaries of all nongrantor accumulation trusts, domestic as well as foreign. It also contained radical changes penalizing only U.S. beneficiaries of nongrantor foreign trusts that accumulate income.

Chapter 11

Small Business Job Protection Act of 1996

This discussion of the 1996 Act is based on Congressional materials and commentary presented by the author in 1995 at the time the Clinton Administration announced its proposals, which ultimately became the Small Business Job Protection Act of 1996 (P.L. 104-188).[196]

11.1 Background

Prior to enactment the 1996 Act (Small Business Job Protection Act of 1996), the following rules existed.

The grantor trust rules (sections 671-679) applied without regard to whether the grantor was a U.S. person or a foreign person. A grantor that retained certain rights or powers, as set forth in the statute, was treated as the owner of the trust's assets. U.S. beneficiaries of the trust were not subject to U.S. tax on distributions from a trust where a foreign grantor was treated as owner of the trust; and it made no difference that no other jurisdiction taxed the trust's income. (As was pointed out in a number of newspaper and magazine articles, the grantor trust rules could be used affirmatively to avoid the payment of taxes by U.S. beneficiaries of foreign grantor trusts.)

A special rule provided that if a U.S. beneficiary of a foreign grantor trust transferred property to the settlor (grantor) of that trust by gift, that U.S. beneficiary was treated as the settlor to the extent of the transferor. This rule is sometimes referred to as the "anti-give-and-go rule." It was aimed at the following situation: a nonresident alien individual, A, who was intending to immigrate to the U.S., transfers property to an individual who, in turn, transfers the property to a trust for the benefit of A. A then becomes a resident alien, or perhaps a U.S. citizen, and receives tax-free distributions from the

[196] Remarks by Charles M. Bruce, International Fiscal Association-Bermuda Branch, Hamilton, Bermuda (February 27, 1995).

foreign non-grantor trust. (This type of trust is sometimes referred to as an "inbound grantor trust.")

Under section 679, a U.S. person that transfers property to a foreign trust generally is treated for U.S. tax purposes as the owner of those assets—although the assets are legally owned by the trustee—for any taxable year in which there is a U.S. beneficiary of the trust. This rule applied to lifetime gifts but not to transfers by reason of death. Also, the rule did not apply to transfers made before the transferor became a U.S. person, or to transfers that represented sales were exchanges of property at fair market value where gain was recognized.

Embedded in the tax rules applicable to accumulation trusts were a set of rules for the taxation of accumulation distributions. These rules applied to distributions in excess of the trust's distributable net income for the taxable year. (Distributable net income (DNI) is similar to taxable income; but taxable income is modified in several ways to arrive at DNI.) A distribution by a foreign nongrantor trust of previously accumulated income—that is, out of undistributed net income—generally was taxed at the U.S. beneficiary's average marginal rate for the prior five years, plus interest. The interest charge was computed at a fixed annual rate of 6 percent; interest was not compounded. (Obviously, by utilizing a fixed rate of interest, sometimes this figure would be too little and sometimes too much.) If adequate trust records were not available, the distribution was treated as an accumulation distributions out of income earned during the first year of the trust.

A special rule in section 665(c) provided that any amount paid from a foreign person to a U.S. person, where the amount was derived (directly or in directly) from a foreign trust that was created by a U.S. person, would be treated as a distribution from the foreign trust. This rule was aimed at the use of intermediaries or nominees to avoid the accumulation distribution rules. It will be noted that the rule calls for unlimited tracing of assets received by the U.S. recipient.

If a foreign nongrantor trust made a loan to one of its U.S. beneficiaries, the amount of a loan generally was not subject to U.S. tax as income to the beneficiary. Thus, the beneficiary could avoid

U.S. tax on the income accumulated in the hands of the trust by obtaining a loan in lieu of taking a distribution.

Under the definitional rules in the Code, a trust was treated as foreign if it was not subject to U.S. income tax on income that was neither derived from U.S. sources nor effectively connected with the conduct of a U.S. trade or business. In other words, if the trust was taxed in a manner similar to a nonresident alien individual, it was characterized as a foreign trust. Any other trust was characterized as a domestic trust. This definition, in section 7701(a)(31), was somewhat circular and imprecise. It was sometimes referred to as the "wavering line" test.

The reach of section 1491—the provision imposing a 35% excise tax on transfers of appreciated property to certain foreign entities, including a foreign trust—was not clear under the statute and the case law. In particular, in the case of a domestic trust that migrated in one fashion or another from the U.S. to a foreign jurisdiction, it was unclear whether there had been a transfer that was subject to the excise tax and, if so, who was the taxpayer.

Since 1962, U.S. tax law has required reporting with respect to foreign trusts. A U.S. person that creates a foreign trust or transfers property to a foreign trust was required to report that occurrence to the IRS without regard to whether the trust was a grantor trust or a nongrantor trust. Also, a U.S. person that transferred property to a foreign trust with U.S. beneficiaries was required to file annual reports where U.S. beneficiaries receiving distributions from a foreign trust were required to pay tax on those distributions in the matter dictated by the Code. Paragraph transfers subject to section 1491 were also reportable.

The penalties for failure to file were as follows. Any person that failed to file a required report with respect to the creation of, or a transfer to, a foreign trust could be subject to a penalty of 5% of the amount transferred. Similarly, any person that failed to file a required annual report could be subject to a penalty of 5% of the value of the corpus of the trust at the close the taxable year. The maximum amount of the penalty imposed under either provision could not exceed $1,000. A reasonable cause exception was available.

There were no special rules for the reporting of gifts or bequests from foreign donors or decedents.

11.2 1996 Act changes

The following discussion is comprised of excerpts from materials prepared by the Joint Committee on Taxation, reordered slightly in order, among other things, to place information about effective dates closer to the substantive amendments affected by the dates. Comments concerning the amendments are inserted.

11.2.1 Grantor trusts

11.2.1.1 Grantor trusts with foreign grantors

The Small Business Act generally applies the grantor trust rules only to the extent such application results, directly or indirectly, in income or other amounts (if any) being currently taken into account in computing the income of a U.S. citizen or resident or a domestic corporation. This rule does not prevent a trust that does not have any income in a year from being treated as a grantor trust provided that income of the trust would be currently includible by a U.S. person if the trust had income. Certain exceptions apply to this rule. Under one exception, the grantor trust rules continue to apply to the portion of a trust where that portion of the trust is revocable by the grantor either without approval of another person or with the consent of a related or subordinate party who is subservient to the grantor. Under another exception, the grantor trust rules continue to apply to the portion of a trust where the only amounts distributable from that portion during the lifetime of the grantor are to the grantor or the grantor's spouse. The general rule denying grantor trust status does not apply to trusts established to pay compensation, and certain trusts in existence as of September 19, 1995 provided that such a trust is treated as owned by the grantor under section 676 or 677 (other than sec. 677(a)(3)).[197] In addition, except as provided in regulations, the grantor trust rules continue to apply where the grantor is a controlled foreign corporation (as defined in sec. 957). Finally, except as provided in

[197] The exception does not apply to the portion of any such trust attributable to any transfers to the trust made after September 19, 1995.

regulations, the grantor trust rules continue to apply in determining whether a foreign corporation is characterized as a passive foreign investment company ("PFIC"). Thus, a foreign corporation cannot avoid PFIC status by transferring its assets to a grantor trust.

If a U.S. beneficiary of an inbound trust transfers property to the foreign "grantor," such beneficiary generally is treated as a grantor of a portion of the trust to the extent of the transfer. This rule applies if, but for section 672(f), the foreign grantor otherwise is treated as the owner of any portion of such trust. However, this rule does not apply if the transfer is a sale of the property for full and adequate consideration or if the transfer is a gift that qualifies for the annual exclusion described in section 2503(b).

The Small Business Act provides a special rule that allows the Secretary of the Treasury to recharacterize a transfer, directly or indirectly, from a partnership or foreign corporation which the transferee treats as a gift or bequest, to prevent the avoidance of the purpose of section 672(f) (e.g., the transfer may be recharacterized as a trust distribution).[198] The Small Business Act treats any amount paid to a U.S. person, where the amount was derived (directly or indirectly) from a foreign trust of which the payor is not the grantor, as if paid by the foreign trust directly to the U.S. person. This rule disregards the role of an intermediary or nominee that may be interposed between a foreign trust and a U.S. beneficiary. Unlike prior law, however, the rule applies regardless of whether the trust was created by a U.S. person. The rule does not apply to a withdrawal from a foreign trust by its grantor, followed by a subsequent gift or other payment to a U.S. person.

In the case where a foreign person (that would be treated as the owner of a trust but for the rules of sec. 672(f)) actually pays tax on the income of the trust to a foreign country, the Congress anticipated that Treasury regulations will provide that, for foreign tax credit purposes, U.S. beneficiaries that are subject to U.S. income tax on the same income will be treated as having paid the foreign taxes that are

---

[198] *See* discussion below for reporting requirements under the Small Business Act with respect to certain foreign gifts and bequests received by a U.S. person.

paid by the foreign grantor. Any resulting foreign tax credits would be subject to applicable foreign tax credit limitations.

Effective dates. The provisions that generally treat grantor trusts with foreign grantors as nongrantor trusts are effective on August 20, 1996 (the date of enactment of the Small Business Act). The Small Business Act provides a transition rule for any domestic trust that has a foreign person that is treated as the owner of the trust under prior law, but becomes a nongrantor trust under the Small Business Act. If such a trust becomes a foreign trust before January 1, 1997, or if the assets of such a trust are transferred to a foreign trust before that date, such trust is exempt from the excise tax on transfers to a foreign trust otherwise imposed by section 1491. However, the Small Business Act's new reporting requirements and penalties are applicable to such a trust and its beneficiaries. The assets of a trust that is treated as a grantor trust under prior law but that becomes a nongrantor trust under the Small Business Act will be treated as if they were recontributed to a nongrantor trust by the foreign grantor, with no recognition of gain or loss, on the date the trust ceases to be treated as a grantor trust. The nongrantor trust willhave the same basis in such assets as did the owner on the date the trust ceases to be treated as a grantor trust.

➔ Taxing U.S. resident beneficiaries of inbound grantor trusts encourages these individuals to remain in the U.S. for less than 122 days on a running average and stay elsewhere the remainder of the time.

➔ Families will use the revocation route. This approach favors settlors from low or zero tax jurisdictions (such as Saudi Arabia) over those from high tax jurisdictions (such as Sweden).

➔ The rule in new section 643(h) (distributions by certain trusts through nominees) appears to require a tracing of assets, which is always difficult, especially in an international setting and where dealing with individuals as opposed, say, to large corporations.

➔ The rule in new section 672(f)(4) requires that the recipient know the source of the gift and the character of the donor. This typically is not the case. Also, it will be difficult for him properly to characterize the donor as partnership or corporation or some other type of entity. ➔ The rule in new section 6039F has been spelled out in Form 3520 and the instructions to the Form. It will be interesting to see what develops in the course of audits of large gifts. Also, the penalties are truly remarkable. The rule permitting a penalty of up to 25% of the amount of the gift is the economic equivalent of partial confiscation, along the lines of some anti-money laundering laws. ➔ Many inbound grantor trusts sold property and made distributions prior to the date of enactment.[199]

11.2.1.2 Grantor trusts with U.S. grantors

The Small Business Act makes the following modifications to the rule which treats a U.S. person that transfers property to a foreign trust as the owner of the portion of the trust attributable to the transferred property for any taxable year in which there is a U.S. beneficiary of the trust (sec. 679(a)):

11.2.1.2.1 Sales or exchanges at market value.

The Small Business Act modifies the prior law exception to the grantor trust treatment under section 679(a)(1) to provide that, except as provided in regulations, obligations issued (or, to the extent provided by regulations, guaranteed) by the trust, by any grantor or beneficiary of the trust, or by any person related to any grantor or

[199] Bruce, "Trustees Need to Act Fast in Face of New Foreign Trust Provisions, Attorney Warns," SPECIAL REPORT, Tax Analysts 96 TNT 162-75 (August 19, 1996).

beneficiary[200] (referred to as "trust obligations") generally are not taken into account in determining whether fair market value is received for property transferred to a trust by any grantor or beneficiary of the trust, or any person related to any grantor or beneficiary. The Congress expected that Treasury regulations will provide an exception from this treatment for loans with arm's-length terms. In applying this exception, the Congress further expected that consideration be given to whether there is a reasonable expectation that a loan will be repaid. Principal payments by the trust on any such trust obligations generally will reduce the portion of the trust of which the transferor is treated as the grantor.

11.2.1.2.2 Other transfers

The Small Business Act adds a new exception to the general rule of section 679(a)(1). Under that exception, a transfer of property to certain charitable trusts is exempt from the application of the rules treating foreign trusts with U.S. grantors and U.S. beneficiaries as grantor trusts.

11.2.1.2.3 Transferors who become U.S. persons

The Small Business Act applies the rule of section 679(a)(1) to certain foreign persons who transfer property to a foreign trust and subsequently become U.S. persons. A nonresident alien individual who transfers property, directly or indirectly, to a foreign trust and then becomes a resident of the United States within 5 years after the transfer generally is treated as making a transfer to the foreign trust on the individual's U.S. residency starting date (as defined in sec. 7701(b)(2)(A)). The amount of the deemed transfer is the portion of the trust (including undistributed earnings) attributable to the property previously transferred. Consequently, such a person generally is

---

[200] For this purpose, a person is treated as related to the grantor or beneficiary if the relationship between such person and the grantor or beneficiary would result in a disallowance of losses under section 267 or 707(b), except that in applying section 267(c)(4) an individual's family includes the spouses of the members of the family.

treated under section 679(a)(1) as the owner of that portion of the trust in any taxable year in which the trust has U.S. beneficiaries.

11.2.1.2.4 Beneficiaries who become U.S. persons

Under the Small Business Act, a beneficiary is not treated as a U.S. person for purposes of determining whether the transferor of property to a foreign trust is taxed as a grantor with respect to any portion of a foreign trust if such beneficiary first became a U.S. person more than 5 years after the transfer.

11.2.1.2.5 Outbound trust migrations

The Small Business Act applies the rule of section 679(a)(1) to a U.S. citizen or resident who transferred property to a domestic trust if the trust subsequently becomes a foreign trust while the transferor is still alive. Such a person is deemed to make a transfer to the foreign trust on the date of the migration. The amount of the deemed transfer is the portion of the trust (including undistributed earnings) attributable to the property previously transferred. Consequently, such a person generally is treated under the rules of section 679(a)(1) as the owner of that portion of the trust in any taxable year in which the trust has U.S. beneficiaries.

11.2.1.2.6 Technical amendment

The Small Business Act conforms the definition of certain foreign corporations the income of which is deemed to be accumulated for the benefit of a U.S. beneficiary to the definition of controlled foreign corporations (as defined in sec. 957(a)).

Effective dates. The amendments to section 679 apply to transfers of property after February 6, 1995.

→ It is not clear why a section 1057 election is not treated as an exception.

→ The treatment of outward migrations appears largely to follow existing law.

→ Protection of assets trusts are not adversely affected provided all required reports are filed.

→ Pre-immigration trusts that take the form of grantor trusts are not adversely affected if they are created within 5 years of immigrating to the U.S.

11.2.2 Distributions of income accumulated by foreign nongrantor trusts

11.2.2.1 Accumulation distribution rules

The Small Business Act changes the interest rate applicable to accumulation distributions from foreign trusts from simple interest at a fixed rate of 6 percent to compound interest determined in the same manner as interest imposed on underpayments of tax under section 6621(a)(2). Simple interest is accrued at the rate of 6 percent through 1995. Beginning on January 1, 1996, however, compound interest based on the underpayment rate is imposed not only on tax amounts determined under the accumulation distribution rules but also on the total simple interest for pre-1996 periods, if any. For purposes of computing the interest charge, the accumulation distribution is allocated proportionately to prior trust years in which the trust has undistributed net income (and the beneficiary receiving the distribution was a U.S. citizen or resident), rather than to the earliest of such years. An accumulation distribution is treated as reducing proportionately the undistributed net income from prior years.

The Small Business Act contains a formula to determine the number of years for which interest is charged on each accumulation distribution. Basically, interest is imposed under the formula for the dollar-weighted number of years that taxation of the accumulated income was deferred (the "applicable number of years"). This dollar-weighted number of years is computed by dividing (a) the product of multiplying the dollar amount of undistributed income for a particular year by the number of years from the year of the accumulation of such income until the year of the accumulation distribution (counting the taxable year in which the accumulated income was recognized, but not counting (1) the taxable year in which the distribution was made and (2) any taxable year during which the trust beneficiary who received the accumulation distribution was not a citizen or resident of the United States) by (b) the aggregate amount of undistributed net income of the trust. The number of years resulting from this formula gives the number of years' interest that is payable computed as if the distributed income had been earned measured back from the date of the distribution by the number of years resulting from the formula. For example, if a foreign nongrantor trust has undistributed net income of $30 for each of years 1 through 3 and the trust makes an accumulation distribution of $45 to a U.S. beneficiary in year 4, the beneficiary has to pay interest on the tax on the $45 using section 6621(a)(2) interest rates as if the income accrued for 2 years.[201] In addition, the accumulation distribution reduces the trust's undistributed net income by $15 for each of years 1 through 3 for purposes of computing the amount of any future accumulation distribution and the applicable number of years attributable to such accumulation distribution.[202]

11.2.2.2 Loans to beneficiaries

In the case of a loan of cash or marketable securities by the foreign trust to a U.S. grantor or a U.S. beneficiary (or a U.S. person related to such grantor or beneficiary,[203] the Small Business Act treats the full amount of the loan as a distribution to the grantor or

---

[201] The number of years is determined as follows:
($30 x 3 years) + ($30 x 2 years) + ($30 x 1 year) + $90 = 2.

[202] That is, the $45 of distribution reduces proportionately the undistributed net income for each of years 1, 2 and 3.

[203] For this purpose, a person is treated as related to the grantor or beneficiary if the relationship between such person and the grantor or beneficiary would result in a disallowance of losses under section 267 or 707(b), except that in applying section 267(c)(4) an individual's family includes the spouses of the members of the family.

beneficiary except to the extent provided by Treasury regulations. The Congress expected that Treasury regulations will provide an exception from this treatment for loans with arm's-length terms. In applying this exception, the Congress further expected that consideration be given to whether there is a reasonable expectation that a loan will be repaid. In addition, any subsequent transaction between the trust and the original borrower regarding the principal of the loan (*e.g.*, repayment) is disregarded for all purposes of the Code. This provision does not apply to loans made to persons that are exempt from U.S. income tax.

Effective dates. The provision to modify the interest charge on accumulation distributions applies to distributions after August 20, 1996. The provision with respect to loans to U.S. grantors, U.S. beneficiaries or a U.S. person related to such a grantor or beneficiary applies to loans made after September 19, 1995.

➔ The changes in the computation of the interest charge greatly increase the complexity of this calculation, which Congress sought to simplify, somewhat, in 1976. Given that other provisions in the package do not take an overly scientific approach, perhaps a simple increase in the flat rate would have been preferable.

➔ In earlier drafts of the legislation, the Clinton Administration proposed a provision intended to tax U.S. persons on the use of assets owned by the foreign trust. For purposes of the accumulation distribution rules (but not the section 6048 reporting rules) , if a "trust participant" directly or indirectly uses any of the trust's property, the use value would be treated as a taxable constructive distribution. There would have been an exemption of up to $2,500 in the aggregate. Use value would have been defined as the fair market value of the use of property less the amount paid for such use by the trust participant or by any person who is related to such participant. The loaning of cash or cash equivalent would be treated as use of property to the full extent of the loan principal (*i.e.*, the approach would be analogous to section 956). Related party could include former spouse. The Treasury Department was persuaded that enforcement of the constructive use rules would lead to a morass.

11.2.3 Anti-abuse regulatory authority

The Small Business Act includes an anti-abuse rule which authorizes the Secretary of the Treasury to issue regulations, on or after the date of enactment, that may be necessary or appropriate to carry out the purposes of the rules applicable to estates, trusts and beneficiaries, including regulations to prevent the avoidance of those purposes.

Effective date. The provision is effective on August 20, 1996.

11.2.4 Residence of trusts

11.2.4.1 Definition

The Small Business Act establishes a two-part objective test for determining for tax purposes whether a trust is foreign or domestic. A trust is treated as domestic if it meets the two following requirements: (1) a U.S. court (*e.g.*, State, or local) exercises primary supervision over the administration of the trust, and (2) one or more U.S. fiduciaries must have the authority to control all substantial decisions of the trust. In applying the second factor, it is intended that a trust be allowed a reasonable period of time to adjust for any inadvertent changes in the trust's fiduciaries.

11.2.4.2 Change in a trust's residence

Under the Small Business Act, if a domestic trust changes its situs and becomes a foreign trust, the trust is treated as having made a transfer of its assets to a foreign trust and is subject to the 35-percent excise tax imposed by section 1491 unless one of the exceptions to this excise tax is applicable.

Effective dates. The provision to modify the treatment of a trust as a U.S. person applies to taxable years beginning after December 31, 1996. The Internal Revenue Service has announced procedures under which a U.S. trust in existence on August 20, 1996 may continue to file returns as a U.S. trust for taxable years beginning after December 31, 1996 if the trustee initiates modification of the trust to conform to the new U.S. trust criteria by the due date for filing the trust's return for its first taxable year beginning after 1996, the trustee completes the modification within two years of such date, and the trustee attaches the required statement to the trust returns for the taxable years beginning after 1996.[204]

If the trustee of a trust so elects, the provision to modify the treatment of a trust as a U.S. person may be applied to the first taxable year ending after August 20, 1996. Notice 96-65 includes guidance regarding the time and manner for making this election. When a trustee makes this election, and as a result changes the situs of a trust from domestic to foreign, the trust is treated as having made an outbound transfer of its assets upon becoming a foreign trust. Consequently, the section 1491 excise tax will apply to such a transfer.

The amendment to section 1491 is effective on August 20, 1996. Notice 96-65 includes guidance regarding the application of section 1491 to a trust the status of which changes from U.S. to foreign by reason of the provisions modifying the treatment of a trust as a U.S. person.

11.2.5 Information reporting and penalties

11.2.5.1 Foreign trust reporting

The Small Business Act generally requires the grantor, transferor or executor (i.e., the "responsible party") to file information returns with the Treasury Department upon the occurrence of certain "reportable events." The term "reportable event" generally means the creation of any foreign trust by a U.S. person, the direct and indirect

[204] *See* Notice 96-65, I.R.B. 1996-52. The approach reflected in Notice 96-65 may require a technical correction.

transfer of any money or property to a foreign trust, including a transfer by reason of death, and the death of a U.S. citizen or resident if the decedent was treated as the owner of any portion of the trust or any portion of a foreign trust was included in the gross estate of the decedent. In addition, the U.S. owner of any portion of a foreign trust generally is required to ensure that the trust files an annual return to provide full accounting of all the trust activities for the taxable year. Finally, any U.S. person that receives (directly or indirectly) any distribution from a foreign trust is required to file a return to report the name of the trust, the aggregate amount of the distributions received, and other information that the Secretary of the Treasury may prescribe. A special rule provides that a U.S. trust that has substantial foreign activities or holds substantial foreign property shall be treated, to the extent provided in regulations, as a foreign trust for purposes of the Small Business Act's rules with respect to information reporting and associated penalties. In exercising its regulatory authority to treat a U.S. trust as a foreign trust for purposes of the information reporting provisions, the Congress expected that the Secretary of the Treasury will take into account the information that such a trust reports under the domestic trust reporting rules.

11.2.5.2 Applicable penalties

Under the Small Business Act, a person that fails to provide the required notice or return in cases involving the transfer of property to a new or existing foreign trust, or a distribution by a foreign trust to a U.S. person, is subject to an initial penalty equal to 35 percent of the gross reportable amount (generally the value of the property involved in the transaction). A U.S. owner's failure to provide an annual reporting of trust activities will result in an initial penalty equal to 5 percent of the gross reportable amount. An additional $10,000 penalty is imposed on the responsible party for continued failure for each 30-day period (or fraction thereof) beginning 90 days after the Treasury Department notifies the responsible party of such failure. In no event will the total amount of penalties exceed the gross reportable amount. Such penalties are subject to a reasonable cause exception. Where an amount that is less than the full gross amount is reported, the penalties will be applied based on the amount that is unreported.

The Small Business Act provides comparable penalties for any failure to file a return required by the Secretary of the Treasury with respect to any transfer described in section 1491 to any foreign entity. For purposes of applying the penalties for failure to report a section 1491 transfer, it is anticipated that the Secretary of the Treasury will take into account information reported under other provisions of the Code in determining whether the reporting requirements have been satisfied with respect to the section 1491 transfer.

11.2.5.3 Appointment of limited U.S. agent

The Small Business Act provides that if a U.S. owner of any portion of a foreign trust fails to appoint a limited U.S. agent to accept service of process with respect to any requests and summons by the Secretary of the Treasury in connection with the tax treatment of any items related to the trust, the Treasury Secretary may determine the tax consequences of amounts to be taken into account under the grantor trust rules. The Congress intended that the Treasury Secretary's exercise of its authority to make such a determination will be subject to judicial review under an arbitrary or capricious standard, which provides a high degree of deference to such determination. In cases where adequate records are not provided to the Treasury Secretary to determine the proper treatment of any distributions from a foreign trust, the distribution is includible in the gross income of the U.S. distributee and is treated as an accumulation distribution from the middle year of a foreign trust (*i.e.*, computed by taking the number of years that the trust has been in existence divided by 2) for purposes of computing the interest charge applicable to such distribution, unless the foreign trust elects to have a U.S. agent for the limited purpose of accepting service of process (as described above).

11.2.5.4 Reporting of foreign gifts

The Small Business Act generally requires any U.S. person (other than certain tax-exempt organizations) that receives purported gifts or bequests from foreign sources totaling more than $10,000 during the taxable year to report them to the Treasury Department. The threshold amount for this reporting requirement is indexed for inflation. The definition of a gift to a U.S. person for this purpose excludes amounts that are qualified tuition or medical payments made on behalf of the U.S. person, as defined for gift tax purposes (sec. 2503(e)(2)), and amounts that are distributions to a U.S. beneficiary of a foreign trust if such amounts are properly disclosed under the reporting requirements of the Small Business Act. If the U.S. person fails, without reasonable cause, to report foreign gifts as required, the Secretary of the Treasury is authorized to determine the tax treatment of the unreported gifts. The Congress intended that the Treasury Secretary's exercise of its authority to make such a determination will be subject to judicial review under an arbitrary or capricious standard, which provides a high degree of deference to such determination. In addition, the U.S. person is subject to a penalty equal to 5 percent of the amount of the gift for each month that the failure continues, with the total penalty not to exceed 25 percent of such amount.

Effective dates. The provisions to amend reporting requirements and applicable penalties generally apply to reportable events or transfers occurring or distributions received after August 20, 1996. The annual reporting requirement and penalties applicable to U.S. grantors apply to taxable years of such persons beginning after December 31, 1995. The Internal Revenue Service has announced that it intends to provide detailed guidance with respect to the information reporting requirements applicable to reportable events (under sec. 6048(a)) and other transfers subject to comparable penalties (under sec. 1494(c)) before 1997.[205] Notice 96-60 suspends the requirement to file an information return under section 6048(a) until a date that is at least 60 days after the issuance of the forthcoming guidance. Any information return submitted within the time period set forth in such guidance will be considered filed on a timely basis. Similarly, no penalty will be imposed under section 1494(c) if a return required with respect to a section 1491 transfer is filed no later than 60 days after the issuance of the forthcoming guidance (or such later date specified in that guidance). The gift reporting rules are to apply to amounts received after August 20, 1996.

---

[205] See Notice 96-60, 1996-49 I.R.B. 7.

➔ Congress tried to avoid directly affecting trustees. However, trustees can be put in a serious bind. They can be required to file returns and statements. If they do not, the trust assets or the U.S. persons will suffer. Penalties and transferee liability can run to the U.S. persons. Yet they may have a fiduciary responsibility not to expose the trust to U.S. taxation and other risks. It is unclear how foreign law will treat these subjects.

➔ The possibility of disclosure of trust information to private parties in the U.S. is a real one due to the workings of the discovery rules. FED. R. CIV. P. 26(b) ("The information sought need not be admissible at trial if the information sought appears reasonably calculated to lead to the discovery of admissible evidence.") It would be difficult to assure that there would not be any disclosure.

➔ The 35% penalty applied to gross value comes close to being a form of currency control. While it is true that it can be avoided by filing the information, some will perceive it to be a control mechanism.

➔ Forms 3520 and 3520-A, and the instructions to the forms, are generally very helpful in setting out the details underlying these rules.

➔ Given their complexity and the confusing mix of responsibilities, it is likely that many taxpayers will be repelled by the rules. Trustees and the advisors for settlors and beneficiaries will have their hands full persuading individuals and families that they should make every effort to comply. Certainly thought should be given to removing some of the burden from taxpayers if they are willing to take reasonable measures to insure compliance.

→ Under amended section 679, a responsible party might be a minor.

Chapter 12

Significant Effective Dates, Transition Rules and Grandfather Provisions; Forthcoming Regulations, Etc.

12.1 Significant effective dates, transition rules and grandfather provisions

These items, generally speaking, are dealt with in Chapter 11 (Small Business Job Protection Act of 1996). This chapter will highlight just a few of the most important provisions.

12.1.1 Inbound grantor trusts with foreign grantors (section 672(f))

The effective date for section 672(f) is the enactment date for the 1996 Act, that is, Aug. 20, 1996. However, section 1904(d)(2) of the Act, which is not made a part of the Code, provides an important exception or "grandfather" provision. It provides that the amendments made to Code section 672(f) will not apply to any trust which existed on September 19, 1995 and which was a grantor trust by virtue of the application of section 676 (relating to the power to revoke) or all but one part of section 677 (relating in general to income for the benefit of the grantor), but only so long as the trust would continue to be so treated under the basic grantor trust rules.[206] The part of section 677 that will be ignored is that part relating to income that without the approval or consent of any adverse party or merely at the discretion of the grantor or a nonadverse party, may be used to pay premiums on life insurance policies on the life of the grantor or the grantor's spouse. Thus, if a trust existed before September 20, 1995 and the grantor or a nonadverse party, or both, had the power to reinvest title to trust assets in the grantor, then the trust would remain a grantor trust. Also, if a trust existed before September 20, 1995 and income of the trust, without the approval or consent of any adverse party or merely at the discretion of the grantor

---

[206] Sections 1.672-3(a)(2)(i) & (b)(4), Proposed Income Tax Regulations.

or a nonadverse party, could be distributed to the grantor or the grantor's spouse or could be held or accumulated for future distribution to the grantor or the grantor's spouse, the trust would remain a grantor trust. This rule, however, does not protect these old trusts from being converted into accumulation trusts at the time of the grantor's death. Also, the grandfather provisions do not apply to post-September 19, 1995 transfers to the trust; these must be separately accounted for.

12.1.2 Interest charge on accumulation distributions (section 668)

In general, the interest charge on accumulation distributions was changed from simple interest at a fixed rate of 6 percent to compound interest determined in the same manner as interest imposed on understatement of tax. A form of transition rule is included in section 668 at subsection (a) (6). Interest for the computation period that occurs before January 1, 1996, will be determined by using the old rules, that is, a 6 percent interest rate without compounding. Mercifully, Congress did not require a splitting of the computation for 1996 between January 1 and August 20, 1996.

12.1.3 Reporting information with respect to certain foreign trusts and giving notice of large gifts and bequests received from foreign persons (Sections 6048 and 6039F)

Section 6048 generally applies to reportable events occurring after the date of enactment of the 1996 Act (August 20, 1996). The grantor trust reporting requirements apply to taxable years of the U.S. person beginning after December 31, 1995. The requirements for the reporting by U.S. beneficiaries apply to distributions received after the aforementioned date of enactment.

Section 6039F applies to amounts received after August 20, 1996.

While strictly speaking these are the effective dates, they have been modified by the Service in a series of pronouncements. The most important of these are Notice 97-34 and Announcement 98-30.[207] Also, it remains to be seen to what extent the Service will abate

[207] Notice 97-34, 1997-1C.B.422; Announcement 98-30, 1998-17 IRB 1.

penalties incurred for late filing. The rules applicable to abatement appear in the Internal Revenue Manual; and they apply to all kinds of situations throughout the tax law. Understanding these rules and how they work as a practical matter is a subject unto itself. With respect to penalties for late reporting under these information reporting provisions, it might be recalled that the regulations explaining these complex provisions have not been issued, and the forms, putting it charitably, are not well-knit and are extremely difficult to follow.

(For a detailed discussion of the dilemma facing taxpayers especially in late 1997 and 1998, see Bruce, "Foreign Trust Tax Compliance: Information Reporting on Transactions With Foreign Trusts and on Large Foreign Gifts; Authorization of U.S. Agent," TNT Doc. 97-31071 (November 14, 1997).)

> ➔ In some instances and to a limited extent, taxpayers may be able to file amended returns for open years.

There are many instances where the final regulations promulgated under the various 1996 Act provisions will have an effective date after the effective date of the provision in the statute. For example, many of the provisions contained in T.D. 8831, which, among other things, finalized regulations under section 672(f), have an effective date of August 10, 1999—the date these regulations were published in the Federal Register.

12.2 Forthcoming regulations

This section will comment on the status of IRS regulations under the major pieces of foreign trusts legislation, beginning with the Tax Reform Act of 1976.

12.2.1 Tax Reform Act of 1976

The regulations under section 679, enacted in 1976, have never been promulgated. The IRS Regulatory Agenda published in April 1999 lists this as a regulations project, but it appears not to have been assigned as an especially high priority. Section 679 was amended to a significant degree in 1996. It is anticipated that the IRS will want to issue "outbound" regulations that include section 679 regulations sometime in the near future—in late 1999 or the first half of 2000. (In May 1997 it was thought that the section 679 regulations might be proposed within a month or two; but obviously this project was postponed.)

12.2.2 The Small Business Act of 1996

In general, this Act dealt with grantor trusts, distributions of income accumulated by foreign nongrantor trusts, anti-abuse regulatory authority, residence of trusts, and information reporting and penalties. Treasury Department officials told the Information Reporting Program Advisory Committee in May 1997 that it hoped to propose regulations determining whether a trust is foreign or domestic under section 7701(a)(31), regulations governing "outbound" trusts under section 679 (foreign trusts created by U.S. persons), and regulations covering "inbound" trusts under sections 672(f) and 643(h) (foreign trusts created by foreign persons with U.S. beneficiaries). It has generally followed this plan and issued a series of notices and new forms as well.

Proposed regulations under section 7701 (REG-251703-96; 62 F.R. 30796-30800 (June 5, 1997)) provide guidance relating to the definition of a trust as a United States person (domestic trust) or foreign trust. These are the so-called "definitional" rules relating to "foreign trust."

These definitional rules have been finalized. T.D. 8813; 64 F.R. 4967-4975 (February 2, 1999).

Proposed regulations under section 672(f) and 643(h) (REG-252487-96 (June 4, 1997)) implement the rules contained in these and related sections enacted as part of the Small Business Job Protection Act of 1996. These rules relate to the application of the grantor trust rules to certain trusts established by foreign persons. The proposed regulations affect primarily United States persons who are beneficiaries of trusts established by foreign persons. These are the so-called "inbound" rules.

The inbound regulations have been finalized and temporary and proposed regulations on the definition of "grantor" have been issued. T.D. 8831; 64 F.R. 43267-43280 (August 10, 1999). This document contains regulations implementing sections 672(f) and 643(h). It also contains temporary and proposed regulations defining the term grantor for purposes of part I of subchapter J, chapter 1 of the Code.

12.2.3 Foreign nonexempt employees' trusts

Proposed regulations aimed in large measure at foreign employees' trusts were published in September 1996, while the 1996 Act was still under consideration. REG-209826-96; 61 F.R. 50778-50787 (September 27, 1996). The proposed regulations clarify that the grantor trust rules generally do not apply to domestic nonexempt employees' trusts, and clarify the interaction between the grantor trust rules, the rules generally governing the taxation of nonqualified deferred compensation arrangements, and the anti-deferral rules for United States persons holding interests in foreign entities. The proposed regulations affect nonexempt employees' trusts funding deferred compensation arrangements, as well as U.S. persons holding interests in certain foreign corporations and foreign partnerships with deferred compensation arrangements funded through foreign nonexempt employees' trusts. In addition, the proposed regulations affect U.S. persons that have deferred compensation arrangements funded through certain foreign nonexempt employees' trusts.

These regulations drew a great deal of comment and have not been finalized.

> ➔ The Treasury Department and IRS seem to be aware of the fact that guidance in all these areas is needed. Because of the "rag-tag" character of some of the reporting forms and instructions, attention is especially needed in this area. It is understandable that the regulations-writing authorities will want to lag the issuance of anti-abuse regulations until they get a good reading on what taxpayers and their advisors are doing in response to the legislation. Also, the IRS will sometimes refuse to issue rulings to taxpayers on matters that are within the scope of regulations proposed or to be proposed.

Chapter 13

Protection of Assets Trusts

13.1 General

Protection of assets trusts for U.S. settlors and U.S. beneficiaries represent one of the most important developments in the field of international trusts in many, many years. If judged by the total value of assets in the trusts, they might well be the most important type of trust—more important than international family trusts, pre-immigration trusts and foreign trusts created by U.S. persons in order to make gifts to non-U.S. persons.

This chapter is intended to give some additional insight into this type of trust.[208]

A protection of assets trust is a foreign grantor trust. The U.S. settlor will be treated as the owner of the assets. The tax and reporting rules described elsewhere in this book will apply to it.

At the time of the 1996 Small Business Job Protection Act, Congress was well aware of the existence and importance of

---

[208] For a more comprehensive treatment of the subject, see "Exploring the Protection of Assets Trusts," TRUST & ESTATES (Nov. & Dec. 1991), Bruce, Gray & Luria. *See also*, Solomon & Serat, ASSET PROTECTION STRATEGIES: TAX AND LEGAL ASPECTS, John Wiley & Sons (1993), Osborne, ASSET PROTECTION: DOMESTIC AND INTERNATIONAL LAW AND TACTICS, Clark Boardman Callahan (1996), Spero, ASSET PROTECTION: LEGAL PLANNING AND STRATEGIES, Warren Gorham & Lamont (1994), Henkel, "Asset Protection Techniques," Remarks at the Meeting of the Estate and Gift Tax Committee of the American Bar Association Section on Taxation (Aug. 9, 1991), Estes, "Asset Protection Trusts For Foreign Persons," INT'L ESTATE PLANNING, Chapter 9 (Mathew Bender), "Foreign Protection of Assets Trusts: What Are They? How Do They Work?," Conference Materials (Feb. 1993) (available from Kluwer Law & Taxation Publishers, Boston, MA); Bruce, Gray & Luria, "Protection Of Assets Trusts: Fallout From Litigation Explosion," N.Y.L.J., Sept. 13, 1991, at 1.

protection of assets trusts. Some thought was given to changing the tax rules in such a way that these trusts would be so adversely affected that as a practical matter they would be abolished.[209] The decision was made not to take this step— probably because to do so would inevitably affect all trusts. The substantive tax rules applicable to protection of assets trust, therefore, were not changed. However, the reporting requirements were increased to an extraordinary degree. Sections 6048 and 6677, it can be said, are directed first and foremost at protection of assets trusts. Congress and the Treasury Department realized that promoters operating at the low-end of the market were encouraging settlors to create APT (Asset Protection Trust) trusts and not report their creation or the income earned by those trusts. About the same time that the new rules were enacted, the IRS initiated a task force aimed at attacking these practices.[210]

13.2 The problem intended to be addressed

Large numbers of Americans feel threatened by risks that arise principally from lawsuits of one type or another. They are worried about rampant litigation, the attraction of plaintiffs to defendants with "deep pockets", the high cost of defending a lawsuit, the large amounts being awarded by juries, and the general unpredictability of results arrived at in the legal system. Alternative methods of safeguarding assets, such as domestic corporations, limited liability corporations and partnerships, and domestic trusts, suffer because attorneys cannot assure the client at the outset that they will succeed in cutting off or limiting liability.[211] Attempts at tort reform have fallen short of their goal.

---

[209] When the use of so-called "Family Trusts"—trusts created to take advantage of lower tax rates then applicable to some trusts—became a problem, assessment of tax rules were changed, and the problem went away.

[210] The IRS training materials on foreign trusts prepared after the enactment of the 1996 Act states "Foreign trusts may be legitimately used for asset protection and estate planning purposes," p. 5-1.

[211] Traditional forms of business protection have been eroded. Notwithstanding the interposition of a corporation, for example, individual officers, directors, and shareholders are personally liable if a claim can be sustained under the United States Racketeer Influenced Corrupt Organizations Act. This act ("RICO"), despite its name, has been applied to a wide range of conduct. Similarly, under the securities laws, particularly 15

As Senator Moynihan (D-NY) observed during the consideration of the foreign trust provisions in the 1996 Act, Protection of Assets Trusts in essence are a form of "self-help tort reform."

In order to address the problem, it is felt that the solution should: (i) divorce the settlor from ownership of the assets to be protected, since judgment creditors stand in the same relation to those assets as does the client; (ii) give to the beneficiaries (and the settlor) a sense of comfort that assets are secure and well-managed; (iii) not cause any additional tax burden, either in terms of income or gift and estate taxes; (iv) not be a violation of any law, whether tax-related, arising from bankruptcy rules, or otherwise; (v) allow the settlor, if desired, a measure of flexibility to influence the investment of assets (by giving advice and indications of an overall direction, level of aggressivity, allocation of assets, etc.); (vi) allow the settlor, when appropriate, to replace one professional trustee with another; (vii) provide the settlor and his or her family with a comprehensive estate plan, with regard to the assets in trust, which is coordinated with the settlor's will and other estate planning; (viii) give to the settlor the freedom to discuss the trust structure truthfully; (ix) permit the settlor to comply honestly, without duplicity, with any court order directed to him/her; (x) remove assets from the U.S., without requiring the settlor to take any extraordinary actions; (xi) permit investment of the assets any place in the world, including the U.S.; (xii) contain mechanisms to permit the settlor to react to changes in his/her personal circumstances; and, most importantly, (xiii) put the settlor and the beneficiaries in a position, in relation to the assets, which is deserving of judicial respect, which comes within traditional principles of equity and trust law, and which starts the running of any statute of limitations on fraudulent

---

U.S.C. Sec. 78t, individual officers, directors, and shareholders may be subject to personal liability for violations of securities rules and regulations by entities which they control. Judges in the United States have latitude to freeze assets and impose liens prior to judgment, even on an *ex parte* basis simultaneously with the filing of a complaint. The ability of a putative creditor to cripple a defendant can be used to pressure a defendant into an unfavorable settlement. *See also* Olson, THE LITIGATION EXPLOSION: WHAT HAPPENED WHEN AMERICA UNLEASHED THE LAWSUIT (1992).

conveyances, so that the mature asset protection plan becomes as legally unassailable as is possible.[212]

13.3 Description of a protection of assets trust

A typical protection of assets trust is established under foreign law. The foreign jurisdiction ordinarily is a common law jurisdiction, not a jurisdiction that deals with trusts only by statute or by civil law, such as the Channel Islands, Liechtenstein and the Netherlands Antilles. There are "flight" provisions that cause the removal of the trust to another non-U.S. jurisdiction in the event of any action that threatens the trust or its assets.[213] The trust will be irrevocable for a term of years selected by the client; the trust indenture will provide that the trustee has the discretion to extend the term of the trust. This extension power protects against the appearance of creditors near the end of the trust's initial term.

The client-settlor determines the dispositive provisions of the trust. The beneficiaries commonly are the settlor's spouse and children. The settlor may be named as a remainderman. The trustee is usually given discretion to sprinkle income and principal to anyone in this class but is not required to do so. Other patterns of distribution may be selected. Thus, if the trustee never distributes any trust income or principal, then, at the end of the trust's term, all trust assets might revert to the settlor. A variety of mechanisms are available to add beneficiaries to the class (or delete them).

---

[212] For a further discussion on the background and rationale for protection of assets trusts, see Bruce, Gray and Luria, "Protection of Assets Trusts: Fallout from Litigation Explosion," N.Y. Law Journal, page 1 (Sept. 13, 1991).

[213] Flight provisions (or flee clauses) are common in trust indentures. They provide for the replacement of the existing trustees by new trustees in another jurisdiction, the law of which becomes the new law governing the trust, when any event specifically named occurs. For such provisions to be effective, the trust assets must be located in a jurisdiction other than that of the original trustees, where they are held by a custodian or nominee. The new trustees are typically in a third jurisdiction. *See* MODERN INTERNATIONAL DEVELOPMENTS IN TRUST LAW, Hayton (Editor) (Kluwer, 1999). Such provisions are intended to protect against sudden political unrest and attacks upon the trust or trust assets.

If the trust terminates due to the death of the settlor, then other dispositive provisions, as selected by the client, are called into play. The trust, acting like a typical will or revocable living trust, carries out the settlor's estate plan with regard to the assets in the trust. Various estate planning options are available to a client who creates an asset protection trust and the provisions of the trust must be coordinated with the client's overall estate plan.

The trust frequently is administered by a single foreign institutional trustee.[214] The trust indenture may call for a Committee of Trust Advisors; and the Committee, which can include the client and a trusted family member or advisor, can have the ability, in effect, to audit the trust accounts and remove the trustee and replace it with a successor institutional trustee. This removal and appointment power may be suspended during any period of duress (*i.e.*, when the trust or the trust's assets are threatened).[215] The Committee also can render non-binding advice to the trustee.

In the version of the asset protection trust preferred by conservative advisors, a settlor will contribute only relatively liquid assets to the trust and will not attempt to place almost all or even most of his or her assets into the trust. There will be no underlying corporations, partnerships or other entities owned by the trust. The trust is used to hold "nest egg" assets and serves several purposes, just one of which is

---

[214] It is submitted that the trustee should be a large, well-reputed corporate trust company. All of the large non-U.S. international trust companies—most of which are owned by large banks having assets in excess of several billion dollars—act as trustees for this type of trust. The fee structures very only slightly. Some of the trust-opening procedures are a little bit more cumbersome for some than for others. Settlors, advised by their attorneys, generally pick a jurisdiction and trustee on the basis of reputation and reliability.

[215] "Duress" is the occurrence of an event that threatens the assets in an assets protection trust. It could be the filing (or threatened filing) of a lawsuit directed at the trustees, the trust assets, etc. Upon a happening of such an event, the service of the existing trustee terminates, and an Emergency Trustee automatically assumes the trusteeship. Previous custodial arrangements may be dissolved, and all assets may be transferred to a new custodian. The effectiveness of the duress and flight provisions of the trust should be carefully researched in advance of creation.

obtaining a measure of protection from unforeseen risks that may arise in the future.

Typically, investment assets placed in the trust—not in an underlying corporation—will not be held directly by the trustee in the jurisdiction of the trust. Instead, the assets might be held by a nominee company (that is a foreign corporation owned by the trust company which is used by it to act as a nominee in many situations) and placed in a custodial account for it with a bank or brokerage firm.[216]

Care should be taken in selecting the foreign jurisdiction in which an assets protection trust is created or relocated. One question that should be answered is whether the English Statute of Elizabeth (1570) applies, and if so, what consequences flow as a result. The Statute of Elizabeth makes it possible to set aside a transfer that is intended to defeat future—but currently unknown—creditors. It is, obviously, a very broad rule. It is difficult to determine in a number of common law jurisdictions whether the Statute of Elizabeth has been incorporated into local law and, if so, to what precise extent. In order to settle this question, a number of jurisdictions have enacted so-called "Statute-of-Elizabeth-Override" statutes. They take various forms; and the desirability of one statute over another can be hotly debated. This subject then becomes part of the overall "selection of a jurisdiction" topic.

> ➔ It is not necessarily the case that a protection of assets trust should be located in a jurisdiction with a "Statute-of-Elizabeth-Override" statute. A well-respected jurisdiction that historically respects common law trusts, such as Bermuda or the Isle of Man, is preferable to a rogue jurisdiction with a bunch of "outlaw" trust statutes.

---

216 In the case of dollar-denominated assets, such as U.S. stocks and bonds, it should be recalled that such assets typically are in non-certificated form. They are usually held by a large custodian under a DTC number and are accounted for in the books of the custodian. Special problems can arise with respect to the proper reporting of holdings under the Federal income tax backup withholding rules. An important criteria in the selection of a trustee should be the ability to deal with these issues.

13.4 Summary of U.S. taxation

At the outset, it should be noted that each asset protection trust must be tailored to the individual client. Thus, given the disparate circumstances of clients and their individually-selected trust distribution patterns, it is not possible to address every imaginable tax fact pattern.

It will be assumed that each settlor and his/her spouse is a U.S. citizen, that the form of the trust indenture is roughly as described, that the settlor serves as Chairman of a Committee of Trust Advisors, and that the trust is operated consistent with the form adopted.

A properly constructed protection of assets trust will produce the following U.S. income, gift, and estate tax results. The trust created to hold the assets will be treated as a trust. The trust will be treated as a "grantor trust," and the settlor will include in his/her personal tax return all items of income, loss, deduction, or credit from the trust with respect to property settled upon the trust by such settlor. No gain or loss will be recognized on transfers of assets to the trust; transfers of assets to the trust will not be completed gifts subject to gift tax. Assets transferred to the trust will remain a part of the settlor's estate. There will be no section 684 tax arising from initial transfers of assets to the trust. In addition, the administrative fees paid for an assets protection trust, to the extent determined to be reasonable, are deductible subject to the 2-percent adjusted gross income rule. The trust is not eligible to be a qualifying Subchapter S shareholder.

13.6 Summary of reporting rules

The reporting rules are covered in detail in Chapters 15 and 16.

Briefly, the settlor of a protection of assets trust must disclose the existence of the trust on her Form 1040, Schedule B. The settlor must also file Form 3520 and must ensure that the foreign trust files Form 3520-A. The trust should appoint a U.S. agent under section 6048(b). All the items of income and expense earned or incurred by the trust must be picked up and reported in the settlor's income tax return. If the trust has a foreign financial account of some type, which is common, in the author's view, a Form 90-22.1 should be filed for this account.[217] If the settlor, who is treated as an owner of the trust, receives a distribution from the trust, she is not required to separately disclose the distribution again on Part III of Form 3520, since a disclosure will have been made elsewhere on the Form.

The beneficiary of a protection of assets trust who receives a distribution during the year should file Form 3520, completing Part III. He should have received a Foreign Grantor Trust Beneficiary Statement from the foreign trust with respect to the distribution. If that is the case, the distribution should not be taxable, and the recipient will not have to complete Schedule A, Part III.

13.6 Ethical considerations and pitfalls

13.7 Observations

Protection of assets trusts present a number of unique and interesting tax issues. Most of these issues—at least those that arise at the time of creation of the trust—would appear to be susceptible to definitive analysis. Clients should ask for, and their advisors should be prepared to render, comprehensive legal opinions on the essential non-tax and tax issues. These opinions may rely in part upon

[217] The application of the requirement for filing a foreign bank accounts report is not clear where a taxpayer is the settlor of a protection of assets trust. The settlor is treated as the owner of all the assets of the trust under section 671 for tax purposes. The legal title holder of the accounts, however, is the trust. (The trust may own an underlying company which, in turn, has foreign accounts. In which case, the problem should be analyzed in this light.) The author's reading of the instructions to the Form 90-22.1 leads him to conclude that the settlor has signature or other authority over the accounts and, therefore, must file the report. He probably does not have a "financial interest" in the accounts because he is not the legal title holder. Accordingly, in the case where the accounts are owned by the trust, the settlor should file the Form, check off item 5, and write in the space following 5(a) the following: "No U.S. person had any financial interest in the foreign accounts." However, it should be noted that he may have a financial interest if he has a present beneficial interest in more than 50 percent of the assets of the trust or he receives from the trust more than 50 percent of its current income. *See* Form 90-22.1, Instructions, General Definitions, "financial interest."

conclusions arrived at by competent foreign counsel. Clients then can get second opinions on these issues.

More difficult matters may arise in connection with the counseling of clients who are contemplating creating such trusts and the non-tax trust law, creditors' rights and procedural issues. Are there more favorable alternatives? If a protection of assets trust is to be used, which assets should be placed in the trust? What are the risks? How should the provisions of the trust be melded with the settlor's overall estate plan? Who will take responsibility, at the outset and in the future, for the proper oversight of the apparatus and all filings? Before proceeding, the client and his/her advisors will want to have clear answers to these questions. In almost every instance, the settlor will want to maintain a good deal of control; and the challenge for the advisor will be to convince the settlor (the person who is normally the client) that less is better.

> ➔ It is natural for the client to want to maintain as much control as possible. However, the smart, mature client will come to understand that he should select the highest quality team of trustee and legal and accounting advisors, understand completely what it is they are advising and follow that advice. If he is not 100% comfortable with this approach, he should do nothing, rather than do something piecemeal or stupid.

Chapter 14

Tax Treatment of Certain Underlying Entities and Insurance Products

14.1 General

A foreign trust can own or participate in a number of different investments and entities. For example, it can own a corporation; it can be a partner in a partnership; it can be the grantor or the beneficiary of another trust; and it can own any number of things, including life and annuity policies. These ownership interests and participations can achieve some desired goals. They can also raise a number of challenging issues.[218]

Also, some insurance products can be used to solve particular problems or act as a substitute for a trust.

This chapter is intended to point out a few practical aspects of these arrangements.

It is beyond the scope of this writing to deal with all the features of such things as controlled foreign corporations, passive foreign investment companies, foreign personal holding companies, life insurance, annuities, etc.[219] Instead, the following summarizes the rules applicable to controlled foreign corporations and passive foreign investment companies and the implications where these entities are

---

[218] For a scholarly discussion of attribution of ownership between discretionary trusts and their beneficiaries, see Goldberg, "Consideration for Underlying Foreign Corporations," International Trust and Estate Planning, ALI-ABA Course Study Materials (Aug. 26-27, 1999).

[219] These subjects are ably handled elsewhere. For an excellent and concise review of the international tax rules applicable to controlled foreign corporations, passive foreign investment companies and the like, see McDaniel & Ault, INTRODUCTION TO UNITED STATES INTERNATIONAL TAXATION (4th revised edition) (Kluwer Law International, 1998).

owned by a foreign trust. A couple of insurance products and how they might be owned by a foreign trust or used in lieu of a trust are also touched upon.

The description of the controlled foreign corporation rules and the passive foreign investment company rules that follows is taken from "Description And Analysis Of Present-Law Rules Relating To International Taxation" prepared by the Staff of the Joint Committee on Taxation. These materials have been abbreviated and modified so as to eliminate some of the details and highlight issues relating to foreign trusts.[220]

In general, the Internal Revenue Code permits U.S. persons to defer current taxation of income earned through a foreign corporation; that is, the income earned is not taxable until it is distributed to the U.S. shareholders. However, there are a number of important exceptions to this rule—so many that is easy to view the exception (income earned through a foreign subsidiary will not be deferred) as the general rule. These exceptions, or anti-deferral rules, are found in the following six sets of provisions: the controlled foreign corporation rules of Subpart F (sections 951-964); the passive foreign investment company rules (sections 1291-1298); the foreign personal holding company rules (sections 551-558); the personal holding company rules (sections 541-547); the accumulated earnings tax rules (sections 531-537); and the foreign investment company rules (section 1246). Special rules apply to the availability of foreign tax credits and the coordination of these various sets of rules. A number of identically or similarly defined terms appear in several sets of rules due to the heavy use of cross-referencing.

The rules applicable to the ownership of life insurance and annuity policies and the taxation of benefits flowing from those policies are spread throughout the Code.

---

220 Staff of the Joint Committee on Taxation, "Description and Analysis of President-Law Rules Relating to Our National Taxation," JCX-40-99 (June 28, 1999).

14.2 Controlled foreign corporations

14.2.1 Statutory rules

The provisions setting forth these rules are found in Subpart F (sections 951 through 964). Broadly speaking, passive income—sometimes referred to as Subpart F income—and certain other types of income earned by a controlled foreign corporation ("CFC"), are taxed to the U.S. shareholders on a current basis. Income, but not losses, will be flowed through to these shareholders. Also, the Subpart F rules generally limit carryovers and carry-backs.

U.S. 10-percent shareholders of a CFC are required to include in income for U.S. tax purposes currently certain income of the CFC (referred to as "Subpart F income"), without regard to whether the income is distributed to the shareholders. In effect, the Code treats the U.S. 10-percent shareholders of a CFC as having received a current distribution of their *pro rata* shares of the CFC's Subpart F income. In addition, the U.S. 10-percent shareholders of a CFC are required to include in income for U.S. tax purposes their *pro rata* share of the CFC's earnings to the extent invested by the CFC in U.S. property. The amounts included in income by the CFC's U.S. 10-percent shareholders under these rules are subject to U.S. tax currently. The U.S. tax on such amounts may be reduced by foreign tax credits.

For this purpose, a U.S. 10-percent shareholder is a U.S. person that owns 10 percent or more of the corporation's stock (measured by vote). A foreign corporation is a CFC if U.S. 10-percent shareholders own more than 50 percent of such corporation's stock (measured by vote or by value).

Example 1. F, a foreign corporation, is owned 50% by a nonresident alien individual and 50% by a U.S. citizen. F is not a controlled foreign corporation.

Example 2. G, a foreign corporation, is owned in equal shares by 11 or more U.S. citizens. G is not a controlled foreign corporation.

In determining stock ownership for purposes of the Subpart F rules, a U.S. person generally is considered to own a proportionate share of stock owned, directly or indirectly, by or for a foreign corporation, foreign partnership, or foreign trust or estate of which the U.S. person is a shareholder, partner, or beneficiary. In addition, constructive ownership rules apply for purposes of determining whether a U.S. person is a U.S. 10-percent shareholder, whether a foreign corporation is a CFC, and whether two persons are related, but not for purposes of requiring the inclusion of amounts with respect to the CFC in a U.S. shareholder's gross income.

Focusing on indirect ownership of the beneficiary through his or her interest in a foreign trust, the determination of a beneficiary's proportionate interest will be made on the basis of all the facts and circumstances in each case. The regulations warn "any arrangement which artificially decreases a United States person's proportionate interest will not be recognized."[221] As elsewhere when applying the Subpart F rules, it is the reality of the situation, not the form, that counts.

The treatment of beneficiaries of a foreign trust is illustrated in the regulations as follows:

> Foreign trust Z was created for the benefit of United States persons D, E, and F. Under the terms of the trust instrument, the trust income is required to be divided into three equal shares. Each beneficiary's share of the income may either be accumulated for him or distributed to him in the discretion of the trustee. In 1970, the trust is to terminate and there is to be paid over to each beneficiary the accumulated income applicable to his share and one-third of the corpus. The corpus of trust Z is composed of 90 percent of the one class of stock in foreign corporation S. By application of this section, each of D, E, and F is considered to own 30 percent (1/3 of 90 percent) of the stock in S corporation.

§ 1.958-1(d), Income Tax Regs. (Example (3)).

The Subpart F rules for determining stock ownership and the constructive ownership of interests in general apply the constructive

[221] § 1.958-1(c)(2), Income Tax Regs.

ownership rules in section 318(a) of the Code; but these are modified somewhat for Subpart F purposes. One of the rules is that stock owned by a nonresident alien individual will not be considered as owned by a U.S. citizen or a resident alien individual; however, this "relaxation" rule does not apply in the case of a foreign trust or foreign estate.

Specific provisions delimit the attribution from and to partnerships, estates, trusts, and corporations. Stock owned, directly or indirectly, by or for any trust—foreign or domestic—will be attributed from the trust to its beneficiaries in proportion to the actuarial interest of such beneficiaries in the trust. If the trust is a grantor trust, the stock will be considered as owned by the person treated as the owner under section 671, *i.e.,* the grantor or the holder of a section 678 power.[222] Conversely, stock owned, directly or indirectly, by or for a beneficiary of trust will be considered as owned by the trust "unless such beneficiary's interest in the trust is a remote contingent interest. For purposes of the preceding sentence, a contingent interest of the beneficiary in a trust shall be considered remote if, under the maximum exercise of discretion by the trustee in favor of such beneficiary, the value of such interest, computed actuarially, is 5 percent or less of the value of the trust property."[223] Stock owned, directly or indirectly, by or for someone who is treated as the owner of the trust under section 671 will be considered as owned by the trust.

Example. J and K, both U.S. individuals and both in their early 40s, are beneficiaries of a foreign nongrantor trust—the J&K Trust. The trust provides that each of them will receive 50 percent of the income of the trust during their life and such additional amounts as the trustee believes, in its sole discretion, is necessary to maintain their lifestyle at the time of the making of the trust. Upon their deaths, the trust property will be distributed *per capita* to their then living children. In default of these provisions, the trust property will be distributed to a charity. The J&K Trust owns 75 percent of the voting common stock of F corporation, which is a foreign corporation. Both J and K will be treated as the owners of 37.5 percent of the stock of F corporation. F will be characterized as a

[222] § 1.958-2(d)(ii), Income Tax Regs.
[223] § 1.958-2(d)(ii), Income Tax Regs.

CFC. J and K will need to file Form 5471 and report income accordingly.

It will be noted that this analysis becomes more problematic where it is difficult to determine the actuarial value of the beneficiaries' interest. For example, what would be the result if in the preceding example there were five beneficiaries, 3 of whom were nonresident aliens; and the trustee was given discretion to make distributions of income and corpus as it saw fit? It seems that the analysis would revert to a broad consideration of all the facts and circumstances, including the pattern of actual distributions.

> ➔ While taxpayers should be concerned about the application of these constructive ownership rules, in fact they do not appear to have been applied very often. This may be because under the old reporting rules, the IRS was not given the opportunity to closely examine cases where the issues might arise. With the filing of new Forms 3520 and 3520-A and increased audit activity, these rules may be called into play more frequently.

Earnings and profits of a CFC that have been included in income by the U.S. 10-percent shareholders are not taxed again when such earnings are actually distributed to such shareholders. Similarly, previously-taxed earnings are not included in income by the U.S. 10-percent shareholders in the event that such earnings are invested by the CFC in U.S. property. In the event that stock in the CFC is transferred subsequent to an income inclusion by a U.S. 10-percent shareholder but prior to the actual distribution of previously taxed income, the transferee shareholder generally is similarly exempt from U.S. tax on the distribution.

Subpart F income typically is passive income or income that is relatively movable from one taxing jurisdiction to another. Subpart F income consists of foreign base company income (defined in section 954), insurance income (defined in section 953), and certain income relating to international boycotts and other violations of public policy (defined in section 952(a)(3)-(5)). Subpart F income does not include income of the CFC that is effectively connected with the conduct of a trade or business within the U.S. (on which income the CFC is subject to current U.S. tax).

> → Some of the harshness of the CFC rules can be avoided by causing the CFC to be engaged in a U.S. trade or business. With respect to foreign trusts, however, section 641(b), by making it clear that a foreign trust will be treated as a nonresident alien individual who is not present in the U.S. at anytime, prevents a foreign trust from simply submitting itself to normal U.S. tax rules.

The Subpart F income of a CFC is limited to its current earnings and profits. Under this rule, current deficits in earnings and profits in any income category reduce the CFC's Subpart F income. In addition, accumulated deficits in a CFC's earnings and profits generated by certain activities in prior years may be used to reduce the CFC's Subpart F income generated by similar activities in the current year.

> → While the differences far outweigh the similarities, there is a certain similarity between the Subpart F earnings and profits rules and the distributable net income/undistributed net income rules in Subpart J. Taxpayers have historically tried to mitigate the adverse effects under Subpart F by wiping clean the earnings and profits slate; and undoubtedly taxpayers will attempt to wipe clean the undistributed net income slate, as well.

Foreign base company income includes five categories of income: foreign personal holding company income, foreign base company sales income, foreign base company services income, foreign base company shipping income, and foreign base company oil related income. In computing foreign base company income, income in these five categories is reduced by allowable deductions properly allocable to such income.

One major category of foreign base company income is foreign personal holding company income. For Subpart F purposes, foreign personal holding company income generally consists of the following: (1) dividends, interest, royalties, rents and annuities; (2) net gains from the sale or exchange of (a) property that gives rise to the preceding types of income, (b) property that does not give rise to income, and (c) interests in trusts, partnerships, and REMICS; (3) net gains from commodities transactions; (4) net gains from foreign currency transactions; (5) income that is equivalent to interest; (6) income from notional principal contracts; and (7) payments in lieu of dividends.

> ➔ These rules are especially important because they are incorporated by cross-reference in the PFIC provisions. Therefore, generally speaking, if income is not Subpart F income for CFC purposes, then it is not passive income for PFIC purposes.

Subpart F foreign personal holding company income generally includes the excess of gains over losses from sales and exchanges of non-income producing property and property that gives rise to certain passive income. However, an exclusion is provided for gains and losses from the sale or exchange of property that is inventory property in the hands of the CFC. Also excluded are gains and losses from the sale or exchange of property (including gains or losses arising out of *bona fide* hedging transactions) by a CFC that is a regular dealer in such property. A temporary exclusion also applies to gains and losses from the sale or exchange of property that gives rise to dividends, interest, rents, royalties, or annuities if such property gives rise to certain active financing income.

Subpart F foreign personal holding company income generally includes the excess of gains over losses from transactions (including futures, forward, and similar transactions) in any commodities. However, exceptions are provided for gains and losses from certain *bona fide* hedging transactions and certain active business transactions.

Subpart F foreign personal holding company income generally includes the excess of foreign currency gains over foreign currency losses attributable to section 988 transactions. An exception is provided for hedging and other transactions directly related to the business needs of the CFC.

Subpart F foreign personal holding income generally includes net income from notional principal contracts. However, income, gain, deduction or loss from a notional principal contract entered into to hedge an item of income in another category of foreign personal holding company income is included in that other category.

Subpart F foreign personal holding company income does not include rents and royalties received by the CFC in the active conduct of a trade or business from unrelated persons. Also generally excluded are dividends and interest received by the CFC from a related corporation organized and operating in the same foreign country in which the CFC was organized, and rents and royalties received by the CFC from a related corporation for the use of property within the country in which the CFC was organized. However, interest, rent, and royalty payments do not qualify for this exclusion to the extent that such payments reduce Subpart F income of the payor.

Temporary exceptions from foreign personal holding company income (as well as foreign base company services income) apply for Subpart F purposes for certain income that is derived in the active conduct of a banking, financing, or similar business, or in the conduct of an insurance business (so-called "active financing income"). These exceptions for active financing income are applicable only for taxable years beginning in 1999.

The 1999 exceptions from Subpart F foreign personal holding company income apply to income derived in the active conduct of a banking, financing, or similar business by a CFC that is predominantly engaged in such business and that conducts substantial activity with respect to such business. Detailed rules apply in determining whether the predominantly engaged and substantial activity requirements are satisfied, as well as whether income is treated as derived in the active conduct of a banking, financing, or similar business. In addition, certain nexus requirements apply, which provide that income derived by a CFC or a qualified business unit ("QBU") of a CFC from transactions with customers is eligible for the exceptions if, among other things, substantially all of the activities in connection with such transactions are conducted directly by the CFC or QBU in its home country, and such income is treated as earned by the CFC or QBU in its home country for purposes of such country's tax laws. Moreover, the 1999 exceptions apply to income derived from certain cross border transactions, provided that certain additional requirements are met. Additional temporary exceptions from foreign personal holding company income apply for certain income derived by a securities dealer within the meaning of section 475 (relating to mark-to-market accounting method for dealers in securities) and for gain from the sale of active financing assets.

The 1999 provision also provides a temporary exception from foreign personal holding company income for certain investment income derived by a qualifying insurance company and by certain qualifying insurance company branches. The exception applies to income (received from a person other than a related person) from investments made by a qualifying insurance company or qualifying insurance company branch of its reserves allocable to exempt contracts or 80 percent of its unearned premiums from exempt contracts.[224]

As previously noted, the U.S. 10-percent shareholders of a CFC generally are subject to U.S. tax currently on their *pro rata* shares of the CFC's Subpart F income. In addition, the U.S. 10-percent shareholders of a CFC are subject to U.S. tax currently on their *pro rata* shares of the CFC's earnings to the extent invested by the CFC in U.S. property.

> ➔ It might be noted that the Section 956 rules taxing U.S. shareholders on earnings that are invested in U.S. property have the effect of "locking out" this income from use in the U.S. A U.S.-controlled group can use these earnings to open a plant in Ireland, but this rule discourages the use of these earnings to expand a plant in the U.S.

If a U.S. person sells or exchanges stock in a foreign corporation, or receives a distribution from a foreign corporation that is treated as an exchange of stock, and, at any time during the five-year period

---

[224] The Treasury Department and the IRS have attempted to characterize certain payments under certain hybrid arrangements as Subpart F income. This area is the subject of considerable controversy. *See* Notice 98-11 and Notice 98-35.

ending on the date of the sale or exchange, the foreign corporation was a CFC and the U.S. person was a U.S. 10-percent shareholder, any gain recognized on the sale or exchange generally is recharacterized as dividend income, to the extent of the earnings and profits of the foreign corporation accumulated during the period that the shareholder held stock while the corporation was a CFC (section 1248). In addition, if a CFC is treated as having gain from the sale or exchange of stock in a foreign corporation, the gain is treated as a dividend to the same extent that it would have been so treated under section 1248 if the CFC were a U.S. person.

For this purpose, earnings and profits of the foreign corporation do not include amounts that already were subject to U.S. tax (whether imposed on the foreign corporation itself or on the U.S. 10-percent shareholders). Detailed rules govern the application of section 1248 in the case of (1) sales or exchanges of certain U.S. stock, (2) certain nonrecognition transactions involving a foreign corporation, and (3) certain indirect transfers of stock of a foreign corporation.

14.2.2 Use of corporate nominees; the Bollinger case

Frequently, foreign trusts, through their trustees, pursue activities and deal with investments through some form of nominee. Trust indentures commonly specifically permit the trustee to hold property through a nominee. For example, a foreign trust might hold a portfolio of stocks and bonds through a foreign corporation—either organized under the same laws as are applicable to the trust or under the laws of a different jurisdiction; this foreign corporation would act as the nominee of the trust. An issue can arise as to whether the nominee foreign corporation will be ignored, so the trust will be viewed as holding the portfolio directly, or it will be treated as a valid, separate entity. If the latter is the case, the corporation may be characterized as a CFC; this will lead to the U.S. shareholders being taxed on all the Subpart F income of the corporation under the sometimes harsh Subpart F rules.

The Supreme Court decision in *Commissioner v. Bollinger, Jr.*, delineates the rules for determining when a corporation will be treated as a straw corporation (that is, looked through or ignored). In *Bollinger*, the taxpayers had formed a series of partnerships to develop apartment complexes. In order to avoid a problem with usury laws in the financing, the partnerships entered into an agreement with a corporation owned by one of the individuals involved in the project, which agreement provided that the corporation would hold title to the property as the partnerships' nominee and agent solely to secure financing. It went on to provide that the partnership would have sole responsibility for the apartment complex, and that the partnership was the principal owner of the property during financing, construction and operation. All the parties who had something to do with the project, including lenders, contractors, managers, employees, and tenants, knew that the corporation was acting merely as the partnerships' agent and regarded the partnerships as the true owners. The IRS treated the corporation as the owner of the property and disallowed losses flowed through to the partners. The Court found that the partnerships were the owners of the projects for federal income tax purposes, since the relationship between them and the corporation was, in both form and substance, an agency with the partnership as principal.

> It seems to us that the genuineness of the agency relationship is adequately assured, and tax-avoiding manipulation adequately avoided, when the fact that the corporation is acting as agent for its shareholders with respect to a particular asset is set forth in a written agreement at the time the asset is acquired, the corporation functions as agent not principal with respect to the asset for all purposes, and a corporation is held out as the agent and not principal in all dealings with third parties relating to the asset.

Commissioner v. Bollinger, Jr., 485 U.S. 340 (1988).

Well-managed trust companies steer clear of this problem by using nominee corporations owned by them that are clearly labeled as a nominee and, what is more, that act for more than just one trust. However, there have been situations where the trust company—perhaps because the settlor insists—utilizes a foreign corporation that masks its identity as a nominee and acts for the sole purpose of holding investments on behalf of a particular trust. This type of arrangement creates a CFC owned constructively by the U.S. shareholders.

14.3 Passive foreign investment companies

Under rules enacted as part of the Tax Reform Act of 1986, U.S. persons that hold stock in a passive foreign investment company ("PFIC") are subject to a special set of rules intended to deny the benefits of tax deferral. A U.S. shareholder of a PFIC generally is subject to U.S. tax, plus an interest charge that reflects the value of the deferral of tax, upon receipt of a distribution from the PFIC or upon a disposition of PFIC stock. (This approach contrasts with the approach taken in Subpart F, which in effect flows through and taxes the income to the U.S. shareholders.) If a "qualified electing fund" election is made, however, the U.S. shareholder is subject to U.S. tax currently on the shareholder's *pro rata* share of the PFIC's total earnings; a separate election may be made to defer payment of such tax, subject to an interest charge, on income not currently received by the shareholder. In addition, with respect to PFIC stock that is marketable, electing shareholders currently take into account as income (or loss) the difference between the fair market value of their PFIC stock as of the close of the taxable year and their adjusted basis in such stock (subject to certain restrictions).

As with controlled foreign corporations, constructive ownership rules apply in determining whether a U.S. person owns stock in a PFIC.[225] Under these rules, a U.S. person generally is treated as owning such person's proportionate share of PFIC stock (1) owned by a partnership, trust or estate of which the person is a partner or beneficiary, (2) owned by a corporation of which the person is a 50-percent or greater shareholder (measured by value), or (3) owned by another PFIC of which the person is a shareholder.

> ➔ Neither the Code provisions nor the regulations provide information about how these constructive ownership rules should apply. One suspects that a court would look to the application of these rules in the context of the CFC provisions.

A foreign corporation is a PFIC if (1) 75 percent or more of its gross income for the taxable year consists of passive income, or (2)

[225] Section 1298(a).

50 percent or more of the average assets of the corporation consists of assets that produce, or are held for the production of, passive income.[226] The 50-percent PFIC asset test generally is applied using fair market value for purposes of measuring the PFIC's assets.[227] For this purpose, fair market value is used for a foreign corporation that is publicly traded. A foreign corporation is treated as publicly traded if stock in such corporation is regularly traded on a national securities exchange that is registered with the Securities and Exchange Commission, the national market system established pursuant to applicable securities laws, or any other exchange or market that the Treasury Secretary determines has rules that adequately ensure a reasonably sound fair market value for the market price of the stock. However, in the case of a foreign corporation that is a CFC that is not publicly traded (or any other foreign corporation that so elects), the asset test for PFIC status is applied using the adjusted bases of the corporation's assets rather than their fair market value.[228]

For this purpose, passive income generally means income that satisfies the definition of foreign personal holding company income under the subpart F provisions.[229] However, except as provided in regulations, passive income does not include certain active-business banking or insurance income. Also excluded from the definition of passive income is certain active-business securities income.

In determining whether a foreign corporation that owns a subsidiary is a PFIC, look-through treatment is provided in certain cases.

In the absence of a qualified electing fund election, a U.S. shareholder of a PFIC is subject to U.S. tax and an interest charge at the time the shareholder receives an "excess" distribution from the PFIC or disposes of stock in the PFIC. Under this rule, gain recognized on receipt of an "excess" distribution or on disposition of PFIC stock generally is treated as ordinary income earned *pro rata* over the shareholder's holding period with respect to the PFIC stock, and is taxed at the highest applicable tax rate in effect for each

---

[226] Section 1297(a).
[227] Section 1297(f).
[228] Section 1297(f)(2).
[229] Section 1297(b).

respective year. Interest is imposed at the underpayment rate on the tax liability with respect to amounts allocated to prior taxable years. Special rules apply for purposes of computing foreign tax credits with respect to such distributions.

An "excess" distribution is any distribution during the current taxable year that exceeds 125 percent of the average amount of distributions received during the three preceding years (or, if shorter, the taxpayer's holding period prior to the current taxable year).

A U.S. person that owns stock in a PFIC may elect that the PFIC be treated as a "qualified electing fund" with respect to that shareholder. Under such election, the U.S. shareholder must include currently in gross income the shareholder's *pro rata* share of the PFIC's total earnings and profits.[230] This inclusion rule generally requires current payment of tax, absent a separate election to defer payment of the tax.

The amount currently included in the income of an electing shareholder is divided between the shareholder's *pro rata* share of the ordinary earnings of the PFIC and the shareholder's *pro rata* share of the net capital gain of the PFIC.[231] The characterization of income, and the determination of earnings and profits, generally is made pursuant to general Code rules.[232]

The distribution of earnings and profits that were previously included in the income of an electing U.S. shareholder under these rules is not taxed as a dividend to the shareholder.[233] The basis of an electing U.S. shareholder's stock in a PFIC is increased by amounts currently included in income under these rules, and is decreased by any amount that is actually distributed but treated as previously taxed.

Foreign tax credits are allowed against U.S. tax on amounts included in income from a qualified electing fund to the same extent, and under the same rules, as in the case of income inclusions from a CFC.

---

[230] Section 1293.
[231] Section 1293(a)(1).
[232] Section 1293(e).
[233] Section 1293(c).

U.S. shareholders generally may elect to defer the payment of U.S. tax on amounts that are included currently in income but for which no current distribution has been received. An election to defer tax is treated as an extension of time to pay tax for which a U.S. shareholder is liable for interest. The disposition of stock in a PFIC terminates all previous extensions of time to pay tax with respect to the earnings attributable to that stock. Any transfer of ownership generally is treated as a disposition for this purpose, regardless of whether the transfer constitutes a realization or recognition event under general Code rules.

For purposes of the PFIC provisions, attribution rules apply to the extent that the effect is to treat stock of a PFIC as owned by a U.S. person.

A shareholder of a PFIC may make a mark-to-market election with respect to the stock of a PFIC, provided that such stock is marketable. Under such an election, the shareholder includes in income each year an amount equal to the excess, if any, of the fair market value of the PFIC stock as of the close of the taxable year over the shareholder's adjusted basis in such stock. The shareholder is allowed a deduction for the excess, if any, of the adjusted basis of the PFIC stock over its fair market value as of the close of the taxable year. However, deductions generally are allowable under this rule to the extent of any net mark-to-market gains with respect to the stock included by the shareholder for prior taxable years.

> ➔ Persons connected with a foreign trust—that is, beneficiaries, grantors and trustees—often would like for the trust to be able to invest in a foreign mutual fund. The PFIC provisions stand in the way. The trust can recognize income each year by selling units in the fund, thus giving up the deferral of income and incurring income for purposes of the DNI/UNI computations. Or the beneficiaries can elect to have the PFIC treated as a "qualified electing fund." Or the beneficiaries can avoid the rules of section 1291 by making an election to mark their marketable PFIC stock to market at the close of

each taxable year. Or they can avoid investing in a mutual fund and instead invest in a corporation that passes the income and assets test in section 1297(a)(1) and (2). Or they can look to invest in the company that has figured out, for the time being, how to earn income that is essentially passive in character and yet avoids characterization as "passive income", *i.e.*, "foreign personal income as defined in section 954(c)."[234] Another possibility, as discussed below, is the purchase of some form of *bona fide* insurance product and letting the investment activity occur inside the policy.

➔ Passive income earned by a foreign accumulation trust will not be taxed to the U.S. beneficiaries until there is an actual distribution and then the "throwback rules" will determine whether and to what extent taxes are due. It is odd that passive income earned in an underlying corporation owned by the trust can pose greater problems for the U.S. beneficiaries, including the possibility of immediate taxation on Subpart F and PFIC income, than direct ownership of the assets by the trust. Some industrious fund manager perhaps should offer investors a choice of either owning units in an incorporated mutual fund or undivided percentage interests in the assets in the fund.

14.4 Insurance products

As is readily apparent, persons involved in a foreign trust, especially the U.S. beneficiaries, generally will want to avoid the build-up of undistributed net income (UNI) followed by a distribution of accumulated earnings that triggers imposition of the "throwback" rules and the interest charge. One thought might be for the trust to invest in a non-U.S. mutual fund and realize income in the trust by selling units in the trust only when income is needed to fund a

[234] Section 1297(b)(1).

distribution. However, the PFIC and other anti-deferral rules, with their constructive ownership provisions, stand in the way. Yet some form of managed investment throwing off passive income is exactly what the settlor and the beneficiaries want.

In addition, some individuals will want to avoid the disclosure and reporting rules that pertain to foreign trusts. In which case, they may be interested in some form of life insurance product that does not involve a trust in any fashion.

There are also a wide variety of special situations, such as a nonresident alien individual intending to immigrate to the U.S., where an insurance product can play a useful role.

Non-U.S. insurance products can have a number of other attractions. Many of the largest insurers in the world are in fact non-U.S. The U.S. tax and regulatory structure, unfortunately, comes at a cost; and this cost sometimes can be reduced by dealing with an insurer that does not have to shoulder some of these domestic costs. For large policies, the policy owner is probably going to be dealing with non-U.S. insurers in one form or another anyway, because most of the reinsurance market is based outside the U.S. (One of the fastest growing reinsurance locations is Bermuda.) Some of the best investment advisory groups are located outside the U.S. Non-U.S. policies ordinarily can be invested in non-U.S. funds that deny access to U.S. investors because of security law prohibitions. Also holding assets within an insurance policy may provide more confidentiality and protection.[235]

14.4.1 Life insurance owned by a foreign trust

A foreign trust—for example, a foreign nongrantor accumulation trust—can own a life insurance policy on the life of any insurable person. This person might be the foreign settlor, or it might be one of the U.S. beneficiaries. The beneficiary of the policy can be the foreign trust or U.S. persons that may be beneficiaries of the trust. Investment advice can be provided by a subadvisor designated by the

---

[235] For an interesting introduction to uses of international life insurance, see Hampton, "International Life Insurance Presents Unique Planning Opportunities," ESTATES, GIFTS AND TRUSTS JOURNAL, pp. 175-188.

insurer, which is acceptable to the settlor (but which is a qualified, professional investment advisor). If, for example, the policy is a variable life insurance policy issued, say, by a *bona fide* insurance company under the laws of Bermuda, it constitutes a life insurance contract under the laws of Bermuda, and it qualifies as an insurance contract under U.S. tax rules, then income earned on the policy in the separate segregated account will not be subject to U.S. tax when earned.[236] The income will not be treated as having been earned by the trust as no constructive ownership rules come into play. The policy owner, the trust, to the extent permitted under the terms of the policy, can borrow funds against the policy and use the funds to make distributions.[237] Such distributions should not "carry out" any UNI/DNI and therefore should not occasion a tax to the beneficiary. The transfer of funds from the foreign trust to the insurer is not subject to any excise tax.[238] Proceeds of the life insurance contract payable by reason of the death of the insured are not taxable as income when received by the U.S. beneficiaries.[239] Also, the proceeds are not subject to U.S. estate taxation since under the U.S. system, the estate, not the heirs, is generally taxable.

> ➔ For the insurance policy to qualify under U.S. rules, it must meet a barrage of tests in section 7702 and the regulations thereunder. Either it must satisfy the Cash Value Accumulation Test or the Guideline

[236] Section 7702 contains rules and definitions applicable to life insurance contracts. Section 817 contains rules requiring diversification of investments where the policy is based on segregated asset accounts. Policy premiums can be paid in one lump sum (single premium) or spread out in such a way as to avoid violating the Modified Endowment Contract (MEC) rules in Section 7702A.

[237] The amount that can be borrowed is somewhat restricted. The policy owner cannot take out all of the funds because the account must contain enough funds continually to cover the costs of insurance and administrative costs. Interest paid on loans might be subject to 30% withholding. Some insurance carriers may make the section 953(d) election by foreign insurance company to be treated as a domestic corporation so as to avoid this problem.

[238] There is a 1% excise tax on premiums paid on insurance policies and similar contracts by U.S. person to non-U.S. insurers; but this would not apply in this instance. Section 4371. This provision was first enacted in 1954 and most recently amended in 1989.

[239] Section 101(a).

> Premium Plus Cash Value Corridor Test. These tests, in general, are intended to "weed out" contracts that are overly investment-oriented and do not call for a sufficient amount of real insurance. With a variable life insurance contract, these tests apply each time the death benefits change and at least once each year. The policy owner must not have a prohibited degree of control over the policy's investment. Persons interested in this approach should rely upon a large, well-known insurer; and they should look for a tax opinion from a highly-qualified U.S. tax advisor. They should be willing to pay for the insurance element and the associated "loads."

14.4.2 Foreign trust/split dollar life insurance—foreign settlor of foreign trust paying the premiums

Another use of life insurance in conjunction with foreign trusts takes the following form. A non-U.S. person establishes a foreign trust ("FT") in a low tax jurisdiction and funds it with sufficient amounts to pay the premiums on a variable cash insurance policy on the life of a U.S. beneficiary. The policy is issued by a non-U.S. insurance carrier. The policy is structured so as not to run afoul of the modified endowment contract rules in section 7702A (relating to modified endowment contract definition). The U.S. beneficiary establishes a foreign trust to act as an insurance trust ("FIT"). The FIT applies for and owns the policy. The policy might allow for the trustee of the FIT to direct the investment of the assets within the policy. The FT and the FIT would enter into a Split Dollar Life Insurance Agreement whereby the FT would retain an interest equal to the aggregate amount of premiums paid by it. Upon the insured's death, FT would be repaid this amount. The FIT would be entitled to amounts in excess of the aggregate amount of premiums paid by FT. During the term of the policy, the FIT could borrow funds against the policy. Upon the insured's death, the death benefit that exceeds the aggregate amount of premiums paid by FT, which are repaid to FT out of the death benefit, is paid to the U.S. beneficiaries of the FIT, who might be the heirs of the U.S. beneficiary. If the parties wish to maximize the lifetime benefits of this type of arrangement, the death benefits can be minimized so as to increase the cash value built up in the policy. If they wish to maximize the death benefits, this can be done as well.

Again, the income earned in the policy is not subject to U.S. tax. The amounts borrowed by the FIT and presumably used to fund distributions to the U.S. beneficiaries again would not occasion a tax.[240] The death benefits would not be subject to U.S. income or gift or estate tax.

A variation on this theme involves the use of a FIT that is established by the non-U.S. person, and this FIT is drafted so as to continue in existence in perpetuity. (There are a number of jurisdictions that now ignore the rule against perpetuities or any mandatory termination period. These are sometimes referred to as "Dynasty Trusts.") A portion of the death benefits that go into the FIT—that portion that is not needed to fund death-time distributions to the heirs of the insured—are used to purchase a policy on the life or lives of the next generation. In this way, the arrangement is repeated. This policy, like the prior one, has an element of death benefits and an element of accessible cash value, which is available to fund policy loans.

14.4.3 Foreign trust/split dollar life insurance—U.S. settlor of foreign trust paying the premiums

Similar to the arrangement described immediately above, a U.S. individual can create a foreign trust ("FT") that owns the life policy on the life of the U.S. individual. The FT pays a portion of the cost of the premiums and another person, perhaps the spouse of the first-named U.S. individual, pays the remainder of the premium. Upon death of the insured, the FT receives the death benefit, and the other party, say the spouse, receives the cash surrender value. (The payment of a portion of the premiums by the spouse is treated in effect as a loan to the FT.) The FT is clearly a foreign grantor trust, but it has no income to be passed on to the grantor. Instead, the income on the assets is earned inside the insurance policy. There will be a gift tax liability on the amounts transferred to the FT to fund a portion of the premiums, but the taxable gift will be greatly reduced

---

[240] This result assumes that the policy has avoided being characterized as a Modified Endowment Contract under section 7702A.

because another person is paying for some of the premiums and the valuation of the amount of the taxable gift is under favorable actuarial tables. The income earned inside the policy is free of U.S. tax; and the death benefits when the policy "falls in" are not taxable.

Again, as above, the FT can be drafted so as to remain in existence for a very long time, assuming this is permitted under applicable law. The build up of value in the structure can be used to purchase insurance on the lives of the next generation; and again a judgement can be made as to whether to lean toward death benefits or lean toward liquidity that can be used to fund loans.

14.4.4 Use of insurance products in lieu of a foreign trust

To a certain extent, a non-U.S. life policy can be treated as a substitute for a foreign trust. It has a number of favorable points. It does not call for the filing of any reports; in this sense, it is the only mechanism for U.S. persons to hold significant investments outside the U.S. and not report the investment under the tax or foreign financial account rules. The income earned inside the policy is not subject to current taxation. The policy can be denominated in a foreign currency.[241] The value of the policy would be subject to U.S. estate tax if it remains in the policy owner's estate. Death benefits are not subject to tax when received by a U.S. beneficiary. Under state creditors' rights laws, there sometimes is a measure of protection afforded the cash surrender value built up in the policy.

---

[241] Most policies that are designed to comply with U.S. tax rules are dollar-denominated.

Chapter 15

Reporting Rules and Penalties

15.1 General

The provisions of the Code dealing with information reporting for foreign trusts and the imposition of penalties where reports are not filed were radically revised in 1996.[242] These rules apply to U.S. grantors and beneficiaries of all types of foreign trusts (except some forms of pension and charitable trusts), and in some cases to the trusts themselves. The trust might be a grantor trust or a nongrantor trust, although, as noted, the population of nongrantor trusts has been greatly reduced by the provisions of section 672(f), enacted in 1996.[243]

15.2 Reporting rules (section 6048)

15.2.1 Section 6048(a)

Section 6048, as amended by the 1996 Act, requires the filing of an information return by a so-called "responsible party" (for example, a person who transfers property to a foreign trust), someone who is treated as the owner of any portion of the assets of a foreign trust under the grantor trust rules, someone who received a distribution from a foreign trust, or someone who received either a large gift or

---

[242] In Notice 97-34, 1997-25 IRB 1 (published June 2, 1997), the Internal Revenue Service provided guidance on the foreign trust and foreign gift reporting provisions added to the Internal Revenue Code by the Small Business Job Protection Act of 1996 (P.L. 104-188). The rules set forth in the Notice, it is anticipated, will be incorporated in regulations issued in the future by the Service. In the meantime, taxpayers must comply with the rules contained in the Notice, including deadlines for the filing of certain notices and returns. On the face of things, the filing deadline for Form 3520 was November 15, 1997, and the filing deadline for Form 3520-A was October 15, 1997.

[243] *See* 97 TNT 167-1 & 97 TNT 165-2. *See also*, Bruce, Foreign Trust Tax Compliance: Urgent Need for Guidance, Tax Notes, Dec. 16, 1996, p. 1365.

bequest (totaling more than $100,000) from a foreign individual or estate or a greater-than-$10,276 gift from a foreign corporation or partnership.[244] The filing is made on Form 3520.

15.2.2 Section 6048(b)

This provision requires that any U.S. person who is treated as the owner of any portion of the assets of a foreign trust must ensure that the foreign trust files an information return regarding trust activities and operations. This filing is made on Form 3520-A.

15.2.3 Section 6048(c)

This subsection requires any U.S. beneficiary who receives a distribution from a foreign trust to file a return, which includes, among other things, the name of the trust and the aggregate amount of the distributions received. If adequate records are not provided to the IRS to determine the proper treatment of the distribution, the distribution will be treated in its entirety as an accumulation distribution includible in the recipient's gross income. However, this harsh result will not apply if the foreign trust elects to appoint a U.S. agent.

15.3 Penalties (Section 6677)

This section prescribes the penalties that apply where the information returns required by section 6048 are not filed.

A foreign grantor trust as to which a U.S. person is treated as an owner of any portion of the trust or any foreign trust that makes a distribution to a U.S. beneficiary may wish to authorize (appoint) a U.S. limited agent in order to avoid the possibility of an adverse tax determination by the IRS under sections 6048(b)(2) or 6048(c)(2)(a). This limited agent can be the U.S. settlor of the trust (if there is one), one of the U.S. beneficiaries, a U.S. attorney, accountant or return preparer, or any other U.S. person.

---

[244] The statute says gifts or bequests of more than $10,000 must be reported; but the IRS "relaxed" the requirement to $100,000. The figure $10,276 is the 1998 figure indexed for inflation.

Also, a U.S. grantor, who is treated as the owner of the assets in the trust, and perhaps the beneficiaries are required to disclose the existence of the trust on their individual federal income tax form (Form 1040) and to make sure that any items that would affect their income tax liability, which items would be reflected on the Forms 3520 and 3520-A, are included in their Form 1040.

15.4 More on reporting responsibilities by responsible person

15.4.1 Transferors to a foreign trust

Section 6048(a) provides that on or before the 90th day after any reportable event, the responsible party must provide written notice of such event to the IRS. The notice takes the form of Form 3520 and includes the amount of money or other property (if any) transferred to the trust and the identity of the trust and of each trustee and beneficiary (or class of beneficiaries) of the trust. A reportable event means the creation of any foreign trust by a U.S. person, the transfer of any money or property (directly or indirectly) to a foreign trust by a U.S. person, including a transfer by reason of death, and the death of a citizen or resident of the U.S. if the decedent was treated as the owner of any portion of a foreign trust under the grantor trust rules of the Code or any portion of a foreign trust was included in the gross estate of the decedent. A "responsible party" means the grantor in the case of the creation of an *inter vivos* trust, the transferor in the case of a reportable event described above and the executor of the decedent's estate in any other case.

Other filings, such as a gift tax return, may be required as well.

Generally, in order to avoid penalties under section 6677 (relating to failure to file information with respect to certain foreign trusts), Form 3520 must be filed as an attachment to the taxpayer's income tax return by the due date (including extensions) of the taxpayer's income tax return. (Thus, the Form need not be filed within the 90-day period stated in the statute.) In addition, unless otherwise provided, a copy of Form 3520 must be sent to the Philadelphia Service Center by the same date.[245]

---

[245] Notice 97-34, however, provides with respect to Form 3520 for the taxable year that includes August 20, 1996 (the "1996 Form 3520"), no such

The penalty under section 6677 is 35% of the gross reportable amount. Gross reportable amount means the gross value of the property involved in the event, determined as of the date of the event. There is a reasonable cause exception so long as the failure is not due to willful neglect.

The grantor of a foreign grantor trust should provide written notice of the creation of the foreign trust to the IRS using Form 3520. If the trust was created on or prior to August 20, 1997, he or she should file a Form 3520 using the old form. If the trust was created after August 20, 1997, he or she should file the new Form.

---

penalties will be imposed if the taxpayer files the 1996 Form 3520 on or before November 15, 1997, with the Philadelphia Service Center. Alternatively, no penalties will be imposed for a failure to file Form 3520 if the taxpayer files the 1996 Form 3520 by the due date (including extensions) for the taxpayer's income tax return for the first taxable year beginning on or after January 1, 1997 (*i.e.*, April 1, 1998 or the extended due date), provided the taxpayer's income tax return for the tax year that includes August 20, 1996, "reflects" the information contained in the 1996 Form 3520. (Disclosure of the creation of a foreign trust on Schedule B of Form 1040 should represent a reflection of the subject information. Apparently, if the taxpayer does not reflect the subject information on his or her income tax return for the relevant year (say, 1996), he or she can amend that return to reflect the information. *See* Example 16, Notice 97-34. The instructions to the 1996 Form 3520 provide that it can be filed by attaching "the form to the timely filed (including extensions) income tax return for the first taxable year beginning on or after January 1, 1997, provided the taxpayer's income tax return for the taxable year that includes August 20, 1996, includes the items (if any) reflected on the form that would affect the U.S. person's income tax liability (for example, any gain recognized by the taxpayer as a result of a section 1057 election, or any interest charge or additional tax resulting from a trust distribution).") Taxpayers who file a Form 3520 that is not revised as described in the Notice 97-34 will not be considered as having complied with the information reporting requirements of revised sections 1494 and 6048. Based on conversations with the Service, it appears that the Service will not take an especially hard line against taxpayers that make a genuine effort to comply with the reporting rules. It acknowledges that the rules are new and complex; and the IRS was late in producing the forms. On the other hand, the IRS is making a concerted effort to pursue aggressive tax schemes involving trusts, of which there are many.

15.4.2 Reporting by foreign trusts with U.S. grantors

Section 6048(b) provides that any person who is treated as an owner of any portion of a foreign trust under the grantor trust rules of the Code must "ensure" that (a) the trust makes a return (*i.e.,* files with the IRS) for the year which sets forth a full and complete accounting of all trust activities and operations for the year, the name of the U.S. agent for such trust, and such other information as the IRS prescribes and (b) the trust furnishes such information as the IRS prescribes (i) to each U.S. person who is treated as the owner of any portion of the trust (under the grantor trust rules) and (ii) to each person who receives any distribution (beneficiary). The amount to be taxed to the U.S. person can be determined by the IRS unless the trust agrees to authorize a U.S. person to act as the trust's limited agent solely for purposes of applying the rules relating to information requests, administrative summons and the like. This authorization is only for tax purposes and does not subject the trust to other forms of legal process. Nor does it cause the foreign trust to be engaged in a U.S. trade or business or to have a permanent establishment in the U.S. In cases where information is not furnished, rules similar to the rules in section 6038A(e) will apply. The taxpayer or presumably its U.S. agent can institute judicial proceedings in a fashion similar to that described in section 6038(A)(e)(4).

In order for the taxpayer to meet its burden of ensuring that the trust files the required return with the Service and furnishes the required information to the person treated as the U.S. owner (typically the grantor) and the U.S. beneficiaries, the trust must file a Form 3520-A. Parts of this Form should be sent to the IRS, parts to the person treated as the U.S. owner (typically the grantor) and parts to the beneficiaries.

If the trust does not file the required return and furnish the required statements, the U.S. owner (typically the grantor) is liable for a penalty under section 6677 equal to 5% of the gross value of the trust's assets. Again, a reasonable cause exception can apply.

Generally, no penalty will be assessed on the U.S. owner of a foreign trust for a failure to file Form 3520-A if the foreign trust files Form 3520-A with the Philadelphia Service Center by the fifteenth day of the third month following the end of the trust's taxable year (or later, if pursuant to an extension of time to file).[246]

The person treated as the owner of the assets in a foreign grantor trust (typically the grantor) should inform the trustee of the trust that he or she wishes for the trust (a) to file a Form 3520-A with the IRS and (b) to furnish the two required statements (a Foreign Grantor Trust Owner Statement to the owner, who is probably the person communicating with the trustee, and a Foreign Grantor Trust Beneficiary Statement to each of the beneficiaries).[247]

15.4.3 Reporting by U.S. beneficiaries of foreign trusts

Section 6048(c) provides that any U.S. person who receives (directly or indirectly) any distribution from a foreign trust must make a return with respect to such trust for such year which includes the name of such trust, the aggregate amount of the distributions so received from such trust during the year, and such other information as the IRS may prescribe. If adequate records are not provided to the IRS to determine the proper treatment of any distribution, such distribution shall be treated as an accumulation distribution (*i.e.*, the calculation may be very complicated and a portion of the amount ordinarily will be taxable). This result can be avoided if the foreign

---

[246] However, with respect to Form 3520-A for the taxable year that includes August 20, 1996 (the "1996 Form 3520-A"), no such penalty will be imposed if the foreign trust files the 1996 Form 3520-A on or before October 15, 1997. Alternatively, no section 6677 penalty will be imposed if the foreign trust files the 1996 Form 3520-A by the due date (including extensions) for the Form 3520-A for the first taxable year beginning on or after January 1, 1997, provided the U.S. owner "reflects" the information contained in the 1996 Form 3520-A on the owner's income tax return for the tax year that includes August 20, 1996. (Again, some disclosure of information relating to the creation of a foreign trust on Form 1040 should represent a reflection of the subject information. Also, if the taxpayer does not reflect the subject information on his or her income tax return for the relevant year (say, 1996), he or she should be able to amend that return to reflect the information. *See* Example 16, Notice 97-34.)

[247] The trustee should check to see that the U.S. person properly reflected any items of income on his or her 1996 return; and, if there is any doubt, that person should amend that return.

trust (which need not be a grantor trust but might be a nongrantor trust) appoints a U.S. limited agent.

As a general rule, a U.S. person who receives a distribution, directly or indirectly, from a foreign trust after August 20, 1996, is required to report on Form 3520 the name of the trust, the aggregate amount of distributions received from the trust during the taxable year, and such other information as the Secretary may prescribe. Reporting is required under section 6048(c) only if the U.S. person knows or has reason to know that the trust is a foreign trust. Special rules apply to loans.

A U.S. beneficiary who fails to report a distribution received after August 20, 1996, will be subject to a 35 percent penalty under section 6677(a) on the gross amount of the distribution.

A U.S. beneficiary will not be forced to treat the entire distribution as an accumulation distribution if the beneficiary obtains from the foreign trust either a Foreign Grantor Trust Beneficiary Statement (included as part of Form 3520-A) or a Foreign Nongrantor Trust Beneficiary Statement (not included as part of Form 3520-A) with respect to the distribution. (The mystery of the missing Foreign Nongrantor Trust Beneficiary Statement is discussed in chapter 16).

If there has been a distribution from a foreign grantor trust, the recipient-beneficiary should file a Form 3520. Generally, the Form should be filed as an attachment to the taxpayer's income tax return by the due date (including extensions) of the taxpayer's income tax return. In addition, unless otherwise provided, a copy of Form 3520 must be sent to the Philadelphia Service Center by the same date.[248]

---

[248] Notice 97-34, however, provides with respect to Form 3520 for the taxable year that includes August 20, 1996 (the "1996 Form 3520"), no such penalties will be imposed if the taxpayer files the 1996 Form 3520 on or before November 15, 1997, with the Philadelphia Service Center. Alternatively, no penalties will be imposed for a failure to file Form 3520 if the taxpayer files the 1996 Form 3520 by the due date (including extensions) for the taxpayer's income tax return for the first taxable year beginning on or after January 1, 1997 (*i.e.*, April 1, 1998 or an extended due date), provided the taxpayer's income tax return for the tax year that includes August 20, 1996, "reflects" the information contained in the 1996 Form 3520. (The problem is that the recipient of a distribution from a foreign Protection of

→ Section 6048(c) provides that domestic trusts with foreign activities, to the extent Treasury Department regulations provide, can be treated as foreign trusts. "To the extent provided in regulations, a trust which is a United States person shall be treated as a foreign trust for purposes of this section and section 6677 if such trust has substantial activities, or holds substantial property, outside the United States." Notice 97-34, 1997-1 CB 422, however, states that the Treasury Department and the IRS are studying the appropriate scope of this particular provision; and until further guidance is issued, all domestic trusts will be treated as domestic trusts, not foreign trusts, pursuant to this provision. In any event, a U.S. grantor trust with a foreign grantor and U.S. beneficiaries, which is administered in the U.S. and invests substantial amounts in the U.S. markets, should not occasion, for the U.S. beneficiaries, the need to file Form 3520. It will be recalled that a trust is "foreign" or "domestic" depending upon the application of the residency rules in section 7701(a)(30) & (31). It makes no difference that the trust is administered in the U.S. and its funds are largely invested in the U.S.

15.4.4 Reports by U.S. recipients of foreign gifts

Section 6039F provides that if the value of aggregate foreign gifts received by a U.S. person during any taxable year exceeds $10,000, such person must file an information return with the IRS. This

---

Assets Trust which is by its nature a grantor trust ordinarily would not reflect the receipt of the distribution on his or her return. In such event, the recipient might file an amended return with an attachment disclosing the receipt of a nontaxable distribution. It is believed, based on discussions with the Service, that not placing an item on the return because it is nontaxable—if this is correct—will be treated as a proper "reflection" of the information; but it is recommended that persons "play safe" by filing an amended return with explanatory attachment.)

threshold amount was raised from $10,000 to $100,000 by the IRS.[249] A foreign gift does not include any amount paid on behalf of an individual as tuition to an educational organization or to any person who provides medical care as payment for such medical care.

Reporting under section 6039F is required on an annual basis on Form 3520. It requires the reporting of general information necessary to determine whether a purported gift is properly classified as a gift or income. For example, limited information is required regarding whether the foreign donor is an individual, corporation, partnership, or estate, and whether the foreign donor was acting as a nominee or intermediary for another person. A brief description of the property received is also required. The form does not require information on the identity of the foreign donor unless the foreign donor is a partnership or foreign corporation, or is acting as a nominee or intermediary for such an entity. However, the U.S. donee may be required to provide additional information, including the identity of the donor, to the IRS upon request.

Distributions from foreign grantor trusts, when accounts are treated as owned by a foreign person are not treated as gifts but are reportable on Form 3520, Part III. Distributions from a domestic grantor trust that is treated as owned by a foreign person, on the other hand, is reportable as a gift from a foreign donor.

If a reportable gift is not reported on Form 3520, the tax consequences of the receipt of the gift shall be determined by the Secretary. Reporting is only required if the U.S. person knows or has reason to know that the donor is a foreign person.

Cases involving a protection of assets trust ordinarily will not entail the receipt of large foreign gifts.

[249] *See* instructions to Form 3620 at p. 9.

15.5 Summary of reporting responsibilities

The various report responsibilities are summarized below.

Form	Comments	Responsible Person
FORM 3520, Creation Of Or Transfers To Certain Foreign Trusts		Grantor, other transferor, beneficiary, etc.
FORM 3520-A, Annual Return Of Foreign Trust With U.S. Beneficiaries		Trustee
Schedule B, Part III, Individual Federal Income Tax Form 1040	The grantor of, or transferor to, a foreign trust that existed during the taxable year, must report this fact, regardless whether he has a beneficial interest in such trust. This report is made by checking "yes" at the bottom of Schedule B-Interest and Dividend Income, Form 1040.	Grantor; transferor
Form 709, Gift Tax Return	A gift tax return should be filed if a U.S. person, such as the grantor of the foreign trust, has made a completed gift. It should be recalled that there can be a completed gift to a grantor trust as well as a nongrantor trust.	Grantor; transferor

Form 56, Notice Concerning Fiduciary Relationship	The trustee of the trust may use Form 56 to notify the IRS of the creation of a fiduciary relationship. The IRS then will be put on notice of the existence of the trust. Generally, Form 56 should be filed when the fiduciary relationship is created. The filing of this form is not mandatory. (The filing of a Form 3520 that complies with section 6048(a) makes the filing of a Form 56 superfluous.)	Trustee (not mandatory)
Form 1041, U.S. Fiduciary Income Tax Return, And Form SS-4, Application For Taxpayer Identification Number	Under the old rules, while a "grantor trust" generally was not required to obtain a tax identification number or to file an annual Form 1041 (Treas. Regs. on Income Tax, § 1.6012-3(a)(9), and § 1.671-4(a) and Treas. Regs. on Procedure and Administration, § 301.6109-1), a grantor trust was required to file a Form 1041 if the *situs* of the trust or any of its assets was not in the U.S. *See* Treas. Regs. on Income Tax, § 1.671-4(b)(3). It is not clear whether a foreign trust, under the new rules, should obtain a taxpayer identification number and file a Form 1041. Form 3520 does not tell the taxpayer to take these steps.	Trustee

Treasury Form 90-22.1, Report Of Foreign Bank And Financial Accounts	For any assets held directly by the trust outside the U.S. in non-U. S. accounts, the settlor may be required to report his/her reversionary interest in such accounts by filing Treasury Form 90-22.1 by June 30 of each year following the close of the preceding year during which such foreign account or accounts existed and had a combined value of more than $10,000 at any time during such year. If such foreign accounts are held by a corporation owned by the trust, the corporation must file this form. Failure to file the return is a felony. The instructions to Form 3520 indicate that a Form 90-22.1 may be required. The IRS Training Materials take the same view.	Person treated as owner of the trust assets (Grantor or holder of a section 678 power)

Customs Form 4790, Report Of International Transportation Of Currency Or Monetary Instruments	Any person who physically transports, mails, or ships monetary instruments of more than $10,000 between the U.S. and a foreign country or who receives in the U.S. from a foreign source monetary instruments of more than $100,000 must file Form 4790. If the person is not carrying the currency or other monetary instrument when departing the U.S., the form can be filed by mail on or before the date of departure, with the Commissioner of Customs in Washington, D.C. Otherwise, the form must be filed at the time of departure with the Customs Officer in charge at the customs port of departure.	Person transporting currency or monetary instruments
Forms W-8 and W-9, Taxpayer Identification Number And Certification	A foreign nongrantor trust or a foreign grantor trust with a foreign settlor should file a W-8 claiming the exemption from domestic back-up withholding. Payments to it will be subject to 30% withholding unless a reduced treaty rate can be claimed. The settlor of a foreign grantor trust should look to the treaty between the U.S. and his/her home country. A foreign grantor trust with a U.S. grantor, in the eyes of the Service, should be subject to 30% withholding, and the U.S. grantor should claim a credit for the tax withheld. IRS Training Materials, p. 4-2. The rules are not clear. Trusts have successfully filed a Form W-9	Trustee

with withholding agents with respect to interest and dividends, in the name of the trust and using its TIN. This approach avoids the withholding of taxes pursuant to sections 1441-1442. Of course the settlor picks up and pays tax on all the income.

Reporting Pursuant to Section 6039C

This provision requires that any foreign person—which includes a corporation, partnership, trust, individual, etc.—holding a direct investment in U.S. real property interests must make a return setting forth its name and address, the description of all U.S. real property interests held and such other information as the IRS prescribes by regulation.

In the case of a trust, the trustee

→ The instructions for Forms 3520 and 3520-A should make clear whether the taxpayer or the trustee should file a Form 1041 and whether the trust must get a tax identification number.

Chapter 16

Reporting Forms

The prior chapter provided a general overview of the reporting rules. This chapter is intended to review the forms in detail. In the process, specific suggestions are made as to how to handle certain issues.

It should be recalled that IRS forms are regularly updated. Therefore, when working on a particular form, the return preparer and the taxpayer should make sure that they are dealing with the correct version. Also, while it may seem odd, the statute may provide one thing, a form may provide another, and the instructions for the form may put everything in a slightly different light. Therefore, it is a good idea to look at everything. Also, some issues are not easily dealt with in the context of one of the forms. The current forms are relatively new. They are, in effect, experiencing a "shakedown" period. This discussion is based on 1998 Forms 3520 and 3520-A. The 1999 version of these forms is identical to the 1998 version except certain lines and spaces that were "reserved" in the 1998 forms were removed in the 1999 forms and some references to pages of the instructions were added.

In several ways, the existing forms simply do not work as they should. In order to "make them work," it is necessary to modify them or create a "make-shift" statement to be attached to the form. These problems perhaps will be corrected as new versions of the forms are issued toward the end of 1998.[250]

> → Since the IRS forms are not well knit, the private provider software is similarly "rough" and difficult to work with. Most software is designed for fiduciaries dealing with domestic trusts. The software packages do not include Forms 3520 and 3520-A, and typically

[250] One can sympathize with the IRS since developing these forms must be extremely difficult. The provisions of the statute are among the most complicated in the tax laws.

they do not tie the trust return with the beneficiary's return. For example, Form 4970 is not part of the fiduciary returns package. For the time being, the best approach may be to use a specially designed spreadsheet that imitates—but where necessary modifies—the calculations in Forms 3520, 3520-A, 1041, and 4970. The actual forms for filing can be generated either by scanning the IRS form and modifying the form or modifying it by hand. (It is not possible to modify the Forms acquired from the IRS from its website or the IRS Forms CD.) The Form 1040NR, it is suggested, should be "modified" either by using a Form 1041, labeling it "Form 1040NR" and proceeding from that point, or by using Form 1040NR, striking out the entire form and attaching a Form 1041, again modified.

➔ The instructions for Form 3520 estimate that on average it may require 62 hours, 10 minutes to complete and file a Form 3520. If the facts surrounding a particular trust and set of distributions are complicated, this figure can be much higher.

Form 3520 and Form 3520-A should be read together since they work in tandem in many respects.

Where there is at least one person treated as a U.S. owner, it is probably best to start with the Form 3520-A, which is signed by the Trustee. Since the U.S. owner is responsible for ensuring that the trust makes a return and furnishes certain information to the U.S. owners and U.S. beneficiaries, in most cases the U.S. owner will somehow take a hand in the preparation of this Form. The Form 3520 might come next. Where there is an accumulation distribution in the picture, the preparation of this Form leads one rapidly to Form 4970 (Taxable Accumulation Distribution Of Trust) (see line 55), and from there to Schedule J of Form 1041. Form 1041 states that in the case of a foreign trust, the taxpayer should use Form 1040NR; but Form 1040NR is not designed for trusts and, in fact, leads the taxpayer back to Form 1041 and Schedule J, saying that the taxpayer should modify Form 1040NR to make it look like Form 1041.

This sequence of forms and cross-referencing is not a pretty sight, and it should be changed in the future. Since after 1977 the accumulation distribution rules and the matrix of forms pertaining to this subject apply in the main to foreign trusts, all the forms should be rewritten.

> ➔ There should be a "Form 1041NR" for foreign trusts (in lieu of the current form 1040NR) and a specially-worded version of Form 4970 (dropping, for example, the references to distributions of income accumulated before the beneficiary was born or reached age 21, which does not apply in the case of distributions from a foreign trust) should be made a part of the Form 1041NR as a statement to be provided to each beneficiary. A new Form 1041NR may have been contemplated and may still be in the works. The IRS Training Materials on foreign trusts state that "As a result of changes made by the 1996 law, non-grantor foreign trusts are expected to begin using a new Form, 1041NR."

As has already been mentioned, in order to complete these forms it is necessary for the taxpayer and his or her return preparer to be able to categorize correctly the trust at issue.

When working with the forms, it is sometimes difficult to determine which provision of the statute or rule in the regulations the form it is addressing. For example, there might be a series of questions, but it is difficult to determine which provision of the law is being dealt with by these questions. This information is provided where it seems especially useful. Understandably, the form and instructions often cannot give a complete explanation of the rules. It is best to review the Code and regulations at the same time you are completing the form. Unfortunately, as of this date, the regulations under sections 665-668 (dealing with the treatment of accumulation distributions) have not been amended to reflect the 1996 Act changes. It is advisable to run the calculation through specially-designed software and not simply rely upon the calculations on the face of the forms. For example, Form 3520 gives very little help understanding "distributable net income" and "undistributed net income." Also, the crediting of foreign and other taxes paid by the trust and the fact that these rules differ depending upon whether the trust is a "garden variety" foreign nongrantor trust or is a foreign nongrantor trust by virtue of the workings of section 672(f), is largely overlooked.[251]

16.1 Form 3520

Form 3520 is entitled "Annual Return To Report Transactions With Foreign Trusts And Receipt Of Certain Foreign Gifts." It is 6 pages in length. The instructions for the Form are 11 pages. Given the complexity of the form and the fact that a good deal of information may be necessary in order to complete it, this is not a form that can be prepared at the last minute—especially if there are accumulation distributions from a foreign nongrantor trust.

> ➔ Whoever is responsible for ensuring that the form is filed (usually the settlor or a beneficiary) should make sure that his or her return preparer is notified of the need to file this form well in advance of the due date—say, six months.
>
> ➔ A good practice is to notify the return preparer in writing, have the return preparer acknowledge receipt, and put the return preparer and the trustee in direct communication so as to avoid a great deal of "toing and froing."

A form, such as Form 3520, can cover a number of subjects. Ordinarily a filing will cover just one of the subjects; and the form will be blank with respect to the other matters.

[251] If the reader grows bored with the U.S. reporting rules and is looking for a new challenge, he can turn his attention to the Canadian rules on foreign trusts, which bear a striking resemblance to the U.S. rules, except Canada only taxes its citizens when resident in that country—which makes life a little simpler. Canadian disclosure forms, however, are every bit as vexing as the U.S. forms.

The 1998 Form 3520 contains a number of spaces that, had the prior law on the excise tax on transfers to certain foreign entites (section 1491) not been repealed, would have reported transactions under that provision. The amendments repealing the excise tax came somewhat late in the day; and therefore the IRS kept the lines and marked them "Reserved." The next version of the Form presumably will be redesigned.

In general, Form 3520 is used to report certain transactions with foreign trusts and receipt of certain large gifts or bequests from foreign persons. A separate Form 3520 must be filed for transactions with each foreign trust. Transactions with different foreign trusts cannot, in effect, be consolidated on one form.

A Form 3520 must be filed by the following persons:

1. Any person who is a "responsible party" for reporting a "reportable event" that occurred in the tax year in question; or any person who held an outstanding obligation of a related foreign trust (or a person related to the trust) that was treated as a "qualified obligation" during the year in question. A "responsible party" means the transferor in the case of a "reportable event" or the executor of the decedent's estate in any other case. A "reportable event" includes the creation of a foreign trust by a U.S. person; the transfer of any money or property, directly or indirectly, to a foreign trust by a U.S. person, including a transfer by reason of death if the transfer was a gratuitous transfer; the death of a citizen or resident of United States if the decedent was treated as the owner of any portion of a foreign trust under the grantor trust rules, or any portion of a foreign trust was included in the gross estate of the decedent; and the transformation of a trust that was not a foreign trust into a foreign trust. A "gratuitous transfer" to a foreign trust is any transfer to the foreign trust other than a transfer for fair market value or a corporate or partnership distribution. It will be noted that a transfer of property to trust can be considered a gratuitous transfer regardless whether the transfer is a gift for gift tax purposes. If a U.S. person transferred property to a trust in exchange for any type of interest in the trust, such an interest in the trust will be disregarded in determining whether fair market value has been received. In addition, a U.S. person will not be treated as making a transfer for fair market value merely because the transferor is deemed to have recognized gain on the transaction. If a

person transfers property to a foreign trust in exchange for an obligation of the trust (or person related to the trust), the transfer will be a gratuitous transfer unless the obligation is a qualified obligation.

> ➔ Executors of estates should be mindful that under certain circumstances they may be obliged to file a Form 3520.

> ➔ The requirement to file a Form 3520 can fall upon a minor. A parent or guardian can act on behalf of the minor.

2. Any person who, during the tax year in question, is treated as the owner of any part of the assets of a foreign trust under the grantor trust rules. It need not be the case that section 679 applies. If any of the grantor trust rules apply, then this reporting requirement comes into play.

3. Any person who, during the year in question, received a distribution from a foreign trust, or a related foreign trust held an outstanding obligation issued by that person (or person related to him or her) that that person treated as a "qualified obligation" during the year. A "qualified obligation" is defined as any obligation if the obligation is reduced to writing by an express written agreement; the term of the obligation does not exceed five years (including options to renew rollovers) and it is repaid within the five-year term; all payments on the obligation are denominated in U.S. dollars; the yield to maturity of the obligation is not less than one percent of the applicable Federal rate under section 1274(d) for the day on which the obligation is issued and not more than 130% of the applicable Federal rate; the U.S. person agrees to extend the period for assessment of any income or transfer tax attributable to the transfer and any consequential income tax changes for each year that the obligation is outstanding, to a date not earlier than three years after the maturity date of the obligation, unless the maturity date of the obligation does not extend beyond the end of the U.S. person's taxable year and is paid within such year; and the U.S. person reports the status of the note, including principal and interest payments, for every year that the loan is outstanding.

4. Any person who, during the year in question, received either more than $100,000 from a nonresident alien individual or a foreign estate (including foreign persons related to that nonresident alien individual or foreign estate) that the recipient treated as gifts or bequests or more than $10,557 from foreign corporations or foreign partnerships (including foreign persons related to such foreign corporations or foreign partnerships) that the recipient treated as gifts.

Some specific transactions need not be reported. These include transfers to foreign trusts described in the sections 402(b) (relating to taxation of the beneficiary of a nonexempt trust), 404(a)(4) (relating to a stock bonus, pension or profit-sharing trust created or organized outside the U.S.), or 404A (relating to deduction for certain foreign deferred compensation plans); fair market value transfers by a U.S. person to a foreign non-grantor trust (other than transfers that are treated as fair market value transfers by reason of the receipt of a qualified obligation); transfers to foreign trusts that have a current determination letter from the IRS recognizing their status as tax-exempt; transfers to, distributions from, and ownership of Certain Canadian Registered Retirement Savings Plans; distributions from foreign trusts that are taxable as compensation for services rendered (within the meaning of section 672(f)(2)(B) and the regulations thereunder), so long as the recipient reports the distribution as compensation income; and distributions from foreign trusts to domestic trusts that have a current determination letter from the IRS recognizing their status as tax-exempt.

Form 3520, in general, is due on the due date for the individual's federal income tax return, including extensions. A copy of the Form should be attached to the individual's income tax return. In addition, the filer should send a copy to the Internal Revenue Service Center in Philadelphia, Pennsylvania. If there are two settlors or transferors to the same foreign trust, or two U.S. beneficiaries of the same foreign trust, they can file a joint Form 3520, but only if they file a joint income tax return as well.

The tax return of the individual who is treated as a U.S. owner of all or some portion of the foreign trust's assets and the tax return of the U.S. beneficiary of the foreign trust must be consistent with the Form 3520-A (Annual Information Return Of A Foreign Trust With A U.S. Owner) filed by the foreign trust unless the inconsistency is reported to the IRS. Such inconsistency should be reported on a Form 8082 (Notice Of Inconsistent Treatment Or Administrative Adjustment Request).

If the return is filed by an individual or a fiduciary, it must be signed by that individual or fiduciary. It cannot be signed by someone acting on behalf of that person or pursuant to a power of attorney.

The Form asks whether the trust appointed a U.S. agent who can provide the IRS with relevant trust information. If the answer is yes, other identifying information must be supplied. If the answer is no (that is, a U.S. agent has not been named), the Form goes on to request, in the last part of Part I, Schedule B, a series of items in lines 16 through 19. It requests the name, address, status (whether the beneficiary is or is not U.S.), and identification number, if any, of the beneficiary; the name, address, and identification number, if any, of the trustee; the name, address and identification number, if any, of other persons having trust powers with respect to the trust, and a description of such powers. The following documents must be attached to the form: summary of all written and oral agreements and understandings relating to the trust, the trust instrument, any memorandum or letters of wishes, subsequent variances to the original trust documents, trust financial statements, "other trust documents." If any of these documents have been attached to Forms 3520 filed within the most recent three years, this need only be noted.

It is interesting to note that, with respect to the financial statements, the instructions state: "These financial statements must reasonably reflect the trust's accumulated income under U.S. income tax principles. For example, the statements must not treat capital gains as additions to trust corpus."

It would appear that the reference to "summary of all written and oral agreements and understandings" refers to a document created by or in the possession of the filer. A file memorandum prepared by the trustee and not shared with the filer is not such a document. Some trustees prefer not to have a letter of wishes or similar document because they can be misinterpreted in a number of ways. They prefer simply to speak with the settlor and prepare a file memorandum based on the conversation. While attaching such a file memorandum to the Form 3520 might be avoided, it should be recalled that an examiner can always ask for information; and if the information is not forthcoming, the IRS can assert that it is as if the U.S. agent had not been appointed.

An interesting question arises as to the effects of this Form on the confidentiality of the trust. If the complete trust indenture is given to the IRS, the information contained therein relating, for example, to the identity of the beneficiaries and the distributions that they will receive, is disclosed to the Service; and this information can be exchanged with other tax authorities. If the indenture is not automatically given to the IRS because a U.S. agent is named, it should be understood that this information can be subsequently requested. Can information about the trust and the trust indenture be provided but the names of the non-U.S. beneficiaries redacted? The problem is that it is impossible to say what will satisfy an international examiner in the course of an audit.

One of the things that everyone forgets (the IRS, Congress, tax advisors, clients) is that information put into a tax return is not protected in all cases. There are provisions in the Code providing confidentiality for so-called taxpayer information.[252] The IRS cannot blithely hand over taxpayer information, for example, to other departments of a government. However, if a settlor of a foreign trust, who has filed a Form 3520, is sued in a private lawsuit, there can be no guarantee that a court will not permit the other party to discover (get a copy of) his or her tax return.[253]

A U.S. agent is defined as a U.S. person that has a binding contract with a foreign trust that allows a U.S. person to act as the trust's authorized U.S. agent in applying sections 7602

[252] Section 6103 (relating to confidentiality and disclosure of returns and return information).

[253] *See* Rule 26, FED. RULES OF CIVIL PROCEDURE ("It is not ground for objection that the information sought will be inadmissible at the trial if the information sought appears to be reasonably calculated to lead to the discovery of admissible evidence.").

(relating to examinations of books and witnesses), section 7603 (relating to the service of summonses) and section 7604 (relating to enforcement of summonses) with respect to any request by the IRS to examine records or produce testimony related to the proper U.S. tax treatment of amounts distributed by, or required to be taken into account under the grantor trust rules with respect to a foreign trust or any summons by the IRS for such records or testimony. The U.S. settlor of the trust, a U.S. beneficiary of the trust or a domestic corporation controlled by the settlor or beneficiary may act as the U.S. agent. The identifying information, however, must be provided. Also, it is said in the instructions to the Form that if the person identified as the U.S. agent does not produce records or testimony requested or summonsed by the IRS, the IRS can redetermine the tax consequences of transactions with the trust and impose appropriate penalties. The agency relationship must be established by the time the U.S. person files the Form 3520 for the relevant taxable year and must continue as long as the statute of limitations remains open for the relevant taxable year. Typically, the statute of limitations period is three years, but it can be six years or longer. If the agent resigns, liquidates, or its responsibility as an agent terminates, a replacement must be put in place.

➔ It is strongly recommended that the person who is required to file not serve as the U.S. agent. He or she might lose or forget to respond to a contact from the IRS, or react in the wrong way to an inquiry. The U.S. agent should be the taxpayer's accountant or attorney.

Part I of the Form deals with transfers by U.S. persons to a foreign trust during the current taxable year. If a foreign trust has been created, the name of the trust creator (settlor) must be shown.

Among other things, the Form asks whether the transfer was a completed gift; and the instructions warn that it may be necessary to file a gift tax return. It also asks whether the person filing the Form will continue to be treated as the owner of the transferred assets after the transfer. In other words, will section 671 apply?

> ➔ In the case of a typical protection of assets trust, the U.S. settlor should complete Part I.

Schedules A and B of Part I deal with obligations of a related trust and gratuitous transfers to a foreign trust. It will be recalled that in the case of a loan of cash or marketable securities by a foreign trust to a U.S. grantor or a U.S. beneficiary (or a U.S. person related to the grantor or beneficiary), the statute (section 643(i)) treats the full amount of the loan as a distribution to the grantor or beneficiary except to the extent provided by Treasury regulations. According to the legislative history, Congress expected that Treasury regulations would provide an exception for loans with arm's-length terms. Congress further expected that consideration would be given to whether there is a reasonable expectation that the loan will be repaid. In addition, any subsequent repayment would be disregarded.[254] In Schedule A, the IRS is searching for transfers of property to a related foreign trust in exchange for an obligation of the trust or person related to the trust. In Schedule B, the Service is searching for transfers to the trust in exchange for no consideration or consideration worth less than the fair market value of the property transferred. Copies of the relevant documents are required to be attached to the Form.

Schedules C and D, lines 20-24, are reserved.

Schedule E deals with qualified obligations outstanding during the taxable year. The filer is asked whether he/she held an outstanding obligation of a related foreign trust that was treated as a "qualified obligation" in the current year. If the answer is yes, information is requested about that obligation. Among other things, the filer is asked whether the obligation still meets the criteria for a

[254] *See* JCT, General Explanation Of Tax Legislation Enacted In The 104th Congress, JCS-12-96 (Dec. 18, 1996).

qualified obligation. The definition of qualified obligation is provided in the instructions.

Part II ("U.S. Owner of a Foreign Trust") must be completed if the filer is considered the owner of any assets of the foreign trust under the grantor trust rules. It will be noted that Parts I and II both can apply where the taxpayer, a U.S. person, transfers property to a foreign trust during the current year and is treated as an owner of the assets of the trust under any of the grantor trust rules. The filer is asked to disclose the name of other foreign trust owners, if any, their address, country of residence, identification number, and the Code section that causes them to be treated as an owner. Information about the country where the trust was created, the country whose laws covered the foreign trust and the date of creation of the foreign trust is also requested. The Form then asks whether the foreign trust filed a Form 3520-A. Any U.S. person who is treated as an owner of assets of a foreign trust under the grantor trust rules is given the responsibility of ensuring that the foreign trust files a Form 3520-A and furnishes certain information (in the form of a Foreign Grantor Trust Owner Statement or a Foreign Grantor Trust Beneficiary Statement, as may be appropriate) to each U.S. person who is treated as an owner of trust's assets or who receives a distribution from the trust. If the answer is yes—the foreign trust did file the Form 3520-A—the filer who has received a Foreign Grantor Trust Owner Statement is requested to attach a copy of that statement. If the answer is no, the filer is asked to complete and attach a substitute Form 3520-A "to the best of your ability." The instructions warn that the filer may be liable for a penalty of 5% of the trust assets that the filer is treated as owning, plus additional penalties for continuing failure to file after notice. The gross value of the portion of the foreign trust that the filer is treated as owning must also the entered on line 29.

Part III focuses on distributions to a U.S. person from a foreign trust during the year in question. This is not the situation where the trust is a grantor trust and the income, in effect, is being "flowed through" to the settlor. Rather, this is the situation where the foreign trust is either a grantor trust (*i.e.*, it fits within one of the exceptions to the rule in section 672(f) (grantor trust rules not to result in foreign ownership) or a nongrantor accumulation trust. Some other questions that appear in other Parts appear here because this Part is directed at beneficiaries. The Form asks for information concerning cash amounts or the fair market value of property received from a foreign trust. It asks for the date of distribution, description of property received, fair market value of property received (determined as of the date of distribution), description of property transferred, and the fair market value of property transferred. It asks whether the filer received a loan from a related foreign trust (including an extension of credit in connection with the purchase of property from the trust). Also, it asks with respect to each obligation that the filer is treating as a "qualified obligation," whether the filer will agree to extend the period for assessment of any tax attributable to the transaction and any consequential income tax changes for each year that the obligation is outstanding to a date 3 years after the maturity date of the obligation. It asks whether the trust held an outstanding obligation of the filer that the filer treated as a "qualified obligation." If so, additional information is requested. Also, the Form asks whether the beneficiary received a Foreign Grantor Trust Beneficiary Statement from the foreign trust with respect to a distribution. If the answer is "yes," the filer must attach the statement but need not complete the remainder of this Part. If "no," the filer must complete Schedule A of Part III. The next question is whether the beneficiary received a Foreign Nongrantor Trust Beneficiary Statement with respect to a distribution. If the answer is "yes," the filer must attach the statement and complete either Schedule A (which is the default calculation for the taxation of trust distributions) or Schedule B (which is the actual calculation for the taxation of trust distributions). If the answer is "no," the filer is required to complete Schedule A (default calculation) with respect to the distribution.

As will be noted when reviewing Form 3520-A, there is no form Foreign Nongrantor Trust Beneficiary Statement that appears as a part of that Form. It is simply missing. The instructions to Form 3520 seem to assume that the statement exists. In any event, the instructions to Form 3520, at p. 7, set forth what such a statement must include. The taxpayer and his or her return preparer can construct a statement based on this information. It should include:

- An explanation of the appropriate U.S. tax treatment of any distribution or deemed distribution, or sufficient information to enable the U.S. beneficiary to establish the appropriate treatment of any distribution or deemed distribution.

- A statement identifying whether the owner of the trust is a partnership or a foreign corporation. (The IRS is on the lookout for situations where purported "gifts" in fact are taxable distributions.)

- A statement that the trust will permit either the IRS or the U.S. beneficiary to inspect and copy the trust's permanent books of account, records, and such other documents that are necessary to establish the appropriate treatment of any distribution or deemed distribution. (A statement is not necessary if the trust has appointed a U.S. agent.)

- The first and last day of the taxable year of the foreign trust to which the statement applies.

- A description of property (including cash) distributed or deemed distributed to the U.S. person during the taxable year, and the fair market value of property distributed.

- A statement as to whether the foreign trust has appointed a U.S. agent. If it has, the name of the agent, the address of the agent and the taxpayer identification number of the agent.

The instructions make clear that Part III is not intended to cover the case of an individual who is treated as the owner of the assets of the trust (for example, the settlor of a grantor trust) and who has properly picked up and reported income under the grantor trust rules.

If the beneficiary has clearly indicated that he believes that he has received a distribution from a foreign nongrantor trust, he must complete either the default calculation of trust distributions in Schedule A of Part III or the actual calculation of trust distributions in Schedule B of Part III. If there has been an accumulation distribution (the amount which would appear on Line 43 or Line 47), the taxpayer will need to calculate the interest charge, as discussed below. As a general rule, a beneficiary is not permitted to use Schedule A in one year and Schedule B in the next (the so-called "consistency rule").

However, a beneficiary can use Schedule B in the year that the trust terminates.

Since the taxpayer is given the choice of completing either Schedule A or Schedule B, naturally he will want to try to complete both and compare the results. It is assumed that the two Schedules work independently of one another, so the taxpayer does not have to pick up any figures from Schedule A to complete Schedule B and *vice versa.*

It is difficult to understand what Schedules A and B are accomplishing; and the instructions, frankly, are not a boatload of help. The following 3 examples are placed on the returns in order to illustrate how the forms work.

Example 1. Foreign complex nongrantor trust was created on July 1, 1994, at which time US$1,000,000 was contributed to the trust. In each of the years 1994, 1995, 1996, 1997, and 1998, the trust earned US$25,000 of ordinary income (interest income) and US$75,000 of capital gains; and it incurred no expenses. In the current year (1998), US$100,000 was distributed. During the 3 preceding years (1997, 1996 and 1995), the trust distributed US$100,000, US$100,000 and US$100,000, for a total of US$300,000; and there were no distributions in 1994. With respect to the current year, -0- was treated as an accumulation distribution. Distributable net income for 1998 was US$100,000.

Example 2. All the facts are the same as in *Example 1*, except in the current year (1998), US$500,000 was distributed. Also, during the 3 preceding years (1997, 1996 and 1995), the trust distributed US$50,000, US$50,000 and US$50,000, for a total of US$150,000. With respect to the current year, US$250,000 was treated as an accumulation distribution. Distributable net income for 1998 was US$100,000.

Example 3. All the facts are the same as in *Example 1*, except in the current year (1998), US$50,000 was distributed. Also, during the 3 preceding years (1997, 1996 and 1995), the trust distributed US$200,000, US$200,000 and US$200,000, for a total of US$600,000. With respect to the current year, -0- was treated as an accumulation distribution. Distributable net income for 1998 was US$100,000.

This exercise, it can be imagined, would be greatly complicated if present were income required to be distributed currently, tax-exempt income, tax credits, multiple trusts, and the like.

	Schedule A - Default Calculation of Trust Distributions			
37	Enter amount from line 33 (total distributions received)	$100,000.00	$500,000.00	$50,000.00
38	Number of years the trust has been a nongrantor trust	5.00	5.00	5.00
39	Enter total distributions received from the foreign trust during the 3 preceding tax years	$300,000.00	$150,000.00	$150,000.00
40	Mutiple line 39 by 1.25	$375,000.00	$187,500.00	$187,500.00
41	Average distribution. Divide line 40 by 3 and enter result	$125,000.00	$62,500.00	$62,500.00
42	Amount treated as ordinary income earned in the current year. Enter the smaller of line 37 or line 41. (This amount should be reported on the beneficiary's Form 1040, Schedule E, Part III.)	$100,000.00	$62,500.00	$62,500.00
43	Amount treated as accumulation distribution. Subtract line 42 from line 37. If -0- or less, enter -0- and do not complete Schedules B and C.	$0.00	$437,500.00	$0.00
44	Compute applicable number of years of trust. Divide line 38 by 2. Enter here		2.50	
	Schedule B - Actual Calculation of Trust Distributions			
45	Enter amount from line 33 (total distributions received)	$100,000.00	$500,000.00	$50,000.00
46	Amount received by the beneficiary that is treated as ordinary income of the trust in the current year	$25,000.00	$25,000.00	$25,000.00
47	Amount treated as accumulation distribution. If -0- or less, enter -0- and do not complete the rest of Part	$0.00	$250,000.00	$0.00

	III.			
48	Amount treated [by the trust] as capital gains in the current year.	$75,000.00	$75,000.00	$25,000.00
49	Amount treated [by the trust] as distribution from trust corpus.	$0.00	$150,000.00	$0.00
50	Enter any other amount received from the foreign trust.	none	none	none
51	Amount of foreign trust's aggregate undistributed net income.	$0.00	$250,000.00	$0.00
52	Amount of foreign trust's weighted undistributed net income.	$0.00	$700,000.00	$0.00
53	Compute applicable number of years of trust. Divide line 52 by like 51. Enter here	0.00	2.80	0.00

It will be noted that only in the case of *Example 2* was there an accumulation distribution (the amount shown on line 43) necessitating the completion of line 44 (that is, showing the "applicable number of years of trust," which is arrived at by dividing line 38 (in these examples, 5) by 2, so as to arrive at, in these examples, 2.5.

As a prerequisite to using Schedule B, the taxpayer must attach a copy of the Foreign Nongrantor Trust Beneficiary Statement to the return. (Interestingly, as previously noted, while a Foreign Grantor Trust Owner Statement and a Foreign Grantor Trust Beneficiary Statement are supplied as part of Form 3520-A, no Foreign Nongrantor Trust Beneficiary Statement is supplied; so the taxpayer will have to create one out of whole cloth.)

Line 46 of Schedule B (where the taxpayer is asked to enter the amount received by him from the foreign trust that is treated as ordinary income of the trust in the current taxable year) is especially confusing. What happens if the trust received half of its income in the form of capital gains and half as ordinary income? How does the beneficiary determine whether the income received by him comes from the ordinary income earnings of the trust or the capital gains of the trust? Also, it is not clear where the rule that capital gains of the trust lose their character (that is, are converted into ordinary income) appears in the form.

Line 47 is similarly confusing. What is the "amount treated as accumulation distribution"? Is it meant "treated by the trust as accumulation distribution"? How is this figure arrived at by the taxpayer? The instructions are not helpful. The taxpayer must go back to sections 665-667 and the regulations. The definition of "accumulation distribution" appears in section 665(b). In general, the term "accumulation distribution" means, for the taxable year of the trust, the amount by which amounts of income other than amounts for such taxable year required to be distributed currently exceed the distributable net income for such year (reduced—but not below zero —by amounts of income for such taxable year required to be distributed currently). The taxpayer also can go to Form 1040NR, which must be modified to look like Form 1041, and develop the accumulation distribution figure.

Line 48 is confusing because of the reference to capital gains. Again, is it meant "treated as capital gains by the trust"? This must be the case. The instructions are silent on this subject.

Line 49 is confusing as well. Is it meant "treated as distribution from trust corpus by the trust"? This must be the case. Again, the instructions do not provide sufficient information. Presumably, the amount treated as a distribution from trust corpus refers only to such amount in the current tax year; but there is no reference on the form or in the instructions to "current tax year."

Schedule C (Calculation of Interest Charge) is intended to calculate the interest charge under section 668 (Interest Charge On Accumulation Distributions From Foreign Trusts). In order to complete the schedule, first it is necessary to complete Form 4970 (Tax on Accumulation Distribution of Trusts). Line 50 of Schedule C asks for the tax on total accumulation distribution from line 28 of Form 4970. Form 4970 will have to be modified to fit the situation since it is designed for distributions from a domestic trust. For example, it refers to distributions of income accumulated before the beneficiary was born or reached age 21; and this provision does not apply to a foreign trust. In order to complete the Form 4970, it will be necessary to complete a Form 1041, including Schedule J of that Form. In this process the taxpayer will develop the figures for "tax on accumulation distribution," "current distribution that is considered distributed in earlier tax years," "distributable net income [for the current year]," "accumulation distribution [for the current taxable year]," and adjusted total income or loss for the trust.

In order properly to prepare the returns flowing from *Example 2*, above, it is necessary to prepare "dummy" Forms 1041 for 1994-1998. In this case, the Forms for 1995-1997 will look the same; the ones for 1994 an 1998 will be different. Next Schedule J (Accumulation Distribution for Certain Complex Trusts), which is an attachment to the 1998 Form 1041, can be prepared. Then Form 4970 can be prepared, picking up figures from Schedule J.

Form 4970 should look like the following. For purposes of this presentation, taxable income figures for 1993 through 1997 have been assumed. (Line 13) Details concerning adjustment to arrive at adjusted income, exemptions, etc. have been ignored. (Line 16) For simplicity's sake, the tax rate used to compute income tax amounts on line 17 is the 1998 single individual tax rate. Tax credits and alternative minimum taxes are ignored. (Lines 20 and 22).

Part I	Average Income and Determination of Computation Years		
1	Amount of current distribuion that is considered distributed in earlier tax years (from Schedule J (Form 1041).		$250,00.00
2	Distributions of income accumulated before you were born or reached age 21		0.00
3	Subtract line 2 from line 1.		$250,00.00
4	Taxes imposed on the trust on amounts from line 3 (from Schedule J (Form 1041), line 37, column (b))		0.00
5	Total (add lines 3 and 4)		$250,00.00
6	Tax-exempt interest included on line 5 (from Schedule J (Form 1041), line 37, column (c))		0.00
7	Taxable part of line 5 (subtract line 6 from line 5)		$250,00.00
8	Number of trust's earlier tax years in which amounts on line 7 are considered distributed		4
9	Average annual amount considered distributed (divide line 3 by line 8)	$62,500	
10	Multiply line 9 by .25	$15,625	
11	Number of earlier tax years to be take into account		4.00
12	Average amount for recomputing tax (divide line 7 by line 11)		$62,500

13	Enter your taxable income before this distribution for the 5 immediately preceding tax years	$100,000	$100,000	$100,000	$100,000	$100,000

Part II Tax Attributable to the Accumulation Distribution				
		(a) 1996	(b) 1995	(c) 1994
14	Enter the amounts from line 13, eliminating the highest and lowest taxable income years	$100,000	$100,000	$100,000
15	Enter amount from line 12 in each column	$62,500	$62,500	$62,500
16	Recomputed taxable income (add lines 14 and 15)	$162,500	$162,500	$162,500
17	Income tax on amounts on line 16	$46,958	$46,958	$46,958
18	Income tax before credits on line 14 income	$25,863	$25,863	$25,863
19	Additional tax before credits (subtract line 18 from line 17)	$21,095	$21,095	$21,095
20	Tax credit adjustment	0.00	0.00	0.00
21	Subtract line 20 from line 19	$21,095	$21,095	$21,095
22	Alternative minimum tax adjustments	0.00	0.00	0.00
23	Combine lines 21 and 22	$21,095	$21,095	$21,095
24	Add columns (a) (b) and (c), line 23			$63,285
25	Divide the line 24 amount by 3			$21,095
26	Multiply the amount on line 25 by the number of years on line 11			$84,380
27	Enter the amount from line 4			0.00
28	Partial tax attributable to the accumulation distribution (subtract line 27 from 26) (If zero or less, enter -0-.)			$84,380

16.2 Form 3520-A

Form 3520-A (Annual Information Return Of Foreign Trust With A U.S. Owner) is required by section 6048(b). If it is comprised of

Part I, General Information, Part II, Foreign Trust Income Statement, Part III, Foreign Trust Balance Sheet, a statement called "Foreign Grantor Trust Owner Statement," including a "Statement Of Foreign Trust Income Attributable To U.S. Owner," and a statement called "Foreign Grantor Trust Beneficiary Statement." This is an annual information return. It applies only where there is a foreign trust with a U.S. owner (for example, where a U.S. person created the trust and is treated as the owner of the trust assets under, say, section 679).

➔ Does a foreign nongrantor trust, that is, a foreign trust that does not have a U.S. owner, have to file a Form 3520-A? Technically, the answer, from the face of the Form, is no. However, if the trust has made a distribution to a U.S. beneficiary, the U.S. beneficiary probablywill want the turst to do two things: one, appoint a U.S. agent (and the appointment, of course, must be signed by the trustee) and, two, file a Foreign Nongrantor Trust Beneficiary Statement (which again must be signed by the trustee). These things can best be done by filing a Form 3520-A, providing the general information called for on Lines 1a-g, answering yes to the question at Line 2 ("Did the foreign trust appoint a U.S. agent...who can provide IRS with all revelant [sic] trust information?"), and attaching the Foreign Nongrantor Trust Beneficiary Statement "made up" following the instructions at page 7 of the Instructions to Form 3520. A copy of the Foreign Nongrantor Trust Beneficiary Statement should be furnished to each U.S. beneficiary who received a distribution during the taxable year. (This should be furnished by the 15th day of the 3rd month following the end of the trust's tax year, or later, if pursuant to an extension of time to file.) A copy of the appointment (or authorization) should also be attached to the form 3520-A. The trust might attach a statement that reads along the following lines: "This trust does not have a U.S. owner. It is a foreign nongrantor trust, but

> because it has a U.S. beneficiary who received a distribution, it is filing this return."

Each U.S. person who is treated as an owner of the foreign trust is responsible for ensuring that the trust files this annual return setting forth a full and complete accounting of trust activities, trust operations and other relevant information. The U.S. owner is similarly responsible for ensuring that the trust furnishes required information—in the form of prescribed statements—to the U.S. owners and U.S. beneficiaries of the trust.

Interesting questions as to liability no doubt will arise. For example, what happens if the foreign trust does not file the Form 3520-A, which includes the appointment of a U.S. agent? A U.S. beneficiary is audited, and the Service determines that he owes additional tax. The U.S. beneficiary is put in the position of having to accept the IRS's inclusion of income in his return because adequate records are not provided and a U.S. agent has not been named. Section 6048(c)(2)(A). Can the beneficiary bring an action against the settlor (the U.S. owner)? Under the circumstances, is the U.S. settlor in the position of a fiduciary with respect to the obligation to ensure that a return is filed? Can the beneficiary bring an action against the trustee for breach of fiduciary duty? The Code puts the onus on the U.S. owner for ensuring that the forms are filed. However, for purposes of determining whether there has been a breach of fiduciary duty, tax rules aside, can it be argued that the trustee knew or should have known that failing to file the required form would result in an additional tax for the beneficiary? Also, it seems that a settlor of the trust can waive liability of the trustee for consequences flowing from failure to file a return or filing an incorrect return; but it is difficult to see how such a waiver might foreclose an action by the beneficiary.

Form 3520-A is due by the 15th day of the third month after the end of the trust's taxable year. By the same date copies of the Foreign Grantor Trust Owner Statement and the Foreign Grantor Trust Beneficiary Statement must be furnished to the intended recipients. An extension of time to file this Form and statements may be granted. Form 4758 (Application For Extension Of Time To File Certain Excise, Income, Information, And Other Returns) should be used for this purpose.

> → The due date for Form 3520-A is one month prior to the due date for Form 3520.

Deferred compensation and charitable trusts do not have to file the Form. Deferred compensation trusts are those described in sections 402(b), 404(a)(4) or 404A. Charitable trusts are those that have been determined by the IRS to be tax-exempt under section 501(c)(3).

The Form must be signed by the trustee. If the Form has been prepared by a return preparer, the return preparer also must sign and provide its Social Security number. If the return is filed by an individual or fiduciary, it must be signed by that individual or fiduciary. If filed by a corporate trustee, it must be signed by the president, vice president, treasurer, assistant treasurer, chief accounting officer, or other corporate officer (such as a tax officer) who is authorized signed. It might be noted that many foreign corporations do not have corporate officers in the same sense that a U.S. corporation has corporate officers; instead, they have directors, some of which are executive directors and others of which are non-executive directors. There might be a managing director.

> → The fiduciary (*i.e.*, the trustee of the foreign trust, which presumably is a corporate trustee) can sign the return itself or, if it wishes, it can cause an agent to sign the return. "The return may be signed for the taxpayer [the fiduciary] by an agent who is duly authorized in accordance with §31.6011(a)-7 to make such return."[255] A power of attorney must accompany a return signed by an agent. The power of attorney should take the form of a Form 2848. Care should be taken to make sure that the Form 2848 is the current version of this Form.

In Part I, the name of the trust, its identification number (if any), address, etc., are provided. The question is asked: "Did the foreign trust appoint a U.S. agent. . . who can provide IRS all relevant trust

[255] § 301.6061-1, Income Tax Regs.

information?" If the answer is yes, there need not be attached a list of items: summary of all written oral agreements and understandings relating to the trust, the trust instrument, memoranda or letters of wishes, subsequent variances to original trust documents, and other trust documents. If the answer is no, these items must be attached, if they exist. The instructions point out that if documents are required to be attached, they should include a summary of the terms of the trust that includes a summary of any oral agreements or understandings with the trustee, whether or not legally enforceable.

The Form asks for the name of the U.S. agent, if one has been appointed, and the identification number, address, etc. for the agent. The instructions state that a U.S. grantor, a U.S. beneficiary, or a domestic corporation controlled by the grantor or beneficiary can act as the U.S. agent. The instructions do not say anything about the appointment of the return preparer, accounting firm, attorney, or other advisor. It is suggested that a U.S. beneficiary or grantor should not act as the U.S. agent, but, instead, the return preparer or an accounting or legal advisor should be named.

For the appointment of the U.S. agent to be valid, the trust and the agent must enter into a binding agreement substantially in the form provided in the instructions. This form authorization, modified slightly to suit a corporate trustee, is as follows:

AUTHORIZATION OF AGENT

> [The John Smith Family Trust] hereby expressly authorizes [ABC Accounting Firm] to act as its agent solely for purposes of sections 7602, 7603, and 7604 of the Internal Revenue Code with respect to a request to examine records or produce testimony relating to the proper treatment of amounts required to be taken into account under the rules of section 6048(b)(1)(a) or to any summons for such records or testimony. The below-designed person hereby certifies that it has the authority to execute this authorization of agent to act on behalf of [the John Smith Family Trust].

Signature of trustee	Title	Date

____
Name of person (type or print)

____
Identification number (if any)

____
Address

[ABC Accounting Firm] hereby accepts this appointment to act as agent for [the John Smith Family Trust] for the above purpose. The below-signed person hereby certifies that it has the authority to execute this authorization of agent to act on behalf of [the John Smith Family Trust] and agrees to accept service of process for the above purposes.

__________________ _____________ ____________
Signature of trustee Title Date

____
Name of person (type or print)

____
Identification number (if any)

____
Address

Line 5 of Part I asks if the trust transferred any property to another entity during the taxable year. If the answer is yes, the instructions tell the preparer what type of statement must be attached. Presumably a distribution to a beneficiary is not covered. Under these circumstances, it is not clear whether "entity" includes an individual. Normally, "entity" means something other than a natural person. The term "person" generally means individuals as well as entities, such as corporations, partnerships and the like. However, the instructions, at page 3, use the term "person." This question is searching for information concerning indirect distributions from the trust—for example, where the trust makes a transfer to a corporation, and the corporation turns around and makes a transfer to one of the beneficiaries. Describing the statement, the instructions say that it should include "to the extent known" a description of any subsequent transfer. Sometimes the trustee, which is the person filing Form 3520-A, will know what course the property traveled after its transfer from the trust; however, sometimes this will not be the case. There is nothing to impute the knowledge of a settlor, beneficiary or trust protector (or Trust advisor) to the trustee.

Part II is the foreign trust income statement taken from the books and records of the foreign trust. Information about the amount and character of the trust income is obviously necessary in the case of a foreign grantor trust. It is also necessary in the case of a foreign non-grantor trust where there has been an accumulation distribution. Trustee and advisor fees are recognized.

Line 17a asks for the total amount of distributions from the trust to all persons whether U.S. or foreign. Lines 17b and 17c ask for the details of distributions to the U.S. owner or U.S. beneficiaries.

➔ The name of the recipient and other detailed information is not required with respect to foreign beneficiaries.

Part III is the Foreign Trust Balance Sheet showing amounts at the beginning of the tax year and the end of the tax year. Line 18 represents the accumulated trust income, that is, the total amount of trust income accumulated and not distributed.

The Foreign Grantor Trust Owner Statement appears on page 3 of the Form. It provides, among other things, the name of the foreign trust, the name of the U.S. agent, the name of the trustee, the taxable year of the owner of the foreign trust to which the statement relates, and the name of the U.S. owner. It will be recalled that the complete Form, including statements, is filed with the IRS Service Center in Philadelphia. A copy of this statement is sent by the filer to each U.S. person who is treated as an owner. If there are two or more owners, each should receive information relating only to his or her portion of the trust.

Line 7 of the Statement asks for an explanation of the facts and law (including the section of the Internal Revenue Code) that establishes that the foreign trust (or portion of the foreign trust) is treated for U.S. tax principles as owned by the U.S. person.

> ➔ For example, if the foreign trust were created by a U.S. person and it fell within the provisions of section 679 because the trust has a U.S. beneficiary, the statement might read: "The trust is treated for U.S. tax purposes as owned by the grantor, Mr. Smith, under section 679."

At the bottom of this Statement there is a statement of foreign trust income attributable to U.S. owner. This statement provides the information regarding income and expenses attributable to the U.S. owner, which that owner must include in his or her income tax return. The instructions remark that the foreign trust might need to furnish the U.S. owner with additional information, including applicable schedules.

The last page of the Form is the Foreign Grantor Trust Beneficiary Statement. This statement provides, among other things, the name of the foreign trust, the name of the U.S. agent, the name of the trustee, the name of the U.S. beneficiary, and a description of the property (including cash) distributed.

Similar to Line 7 of the Foreign Grantor Trust Owner Statement, Line 8 of this Statement asks for an explanation of the facts and law (including the section of the Internal Revenue Code) that establishes that the foreign trust (or portion of the foreign trust) is treated for U.S. tax principles as owned by another person.

> ➔ This explanation can be drafted in a way that does not disclose the name of the U.S. owner. For example, the explanation might read: "The trust is treated under section 679 as owned by another person (that is, as a grantor trust) because it was created by a

> U.S. person—not the U.S. beneficiary name above—and it has U.S. beneficiaries."

Line 9 asks if the foreign trust owner is an individual, partnership or corporation. It does not ask for additional details. (The owner of the trust—that is, the grantor of a grantor trust—might, in fact, be a trust.)

Chapter 17

Compliance Issues; Collection and Enforcement; Trusts in Treaties

17.1 General

Taxpayers have the obligation to report properly their income and expenses. This is a general requirement that appears in the tax law. To this, as has been discussed in Chapter 9, there are special requirements relating to a foreign trust.

Also, in any challenge made by a taxpayer of the IRS assessment, the taxpayer generally has the burden of proving the correctness of his position.

The IRS will audit foreign trusts; that is, it will audit the U.S. person who creates a trust or receives distributions from the trust. It can be anticipated that it also will audit large gifts and bequests from foreign donors to U.S. recipients.

17.2 IRS audits; IRS Training Materials

Until just a few years ago, it might be said that IRS International Examiners were not very knowledgeable on the subject of the taxation of foreign trusts. The Service did not pay much attention to the subject of foreign trusts. It directed almost all of its attention in the international tax area to large case audits, many of them having to do with the allocation of income and expenses under section 482. But this has changed.

Recently, the IRS Training Materials, called FOREIGN TRUSTS AND THE IRS, were made public.[256] This publication is a guide (a

[256] The materials are reprinted in Bruce (Editor), UNITED STATES INTERNAL REVENUE SERVICE INTERNATIONAL TAX COMPLIANCE INFORMATION, Vol. 7 (Kluwer, 1998) ("IRS Training Materials"). They were obtained by the author for the publisher Kluwer Law International pursuant to a Freedom of Information Act request.

set of course materials) prepared under the auspices of the International Institute in the Corporate Education School of Taxation of the IRS. It grew out of an audit guide written by the Project Office for Foreign Trust Compliance managed by the Los Angeles District Office. It is based largely on the experiences of 25 examiners, attorneys and managers.

The guide contains ten lessons and five appendices. The lessons are: Definitions and Structure; Trust Creation and Termination; Taxation of Income; Other Tax Issues; Uses of Foreign Trusts; Examples of Abuse of Foreign Trusts; Audit Techniques; Sources of Information; Obtaining Information from Taxpayers. The appendices are: Form 3520-A Pre-Audit Checklist; Initial Interview Questions; Initial Information Document Request; Typical Foreign Trust Jurisdictions; and Code and Regulations.

The materials take into consideration the new rules enacted in August of 1996 (the Small Business Job Protection Act of 1996 (P.L. 104-188)). They pre-date, however, Notice 97-34 (which deals with the details of the new law in advance of regulations), the revised Form 3520-A and Announcement 98-30 (which provides limited relief from section 6677 penalties for U.S. owners of some foreign trusts that fail to file their 1997 information returns on time). Thus, some of the details concerning the reporting rules and deadlines are not included. They also predate the replacement of section 1491 with section 684.

The problem so far as the IRS is concerned, it is said in the Introduction to the IRS Training Materials, is essentially a tax haven problem. "Trustees in tax havens and their clients know that their actions are veiled from tax authorities by banking and commercial secrecy laws and by lack of tax treaties or tax information exchange agreements. They can create paper entities to disguise the real parties to the transactions, and many are willing to create false documents to disguise the real nature of transactions." This view indicates that the IRS's primary focus is on relatively blatant fraudulent schemes; but it also is the case that much of what is taught in the guide bears on far more sophisticated arrangements.

The materials are too voluminous to quote at length, but there follows some of the highlights.

- For a trust to be recognized as such, the beneficiary must not control the property.

- A "trust protector" with unlimited power of removal holds unlimited power over the trustee's actions and may subvert the trustee's independence.

- As to Form 926 (Return by a Transferor of Property to a Foreign Corporation, Foreign Estate of Trust, or Foreign Partnership), it is said that this form is required to be filed on any transfer of property abroad, even if section 1491 does not apply and the transfer is not taxable. (This form is now out of date, given the repeal of section 1491.)

- A discussion of the excise tax on incomplete gifts delves into the problems of a section 1491 excise tax at the time of the death of a grantor. (After the repeal of section 1491 and the enactment of section 684, the question is how section 684 should apply.)

- When it comes to the actual computation of tax on accumulation distributions, the examiner is advised to get help. "Determination of accumulation distributions is complicated because of numerous special rules."

- Withholding tax is required on payments of fixed or determinable annual or periodic income from U.S. sources paid to a foreign trust even if the U.S. grantor is treated as the owner of the trust assets. The grantor has to ask for a credit.

- "Withholding agents who make payments to foreign fiduciaries are required to file a separate 1042S for each ultimate recipient of income, if known. It is common for a foreign bank, acting as trustee, to invest trust funds in the United States through an American affiliate. In some cases, the affiliate files a single 1042S showing the trustee bank as recipient of the income. In fact, the American affiliate often knows or can learn the identities of the ultimate recipients. Some banks have refused to provide the information to conceal the identities of their clients despite penalties."

- "Foreign trusts may be legitimately used for asset protection and estate planning purposes." Also, "American grantors can still use foreign trusts to make gifts to foreigners tax free to them [the recipients]."

- Examiners are told of the usefulness of Fin CEN, which is a Treasury Department organization geared primarily to money laundering.

- A U.S. person who has a beneficial interest in more than 50% of the assets of a trust or from which he/she receives more than 50% of the current income (for example, someone who is the grantor of a foreign trust) must file a Form TD F 90-22.1 for bank accounts as to which the trust is owner of record or holder of legal title.

- All Forms 3520 and 3520-A are sent to the Foreign Trust Desk at the IRS Facility at La Mirada, California. "Each item in the database has been screened for potential audit issues and incomplete filings."

- Regarding summonses, if a settlor chooses a foreign branch of a U.S. bank, or presumably an affiliate of that bank, to be its trustee, a summons may be issued to the U.S bank to produce its branch records.

Under the discussion of abusive trusts contained in the materials, there is an informative exploration of the use of U.S. family limited partnerships in connection with a foreign trust. There have been thousands of such arrangements created with the help of aggressive U.S. attorneys. These are being scrutinized by the Service.

Oddly, the IRS Training Materials place an emphasis on "business purpose" in a number of places throughout the materials. For example, under audit techniques, "Any time agents encounter use of tax haven trust they should determine why the taxpayer is using them and whether that is a real business purpose." There is no business purpose test for the validity of a trust. Trusts, almost as a matter of definition, never have a business purpose.

17.3 Observations

Stepping back from these materials, it can be said that the IRS is clearly focused on abusive situations, of which there would appear to be many.

Taxpayers should not be afraid to file the necessary returns. First, and most important, the returns must be filed in order to comply with the laws. Secondly, the rules relating to foreign trusts are sufficiently clear that taxpayers, in most instances, can "live with" them quite comfortably.

If the taxpayer is audited, the U.S. agent, assuming one is in place, and the taxpayer's legal and accounting advisers should be able to handle any questions in relatively short order. Many foreign trusts really do not have much to do with taxes but with family-related matters. The IRS will only be interested in those that are producing miraculous tax results for the U.S. taxpayers.

Again, the taxpayer has the burden of proof. If a U.S. agent has been appointed, this person can act as a point of contact for information requests and administrative summons. It should also be recalled that the IRS can use the provisions of section 982, which relates to Formal Document Requests for documents located outside the U.S. Once a Formal Document Request has been issued by the Service, the taxpayer has 90 days to comply with the request. If a taxpayer fails to comply substantially with a Formal Document Request, then any court having jurisdiction of a civil proceeding can prohibit the introduction by the taxpayer of any of the records covered by the request.

As time goes on, it will be interesting to see how audit practices evolve. There will no doubt be a number of interesting issues that arise. The foreign trust reporting and penalty rules are modeled on those that were previously put in place for U.S. corporations owned by foreign groups.[257] What must be recalled, however, is that individuals and family groups do not behave like business entities.

[257] Section 6038A (relating to information with respect to certain foreign-owned corporations).

Also, it would seem, there is a legitimate issue concerning privacy. The trustee of a foreign trust will feel obliged to safeguard information about the trust. For example, what will be required to prove that the settlor of a foreign grantor trust (one which falls within the rule that a foreign trust can be a grantor trust because it is revocable) is still alive? Also, with respect to large gifts, what will the U.S. recipient need to prove? If he received a $200,000 gift from a foreign donor, will a letter from the donor declaring that the gift is just that, a gift, suffice? It seems that this topic is left to the general law concerning burden of proof. If the IRS does not believe the taxpayer, then the taxpayer will have to be prepared to make his case in a convincing fashion before the United States Tax Court or some other court.[258]

> ➔ When selecting a trustee, depending upon the circumstances, it might be useful to choose one who would actually meet with the IRS and, if necessary, give testimony in court, There are not many individual trust officers who could perform this role well.

17.4 Liability of trustees

There are several types of liability that the trustee of a foreign trust should be aware of. The first derives from U.S. statutory provisions imposing personal liability on fiduciaries for unpaid taxes. The second is in the nature of a liability for breach of fiduciary duty when some act or omission of the trustee in connection with the reporting or payment of U.S. taxes causes someone else, for example, the beneficiaries, to be harmed. Another type of liability might arise in the more extreme case where a trustee engages in a fraud.

---

[258] Courts can be quite skeptical when information is located outside United States and it is suspected that the taxpayer could obtain that information if he or she wished. The subject has arisen in a number of contexts. For an interesting "playing out" of the subject in a case involving foreign corporations, see *Gerling Int'l Ins. Co. v. Commissioner*, 86 T.C. 468 (1986) (J. Tannenwald), *reversed and remanded*, 839 F. 2d 131 (3rd Cir. 1988).

The purpose of this discussion is simply to raise the issues—not exhaustively analyze the rules or their application.

17.4.1 Fiduciary liability for unpaid taxes

Since 1799, U.S. law has contained provisions imposing personal liability on fiduciaries, such as executors of estates and trustees of trusts, for unpaid taxes. The underlying concept is that a fiduciary must not pay other debts before paying a tax claim of the Government where this amounts to a preferring of others over the Government. It will be noted that fiduciary liability does not depend upon the trustee benefiting in any way, but upon paying amounts or transferring property to persons other than the Government when the Government is entitled to the status of a high-priority but unsecured general creditor. Fiduciary liability can be collected out of any assets belonging to the fiduciary; the funds need not be traceable to the individuals and transactions involved in the matter. For fiduciary liability to attach, it would appear that the taxpayer—which might be the grantor, the beneficiary or the trust itself—must be insolvent and the fiduciary's payment or transfer must have occurred at a time when the Government's claims remained unsatisfied. In other words, the payment or transfer must have defeated the Government's collection of its tax claim. Distributions to beneficiaries can be treated as payments to creditors. The tax claim need not have ripened into an assessment.

There is little authority with respect to foreign fiduciaries and it is difficult to envision situations where personal liability, as a practical matter, might come into play. With most foreign trusts, the taxpayer will either be the grantor (with a foreign grantor trust, the grantor would be the taxpayer) or a beneficiary of the trust (with a foreign nongrantor trust, the trust will not be subject to U.S. tax—in fact, it is cast by section 641(b) as a nonresident alien individual who is not present in the United States at any time; but the U.S. beneficiaries frequently will be subject to tax on distributions). With a grantor trust, there may be a situation where the trustee, under the influence of a protector or the grantor, makes distributions or makes payments to third parties at a time when the grantor owed taxes. It would seem that if the trust is to be respected as a valid trust, the trustee has no obligation to pay the taxes in question and is not preferring others over the U.S. Government. The case becomes more difficult if, in fact, the trust is a "sham;" in which case, the trustee might be said to hold the assets for the putative grantor and his or her creditors, including the U.S. Government. Unique issues may also arise where the grantor of a foreign grantor trust dies and the foreign trustee must make distributions to the grantor's heirs, much in the same way as the executor of an estate.

17.4.2 Fiduciary liability for breach of fiduciary responsibility

Statutory and case law rules exist in all common law jurisdictions and many other jurisdictions imposing liability on a fiduciary for breach of a fiduciary responsibility that results in damages for the beneficiaries. This is a fundamental concept of trust law. The action can be brought in any jurisdiction where the trustee is subject to suit; but normally it would be brought in the "home" jurisdiction of the trustee. A number of interesting questions arise including which law should apply.

The new reporting rules and penalties imposed by the Small Business Job Protection Act of 1996 raise a number of issues that did not exist in the past. How these issues are decided remains to be seen; it is too early to say at this date.

For example, assume that the grantor of a foreign grantor trust notifies the foreign trustee that it should file a Form 3520-A and complete and send the appropriate statements forming a part of the Form. The trustee forgets to take any action. As a result, the U.S. grantor is determined to have failed to file information required by section 6048 and is assessed with a penalty equal to 35 percent of the gross reportable amount under section 6677. Will the grantor be able to recover damages in an action against the trustee in the jurisdiction where the trustee resides?

> ➔ It is possible to think of many situations where this type of controversy can arise. This being the case, it would seem that trustees of foreign trusts with U.S. settlors and beneficiaries will want carefully to review the terms of their role as trustee and institute procedures that will reasonably assure performance of those services for which they are responsible. With respect to the filing of U.S.

information and other returns, all concerned parties might agree that these returns will be prepared by a competent U.S. return preparer and, perhaps, reviewed by the grantor and/or beneficiaries, or representatives nominated by them. There is probably not one "correct" approach to the problem. But it is necessary for the trustee to give the issue careful attention.

17.4.3 Fiduciary liability for fraud

There have been instances where foreign trustees have clearly cooperated with U.S. promoters and "settlors" in the creation and operation of a fraudulent foreign trust. These trusts were fraudulent, for example, because with the knowing participation of the parties, they presented one picture to the tax authorities when, in fact, the reality was quite different. For example, a trust might report holdings in entities that were neither controlled foreign corporations nor passive foreign investment companies; but the truth of the matter—known to the trustee—might be that a company owned by the trust is owned, through nominees provided by the trust company, by the settlor; and the trustee knew the tax consequences flowing from this misrepresentation. This action is a fraudulent misrepresentation of the facts. Query whether the United States could bring an action against the trust company in its home jurisdiction for what amounts to common law fraud.

→ U.S. settlors, beneficiaries and advisers have been known to conjure up some very aggressive strategies for reducing U.S. taxes. Since the U.S. tax rules are quite complex, it is often difficult for the non-U.S. trustee to judge whether the plan is acceptable. Anything that is based on a misrepresentation obviously is unacceptable. However, there can be situations where it is difficult to determine where a proposed plan falls. The parties should set aside any thought that the standard of conduct is different for entities and transactions outside the U.S. as opposed to those inside the U.S. In fact, a good habit is to assume that everything is located across the street from the Treasury Department building at the intersection of 15th Street and Pennsylvania Avenue in Washington D.C.

17.5 Transferee liability

The Internal Revenue Code contains provisions for the collection of taxes assessed against one person from others to whom the delinquent taxpayer has transferred property for less than adequate and full consideration. These rules are generally contained in Chapter 71 (transferees and fiduciaries). In general, the amounts of income, estate, gift, and other tax are assessed and collected in the same manner and subject to the same provisions and limitations as in the case of taxes with respect to which the liabilities were incurred. The burden of proof is on the IRS to show that a person is liable as a transferee of the property of a taxpayer, but this burden does not extend to showing that the taxpayer-transferor was liable for the tax.

A U.S. beneficiary that receives distributions from a foreign trust might easily incur transferee liability with respect to a tax liability of the grantor. For example, a U.S. gift tax liability might arise upon the distribution of assets to the U.S. beneficiary. If this is not paid by the U.S. grantor, the IRS could assess the liability to the beneficiary.

In theory the trustee of a foreign trust could be treated as a transferee. For example, assume that a U.S. transferor transfers funds to a foreign trust and in doing so makes a completed gift and incurs the U.S. gift tax. The foreign trustee could be viewed as a transferee for purposes of these provisions; however, it is difficult to imagine how the foreign trustee might be the subject of assessment and collection activity that would result in it deciding to file a petition in the United States Tax Court or otherwise challenge assessment or collection in a U.S. court.

Foreign trustees should be wary of arrangements whereby they and the U.S. parties cooperate in defeating IRS tax claims against the U.S. persons as transferees. For example, beneficiaries may ask that distributions be disguised as *bona fide* payments for value so as to make it less likely that the IRS can levy on the funds.

17.6 Proceeds of crime ("money laundering") issues

Trustees and advisors will want to be aware of the possible application of so-called "proceeds of crime" or "money laundering" provisions. First, they will not want to violate these rules in any jurisdiction. Secondly, they will want to be fully aware of the implications in their business. For example, a number of jurisdictions have or are moving toward instituting rules that require them to report as suspicious transactions situations where a settlor or a beneficiary apparently is not reporting tax in his or her home jurisdiction. The exact parameters of these rules should be examined very carefully. Sometimes the rule is not triggered if the failure to report is not an indictable crime in the jurisdiction of the trust and the trustee.

In addition, careful attention should be paid to the rules permitting a foreign jurisdiction, such as the United States, the United Kingdom, or Argentina, to obtain a confiscation order to obtain the funds traceable, for example, to criminal tax evasion.

These are not areas where common sense or generalities can be relied upon. A detailed examination of the facts and law is necessary.

As these rules come into existence, trust companies will want to make sure that their clients are not engaged in illegal activities. Rather than rely upon the representations of the client, the trust company will want an attorney or accountant in the client's home country to represent to it that everything is generally proper. If there are troublesome issues, these should be "cleaned up" before proceeding.

The application of money laundering laws to trusts, settlors, beneficiaries, trust companies, and advisors is a difficult and rapidly evolving subject.

Chapter 18

Large Gifts Received by U.S. Persons; Individuals Immigrating to and Expatriating from the U.S.; What Happens When the Grantor Dies?

18.1 Large gifts received by U.S. persons

Under U.S. tax laws, the recipient of a gift is not taxable under the income, or estate and gift, or any other tax rules.[259] Section 102 (relating to gifts and inheritances) specifically provides that gross income does not include the value of property acquired by gift, bequest, devise, or inheritance.[260]

U.S. gift tax taxes the donor, not the donee.[261] In fact, the workings of the U.S. gift tax where some of the parties or property are not U.S. or are located outside the U.S., are a bit convoluted. The U.S. gift tax is imposed on the transfer of property, wherever situated, by gift during the calendar year in question by any individual, resident or nonresident. Individuals who are not resident in the United States, *i.e.*, nonresident alien individuals, are not excluded from this rule. Going on, the rule states that the gift tax will not apply to the transfer of intangible property by a "nonresident not a citizen of United States" (a nonresident alien individual).[262] Continuing, it is

[259] The gift tax provisions are contained in sections 2501 through 2524 of the Code. The gift tax works hand-in-hand with the estate tax; in other words, they form a unified system applicable to lifetime and death-time transfers. The estate tax provisions are found in sections 2001 through to 2210.

[260] This exclusion does not cover income earned on the property received or a gift, bequest, etc., of income from property. For example, if an individual receives a gift in the form of an assignment of income from an economic interest in an oil and gas lease, he will be taxed on the income. Section 102(b).

[261] § 2501(c), Income Tax Regs. ("The tax imposed by section 2501 shall be paid by the donor.").

[262] There are special rules aimed at catching individuals who have expatriated for tax avoidance purposes.

provided that in the case of a nonresident alien individual, the rule will apply to a transfer only if the property is situated within the United States. Put differently, U.S. citizens and residents are taxable on all types of gifts; this is so even though the taxpayer is resident outside the U.S. at the time of making the gift and the property is outside the U.S. Nonresident alien individuals will be taxed on transfers of tangible real and personal property situated within the U.S., but not other transfers.[263]

In order to guard against circumvention of the rules aimed at taxing distributions from foreign accumulation trusts and the rules denying the benefits of the grantor trust rules to many foreign trusts, it was felt necessary to increase the reporting for recipients of gifts given by non-U.S. donors. Therefore, in 1996, Congress enacted a new information reporting rule—section 6039F. This is not a rule that creates a tax liability; it merely calls for the filing of a report. The Service then, if it wishes, can audit the recipient not for a possible gift tax liability but likely for a liability under the provisions applicable to beneficiaries of a foreign trust.

Section 6039F provides, in general, that if the aggregate value of foreign gifts received by a U.S. person during the taxable year exceeds $10,000, the person must make a report to the IRS. An exception is provided for any charitable organization that is a tax-exempt organization. The term "foreign gift" is defined as any amount received from a person other than a U.S. person that the recipient treats as a gift or bequest. A distribution from a foreign trust that is properly subject to disclosure under section 6048(c) is not treated as a "foreign gift." Also, transfers falling within section 2503(b)(2) are excluded from the definition. These transfers are amounts paid on behalf of an individual as tuition to an educational organization, such as a college or university, or to any person who provides medical care for the individual, as payment for that care.

---

[263] The gift tax regulations, speaking of the *situs* of property, state that real property and tangible personal property constitute property within the United States only if they are physically situated therein. Gift Tax Regs. § 25.2511-3 (b)(1). Debt obligations, including a bank deposit, are treated as intangible property. Currency, according to the regulations, is not a debt obligation. Therefore, one might conclude that cash is personal property and, if situated in the U.S., might cause a nonresident alien individual to be taxable.

➔ This disclosure rule applies to the receipt of a bequest as well as a gift. Also, the recipient need not be an individual; the rule applies to any person, including a corporation, partnership, trust, etc.

The $10,000 figure is subject to a cost-of-living adjustment. The adjusted amount is derived by multiplying $10,000 by the cost-of-living adjustment under section 1(f)(3) (relating to adjustments in tax tables so that inflation will not result in tax increases); or the taxpayer or his or her return preparer can simply look for the most recent IRS Revenue Procedure referencing Code section 6039F. (For 1998, the amount is $10,557.[264])

The penalty for failure to file is contained in the provision itself—section 6039F(c). The penalty is, first, the tax consequences of the gift will be determined by the IRS and, second, the recipient will have to pay an amount equal to 5% of the amount of the foreign gift for each month for which the failure continues, up to a maximum of 25% of the aggregate amount.

Prior to the form, Form 3520, becoming available in mid-November 1997, the IRS issued a lengthy Notice (Notice 97-34) providing information on reporting by U.S. recipients of foreign gifts and bequests, as well as U.S. grantors of a foreign trust, transferors to a foreign trust, and beneficiaries of a foreign trust.[265] This Notice will stand as an important authority for some time to come. Much of the information contained in the Notice appeared, or was reflected in some fashion, in Form 3520 when it was finally issued.

The Notice provides in part as follows:

> Form 3520 will only require the reporting of general information necessary to determine whether a purported gift is properly classified as a gift or income. For example, limited information will be required regarding whether the foreign donor is an

[264] Rev. Proc. 97-57, I.R.B. 1997-52, 20.

[265] Notice 97-34, I.R.B. 1997-25. This Notice was published on June 2, 1997.

> individual, corporation, partnership, or estate, and whether the foreign donor was acting as a nominee or intermediary for other person. Also, a brief description of the property received will be required. It is expected that the form will not require information on the identity of the foreign donor unless the foreign donor is a partnership or foreign corporation, or is acting as a nominee or intermediary for such an entity. However, the U.S. donee may be required to provide additional information, including the identity of the donor, to the IRS upon request. . . .
>
> Reporting is only required under section 6039F for gifts actually or constructively received by a U.S. person. Furthermore, reporting is required under section 6039F only if the U.S. person knows or has reason to know that the donor is a foreign person.

Notice 97-34, I.R.B. 1997-25 at Section VI.

The Notice also announced that the reporting threshold would be increased from $10,000 (adjusted for cost-of-living increases) to $100,000. If the $100,000 threshold is exceeded, however, the donee will be required to separately identify each gift in excess of $5,000; but he will not have to identify the donor.

> ➔ The IRS's lifting of the threshold amount from $10,000 to $100,000 will take many people out of the scope of this reporting rule—especially as transfers to colleges and health providers are also excluded.

Form 3520, Part IV, Line 60 (the 1998 version), asks whether the person filing received more than $100,000 in the form of gifts or bequests; and if so, he must give information about each gift or bequest in excess of $5,000. All that is requested is the date of the gift or bequest, a description of the property received, and the fair market value the property received. Line 61 asks whether the filer received more than $10,557 (the adjusted figure) as gifts from a foreign corporation or foreign partnership. If the answer is yes, he must give information with respect to each such gift. The information is: date of gift, name of donor, address of donor, identification number, if any, of the donor, whether the donor is a corporation or a partnership, a description of the property received, and the fair market value of property received. Lastly, Line 62 asks "Do you have any reason to believe that the foreign donor, in making any gift or bequest described in Lines 60 and 61, was acting as a nominee or intermediary for any other person?"

Both Notice 97-34 and the instructions to Form 3520 are helpful with respect to distributions from and contributions to trusts. If it is a distribution to a U.S. beneficiary, the beneficiary should report the amount as a distribution from a foreign trust under Part III of the Form, and not as a gift under Part IV. Contributions of property by foreign persons to a domestic or foreign trust that has U.S. beneficiaries are not reportable under section 6039F by the U.S. beneficiaries unless the U.S. persons are treated as receiving the contribution in the year of the transfer; that is, unless the beneficiary is treated as an owner of the trust because, for example, the U.S. person has a power to appoint income to himself. A domestic trust that is not treated as owned by another person (*i.e.*, a nongrantor trust) is required to report the receipt of a contribution to the trust from a foreign person. A domestic trust that is owned by a foreign person (*i.e.*, a domestic grantor trust, the grantor of which is foreign) is not required to report the receipt of a contribution from a foreign person. However, a U.S. person who receives a distribution from such a trust—at the time of receipt or subsequently—should report the distribution as a gift from a foreign person at the time the distribution (treated as a gift) is made.

> ➔ In normal circumstances, the recipient of a distribution from a domestic trust may not know or have any reason to suspect that the trust is a grantor trust and the grantor is foreign.

The Notice and the instructions to the Form point out that aggregation rules apply to the calculation of the threshold amount. The person filing must aggregate gifts from different foreign nonresident aliens and foreign estates if the filer knows (or has reason to know) that these persons are related to each other or one is acting as the nominee for the other. No definition of "related" is given.

→ When the provisions in the 1996 Act were being formulated by the Administration, serious thought was given to changing the gift tax rules to provide that while the donor would remain the primary taxpayer, in cases where the donor was not subject to tax (in other words, the donor was foreign and the property was not real or personal property situated in the U.S.), then the donee-recipient would become the taxpayer. This change would have constituted a very big change. Without knowing for sure, one can guess that there are many more gifts traveling from U.S. givers to foreign recipients than *vice versa*; and it would be very upsetting to many people if other countries enacted rules like the one contemplated. In any event, this idea was dropped. Today, gifts coming into the U.S. and distributions from foreign grantor trusts (for example, foreign trusts that are revocable), which are the economic equivalent of a direct gift from the grantor, remain free of U.S. tax.

Where there are a foreign grantor (revocable) trust and U.S. beneficiaries, payments to U.S. beneficiaries can be effected in one of two ways: a distribution can be made from the trust or the grantor can make a partial revocation followed by a gift to the U.S. persons. If the first approach is used, the recipient has to fill out Part III of Form 3520 and the trust has to complete Form 3520-A, including the Foreign Grantor Trust Beneficiary Statement. If the latter approach is used, the recipient need only complete Part IV of Form 3520, which is relatively straightforward. Most people, one suspects, will choose the latter.[266]

In the case of the receipt of a gift, any audit will be directed at the recipient. "Gifts" from individuals other than members of the family or long-term friends may be examined more closely. The Supreme Court's decisions in *Commissioner v. Duberstein* and *Bogardus v.*

[266] There have been proposals circulated among Members of Congress to make gifts or bequests from individuals who expatriated taxable to the recipient. These proposals are generally attached to some form of "exit tax."

Commissioner provide a picture of what is intended by the term "gift."

> The course of decision here makes it plain that the statute does not use the term "gift" in the common-law sense, but in a more colloquial sense. This Court has indicated that a voluntary executed transfer of his property by one to another, without any consideration or compensation therefor, though a common-law gift, is not necessarily a "gift" within the meaning of the statute. For the Court has shown that the mere absence of the legal or moral obligation to make such a payment does not establish that it is a gift. And, importantly, if the payment proceeds primarily from "the constraining force of any moral or legal duty," or from "the incentive of anticipated benefit" of an economic nature, it is not a gift. And, conversely, "[w]here the payment is in return for services rendered, it is irrelevant that the donor derives no economic benefit from it." A gift in the statutory sense, on the other hand, proceeds from a "detached and disinterested generosity;" "out of affection, respect, admiration, charity or like impulses." And in this regard, the most critical consideration, as the Court was agreed in the leading case here, is the transferor's "intention." "What controls is the intention with which payment, however voluntary, has been made."

Commissioner v. Duberstein, 363 U.S. 278 (1960).

It is recommended that whoever receives a reportable gift should have in his or her possession a letter from the donor, written at about the time of the gift, establishing the date, amount, description of the property (cash, personal property, etc.), and donative intent of the donor. This letter should not be dashed off with little thought; and, of course, it is not enough simply to pen a few magic words. The donor's characterization is not determinative; the individuals involved must prepare for an objective inquiry as to whether what is called a gift amounts to one in reality. Where appropriate, the letter might alert the recipient to the fact that the filing of an IRS form may be required.

Sample Letter. A letter from the donor to the recipient might look like this.

> *Margaret Brown*
> *Turtle Bay*
> *New York, NY*
>
> *Dear Margaret,*
>
> *This letter relates to the gift that I gave you in December of last year.*
>
> *I gave you $150,000, which was transferred from my bank account in London to your account at the same bank in London.*
>
> *While we are not related by blood, you have been my good friend for almost 20 years; and it gives me great pleasure to help you in this way. My intention is simply to express my affection for you.*
>
> *Since I am not a U.S. citizen or resident under U.S. tax laws, you may wish to inquire of your return preparer whether you need to file a special tax form (Form 3520) regarding this matter. That person can also advise you as to whether you need to file a report regarding your London bank account. Of course, these filings must remain solely your responsibility.*
>
> *With every best wish, I am,*
>
> *Very truly yours,*
>
> *Cynthia Jones*
> *Cadogan Place*
> *London, England*

18.2 Individuals immigrating to and expatriating from the U.S.

18.2.1. Individuals immigrating to the U.S.

The U.S. taxation of individuals immigrating to the U.S. and individuals emigrating from the U.S. need not be the subject of a lengthy treatment here. Only a few points will be noted.

Individuals immigrating to the U.S. will want to note the existence of the five-year rule in section 679(a)(4). If he or she immigrates to the U.S. within 5 years after having created a foreign trust, he/she will be treated as the owner of all the assets in the trust and will be taxed on all the income and losses earned by the trust. Therefore, a little advance planning will come in handy.

Also, the anti-"give-and-go" rule in section 672(f)(5) must be taken into account. There is no time period or "window" with respect to the application of this rule, so no amount of advance planning will help. What is useful is a wealthy member of the family who wishes to remain a nonresident alien residing outside the U.S. This individual can create foreign grantor trusts that are revocable. These trusts can be used to make tax-free distributions to U.S. beneficiaries. Of course, all the reporting forms would have to be filed, but there should be no difficulties in the event of an audit.

Still focusing on the pre-immigration situation, an individual coming to the U.S. will want to take note of the relatively new provisions for taxing a long-term resident who "lifts" his or her status as a lawful permanent resident. "Long-term resident" means any individual who is a lawful permanent resident of the U.S. at least 8 taxable years during the period of 15 taxable years ending with the taxable year during which the "lifting" occurs. In other words, in individual who has had a "green card" for 8 out of 15 years, can run into this problem. This individual will be taxed the same as a U.S. citizen who expatriates for tax purposes. He will be taxed for the following 10 years on U.S. source income; and the definition of U.S. source income is somewhat expanded for these purposes. The U.S. estate tax can also continue to apply. The immigrating individual can elect to "step up" the basis of his assets to their fair market value at the time he comes to the U.S. Also, it may be possible to get a ruling from the IRS that his ceasing to be a resident is not for tax avoidance purposes and, therefore, does not cause the application of this rule.

18.2.2 Individuals expatriating from the U.S.

The presence of trusts, especially foreign trusts, can complicate the planning for an individual who wishes to give up his U.S. citizenship. Among other things, it should be noted that when testing under section 877(a)(2) (these rules contain an average net income tax test and a net worth test) it may be necessary to take into account the value of interests in a trust, regardless of the fact that the value of these interests may be difficult to assess. Notice 97-19, which deals at length with the new rules under section 877, sets forth special rules for determining beneficial interests in trust. These are novel and far-reaching. Also, it should be noted that an interest in the right to use property will be treated as an interest in such property. This approach contrasts with that in the trust distributions area, where the right to use property owned by a trust is not treated as a constructive distribution.[267]

18.3 What happens when the grantor dies?

When the grantor dies, the grantor trust—whether a domestic trust or foreign trust—loses its status as a grantor trust and, unless there are specific provisions in the trust indenture, it will be treated after the date of death as a nongrantor trust. "This may be because at death the grantor ceases to hold any interest or power described in the identification provisions of Subpart E. Or it may be because at death the grantor ceases to be a 'grantor.'"[268] (The same phenomenon occurs when, absent the grantor's death, grantor trust status is lost due to the relinquishment by the grantor or some other person of the

---

[267] Notice 97-19, 1997-1 CB 394, *modified by* Rev. Proc. 98-1, I.R.B. 1998-1, 7 and Notice 98-34, I.R. B. 1998-27, 30.

[268] Ferguson, Freeland & Ascher, FEDERAL INCOME TAXATION OF ESTATES, TRUSTS, AND BENEFICIARIES (3rd Ed.) (Aspen Law & Business 1998), p. 10-51, *citing D.G. McDonald Trust,* 19 T.C. 672 (1953), *acq.*, 1953-2 C.B. 3, *aff'd sub nom. Chase Nat'l Bank v. Commissioner*, 225 F.2d 621 (8th Cir. 1955), *cert. denied,* 350 U.S. 965 (1956) and Rev. Rul. 57-51, 1957-1 C.B. 171 ("[U]pon the death of the grantor the trust [becomes] a separate entity for Federal income tax purposes for the first time").

interests or powers that caused the trust to fall within the grantor trust provisions.)

As a result, the grantor immediately ceases to be treated as the owner of the trust assets under section 671. A deceased grantor is taxable only on the trust's income through the date of death; income arising during that portion of the taxable year following the date of death will not be taxable to him. The assets thereafter will be treated as owned by the trust and taxed to it or the beneficiaries in accordance with the normal rules applicable to nongrantor trusts—whether simple or complex. The basis of those assets will be the same as they were in the hands of the grantor (the prior owner); as a separate matter, the assets should be treated as included or not included in the decedent's estate. It will be recalled that the grantor trust rules operate for income tax purposes only.[269]

Where there is a foreign grantor trust, which remains under the new rules "grantor" because, for instance, it is revocable, and the grantor dies, the trust becomes a nongrantor trust. While the grantor is alive, distributions can be made to U.S. beneficiaries without the imposition of a tax. When he is dead, this can no longer be done. Starting with his death, income will be earned and either accumulated or distributed. If current income is not distributed, the trust's undistributed net income account will begin to build. The problem of getting distributions out of a foreign nongrantor (accumulation) trust to its U.S. beneficiaries in a tax-efficient manner is one of the most vexing problems around today. To whatever degree the statute permits, the trust and beneficiaries can take steps to mitigate the problem.[270] For example, capital gains on low-basis property should be realized and distributed as current income, so as to avoid the obliteration of capital gains character.

---

[269] The gift and estate tax rules and the section 1014 basis rules apply separately; that is, they stand apart from the grantor trust rules. When creating a foreign grantor trust, a grantor can choose to make a completed gift or not. If he chooses to make a completed gift, he will incur a gift tax and property will be removed from his estate. Upon his death, the property will not receive a stepped-up basis. If he chooses not to make a completed gift, no gift tax will be incurred, the property will be in his estate at the time of his death, and the property will receive a stepped-up basis.

[270] At some point, the IRS may want to issue anti-abuse rules under section 643(a)(7).

> ➔ When drafting the indenture of a foreign grantor trust, the attorney may wish to consider whether to include language to the effect that should the trust be converted into a nongrantor trust, the trustee shall be required to distribute income currently. Otherwise, the trust may not be able to qualify as a simple trust. Capital gains of a foreign nongrantor accumulation trust should nevertheless retain their character provided they are paid out currently and not accumulated.

Where there is a foreign grantor trust with a U.S. grantor and the grantor dies, again the trust is converted into a nongrantor trust. The U.S. grantor is no longer the owner of the assets. The assets thereafter are treated as owned for tax purposes by the trust. The character of the trust as "foreign" remains the same.

In this event, should section 684 (recognition of gain on certain transfers to certain foreign trusts and estates) apply? Put differently, assuming there are appreciated assets in the trust, will the death of the grantor, which causes a change in the status of the trust, be viewed the same as a transfer of property by a U.S. person to the foreign trust? The answer would appear to be no.

Section 684—in a sense, the replacement for section 1491—provides that "certain transfers" to certain foreign trusts and estates will cause the recognition of gain. It provides that in the case of any transfer of property by a U.S. person to a foreign estate or trust, for purposes of this subtitle (Subtitle A, dealing with income taxes), such transfer shall be treated as a sale or exchange for an amount equal to the fair market value of the property transferred. The provision goes on to explain how the amount of gain to be recognized is calculated. A specific exception is provided for transfers from a U.S. person to a foreign grantor trust as to which any person is treated as the owner of all the assets under section 671. Specifically subjected to the rule is the case of a domestic trust that converts into a foreign trust; in which event, the domestic trust, not the original settlor, is treated as the taxpayer.

There is nothing in the Code providing that the death of a grantor, causing the conversion of a grantor trust into a nongrantor trust, is or should be treated as a "transfer." When Congress has wanted an event that is not actually a transfer to be treated as such, it has explicitly provided for this result. For example, when Congress wanted the outward migration of a trust to be treated as a transfer, it said so in a specific statutory provision. If it had wanted the conversion of a grantor trust into a nongrantor trust to be treated as a transfer, likewise, it presumably would have so provided. Moreover, even if the conversion is tantamount to a transfer, it is apparent that Congress only intended in section 684 to address certain transfers and not others.

When Congress wanted actual—as opposed to constructive—transfers occasioned by death to be dealt with in a given context, in particular, section 679, it provided a clear rule. Section 679(a)(2)(A) specifically removes transfers by reason of death from the general rule of section 679. Also, it will be noted that a death-time transfer of appreicated property owned by the decedent directly, rather than in the form of a grantor trust, will not be affected by section 684 because the estate will enjoy a step-up in the basis of the assets under section 1014. There is no reason why a death-time transfer where the decedent owned the assets by means of a grantor trust should be treated any differently than such a transfer where the decedent owned the assets directly. Put differently, why should a U.S. citizen who owns a house in London through an English living trust be treated any differently than a U.S. citizen who owns a house in London and transfers it by will to an English trust for his children?

At the time of consideration of the 1996 foreign trust amendments and the substitution of section 684 for section 1491 in 1997, Congress looked closely at this area. It certainly cannot be said that its failure to make the death of a grantor under the circumstances (or other event causing the conversion of a grantor trust) a taxable event was due to oversight.[271] Also, it should be recalled that Congress in various

[271] Old section 1491 was repealed and new section 684 was enacted as part of Title XI, (sections 1131, 1141-1145, and 1151) of the Taxpayer Relief Act of 1997 (P.L. 105-34). The provisions enacting new section 684 were contained in section 1131(b). it was estimated by the Joint Committee on

contexts has considered applying a capital gains tax at death; and it has very deliberately decided against such a measure.[272]

None of the versions of Form 3520 and Notice 97-34 give any indication that a section 684 tax (or the predecessor section 1491 excise tax) may be triggered and the estate may need to file a Form 926 and pay a tax at the time of death.

This same question arose under old section 1491.[273]

---

taxation that these provisions, together with the repeal of section 1491 and other provisions to simplify the formation and operation of international joint ventures, would result in a modest loss of revenue (a reduction in Federal fiscal year budget receipts by less than $500,000 in 1998, less than $500,000 in 1999, $1 million in 2000, $1 million in 2001, $1 million in 2002, $1 million in 2003, $1 million in 2004, $1 million in 2005, $1 million in 2006, and $2 million in 2007). GENERAL EXPLANATION OF TAX LEGISLATION ENACTED IN 1997, Staff Of The Joint Committee On Taxation, JCS-23-97 (dec. 17, 1997). If this provision was drafted to affect foreign grantor trusts with respect to which the U.S. grantor died, the revenue increase, not reduction, would have been substantial.

[272] While there is nothing in the 1976 Act or subsequent legislation suggesting that there should be a triggering of a tax under section 1491 or its successor, this issue may be addressed in the section 679 "outbound" trust regulations, which may be issued in proposed form in early 2000. Regulations under section 679, enacted in 1976, have never been promulgated. The amendments to this section in 1996 provide a good reason for doing so now.

[273] There may be differences, however, between the application of old section 1491 and new section 684 because the excise tax sat alone in Chapter 5, Subtitle A, whereas section 684 sits in Subpart F, of Subchapter J (dealing with estates, trusts, beneficiaries, and descendants), of Chapter I (dealing with normal taxes and surtaxes). Section 671 (trust income, deductions, and credits attributable to grantors and others as substantial owners) provides that where the grantor is treated as the owner of the trust assets by virtue of the grantor trust rules, there will be included in his income all items of income, deductions, and credits of the trust to the extent that such items would be taken into account under Chapter I in computing the taxable income, separate, of an individual. Congress clearly traipsed through this part of the statute in 1996 and again in 1997; and it was fully aware of the existence of this type of trust.

The IRS Training Materials, which were written prior to the enactment of section 684 in 1997, come down in favor of the imposition of the section 1491 excise tax when the grantor dies or, in the case of a foreign grantor

In any event, the possible imposition of the section 684 tax may be avoided by providing that a U.S. person other than the settlor of the foreign trust shall have a section 678 power to vest the corpus in himself upon the settlor's death.[274] The settlor would remain the owner of the assets under section 6712 until his death. Section 684(b) provides that the section 684(a) tax willnot apply to a transfer to a trust by a U.S. person to the extent that any U.S. person is treated as the owner of such trust under section 671. It is possible that the power to vest need only last for a limited period of time. If the assets in the trust remained in the decedent-settlor's estate and were subject to estate tax, the bases of the assets would be stepped up.

trust which is "grantor" only under section 679, the trust ceases to have a U.S. beneficiary. No statutory or case law authority is cited for this proposition. It should be noted that Training Materials are designed for training purposes only and cannot be cited as authority for a technical position.

[274] Section 678(b).

INDEX

R

S

T

U

W

Appendix A: Forms and Instructions

The following forms relate to the taxation of foreign trusts and U.S. beneficiaries of foreign trusts and their reporting responsibilities.

The IRS forms are the 1998 forms. The 1999 forms are in substance the same. Some lines that were "reserved" on the 1998 forms due to last minute changes in the law were removed in the 1999 forms; and references to various pages in the instructions were added. There was also some slight editing of the text—to the extent of a few words.

The Department of Treasury Form TD F 90-22.1 is the current form.

Form 1040NR-Instructions	1998	Only page 2, which refers to filing for an Estate or Trust, is provided.
Form 3520 Annual Return To Report Transactions With Foreign Trust And Receipt Of Certain Foreign Gifts	1998	
Form 3520-Instructions	1998	Pages 10 and 11, which list abbreviations for foreign countries, have been omitted.
Form 3520-A Annual Information Return Of Foreign Trust With A U.S. Owner	1998	
Form 3520-A-Instructions	1998	
Form 1041 U.S. Income Tax Return For Estates And Trusts	1998	
Form 1041-Schedule J Accumulation Distribution From Certain Complex Trusts	1998	
Form 1041-Instructions	1998	
Form 4970 Tax On Accumulation Distribution Of Trusts	1998	
Department of Treasury Form TD F 90-22.1 (With Instructions)	Current	

1998

Department of the Treasury
Internal Revenue Service

Instructions for Form 1040NR

U.S. Nonresident Alien Income Tax Return

Section references are to the Internal Revenue Code unless otherwise noted.

General Instructions

TIP: For details on these and other changes, see **Pub. 553** or see **What's Hot** at www.irs.ustreas.gov.

What's New for 1998?

Student Loan Interest Deduction

If you paid interest on a qualified student loan, you may be able to deduct up to $1,000 of the interest on line 25. See the instructions for line 25 on page 9 for details.

New Child Tax Credits

Do you have a dependent child (see the instructions for line 7c on page 6 for a list of filers who are allowed to claim a dependent on Form 1040NR) who was under age 17 at the end of 1998?

If so, you may be able to claim either or both of these new credits:

- The Child Tax Credit
- The Additional Child Tax Credit

The total of these credits cannot be more than $400 for each qualifying child. Figure the child tax credit first. If you have three or more qualifying children and you are not able to claim the full $400 child tax credit for each child, you may be able to claim the additional credit.

The **additional child tax credit** is refundable; that is, it may give you a refund even if you do not owe any tax.

These credits are in addition to the child and dependent care credit that you may be able to claim.

Who Is a Qualifying Child? The child must be your dependent and must meet certain other requirements. See **Qualifying Child for Child Tax Credit** in the instructions for line 7c, column (4), on page 6.

Caution: *If the child meets those requirements, check the box in column (4) on line 7c of your return.*

Where Do You Claim These Credits?

Child Tax Credit. If you have at least one qualifying child, follow the instructions that begin on page 10. Enter the credit on Form 1040NR, line 41.

Additional Child Tax Credit. Use **Form 8812** to figure this credit and attach it to your return. Enter the additional child tax credit on Form 1040NR, line 56.

Sale of Your Home

If you sold your main home in 1998 and **all four** of the following apply, you do not have to report the sale on your tax return.

1. No part of the home was used for business or rental purposes.

2. You owned and lived in the home as your main home for at least 2 years within the 5-year period ending on the date of sale.

3. You have not sold or exchanged another main home after May 6, 1997.

4. The selling price of the home is not over $250,000.

If all four of the conditions do not apply, see **Pub. 523** to find out if you have to report the sale on your return and, if you do, how to do so.

Self-Employed Health Insurance

You may be able to deduct up to 45% of your health insurance. See the instructions for line 28 on page 10 for details.

IRA Deduction Restored for Some People Covered by Retirement Plans

You may be able to take an IRA deduction if you were covered by a retirement plan and your modified adjusted gross income is less than $40,000 if you checked filing status box 1, 2, 3, 4, or 5; or $60,000 if qualifying widow(er) (filing status box 6). See the instructions for line 24 on page 9.

Conversions From Traditional IRAs to Roth IRAs

If you converted part or all of a traditional, SEP, or SIMPLE IRA to a Roth IRA in 1998, you may have to file **Form 8606.** See Form 8606 and its instructions for details.

Penalty-Free IRA Distributions

The additional tax on an early distribution from an IRA may not apply if you paid higher education expenses for yourself, your spouse, or your children or grandchildren. The tax also may not apply if you pay expenses related to the purchase of a home by a first-time homebuyer. See **Form 5329** and its instructions for details.

Estimated Tax Penalty

You generally will not owe an estimated tax penalty if the amount you owe on line 67 is less than $1,000. See the instructions for line 68 on page 13.

Credit for Federal Tax Paid on Kerosene

If you bought undyed kerosene after June 30, 1998, for heating or certain other nonhighway uses, you may be able to take a credit of 24.4 cents for each gallon. You can get a refund even if you do not owe tax. See **Form 4136.**

Payment of Tax

If you owe tax, make your check or money order payable to the **"United States Treasury."** See the instructions for line 67 on page 13 for more details.

Standard Mileage Rates

The rate for business use of a vehicle has increased to 32.5 cents a mile. Starting this year, you can use the business rate even if you lease your vehicle. For charitable contributions, the rate has increased to 14 cents a mile.

What To Look for in 1999

Child Tax Credits. The total of the child tax credit and the additional child tax credit can be as much as $500 for each qualifying child.

Student Loan Interest Deduction. You may be able to deduct up to $1,500 of the interest you pay on a qualified student loan.

Self-Employed Health Insurance Deduction. You may be able to deduct up to 60% of your health insurance.

IRA Deduction Allowed to More Taxpayers Covered by a Retirement Plan. You may be able to take an IRA deduction if you are covered by a retirement plan and your 1999 modified adjusted gross income is less than: $41,000 if single or married filing separately and you lived apart from your spouse for all of 1999; or $61,000 if qualifying widow(er).

Items To Note

Form 1040NR-EZ. You may be able to use **Form 1040NR-EZ,** U.S. Income Tax Return for Certain Nonresident Aliens With No Dependents, if your only income from U.S. sources is wages, salaries, tips, taxable refunds of state and local income taxes, and scholarship or fellowship grants. Also, if married, you cannot claim an exemption for your spouse. For more details, see Form 1040NR-EZ and its instructions.

Other Reporting Requirements. If you meet the closer connection to a foreign country exception to the substantial presence test you must file **Form 8840,** Closer Connection Exception Statement for Aliens. If you exclude days of presence in the United States for purposes of the substantial presence test, you must file **Form 8843,** Statement for Exempt Individuals and Individuals With a Medical Condition. This rule does not apply to foreign-government-related individuals who exclude days of presence in the United States. Certain dual-resident taxpayers who claim tax treaty benefits must file **Form 8833,** Treaty-Based Return Position Disclosure Under Section 6114 or 7701(b). A dual-resident taxpayer is one who is a resident of both the United States and another country under each country's tax laws.

Additional Information

If you need more information, our free publications may help you. **Pub. 519,** U.S. Tax Guide for Aliens, will be the most important, but the following publications may also help.

Pub. 525, Taxable and Nontaxable Income

Pub. 529, Miscellaneous Deductions

Pub. 552, Recordkeeping for Individuals

Pub. 597, Information on the United States-Canada Income Tax Treaty

Pub. 901, U.S. Tax Treaties

Pub. 910, Guide to Free Tax Services (includes a list of all publications)

These free publications and the forms and schedules you will need are available on request from the Internal Revenue Service. If you have a foreign address, send your order to the Eastern Area Distribution Center, P.O. Box 85627, Richmond, VA 23285-5627, U.S.A.

Resident Alien or Nonresident Alien

If you are not a citizen of the United States, specific rules apply to determine if you are a resident alien or a nonresident alien for tax purposes. Generally, you are considered a resident alien if you meet either the **green card test** or the **substantial presence test** for 1998. If you do not meet either of these tests for 1998 but you meet the substantial presence test for 1999, you may be able to choose to be treated as a resident alien for part of 1998. But you must have been physically present in the United States for at least 31 days in a row during 1998 to do so. This choice does not apply if you met either the green card test or the substantial presence test for 1997. For more details, see Pub. 519.

You are considered a nonresident alien for the year if you are not a U.S. resident under either of these tests. You are also considered a nonresident alien if you otherwise meet the substantial presence test but you come under any of the three exceptions described below.

For more details on resident and nonresident status, the tests for residence and the exceptions to them, see Pub. 519.

Green Card Test. You are a resident for tax purposes if you were a lawful permanent resident (immigrant) of the United States at any time during 1998.

Substantial Presence Test. You are considered a U.S. resident if you meet the substantial presence test for 1998. You meet this test if you were physically present in the United States for at least:

1. 31 days during 1998, and

2. 183 days during the period 1998, 1997, and 1996, counting all the days of physical presence in 1998 but only ⅓ the number of days of presence in 1997 and only ⅙ the number of days in 1996.

Generally, you are treated as present in the United States on any day that you are physically present in the country at any time during the day.

Exceptions. The following are exceptions to the substantial presence test.

1. Exempt Individual. You do not count days for which you are an exempt individual. In general, an exempt individual is someone who is a:

a. foreign-government-related individual,

b. teacher or trainee,

c. student, or

d. professional athlete who is temporarily in the United States to compete in a charitable sports event.

Note: *Alien individuals with "Q" visas are treated as either students, teachers, or trainees and, as such, are exempt individuals for purposes of the substantial presence test if they otherwise qualify. "Q" visas are issued to aliens participating in certain international cultural exchange programs.*

2. Medical condition. You do not count any day that you intended to leave the United States but were unable to leave because of a medical condition or medical problem that arose while you were present in the United States.

Note: *This exception does not apply to pre-existing medical conditions or problems. For more details, see Pub. 519.*

3. Closer connection to foreign country. Even though you would otherwise meet the substantial presence test, you are not treated as having met that test for 1998 if you:

a. were present in the United States for fewer than 183 days during 1998,

b. establish that during 1998 you had a tax home in a foreign country, and

c. establish that during 1998 you had a closer connection to one foreign country in which you had a tax home than to the United States unless you had a closer connection to two foreign countries.

Who Must File

File Form 1040NR if any of the following four conditions applies to you.

1. You were a nonresident alien engaged in a trade or business in the United States during 1998. You must file even if—

a. none of your income came from a trade or business conducted in the United States,

b. you have no U.S. source income, or

c. your income is exempt from U.S. tax.

In any of the above three cases, do not complete the schedules for Form 1040NR. Instead, attach a list of the kinds of exclusions you claim and the amount of each.

Note: *If you were a nonresident alien student, teacher, or trainee who was temporarily present in the United States under an "F," "J," "M," or "Q" visa, you must file Form 1040NR (or Form 1040NR-EZ)* ***only*** *if you have income that is subject to tax under section 871 (i.e., the income items listed on lines 8 through 21 on page 1 of Form 1040NR and on lines 69 through 79 on page 4 of Form 1040NR).*

2. You were a nonresident alien not engaged in a trade or business in the United States during 1998 and not all U.S. tax that you owe was withheld from your income.

3. You represent a deceased person who would have had to file Form 1040NR.

4. You represent an estate or trust that has to file Form 1040NR.

Exception for Children Under Age 14. If your child was under age 14 on January 1, 1999, had income **only** from interest and dividends that are effectively connected with a U.S. trade or business, and that income totaled less than $6,500, you may be able to elect to report your child's income on your return. But you must use **Form 8814,** Parents' Election To Report Child's Interest and Dividends, to do so. If you make this election, your child does not have to file a return. For more details, see Form 8814.

Filing a Deceased Person's Return. The personal representative must file the return for a deceased person who was required to file a return for 1998. A personal representative can be an executor, administrator, or anyone who is in charge of the deceased person's property.

Filing for an Estate or Trust. If you are filing Form 1040NR for a nonresident alien estate or trust, change the form to reflect the provisions of Subchapter J, Chapter 1, of the Internal Revenue Code. You may find it helpful to refer to **Form 1041,** U.S. Income Tax Return for Estates and Trusts, and its instructions.

When To File

Individuals. If you were an employee and received wages subject to withholding, file Form 1040NR by the 15th day of the 4th month after your tax year ends. A return for the 1998 calendar year is due by April 15, 1999.

If you did not receive wages as an employee subject to U.S. income tax withholding, file Form 1040NR by the 15th day of the 6th month after your tax year ends. A return for the 1998 calendar year is due by June 15, 1999.

Estates and Trusts. If you file for a nonresident alien estate or trust that has an office in the United States, file the return by the 15th day of the 4th month after the tax year ends. If you file for a nonresident alien estate or trust that does not have an office in the United States, file the return by the 15th day of the 6th month after the tax year ends.

Note: *If the regular due date for filing falls on a Saturday, Sunday, or legal holiday, file by the next business day.*

Extension of Time To File. If you cannot file your return by the due date, you should file **Form 4868,** Application for Automatic Extension of Time To File U.S. Individual Income Tax Return. You must file Form 4868 by the regular due date of the return.

Note: *Form 4868 does not extend the time to pay your income tax. The tax is due by the regular due date of the return.*

Where To File

File Form 1040NR with the Internal Revenue Service Center, Philadelphia, PA 19255, U.S.A.

Private Delivery Services

You can use certain private delivery services designated by the IRS to meet the "timely mailing as timely filing/paying" rule for tax returns and payments. The IRS publishes a list of the designated private delivery services in September of each year. The list published in September 1998 includes only the following:

- Airborne Express (Airborne): Overnight Air Express Service, Next Afternoon Service, and Second Day Service.
- DHL Worldwide Express (DHL): DHL "Same Day" Service, and DHL USA Overnight.
- Federal Express (FedEx): FedEx Priority Overnight, FedEx Standard Overnight, and FedEx 2Day.
- United Parcel Service (UPS): UPS Next Day Air, UPS Next Day Air Saver, UPS 2nd Day Air, and UPS 2nd Day Air A.M.

The private delivery service can tell you how to get written proof of the mailing date.

Caution: *Private delivery services cannot deliver items to P.O. boxes. You must use the*

Form **3520**

Department of the Treasury
Internal Revenue Service

Annual Return To Report Transactions With Foreign Trusts and Receipt of Certain Foreign Gifts

File in duplicate. Instructions are separate.

OMB No. 1545-0159

1998

All information must be in English. Show all amounts in U.S. dollars. File a separate Form 3520 for each foreign trust.

For calendar year 1998, or tax year beginning , 19 , ending , 19 .

Check appropriate box(es): See instructions. ☐ Initial return ☐ Final return ☐ Amended return

Check box that applies to U.S. person filing return: ☐ Individual ☐ Partnership ☐ Corporation ☐ Trust ☐ Executor

Check all applicable boxes:

☐ (a) You are a U.S. transferor who, directly or indirectly, transferred money or other property during the current tax year to a for eign trust, or (b) You held an outstanding obligation of a related foreign trust (or a person related to the trust) issued during the current tax year, that you treated as a "qualified obligation" (defined on page 2 of the instructions) during the current tax year. See the instructions for P art I.

☐ You are a U.S. owner of all or any portion of a foreign trust at any time during the tax year. See the instructions for Part II .

☐ (a) You are a U.S. person who, during the current tax year, received a distribution from a foreign trust, or (b) A related foreign trust held an outstanding obligation issued by you (or a person related to you) during the current tax year that you treated as a "qualified ob ligation" (defined on page 2 of the instructions) during the current tax year. See the instructions for Part III.

☐ You are a U.S. person who, during the current tax year, received certain gifts or bequests from a foreign person. See the instr uctions for Part IV.

Service Center where U.S. person filing this return files its income tax return ▶

1a Name of U.S. person(s) filing return			b Identification number
c Number, street, and room or suite no. (If a P.O. box, see instructions.)			d Spouse's identification number (see instr.)
e City or town	f State or province	g ZIP or postal code	h Country
2a Name of foreign trust (if applicable)	b Identification number (if any)		c Number, street, and room or suite no.
d City or town	e State or province	f ZIP or postal code	g Country

3 Did the foreign trust appoint a U.S. agent (defined on page 3 of the instructions) who can provide the IRS with all relevant trust information? . . . . ☐ Yes ☐ No

If "Yes," complete lines 3a through 3g.

3a Name of U.S. agent	b Identification number (if any)		c Number, street, and room or suite no.
d City or town	e State or province	f ZIP or postal code	g Country
4a Name of U.S. decedent (see instr.)	b Address		c TIN of decedent
d Date of death			e EIN of estate

Part I Transfers by U.S. Persons to a Foreign Trust During the Current Tax Year (See instructions.)

5a Name of trust creator (if different from line 1a)	b Address	c Identification number (if any)
6a Country code of country where trust was created	b Country code of country whose law governs the trust	c Date trust was created

7a Will any other person be treated as the owner of the transferred assets after the transfer? . . . . ☐ Yes ☐ No

b Name of other foreign trust owners, if any (a)	Address (b)	Country of residence (c)	Identification number, if any (d)	Relevant code section (e)

Under penalties of perjury, I declare that I have examined this return, including any accompanying reports, schedules, or state ments, and to the best of my knowledge and belief, it is true, correct, and complete.

Signature | Title | Date

Preparer's signature | Preparer's identification number | Date

For Paperwork Reduction Act Notice, see page 9 of the instructions. Cat. No. 19594V Form 3520 (1998)

Part I (Continued)

8	Was the transfer a completed gift or bequest? If "Yes," see instructions	☐ Yes	☐ No
9a	Can any part of the income or corpus of the trust benefit, now or in the future, any U.S. beneficiary?	☐ Yes	☐ No
b	If "No," could the trust be revised or amended to benefit a U.S. beneficiary?	☐ Yes	☐ No
10	Will you continue to be treated as the owner of the transferred asset(s) after the transfer?	☐ Yes	☐ No

Schedule A—Obligations of a Related Trust (See instructions.)

11a During the current tax year, did you transfer property (including cash) to a related foreign trust in exchange for an obligation of the trust or a person related to the trust? See instructions . . . ☐ Yes ☐ No

If "Yes," complete Schedule A, as applicable. If "No," go to Schedule B.

b Was the obligation you received a qualified obligation? . . . ☐ Yes ☐ No

If "Yes," complete Schedule A with respect to that obligation. If "No," go to Schedule B.

Note: The FMV of an obligation (column (d)) is -0- unless it is a qualified obligation.

Date of transfer giving rise to obligation (a)	Maximum term (b)	Yield to maturity (c)	FMV of obligation (d)

12 With respect to each obligation you treated as a "qualified obligation" on line 11b: Do you agree to extend the period of assessment of any income or transfer tax attributable to the transfer and any consequential income tax changes for each year that the obligation is outstanding, to a date 3 years after the maturity date of the obligation? ☐ Yes ☐ No

Note: You generally must answer "Yes," if you checked "Yes" to question 11b.

Schedule B—Gratuitous Transfers (See instructions.)

13 During the current tax year, did you make any transfers (directly or indirectly) to the trust and receive less than FMV, or no consideration at all, for the property transferred? . . . ☐ Yes ☐ No

If "Yes," complete columns (a) through (i) below and the rest of Schedule B, as applicable.

If "No," do not complete the rest of Schedule B and go to Schedule E.

Date of transfer (a)	Description of property transferred (b)	FMV of property transferred (c)	U.S. adj. basis of property transferred (d)	Gain recognized at time of transfer (e)	Excess, if any, of column (c) over the sum of columns (d) and (e) (f)	Description of property received, if any (g)	FMV of property received (h)	Excess of column (c) over column (h) (i)
Totals ▶					$			$

14 Reserved.

15 You are required to attach a copy of each sale or loan document entered into in connection with a transfer reported on line 13. If these documents have been attached to a Form 3520 filed within the previous 3 years, attach only relevant updates.

	Have you attached a copy of:	Yes	No	Attached Previously	Year Attached
a	Sale document?	☐	☐	☐	
b	Loan document?	☐	☐	☐	
c	Subsequent variances to original sale or loan documents?	☐	☐	☐	

Part I (Continued)

Note: Complete lines 16 through 19 only if you answered "No" to line 3.

16

Name of beneficiary (a)	Address of beneficiary (b)	U.S. beneficiary? (c) Yes	U.S. beneficiary? (c) No	Identification number, if any (d)

17

Name of trustee (a)	Address of trustee (b)	Identification number, if any (c)

18

Name of other persons with trust powers (a)	Address of other persons with trust powers (b)	Description of powers (c)	Identification number, if any (d)

19 You are required to attach a copy of all trust documents as indicated below. If these documents have been attached to a Form 35 20-A filed within the previous 3 years, attach only relevant updates.

Have you attached a copy of:	Yes	No	Attached Previously	Year Attached
a Summary of all written and oral agreements and understandings relating to the trust?	☐	☐	☐	
b The trust instrument?	☐	☐	☐	
c Memoranda or letters of wishes?	☐	☐	☐	
d Subsequent variances to original trust documents?	☐	☐	☐	
e Trust financial statements?	☐	☐	☐	
f Other trust documents?	☐	☐	☐	

Schedule C—Reserved.

20–23. Reserved.

Part I Schedule D—Reserved.

24 Reserved.

Schedule E—Qualified Obligations Outstanding in the Current Tax Year (See instructions.)

25 Did you, at any time during the tax year, hold an outstanding obligation of a related foreign trust (or a person related to the trust) that you treated as a "qualified obligation" in the current tax year? . . . . ☐ Yes ☐ No
If "Yes," complete columns (a) through (e) below.

Date of original obligation (a)	Tax year qualified obligation first reported (b)	Amount of principal payments made during the tax year (c)	Amount of interest payments made during the tax year (d)	Does the obligation still meet the criteria for a qualified obligation? (e)	
				Yes	No

Part II U.S. Owner of a Foreign Trust (See instructions.)

26 Name of other foreign trust owners, if any (a)	Address (b)	Country of residence (c)	Identification number, if any (d)	Relevant code section (e)

27 Country code of country where foreign trust was created (a)	Country code of country whose law governs the foreign trust (b)	Date foreign trust was created (c)

28 Did the foreign trust file Form 3520-A for the current year? . . . . ☐ Yes ☐ No
If "Yes," attach the Foreign Grantor Trust Owner Statement you received from the foreign trust. If "No," to the best of your ability, complete and attach a substitute Form 3520-A for the foreign trust. See instructions for information on penalties.

29 Enter the gross value of the portion of the foreign trust that you are treated as owning . . . . ▶ $

Part III Distributions to a U.S. Person From a Foreign Trust During the Current Tax Year (See instructions.)

30 Cash amounts or FMV of property received, directly or indirectly, during the current tax year, from the foreign trust (exclude loans included on line 31).

Date of distribution (a)	Description of property received (b)	FMV of property received (determined on date of distribution) (c)	Description of property transferred, if any (d)	FMV of property transferred (e)	Excess of column (c) over column (e) (f)
Totals . . . . ▶					$

Part III (Continued)

31 During the current tax year, did you (or a person related to you) receive a loan from a related foreign trust (including an extension of credit upon the purchase of property from the trust)? . . . . ☐ Yes ☐ No
If "Yes," complete columns (a) through (g) below with respect to such loans.
Note: The FMV of an obligation (column (f)) is -0- unless it is a "qualified obligation."

FMV of loans proceeds (a)	Date of original loan transaction (b)	Maximum term of repayment of obligation (c)	Interest rate of obligation (d)	Is the obligation a "qualified obligation"? (e)		FMV of obligation (f)	Amount treated as distribution from the trust (subtract column (f) from column (a)) (g)
				Yes	No		
Total . . . . ▶							$

32 With respect to each obligation you treated as a "qualified obligation" on line 31: Do you agree to extend the period of assessment of any income or transfer tax attributable to the transaction, and any consequential income tax changes for each year that the obligation is outstanding, to a date 3 years after the maturity date of the obligation? ☐ Yes ☐ No
Note: You generally must answer "Yes" if you checked "Yes" in column (e) of line 31. . . . .

33 Total distributions received during the current tax year. Add line 30, column (f), and line 31, column (g) . . ▶ $

34 Did the trust, at any time during the tax year, hold an outstanding obligation of yours (or a person related to you) that you treated as a "qualified obligation" in the current tax year? . . . . ☐ Yes ☐ No
If "Yes," complete columns (a) through (e) below with respect to each obligation.

Date of original loan transaction (a)	Tax year qualified obligation first reported (b)	Amount of actual principal payments made during the tax year (c)	Amount of actual interest payments made during the tax year (d)	Does the loan still meet the criteria of a qualified obligation? (e)	
				Yes	No

35 Did you receive a Foreign Grantor Trust Beneficiary Statement from the foreign trust with respect to a distribution? ☐ Yes ☐ No
If "Yes," attach the statement and do not complete the remainder of Part III with respect to that distribution.
If "No," complete Schedule A with respect to that distribution.

36 Did you receive a Foreign Nongrantor Trust Beneficiary Statement from the foreign trust with respect to a distribution? ☐ Yes ☐ No
If "Yes," attach the statement and complete either Schedule A or Schedule B below. If "No," complete Schedule A with respect to that distribution.

Schedule A—Default Calculation of Trust Distributions (See instructions.)

37 Enter amount from line 33 . . . .
38 Number of years the trust has been a nongrantor trust (see instructions). ▶ ________
39 Enter total distributions received from the foreign trust during the 3 preceding tax years (or the number of years the trust has been a nongrantor trust, if fewer than 3) . . . .
40 Multiply line 39 by 1.25 . . . .
41 Average distribution. Divide line 40 by 3 (or the number of years the trust has been a nongrantor trust, if fewer than 3) and enter the result . . . .
42 Amount treated as ordinary income earned in the current year. Enter the smaller of line 37 or line 41 . . . .
43 Amount treated as accumulation distribution. Subtract line 42 from line 37. If -0- or less, enter -0- and do not complete the rest of Part III . . . .
44 Compute applicable number of years of trust. Divide line 38 by 2 and enter here ▶

Schedule B—Actual Calculation of Trust Distributions (See instructions.)

45 Enter amount from line 33 . . . .
46 Amount treated as ordinary income in the current tax year . . . .
47 Amount treated as accumulation distribution. If -0- or less, enter -0- and do not complete the rest of Part III .
48 Amount treated as capital gains in the current tax year . . . .
49 Amount treated as distribution from trust corpus . . . .
50 Enter any other amount received from the foreign trust (attach explanation) . . . .
51 Amount of foreign trust's aggregate undistributed net income . . . .
52 Amount of foreign trust's weighted undistributed net income . . . .
53 Compute applicable number of years of trust. Divide line 52 by line 51 and enter here ▶

Part III (Continued)

Schedule C—Calculation of Interest Charge (See instructions.)

54	Enter accumulation distribution from line 43 or 47, as applicable	
55	Enter tax on total accumulation distribution from line 28 of Form 4970	
56	Enter applicable number of years of foreign trust from line 44 or 53, as applicable (round to nearest half-year). ▶ ______	
57	Combined interest rate imposed on the total accumulation distribution. See Table B on page 8 of instructions	
58	Interest charge. Multiply the amount on line 55 by the combined interest rate on line 57	
59	Tax attributable to accumulated distributions. Add lines 55 and 58. Enter here and as "additional tax" on your income tax return	

Part IV U.S. Recipients of Gifts or Bequests Received During the Current Tax Year From Foreign Persons (See instructions.)

60 During the current tax year, did you receive more than $100,000 during the tax year that you treated as gifts or bequests from a nonresident alien or a foreign estate? See instructions regarding related donors . . . . . . ☐ Yes ☐ No

If "Yes," complete columns (a) through (c) with respect to each such gift or bequest in excess of $5,000. If more space is needed, attach schedule.

Date of gift or bequest (a)	Description of property received (b)	FMV of property received (c)
Total	▶	$

61 During the current tax year, did you receive more than $10,557 that you treated as gifts from a foreign corporation or a foreign partnership? See instructions regarding related donors . . . . . . ☐ Yes ☐ No

If "Yes," complete columns (a) through (g) with respect to each such gift. If more space is needed, attach schedule.

Date of gift (a)	Name of donor (b)	Address of donor (c)	Identification number, if any (d)

Check the box that applies to the foreign donor (e)		Description of property received (f)	FMV of property received (g)
Corporation	Partnership		

62 Do you have any reason to believe that the foreign donor, in making any gift or bequest described in lines 60 and 61, was acting as a nominee or intermediary for any other person? If "Yes," see instructions. . . . . . . ☐ Yes ☐ No

1998

Department of the Treasury
Internal Revenue Service

Instructions for Form 3520

Annual Return To Report Transactions With Foreign Trusts and Receipt of Certain Foreign Gifts

Section references are to the Internal Revenue Code unless otherwise noted.

A Change To Note

Due to the repeal of the excise tax provision under sections 1491 through 1494, lines 14 and 20 through 24 of the 1997 form are no longer needed. Because of the short time span between the release of the 1997 and 1998 forms and the need to limit the amount of reprogramming required, we have retained the 1997 numbering. Lines 14 and 20 through 24 will remain on the 1998 form followed by the word "Reserved."

General Instructions

Purpose of Form

U.S. persons file Form 3520 to report:

- Certain transactions with foreign trusts, and
- Receipt of certain large gifts or bequests from certain foreign persons.

A separate Form 3520 must be filed for transactions with **each** foreign trust.

Who Must File

File Form 3520 if:

1. You are the **responsible party** for reporting a **reportable event** that occurred during the current tax year, or you held an outstanding obligation of a related foreign trust (or a person related to the trust) that you treated as a **qualified obligation** during the current tax year. **Responsible party, reportable event,** and **qualified obligation** are defined on pages 2 and 3.

Complete the first part of page 1 and the relevant portions of Part I. See the instructions for Part I.

2. You are a U.S. person who, during the current tax year, is treated as the owner of any part of the assets of a foreign trust under the grantor trust rules.

Complete the first part of page 1 and Part II. See the instructions for Part II.

3. You are a U.S. person who, during the current tax year, received a distribution from a foreign trust, or a related foreign trust held an outstanding obligation issued by you (or a person related to you) that you treated as a **qualified obligation** (defined on page 2) during the current tax year.

Complete the first part of page 1 and Part III. See the instructions for Part III.

4. You are a U.S. person who, during the current tax year, received either:

a. More than $100,000 from a nonresident alien individual or a foreign estate (including foreign persons related to that nonresident alien individual or foreign estate) that you treated as gifts or bequests, or

b. More than $10,557 from foreign corporations or foreign partnerships (including foreign persons related to such foreign corporations or foreign partnerships) that you treated as gifts.

Complete the first part of page 1 and Part IV. See the instructions for Part IV.

Note: *You may also be required to file* ***Form TD F 90–22.1,*** *Report of Foreign Bank and Financial Accounts.*

Exceptions to filing Form 3520: Form 3520 does not have to be filed to report the following transactions:

- Transfers to foreign trusts described in sections 402(b), 404(a)(4), or 404A.
- Fair market value (FMV) transfers by a U.S. person to a foreign nongrantor trust (other than transfers that are treated as FMV transfers by reason of the receipt of a qualified obligation).
- Transfers to foreign trusts that have a current determination letter from the IRS recognizing their status as exempt from income taxation under section 501(c)(3).
- Transfers to, distributions from, and ownership of Canadian Registered Retirement Savings Plans if the trust would qualify for treaty benefits under the Convention Between the United States of America and Canada with Respect to Taxes on Income and on Capital. However, if for any taxable year you rely on the tax treaty with Canada to avoid information reporting, you are required to disclose this position pursuant to section 6114. See **Pub. 901,** U.S. Tax Treaties.
- Distributions from foreign trusts that are taxable as compensation for services rendered (within the meaning of section 672(f)(2)(B) and its regulations), so long as the recipient reports the distribution as compensation income on its applicable Federal income tax return.
- Distributions from foreign trusts to domestic trusts that have a current determination letter from the IRS recognizing their status as exempt from income taxation under section 501(c)(3).

When and Where To File

In general, Form 3520 is due on the date that your income tax return is due, including extensions. Attach the form to your income tax return. In addition, send a copy to the Internal Revenue Service Center, Philadelphia, PA 19255.

Form 3520 must have all required attachments to be considered complete.

Joint Returns

Two transferors or grantors of the same foreign trust, or two U.S. beneficiaries of the same foreign trust, may file a joint Form 3520, but only if they file a joint income tax return.

Inconsistent Treatment of Items

The U.S. beneficiary and U.S. owner's tax return must be consistent with the **Form 3520-A,** Annual Information Return of a Foreign Trust With a U.S. Owner, filed by the foreign trust unless you report the inconsistency to the IRS. If you are treating items on your tax return differently from the way the foreign trust treated them on its return, file **Form 8082,** Notice of Inconsistent Treatment or Administrative Adjustment Request (AAR). Get Form 8082 for more details.

Definitions

A **distribution** is any gratuitous transfer of money or other property from a trust, whether or not the trust is treated as owned by another person under the grantor trust rules, and without regard to whether the recipient is designated as a beneficiary by the terms of the trust. A distribution includes the receipt of trust corpus and the receipt of a gift or bequest described in section 663(a).

A distribution also includes constructive transfers from a trust. For example, if charges you make on a credit card are paid by a foreign trust or guaranteed or secured by the assets of a foreign trust, the amount charged will be treated as a distribution to you by the foreign trust. Similarly, if you write checks on a foreign trust's bank account, the amount will be treated as a distribution.

Also, if you receive a payment from a foreign trust in exchange for property transferred to the trust or services rendered to the trust, and the fair market value (FMV) of the payment received exceeds the FMV of the property transferred or services rendered, the excess will be treated as a distribution to you.

For example:

- If you sell stock with a FMV of $100 to a foreign trust and receive $150 in exchange, you have received a distribution of $50.
- Similarly, if you receive $100 from the trust for services performed by you for the trust, and the services have a FMV of $20, you have received a distribution of $80.

See the instructions for Part I, Schedule A, and Part III, for special rules with respect to obligations made to, or received from, a foreign trust.

A **foreign trust** is any trust other than a domestic trust. A domestic trust is any trust if:

1. A court within the United States is able to exercise primary supervision over the administration of the trust, and

2. One or more U.S. persons have the authority to control all substantial decisions of the trust.

A **grantor** is any person who creates a trust or transfers cash or other property to a trust. A grantor includes any person treated as the owner of any part of a foreign trust's assets under sections 671 through 679, excluding section 678.

A **grantor trust** is any trust to the extent that the assets of the trust are treated as owned by a person other than the trust. See the **grantor trust rules** below. A part of the trust may be treated as a grantor trust to the extent that only a portion of the trust assets are owned by a person other than the trust.

The **grantor trust rules** are contained in subpart E of Part I of subchapter J (sections 671 through 679).

A **gratuitous transfer** to a foreign trust is any transfer to the trust other than **(a)** a transfer for FMV, or **(b)** a corporate or partnership distribution. A transfer of property to a trust may be considered a gratuitous transfer without regard to whether the transfer is a gift for gift tax purposes (see Chapter 12 of Subtitle B of the Code).

For purposes of this determination, if a U.S. person contributed property to a trust in exchange for any type of interest in the trust, such interest in the trust will be disregarded in determining whether FMV has been received. In addition, a U.S. person will not be treated as making a transfer for FMV merely because the transferor is deemed to recognize gain on the transaction.

If you transfer property to a foreign trust in exchange for an obligation of the trust (or a person related to the trust), it will be a gratuitous transfer unless the obligation is a **qualified obligation** (defined below).

Gross reportable amount is:

- The gross value of property involved in the creation of a foreign trust or the transfer of property to a foreign trust (including a transfer by reason of death);
- The gross value of any portion of a foreign trust treated as owned by a U.S. person under the grantor trust rules or any part of a foreign trust that is included in the gross estate of a U.S. citizen or resident;
- The gross value of assets deemed transferred at the time a domestic trust to which a U.S. citizen or resident previously transferred property becomes a foreign trust, provided such U.S. citizen or resident is alive at the time the trust becomes a foreign trust (see section 679(a)(5)); or
- The gross amount of distributions received from a foreign trust.

Gross value is the FMV of property as determined under section 2031 and its regulations as if the owner had died on the valuation date. Although formal appraisals are not generally required, you should keep contemporaneous records of how you arrived at your good faith estimate.

A **guarantee**:

- Includes any arrangement under which a person, directly or indirectly, assures, on a conditional or unconditional basis, the payment of another's obligation;
- Encompasses any form of credit support, and includes a commitment to make a capital contribution to the debtor or otherwise maintains its financial viability; or
- Includes an arrangement reflected in a "comfort letter," regardless of whether the arrangement gives rise to a legally enforceable obligation. If an arrangement is contingent upon the occurrence of an event, in determining whether the arrangement is a guarantee, you must assume that the event has occurred.

A **nongrantor trust** is any trust to the extent that the assets of the trust are not treated as owned by a person other than the trust. Thus, a nongrantor trust is treated as a taxable entity. A trust may be treated as a nongrantor trust with respect to only a portion of the trust assets. See the grantor trust rules.

An **owner** of a foreign trust is the person that is treated as owning any of the assets of a foreign trust pursuant to the grantor trust rules.

A **qualified obligation,** for purposes of this form, is any obligation if:

1. The obligation is reduced to writing by an express written agreement,

2. The term of the obligation does not exceed 5 years (including options to renew and rollovers) and it is repaid within the 5-year term,

3. All payments on the obligation are denominated in U.S. dollars,

4. The yield to maturity of the obligation is not less than 100% of the applicable Federal rate under section 1274(d) for the day on which the obligation is issued and not greater than 130% of the applicable Federal rate,

5. The U.S. person agrees to extend the period for assessment of any income or transfer tax attributable to the transfer and any consequential income tax changes for each year that the obligation is outstanding, to a date not earlier than 3 years after the maturity date of the obligation, unless the maturity date of the obligation does not extend beyond the end of the U.S. person's taxable year and is paid within such period (this is done on Part I, Schedule A, and Part III, as applicable), and

6. The U.S. person reports the status of the note, including principal and interest payments, on Part I, Schedule A, and Part III, as applicable, for every year that the loan is outstanding.

A **related person** generally includes any person who is related to you for purposes of sections 267 and 707(b). This includes, but is not limited to:

- A member of your family – your brothers and sisters, half-brothers and half-sisters, spouse ancestors (parents, grandparents, etc.), lineal descendants (children, grandchildren, etc.), and the spouses of any of these persons.
- A corporation in which you, directly or indirectly, own more than 50% in value of the outstanding stock. See section 643(i)(2)(B). In addition, see the regulations pursuant to sections 267 and 707(b) for further guidance on related parties.

A **related foreign trust**. A person is related to a foreign trust if such person, without regard to the transfer at issue, is a grantor of the trust, a beneficiary of the trust, or is related to any grantor or beneficiary of the trust. See definition of a **related person** above.

A **reportable event** includes:

1. The creation of a foreign trust by a U.S. person.

2. The transfer of any money or property, directly or indirectly, to a foreign trust by a U.S. person, including a transfer by reason of death if the transfer was a **gratuitous transfer** (defined on page 2).

3. The death of a citizen or resident of the United States if:

a. The decedent was treated as the owner of any portion of a foreign trust under the grantor trust rules, or

b. Any portion of a foreign trust was included in the gross estate of the decedent.

4. A trust that was not a foreign trust becomes a foreign trust.

Responsible party means:

- The transferor in the case of a **reportable event** (defined above).
- The executor of the decedent's estate in any other case.

A **transfer** includes both direct and indirect transfers to a foreign trust. A transaction is considered a transfer without regard to whether the transferor receives consideration from the trust or whether the transfer constitutes a sale or exchange of the property to the trust.

The **transferor** is any person who:

1. Creates or settles a foreign trust,

2. Directly or indirectly transfers money or property to a foreign trust,

3. Makes a sale to a foreign trust if the sale was at other than arm's-length terms or was to a related foreign trust, or makes (or guarantees) a loan to a related foreign trust,

4. Is the executor of the estate of a U.S. person, and

a. The decedent made a testamentary transfer (a transfer by reason of death) to a foreign trust,

b. Immediately prior to death, the decedent was treated as the owner of any portion of a foreign trust under the grantor trust rules, or

c. Any portion of a foreign trust's assets were included in the estate of the decedent.

5. In the case of a trust described in item 4 of the definition of **reportable event:**

a. If an individual who is a citizen or resident of the United States transferred property to the trust when it was not a foreign trust, and that individual is alive when the trust becomes a foreign trust, that individual is the transferor (see section 679(a)(5)).

b. In all other events, the trust is the transferor.

Generally, the person defined as the transferor is the **responsible party** (defined above) who must ensure that required information be provided or pay appropriate penalties.

A **U.S. agent** is a **U.S. person** (defined on page 4) that has a binding contract with a foreign trust that allows the U.S. person to act as the trust's authorized U.S. agent in applying sections 7602, 7603, and 7604 with respect to:

- Any request by the Service to examine records or produce testimony related to the proper U.S. tax treatment of amounts distributed by, or required to be taken into account under the grantor trust rules with respect to, a foreign trust, or
- Any summons by the Service for such records or testimony.

A U.S. grantor, a U.S. beneficiary, or a domestic corporation controlled by the grantor or beneficiary may act as a U.S. agent. However, you may not treat the foreign trust as having a U.S. agent unless you enter the name, address, and taxpayer identification number of the U.S. agent on lines 3a through 3g. If the person identified as the U.S. agent does not produce records or testimony when requested or summonsed by the IRS, the IRS may redetermine the tax consequences of your transactions with the trust and impose appropriate penalties under section 6677.

The agency relationship must be established by the time the U.S. person files Form 3520 for the relevant taxable year and must continue as long as the statute of limitations remains open for the relevant taxable year. If the agent resigns, liquidates, or its responsibility as an agent of the trust is terminated, see Notice 97-34, 1997-1 C.B. 422.

A **U.S. beneficiary** includes any person that could possibly benefit (directly or indirectly) from the trust (including an amended trust) at any time, whether or not the person is named in the trust instrument as a beneficiary and whether or not the person can receive a distribution from the trust in the current year. In addition, a U.S. beneficiary includes:

• A foreign corporation that is a controlled foreign corporation (as defined in section 957(a)),

• A foreign partnership if a U.S. person is a partner of the partnership, and

• A foreign estate or trust if the estate or trust has a U.S. beneficiary.

A foreign trust will be treated as having a U.S. beneficiary unless the terms of the trust instrument specifically prohibit any distribution of income or corpus to a U.S. person at any time, even after the death of the U.S. transferor, and the trust cannot be amended or revised to allow such a distribution.

A **U.S. person** is:

• A citizen or resident alien of the United States (see **Pub. 519**, U.S. Tax Guide for Aliens, for guidance on determining resident alien status),

• A domestic partnership,

• A domestic corporation,

• Any estate (other than a foreign estate, within the meaning of section 7701(a)(31)), and

• Any trust if it is not a **foreign trust** (defined on page 2).

Penalties

A penalty generally applies if Form 3520 is not timely filed or if the information is incomplete or incorrect. Generally, the penalty is:

1. 35% of the gross value of any property transferred to a foreign trust for failure by a U.S. transferor to report the transfer,

2. 35% of the gross value of the distributions received from a foreign trust for failure by a U.S. person to report receipt of the distribution, or

3. 5% of the amount of certain foreign gifts for each month for which the failure to report continues (not to exceed a total of 25%). See section 6039F(c).

In addition, if a foreign trust has a U.S. owner and the trust fails to file the required annual reports on trust activities and income, the U.S. owner is subject to a penalty equal to 5% of the gross value of the portion of the trust's assets treated as owned by the U.S. person (the gross reportable amount). See Form 3520-A.

Additional penalties may be imposed if noncompliance continues after the IRS mails a notice of failure to comply with required reporting. However, this penalty may not exceed the gross reportable amount. Also, penalties will only be imposed to the extent that the transaction is not reported. Thus, if a U.S. person transfers property worth $1 million to a foreign trust, but only reports $400,000 of that amount, penalties could only be imposed on the unreported $600,000.

For more information, see section 6677.

Reasonable cause. No penalties will be imposed if the taxpayer can demonstrate that the failure to comply was due to reasonable cause and not willful neglect.

Note: *The fact that a foreign country would impose penalties for disclosing the required information is not reasonable cause. Similarly, reluctance on the part of a foreign fiduciary or provisions in the trust instrument that prevent the disclosure of required information, is not reasonable cause.*

Who Must Sign

If the return is filed by an individual or a fiduciary, it must be signed by that individual or fiduciary. If it is filed by a partnership, it must be signed by a general partner or limited liability company member. If it is filed by a corporation, it must be signed by the president, vice president, treasurer, assistant treasurer, chief accounting officer, or other corporate officer (such as a tax officer) who is authorized to sign. The paid preparer must complete the required preparer information and:

• Sign the return, by hand, in the space provided for the preparer's signature (signature stamps are not acceptable).

• Give a copy of the return to the filer.

Identification Numbers and Addresses

Use social security numbers or individual taxpayer identification numbers to identify individuals. Use employer identification numbers to identify estates, trusts, partnerships, and corporations.

Include the suite, room, or other unit number after the street address. If the Post Office does not deliver mail to the street address and the U.S. person has a P.O. box, show the box number instead of the street address.

Foreign address. Enter the information in the following order: city, province or state, and country. Follow the country's practice for entering the postal code, if any. Please do not abbreviate the country name.

Specific Instructions

See **Who Must File** for which parts of the form to complete. All filers must check any applicable box for initial, final, or amended return.

Initial return. If this is the first return you are filing with respect to the foreign trust identified, check the box for Initial return.

Final return. If you do not have to file any further returns for transactions with the foreign trust, check the box for Final return. For example, if you annually filed Part II, Form 3520 because you were the owner of the trust for U.S. income tax purposes and the trust has terminated within the taxable year, that year's return would be a final return with respect to that foreign trust.

Amended return. If this Form 3520 is filed to amend a Form 3520 that you filed previously, check the box for Amended return.

Line 1. This line identifies the U.S. person that is filing the Form 3520. If you and your spouse are both making transfers to the same trust and you file joint returns, you may file only one Form 3520. Put the names and taxpayer identification numbers in the same order as they appear on your Form 1040.

Line 3. If you know that the foreign trust has appointed a U.S. agent for purposes of section 6048(b), answer "Yes" and complete lines 3a through 3g. See definition of **U.S. agent** on page 3.

Line 4. If you are the executor of the estate of a U.S. citizen or resident, you must identify the decedent on this line.

Part I
Transfers by U.S. Persons to a Foreign Trust During the Current Tax Year

Complete Part I for information on a **reportable event** (defined on page 3).

Line 5. If you are not the trust creator, enter the name of the person that created or originally settled the foreign trust.

Line 6. See the list of country codes on pages 10 and 11 of these instructions. If the country is not included in the list, write in "OC" for "other country" and write out the country name.

Lines 7, 8, and 10. If you are reporting multiple transfers to a single foreign trust and the answers to lines 7, 8, or 10 are different for various transfers, complete a separate line for each transfer on duplicate copies of the relevant pages of the form.

Line 7a. If "Yes," you must comply with the reporting requirements that would apply to a direct transfer to that other person. For example, if that other person is a foreign partnership, you must comply with the reporting requirements for transfers to foreign partnerships.

Line 8. If the transfer was a completed gift (see Regulations section 25.2511), or bequest, you may have to file **Form 706,** United States Estate (and Generation-Skipping Transfer) Tax Return, or **Form 709,** United States Gift (and Generation-Skipping Transfer) Tax Return.

Line 9. See definition of **U.S. beneficiary** on page 3.

Line 10. If you are treated as the owner of any portion of the foreign trust under the grantor trust rules, answer "Yes" to this question.

Schedule A Obligations of a Related Trust

Line 11a. The FMV of an obligation of the trust (or person related to the trust) that you receive in exchange for the transferred property equals zero, unless the obligation meets the requirements of a qualified obligation. See pages 2 and 3 for definitions of **qualified obligation** and **related foreign trust.**

Lines 12 and 32. If you answered "Yes" to line 11b (line 31, column (e)) with respect to any obligation, you generally must answer "Yes" to line 12 (line 32). By so doing, you agree to extend the period of assessment of any income or transfer tax attributable to the transfer and any consequential income tax changes for each year that the obligation is outstanding. This form will be deemed to be consented to and signed by the Service Center Director or the Assistant Commissioner (International) for purposes of Regulations section 301.6501(c)-1(d).

If you answer "No" to line 12 (line 32), you generally may not treat an obligation as a qualified obligation on line 11b (line 31, column (e)). The one exception to this is if the maturity date of the obligation does not extend beyond the end of your taxable year for which you are reporting and such obligation is paid within that taxable year.

Schedule B Gratuitous Transfers

Complete the applicable portions of Schedule B with respect to all **reportable events** (as defined on page 3) that took place during the current tax year.

Note: *If a **reportable event** causes you to be treated as the owner of any portion of the foreign trust under the grantor trust rules, you must also complete Part II of this form.*

Line 13.

- In your description, indicate whether the property is tangible or intangible.
- You may aggregate transfers of cash during the year on a single line of line 13.
- If there is not enough space on the form, please attach a statement.
- If any transfers are reported on attachments, you must enter "Attachment" on one of the lines in column (b), and enter the total amount of transfers reported on the attachment on line 13, columns (c), (d), (e), (f), (h), and (i).

Note: *Failure to report amounts that should be reported here, may cause penalties to be imposed. See item 1 of **Penalties** on page 4.*

Line 13, column (e). Only include gain that is immediately recognized at the time of the transfer.

Note: *With respect to any transfer by a U.S. person to a foreign nongrantor trust after August 4, 1997, the transfer is treated as a sale or exchange and the transferor must recognize as a gain the excess of the FMV of the transferred property over its adjusted basis. Although the gain is not reported on Form 3520, it is to be reported on the appropriate form or schedule of the transferor's income tax return. See section 684.*

Line 13, column (f). Generally, if the reported transaction is a sale, you should report the gain on the appropriate form or schedule of your income tax return.

Line 16. Enter the name, address, whether the person is a **U.S. beneficiary** (defined on page 3), and taxpayer identification number, if any, of all specified beneficiaries. Include specified beneficiaries, classes of discretionary beneficiaries, and names or classes of any beneficiaries that could be named as additional beneficiaries. If there is not enough space on the form, please attach a statement.

Line 18. Enter the name, address, and taxpayer identification number (if any) of any persons other than those listed on line 17, if those persons have significant powers over the trust (e.g., "protectors," "enforcers," any person that must approve of trustee decisions or otherwise direct the trustee, any person with a power of appointment, any person with a power to remove or appoint trustees, etc.). Include a description of each person's power. If there is not enough space, please attach a statement.

Line 19. Attach:

- A summary of the terms of the trust that includes a summary of any oral agreements or understandings you have with the trustee, whether or not legally enforceable.
- A copy of all trust documents (and any revisions), including the trust instrument, any memoranda of wishes prepared by the trustees summarizing the settlor's wishes, any letter of wishes prepared by the settlor summarizing his or her wishes, and any similar documents.

If you checked "No," also attach a copy of the trust's financial statements, including a balance sheet and an income statement similar to those shown in Form 3520–A. These financial statements must reasonably reflect the trust's accumulated income under U.S. income tax principles. For example, the statements must not treat capital gains as additions to trust corpus.

Schedule E
Qualified Obligations Outstanding in the Current Tax Year

Line 25. Provide information on the status of any outstanding obligation of the foreign trust (or a person related to the foreign trust) that you reported as a qualified obligation in the current tax year. This information is required in order to retain the obligation's status as a qualified obligation. If relevant, attach a statement describing any changes to the terms of the qualified obligation.

If the obligation fails to retain the status of a qualified obligation, you will be treated as having made a gratuitous transfer to the foreign trust, which must be reported on Schedule B, Part I. See Notice 97-34.

Part II
U.S. Owner of a Foreign Trust

Complete Part II if you are considered the owner of any assets of a foreign trust under the grantor trust rules during the taxable year. You are required to enter a taxpayer identification number for such a foreign trust on line 2b.

Line 26. Enter information regarding any person other than yourself who is considered the owner of any portion of the trust under the grantor trust rules. Also, enter in column (e) the specific Code section that causes that person to be considered an owner for U.S. income tax purposes. See the grantor trust rules under sections 671 through 679.

Line 27. See the list of country codes on pages 10 and 11 of these instructions. If the country is not included in the list, write in "OC" for "other country" and write out the country name.

Line 28. If "Yes," the copy of the Foreign Grantor Trust Owner Statement (page 3, Form 3520-A) should show the amount of the foreign trust's income that is attributable to you for U.S. income tax purposes. See Section IV of Notice 97-34.

If "No," you may be liable for a penalty of 5% of the trust assets that you are treated as owning, plus additional penalties for continuing failure to file after notice by the Secretary. See section 6677.

Line 29. Your gross reportable amount is the FMV of the trust assets that you are treated as owning. Include all assets at FMV as of the end of the taxable year. For this purpose, disregard all liabilities. The trust should send you this information in connection with its Form 3520-A. If you did not receive such information (line 9 of the Foreign Grantor Trust Owner Statement) from the trust, complete line 29 to the best of your ability. At a minimum, include the value of all assets that you have transferred to the trust. Also use Form 8082 to notify the IRS that you did not receive a Foreign Grantor Trust Owner Statement. However, filing Form 8082 does not relieve you of any penalties that may be imposed under section 6677. See **Penalties** on page 4.

Part III
Distributions To a U.S. Person From a Foreign Trust During the Current Tax Year

If you received an amount from a portion of a foreign trust of which you are treated as the owner and you have correctly reported any information required on Part II and the trust has filed a Form 3520-A with the IRS, do not separately disclose distributions again in Part III. If you received an amount from a foreign trust that would require a report under both Parts III and IV (gifts and bequests) of Form 3520, report the amount only in Part III.

Line 30. Report any cash or property that you received (actually or constructively, directly or indirectly) during the current tax year, from a foreign trust, whether or not taxable, unless the amount is a loan to you from the trust that is to be reported on line 31. For example, if you are a partner in a foreign partnership that receives a distribution from a foreign trust, you must report your allocable share of such payment as an indirect distribution from the trust.

Line 31. If you, or a person related to you, received a loan from a related foreign trust, it will be treated as a distribution to you unless the obligation you issued in exchange is a qualified obligation.

For this purpose, a loan to you by an unrelated third party that is guaranteed by a foreign trust is generally treated as a loan from the trust.

Line 31, column (e). Answer "Yes" if your obligation given in exchange for the loan is a **qualified obligation** (defined on page 2).

Line 32. See instructions for lines 12 and 32 on page 5.

Line 33. Failure to report distributions that should be reported here, may cause penalties to be imposed.

See item **2** of **Penalties** on page 4.

Line 34. Provide information on the status of any outstanding obligation to the foreign trust that you reported as a qualified obligation in the current tax year. This information is required in order to retain the obligation's status as a qualified obligation. If relevant, attach a statement describing any changes to the terms of the qualified obligation. If the obligation fails to retain the status of a qualified obligation, you will be treated as having received a distribution from the foreign trust, which must be reported in Part III. See Notice 97-34.

Lines 35 and 36. If any of the six items required for the Foreign Grantor Trust Beneficiary Statement or for the Foreign Nongrantor Trust Beneficiary Statement (see page 7) is missing, you must check "No" to line 35 or line 36, as applicable.

Also, if you answer "Yes" to line 35 or line 36, and the foreign trust or U.S. agent does not produce records or testimony when requested or summonsed by the IRS, the IRS may redetermine the tax consequences of your transactions with the trust and impose appropriate penalties under section 6677.

Line 35. If "Yes," attach the Foreign Grantor Trust Beneficiary Statement from the foreign trust and do not complete the remainder of Part III with respect to the distribution. If a U.S. beneficiary receives a complete Foreign Grantor Trust Beneficiary Statement with respect to a distribution during the tax year, the beneficiary should treat the distribution for income tax purposes as if it came directly from the owner. For example, if the distribution is a gift, the beneficiary should not include the distribution in gross income.

This statement must contain these items:

1. The first and last day of the taxable year of the foreign trust to which this statement applies.

2. An explanation of the facts necessary to establish that the foreign trust should be treated for U.S. tax purposes as owned by another person. (The explanation should identify which Code section treats the trust as owned by another person.)

3. A statement identifying whether the owner of the trust is an individual, corporation, or partnership.

4. A description of property (including cash) distributed or deemed distributed to the U.S. person during the taxable year, and the FMV of the property distributed.

5. A statement that the trust will permit either the IRS or the U.S. beneficiary to inspect and copy the trust's permanent books of account, records, and such other documents that are necessary to establish that the trust should be treated for U.S. tax purposes as owned by another person. This statement is not necessary if the trust has appointed a U.S. agent.

6. A statement as to whether the foreign trust has appointed a **U.S. agent** (as defined on page 3). If the trust has a U.S. agent, include the name, address, and taxpayer identification number of the agent.

Line 36. If "Yes," attach the Foreign Nongrantor Trust Beneficiary Statement from the foreign trust. A Foreign Nongrantor Trust Beneficiary Statement must include the following items:

1. An explanation of the appropriate U.S. tax treatment of any distribution or deemed distribution for U.S. tax purposes, or sufficient information to enable the U.S. beneficiary to establish the appropriate treatment of any distribution or deemed distribution for U.S. tax purposes.

2. A statement identifying whether the owner of the trust is a partnership or a foreign corporation.

3. A statement that the trust will permit either the IRS or the U.S. beneficiary to inspect and copy the trust's permanent books of account, records, and such other documents that are necessary to establish the appropriate treatment of any distribution or deemed distribution for U.S. tax purposes. This statement is not necessary if the trust has appointed a U.S. agent.

4. The Foreign Nongrantor Trust Beneficiary Statement must also include items 1, 4, and 6, as listed for line 35 on page 6.

Schedule A
Default Calculation of Trust Distributions

If you answered "Yes" to line 36, you may complete either Schedule A or Schedule B. Generally, however, if you complete Schedule A in the current year (or did so in the prior year), you must continue to do so for all future years, even if you are able to answer "Yes" to line 36 in that future year. (The only exception to this consistency rule is that you may use Schedule B in the year that a trust terminates, but only if you are able to answer "Yes" to line 36 in the year of termination.)

Line 38. To the best of your knowledge, state the number of years the trust has been in existence as a nongrantor trust and attach an explanation of your basis for this statement. Consider any portion of a year to be a complete year. If this is the first year that the trust has been a nongrantor trust, skip lines 39 through 41 and enter the amount from line 37 on line 42.

Line 39. Enter the total amount of distributions that you received during the 3 preceding tax years (or the number of years the trust has been a nongrantor trust, if less than 3). For example, if a trust distributed $50 in year 1, $120 in year 2, and $150 in year 3, the amount reported on line 39 would be $320 ($50 + $120 + $150).

Line 41. Divide line 40 by 3 (or the number of years the trust has been a nongrantor trust if less than 3). Consider any portion of a year to be a complete year. For example, a nongrantor trust created on July 1, 1997, would be treated on a 1999 calendar year return as having two preceding years (1997 and 1998). In this case, you would calculate the amount on line 41 by dividing line 40 by 2. Do not disregard tax years in which no distributions were made. The IRS will consider your proof of these prior distributions as adequate records to demonstrate that any distribution up to the amount on line 37 is not an accumulation distribution in the current taxable year.

Line 42. Enter this amount as ordinary income on your tax return. Report this amount on the appropriate schedule of your tax return (e.g., Schedule E (Form 1040), Part III).

Note: *If there is an amount on line 43, you must also complete line 44 and Schedule C to determine the amount of any interest charge you may owe.*

Schedule B
Actual Calculation of Trust Distributions

You may only use Schedule B if:

- You answered "Yes" to line 36,
- You attach a copy of the Foreign Nongrantor Trust Beneficiary Statement to this return,
- You have never before used Schedule A for this foreign trust or this foreign trust terminated during the taxable year.

Line 46. Enter the amount received by you from the foreign trust that is treated as ordinary income of the trust in the current tax year. Ordinary income is all income that is not capital gains.

Line 50. Enter any other distributed amount that is not included in lines 46, 47, 48, and 49.

Line 51. Enter the foreign trust's aggregate undistributed net income (UNI). For example, assume that a trust was created in 1992 and has made no distributions prior to 1998. Assume the trust's ordinary income was $0 in 1997, $60 in 1996, $124 in 1995, $87 in 1994, $54 in 1993, and $25 in 1992. Thus, for 1998, the trust's UNI would be $350. If the trust earned $100 and distributed $200 during 1998 (so that $100 was distributed from accumulated earnings), the trust's 1999 aggregate UNI would be $250 (i.e., $350 + $100 - $200).

Line 52. Enter the foreign trust's weighted undistributed net income (weighted UNI). The trust's weighted UNI is its accumulated income that has not been distributed, weighted by the years that it has accumulated income. To calculate weighted UNI, multiply the undistributed income from each of the trust's years by the number of years since that year, and then add each year's result. Using the example from line 51, the trust's weighted UNI in 1998 would be $1,260, calculated as follows:

Year	No. of years since that year	UNI from each year	Weighted UNI
1997	1	$ 0	$ 0
1996	2	60	120
1995	3	124	372
1994	4	87	348
1993	5	54	270
1992	6	25	150
TOTAL		$350	$1,260

To calculate the trust's weighted UNI in 1999, the trust could repeat this calculation, or the weighted UNI shown on line 52 of the 1998 Form 3520 could simply be updated using the following formula:

- Begin with 1998 weighted UNI,
- Add UNI at the beginning of 1998,
- Add trust earnings in 1998,
- Subtract trust distributions in 1998, and
- Subtract weighted trust accumulated distributions in 1998. (Weighted trust accumulation distributions are the trust accumulation distributions in 1998 multiplied by the applicable number of years from 1998.)

Using the examples on page 7, the trust's 1999 weighted UNI would be $1,150, calculated as follows.

1998 weighted UNI	$1,260
UNI at beginning of 1998	+ 350
Trust earnings in 1998	+ 100
Trust distributions in 1998	− 200
Weighted trust accumulation distributions in 1998 ($100 X 3.6)	− 360
1999 weighted UNI	$1,150

Line 53. Calculate the trust's applicable number of years by dividing line 52 by line 51. Using the examples in the instructions for lines 51 and 52, the trust's applicable number of years would be 3.6 in 1998 (1,260/350) and 4.6 in 1999 (1,150/250).

Note: *Include as many decimal places as there are digits in the UNI on line 51 (e.g., using the example in the instructions to line 51, include three decimal places).*

Schedule C Calculation of Interest Charge

Complete Schedule C if you entered an amount on line 43 or line 47.

Line 55. Enter the amount from line 54 of this form on line 1, Form 4970. Then compute the tax on the total accumulation distribution using lines 1 through 28 of Form 4970. Enter on line 55 the tax from line 28 of Form 4970.

Note: *Use Form 4970 as a worksheet and attach it to Form 3520.*

Line 57. Interest accumulates on the tax (line 55) for the period beginning on the date that is the applicable number of years (as rounded on line 56) prior to the applicable date and ending on the applicable date. For purposes of making this interest calculation, the applicable date is the date that is mid-year through the taxable year for which reporting is made (e.g., in the case of a 1998 calendar-year taxpayer, the applicable date would be June 30, 1998). Alternatively, if you received only a single distribution during the taxable year that is treated as an accumulation distribution, you may use the date of that distribution as the applicable date.

For portions of the interest accumulation period that are prior to 1996 (and after 1976), interest accumulates at a simple rate of 6% annually, without compounding. For portions of the interest accumulation period that are after 1995, interest is compounded daily at the rate imposed on underpayment of tax under section 6621(a)(2). This compounded interest for periods after 1995 is imposed not only on the partial tax, but also on the total simple interest attributable to pre-1996 periods.

If you are a 1998 calendar-year taxpayer and you use June 30, 1998, as the applicable date for calculating interest, use Table B below to determine the combined interest rate and enter it on line 57. If you are not a 1998 calendar-year taxpayer or you choose to use the actual date of the distribution as the applicable date, calculate the combined interest rate using the above principles and enter it on line 57.

Table B
Combined Interest Rate Imposed on the Total Accumulation Distribution

Look up the applicable number of years of the foreign trust that you entered on line 56. Read across to find the combined interest rate to enter on line 57. Use this table only if you are a 1998 calendar year taxpayer and are using June 30, 1998 as the applicable date.

Applicable number of years of trust (from line 56)	Combined interest rate (enter on line 57)
1.0	0.0875
1.5	0.1354
2.0	0.1854
2.5	0.2376
3.0	0.4083
3.5	0.4506
4.0	0.4928
4.5	0.5351
5.0	0.5773
5.5	0.6196
6.0	0.6618
6.5	0.7041
7.0	0.7463
7.5	0.7886
8.0	0.8308
8.5	0.8731
9.0	0.9153
9.5	0.9576
10.0	0.9998
10.5	1.0421
11.0	1.0843
11.5	1.1266
12.0	1.1688
12.5	1.2111
13.0	1.2533
13.5	1.2956
14.0	1.3378
14.5	1.3801
15.0	1.4223
15.5	1.4646
16.0	1.5068
16.5	1.5491
17.0	1.5913
17.5	1.6336
18.0	1.6758
18.5	1.7181
19.0	1.7603
19.5	1.8026
20.0	1.8448
20.5	1.8871
21.0	1.9293
All years greater than 21.0	1.9716

(**Note:** *Interest charges began in 1977.*)

Line 59. Report this amount as additional tax (ADT), on the appropriate line of your income tax return (e.g., for Form 1040 filers, include this amount on line 56 of your

1998 Form 1040). Write "ADT" to the left of the line 56 entry space.

Part IV
U.S. Recipients of Gifts or Bequests Received During the Current Tax Year From Foreign Persons

Note: *Failure to report gifts that should be reported, may cause penalties to be imposed. See item **3** of **Penalties** on page 4.*

A gift to a U.S. person does not include any amount paid for qualified tuition or medical payments made on behalf of the U.S. person.

If a foreign trust makes a distribution to a U.S. beneficiary, the beneficiary is to report the amount as a distribution in Part III, rather than as a gift in Part IV.

Contributions of property by foreign persons to domestic or foreign trusts that have U.S. persons as beneficiaries are not reportable by those beneficiaries unless they are treated as receiving the contribution in the year of the transfer (e.g., the beneficiary is an owner of that portion of the trust under section 678).

A domestic trust that is not treated as owned by another person is required to report the receipt of a gift or bequest from a foreign person under Part IV.

A domestic trust that is treated as owned by a foreign person is not required to report the receipt of a contribution to the trust from a foreign person. However, a U.S. person should report the receipt of a distribution from such a trust as a gift from a foreign person under Part IV.

Line 60. To calculate the threshold amount ($100,000), you must aggregate gifts from different foreign nonresident aliens and foreign estates if you know (or have reason to know) that those persons are related to each other or one is acting as the nominee for the other. For example, if you receive a gift of $75,000 from nonresident alien individual A and a gift of $40,000 from nonresident alien individual B, and you know that A and B are related, you must answer "Yes" and complete columns (a) through (c) for each gift.

Line 61. Answer "Yes" if: you received aggregate amounts in excess of $10,557 during the current tax year, that you treated as gifts from foreign corporations or foreign partnerships (or any persons that you know (or have reason to know) are related to such foreign corporations or foreign partnerships).

For example, if you, a calendar-year taxpayer during 1998, received $5,000 from foreign corporation X that you treated as a gift, and $8,000 that you received from nonresident alien A that you treated as a gift, and you know that X is wholly owned by A, you must complete columns (a) through (g) for each gift.

Note: *Gifts from foreign corporations or foreign partnerships are subject to recharacterization by the IRS under section 672(f)(4).*

Line 62. If "Yes," and the ultimate donor on whose behalf the reporting donor is acting is a foreign corporation or foreign partnership, attach an explanation including the ultimate foreign donor's name, address, identification number (if any), and status as a corporation or partnership.

If the ultimate donor is a foreign trust, treat the amount received as a distribution from a foreign trust and complete Part III.

Paperwork Reduction Act Notice. We ask for the information on this form to carry out the Internal Revenue laws of the United States. You are required to give us the information. We need it to ensure that you are complying with these laws and to allow us to figure and collect the right amount of tax.

You are not required to provide the information requested on a form that is subject to the Paperwork Reduction Act unless the form displays a valid OMB control number. Books or records relating to a form or its instructions must be retained as long as their contents may become material in the administration of any Internal Revenue law. Generally, tax returns and return information are confidential, as required by section 6103.

The time needed to complete and file this form and related schedules will vary depending on individual circumstances. The estimated average times are:

Recordkeeping	50 hr., 28 min.
Learning about the law or the form	4 hr., 44 min.
Preparing the form	6 hr., 42 min.
Sending the form to the IRS	16 min.

If you have comments concerning the accuracy of these time estimates or suggestions for making this form simpler, we would be happy to hear from you. See the instructions for the tax return with which this form is filed.

Country Codes

Enter on lines 6a, 6b, and line 27, columns (a) and (b) the codes from the list below.

Country	Code
Afghanistan	AF
Albania	AL
Algeria	AG
American Samoa	AQ
Andorra	AN
Angola	AO
Anguilla	AV
Antarctica	AY
Antigua and Barbuda	AC
Argentina	AR
Armenia	AM
Aruba	AA
Ashmore and Cartier Islands	AT
Australia	AS
Austria	AU
Azerbaijan	AJ
Azores	PO
Bahamas, The	BF
Bahrain	BA
Baker Island	FQ
Bangladesh	BG
Barbados	BB
Bassas da India	BS
Belarus	BO
Belgium	BE
Belize	BH
Benin	BN
Bermuda	BD
Bhutan	BT
Bolivia	BL
Bosnia-Herzegovina	BK
Botswana	BC
Bouvet Island	BV
Brazil	BR
British Indian Ocean Territory	IO
Brunei	BX
Bulgaria	BU
Burkina Faso	UV
Burma	BM
Burundi	BY
Cambodia	CB
Cameroon	CM
Canada	CA
Canary Islands	SP
Cape Verde	CV
Cayman Islands	CJ
Central African Republic	CT
Chad	CD
Chile	CI
China, People's Republic of	CH
Christmas Island (Indian Ocean)	KT
Clipperton Island	IP
Cocos (Keeling) Islands	CK
Colombia	CO
Comoros	CN
Congo	CF
Cook Islands	CW
Coral Sea Islands Territory	CR
Corsica	VP
Costa Rica	CS
Cote D'Ivoire (Ivory Coast)	IV
Croatia	HR
Cuba	CU
Cyprus	CY
Czech Republic	EZ
Denmark	DA
Djibouti	DJ
Dominica	DO
Dominican Republic	DR
Ecuador	EC
Egypt	EG
El Salvador	ES
Equatorial Guinea	EK
Eritrea	ER
Estonia	EN
Ethiopia	ET
Europa Island	EU
Falkland Islands (Islas Malvinas)	FK
Faroe Islands	FO
Fiji	FJ
Finland	FI
France	FR
French Guiana	FG
French Polynesia	FP
French Southern and Antarctic Lands	FS
Gabon	GB
Gambia, The	GA
Gaza Strip	GZ
Georgia	GG
Germany	GM
Ghana	GH
Gibraltar	GI
Glorioso Islands	GO
Greece	GR
Greenland	GL
Grenada	GJ
Guadeloupe	GP
Guam	GQ
Guatemala	GT
Guernsey	GK
Guinea	GV
Guinea-Bissau	PU
Guyana	GY
Haiti	HA
Heard Island and McDonald Islands	HM
Honduras	HO
Hong Kong	HK
Howland Island	HQ
Hungary	HU
Iceland	IC
India	IN
Indonesia	ID
Iran	IR
Iraq	IZ
Ireland	EI
Isle of Man	IM
Israel	IS
Italy	IT
Jamaica	JM
Jan Mayen	JN
Japan	JA
Jersey	JE
Johnston Atoll	JQ
Jordan	JO
Juan de Nova Island	JU
Kazakhstan	KZ
Kenya	KE
Kingman Reef	KQ
Kiribati	KR
Korea, Democratic People's Republic of (North)	KN
Korea, Republic of (South)	KS
Kuwait	KU
Kyrgyzstan	KG
Laos	LA
Latvia	LG
Lebanon	LE
Lesotho	LT
Liberia	LI
Libya	LY
Liechtenstein	LS
Lithuania	LH
Luxembourg	LU
Macau	MC
Macedonia	MK

Country	Code	Country	Code
Madagascar	MA	San Marino	SM
Malawi	MI	Sao Tome and Principe	TP
Malaysia	MY	Saudi Arabia	SA
Maldives	MV	Senegal	SG
Mali	ML	Serbia	SR
Malta	MT	Seychelles	SE
Marshall Islands	RM	Sierra Leone	SL
Martinique	MB	Singapore	SN
Mauritania	MR	Slovakia	LO
Mauritius	MP	Slovenia	SI
Mayotte	MF	Solomon Islands	BP
Mexico	MX	Somalia	SO
Micronesia, Federated States of	FM	South Africa	SF
Midway Islands	MQ	South Georgia and the South Sandwich Islands	SX
Moldova	MD	Spain	SP
Monaco	MN	Spratly Islands	PG
Mongolia	MG	Sri Lanka	CE
Montenegro	MW	Sudan	SU
Montserrat	MH	Suriname	NS
Morocco	MO	Svalbard	SV
Mozambique	MZ	Swaziland	WZ
Namibia	WA	Sweden	SW
Nauru	NR	Switzerland	SZ
Navassa Island	BQ	Syria	SY
Nepal	NP	Taiwan	TW
Netherlands, The	NL	Tajikistan	TI
Netherlands Antilles	NT	Tanzania, United Republic of	TZ
New Caledonia	NC	Thailand	TH
New Zealand	NZ	Togo	TO
Nicaragua	NU	Tokelau	TL
Niger	NG	Tonga	TN
Nigeria	NI	Trinidad and Tobago	TD
Niue	NE	Tromelin Island	TE
Norfolk Island	NF	Tunisia	TS
Northern Ireland	UK	Turkey	TU
Northern Mariana Islands	CQ	Turkmenistan	TX
Norway	NO	Turks and Caicos Islands	TK
Oman	MU	Tuvalu	TV
Pakistan	PK	Uganda	UG
Palau, Republic of	PS	Ukraine	UP
Palmyra Atoll	LQ	United Arab Emirates	TC
Panama	PM	United Kingdom	UK
Papua New Guinea	PP	United States of America	US
Paracel Islands	PF	Uruguay	UY
Paraguay	PA	Uzbekistan	UZ
Peru	PE	Vanuatu	NH
Philippines	RP	Vatican City	VT
Pitcairn Island	PC	Venezuela	VE
Poland	PL	Vietnam	VM
Portugal	PO	Virgin Islands (British)	VI
Puerto Rico	RQ	Virgin Islands (U.S.)	VQ
Qatar	QA	Wake Island	WQ
Reunion	RE	Wallis and Futuna	WF
Romania	RO	West Bank	WE
Russia	RS	Western Sahara	WI
Rwanda	RW	Western Samoa	WS
St. Kitts and Nevis	SC	Yemen	YM
St. Helena	SH	Zaire	CG
St. Lucia	ST	Zambia	ZA
St. Pierre and Miquelon	SB	Zimbabwe	ZI
St. Vincent and the Grenadines	VC	Other Countries	OC

Form **3520-A**

Department of the Treasury
Internal Revenue Service

Annual Information Return of Foreign Trust With a U.S. Owner

(Under section 6048(b))

► Certain foreign trusts may have to issue a Foreign Grantor Trust Owner Statement(s) or a Foreign Grantor Trust Beneficiary Statement(s) (pages 3 and 4). See separate instructions.

OMB No. 1545-0160

1998

Note: All information must be in English. Show all amounts in U.S. dollars.

For calendar year 1998, or tax year beginning , 19 , and ending , 19

Part I General Information (See instructions.)

1a Name of foreign trust	b Identification number
c Number, street, and room or suite no. (if a P.O. box, see instructions)	

d City or town	e State or province	f ZIP or postal code	g Country

2 Did the foreign trust appoint a U.S. agent (defined on page 2 of the instructions) who can provide IRS with all revelant trust information? . . . ☐ Yes ☐ No

If "Yes," skip lines 2a through 2e and go to line 3.

If "No," you are required to attach a copy of all trust documents as indicated below. If these documents have been attached to a Form 3520-A filed within the previous 3 years, attach only relevant updates.

Have you attached a copy of:	Yes	No	Attached Previously	Year Attached
a Summary of all written and oral agreements and understandings relating to the trust?	☐	☐	☐	______
b The trust instrument?	☐	☐	☐	______
c Memoranda or letters of wishes?	☐	☐	☐	______
d Subsequent variances to original trust documents?	☐	☐	☐	______
e Other trust documents?	☐	☐	☐	

3a Name of U.S. agent	b Identification number
c Number, street, and room or suite no. (if a P.O. box, see instructions)	

d City or town	e State or province	f ZIP or postal code	g Country

4a Name of trustee	b Identification number, if any
c Number, street, and room or suite no. (if a P.O. box, see instructions)	

d City or town	e State or province	f ZIP or postal code	g Country

5 Did the trust transfer any property to another entity during the tax year? . . . ☐ Yes ☐ No
If "Yes," attach statement. See instructions.

Under penalties of perjury, I declare that I have examined this return, including any accompanying reports, schedules, or state ments, and to the best of my knowledge and belief, it is true, correct, and complete.

Trustee's Signature ______________________ Title ______________________ Date ________

Preparer's Signature Preparer's social security number Date

Part II Foreign Trust Income Statement. Totals from books and records of foreign trust. (See instructions.)

Income	1 Interest	
	2 Dividends	
	3 Gross rents and royalties	
	4 Income (loss) from partnerships and fiduciaries	
	5 Capital gains:	
	a Net short-term capital gain (loss)	
	b Net long-term capital gain (loss)	
	6 Ordinary gains (losses)	
	7 Other income (attach schedule)	
	8 Total income (add lines 1 through 7)	
Expenses	9 Interest expense	
	10a Foreign taxes (attach schedule)	
	b State and local taxes	
	11 Amortization and depreciation (depletion)	
	12 Trustee and advisor fees	
	13 Charitable contributions	
	14 Other expenses (attach schedule)	
	15 Total expenses (add lines 9 through 14)	
	16 Net income (loss) (subtract line 15 from line 8)	
	17a Enter FMV of total distributions from the trust to all persons whether U.S. or foreign persons ▶	

b Distributions to U.S. owner:

(a) Name of owner	(b) Identification number	(c) Date of distribution	(d) FMV

c Distributions to U.S. beneficiaries:

(a) Name of beneficiary	(b) Identification number	(c) Date of distribution	(d) FMV

Part III Foreign Trust Balance Sheet

	Beginning of Tax Year		End of Tax Year	
	(a) Amount	(b) Total	(c) Amount	(d) Total
Assets				
1 Cash				
2 Accounts receivable				
3 Mortgages and notes receivable				
4 Inventories				
5 Government obligations				
6 Other marketable securities				
7 Other nonmarketable securities				
8a Depreciable (depletable) assets				
b Less: accumulated depreciation (depletion)				
9 Real property				
10 Other assets (attach schedule)				
11 Total assets				
Liabilities				
12 Accounts payable				
13 Contributions, gifts, grants, etc, payable				
14 Mortgages and notes payable				
15 Other liabilities (attach schedule)				
16 Total liabilities				
Net Worth				
17 Contributions to trust corpus				
18 Accumulated trust income				
19 Other (attach schedule)				
20 Total net worth (add lines 17 through 19)				
21 Total liabilities and net worth (add lines 16 and 20)				

1998 Foreign Grantor Trust Owner Statement
(See instructions.)

1a Name of foreign trust	b Identification number
c Number, street, and room or suite no. (if a P.O. box, see page 2 of instructions)	

d City or town	e State or province	f ZIP or postal code	g Country

2 Did the foreign trust appoint a U.S. agent (defined on page 2 of the instructions) who can provide IRS with all revelant trust information? . . . ☐ Yes ☐ No
If "Yes," complete lines 3a through 3g.

3a Name of U.S. agent	b Identification number
c Number, street, and room or suite no. (if a P.O. box, see instructions)	

d City or town	e State or province	f ZIP or postal code	g Country

4a Name of trustee	b Identification number, if any
c Number, street, and room or suite no. (if a P.O. box, see instructions)	

d City or town	e State or province	f ZIP or postal code	g Country

5 The tax year of the owner of the foreign trust to which this statement relates ▶

6a Name of U.S. owner	b Identification number
c Number, street, and room or suite no. (if a P.O. box, see instructions)	

d City or town	e State or province	f ZIP or postal code	g Country

7 Attach an explanation of the facts and law (including the section of the Internal Revenue Code) that establishes that the forei gn trust (or portion of the foreign trust) is treated for U.S. tax principles as owned by the U.S. person.

8 If the trust did not appoint a U.S. agent, list the trust documents attached to Form 3520-A.

9 Gross value of the portion of the trust treated as owned by the U.S. owner . . . . $

1998 Statement of Foreign Trust Income Attributable to U.S. Owner (See instructions.)
Report each item on the proper form or schedule of your tax return.

Income	1	Interest . . .	
	2	Dividends . . .	
	3	Gross rents and royalties . . .	
	4	Income from partnerships and fiduciaries . . .	
	5	Capital gains (losses) . . .	
	6	Ordinary gains and (losses) . . .	
	7	Other income (attach schedule) . . .	
Expenses	8	Interest expenses . . .	
	9a	Foreign taxes (attach schedule) . . .	
	b	State and local taxes . . .	
	10	Amortization and depreciation (depletion) . . .	
	11	Trustee and advisor fees . . .	
	12	Charitable contributions . . .	
	13	Other expenses (attach schedule) . . .	

Under penalties of perjury, I declare that I have examined this return, including any accompanying reports, schedules, or state ments, and to the best of my knowledge and belief, it is true, correct, and complete.

Trustee Signature ____________ Title ____________ Date ______

1998 Foreign Grantor Trust Beneficiary Statement

1a Name of foreign trust			b Identification number
c Number, street, and room or suite no. (if a P.O. box, see page 2 of instructions)			
d City or town	e State or province	f ZIP or postal code	g Country

2 Did the foreign trust appoint a U.S. agent (defined on page 2 of the instructions) who can provide IRS with all revelant trust information? . . . . . ☐ Yes ☐ No

If "Yes," complete lines 3a through 3g.

If "No," do you agree that either the IRS or the U.S. beneficiary can inspect and copy the trust's permanent books of account, records, and such other documents that are necessary to establish that the trust should be treated for U.S. tax purposes as owned by another person? . . . . . ☐ Yes ☐ No

3a Name of U.S. agent			b Identification number
c Number, street, and room or suite no. (if a P.O. box, see instructions)			
d City or town	e State or province	f ZIP or postal code	g Country
4a Name of trustee			b Identification number (if any)
c Number, street, and room or suite no. (if a P.O. box, see instructions)			
d City or town	e State or province	f ZIP or postal code	g Country

5 The first and last day of the tax year of the foreign trust to which Form 3520-A applies ▶

6a Name of U.S. beneficiary			b Identification number
c Number, street, and room or suite no. (if a P.O. box, see instructions)			
d City or town	e State or province	f ZIP or postal code	g Country

7 Description of property (including cash) distributed, or treated as distributed, to the U.S. person during the tax year. (See i nstructions to Part III of Form 3520 for U.S. tax treatment of these amounts.)

(a) Description of property	(b) FMV

8 Attach an explanation of the facts and law (including the section of the Internal Revenue Code) that establishes that the forei gn trust (or portion of the foreign trust) is treated for U.S. tax principles as owned by another person.

9 Owner of the foreign trust is (check one)

☐ individual ☐ partnership ☐ corporation

Under penalties of perjury, I declare that I have examined this return, including any accompanying reports, schedules, or state ments, and to the best of my knowledge and belief, it is true, correct, and complete.

Trustee Signature ▶ Title ▶ Date ▶

1998

Department of the Treasury
Internal Revenue Service

Instructions for Form 3520-A

Annual Information Return of Foreign Trust With a U.S. Owner

Section references are to the Internal Revenue Code unless otherwise noted.

General Instructions

Purpose of Form

Form 3520-A is the annual information return of a foreign trust with at least one U.S. owner. The form provides information about the foreign trust, its U.S. beneficiaries, and any U.S. person who is treated as the owner of any portion of the foreign trust.

Who Must File

A foreign trust must file Form 3520-A to satisfy its annual information reporting requirements. Each U.S. person treated as an owner of a foreign trust under sections 671 through 679 is responsible for ensuring that the foreign trust files an annual return setting forth a full and complete accounting of all trust activities, trust operations, and other relevant information. In addition, the U.S. owner is responsible for ensuring that the trust annually furnishes such information (as the Secretary prescribes) to U.S. owners and U.S. beneficiaries of the trust.

Exceptions to filing Form 3520-A: Form 3520-A does not have to be filed by the following foreign trusts:

- A trust that is a Canadian Registered Retirement Savings Plan if the trust would qualify for treaty benefits under the Convention Between the United States of America and Canada with Respect to Taxes on Income and on Capital. However, if for any taxable year the trust relies on the tax treaty with Canada to avoid information reporting, the U.S. owner is required to disclose this position pursuant to section 6114. See **Pub. 901,** U.S. Tax Treaties.
- A foreign trust described in section 402(b), 404(a)(4), or 404A.

When and Where To File

File a complete Form 3520-A with the Internal Revenue Service Center, Philadelphia, PA 19255, by the 15th day of the 3rd month after the end of the trust's tax year. Furnish copies of the Foreign Grantor Trust Owner Statement and the Foreign Grantor Trust Beneficiary Statement to the U.S. owners and U.S. beneficiaries by the 15th day of the 3rd month after the end of the trust's tax year. An extension of time to file Form 3520-A (including the statements) may be granted. For details, get **Form 2758**, Application for Extension of Time To File Certain Excise, Income, Information, and Other Returns.

Definitions

A **distribution** is any gratuitous transfer of money or other property from a trust, whether or not the trust is treated as owned by another person under the grantor trust rules, and without regard to whether the recipient is designated as a beneficiary by the terms of the trust. A distribution includes the receipt of trust corpus and the receipt of a gift or bequest described in section 663(a).

A distribution also includes constructive transfers from a trust. For example, if charges you make on a credit card are paid by a foreign trust or guaranteed or secured by the assets of a foreign trust, the amount charged will be treated as a distribution to you by the foreign trust. Similarly, if you write checks on a foreign trust's bank account, the amount will be treated as a distribution.

Also, if you receive a payment from a foreign trust in exchange for property transferred to the trust or services rendered to the trust, and the fair market value (FMV) of the payment received exceeds the FMV of the property transferred or services rendered, the excess will be treated as a distribution to you.

For example:

- If you sell stock with an FMV of $100 to a foreign trust and receive $150 in exchange, you have received a distribution of $50.
- Similarly, if you receive $100 from the trust for services performed by you for the trust, and the services have an FMV of $20, you have received a distribution of $80.

If you, or a person related to you, received a loan from a related foreign trust, it will be treated as a distribution to you unless the obligation you issued in exchange is a qualified obligation.

A **foreign trust** is any trust other than a domestic trust. A domestic trust is any trust if:

1. A court within the United States is able to exercise primary supervision over the administration of the trust, and

2. One or more U.S. persons have the authority to control all substantial decisions of the trust.

A **grantor** is any person who creates a trust or transfers cash or other property to a trust. A grantor includes any person treated as the owner of any part of a foreign trust's assets under sections 671 through 679, excluding section 678.

A **grantor trust** is any trust to the extent that the assets of the trust are treated as owned by a person other than the trust. See **grantor trust rules** below. A part of the trust may be treated as a grantor trust to the extent that only a portion of the trust assets are owned by a person other than the trust.

The **grantor trust rules** are contained in subpart E of Part I of subchapter J (sections 671 through 679).

Gross value is the FMV of property as determined under section 2031 and the regulations thereunder as if the owner had died on the valuation date. Although formal appraisals are not generally required, you should keep contemporaneous records of how you arrived at your good faith estimate.

A **nongrantor trust** is any trust to the extent that the assets of the trust are not treated as owned by a person other than the trust. Thus, a nongrantor trust is treated as a taxable entity. A trust may be treated as a nongrantor trust with respect to only a portion of the trust assets. See the grantor trust rules.

An **owner** of a foreign trust is the person that is treated as owning any of the assets of a foreign trust pursuant to the grantor trust rules.

A **U.S. agent** is a **U.S. person** (defined on page 2) that has a binding contract with a foreign trust that allows the U.S. person to act as the trust's authorized U.S. agent (see instructions for Part I, **Lines 3a through 3g, U.S. agent,** on page 2) in applying sections 7602, 7603, and 7604 with respect to:

• Any request by the Service to examine records or produce testimony related to the proper U.S. tax treatment of amounts distributed by, or required to be taken into account under the grantor trust rules with respect to, a foreign trust, or

• Any summons by the Service for such records or testimony.

A U.S. grantor, a U.S. beneficiary, or a domestic corporation controlled by the grantor or beneficiary may act as a U.S. agent. However, you may not treat the foreign trust as having a U.S. agent unless you enter the name, address, and taxpayer identification number of the U.S. agent on lines 3a through 3g. If the person identified as the U.S. agent does not produce records or testimony when requested or summonsed by the IRS, the IRS may redetermine the tax consequences of your transactions with the trust and impose appropriate penalties under section 6677.

The agency relationship must be established by the time the U.S. person files Form 3520-A for the relevant taxable year and must continue as long as the statute of limitations remains open for the relevant taxable year. If the agent resigns, liquidates, or its responsibility as an agent of the trust is terminated, see Notice 97-34, 1997–1 C.B. 422.

A **U.S. beneficiary** includes any person that could possibly benefit (directly or indirectly) from the trust (including an amended trust) at any time, whether or not the person is named in the trust instrument as a beneficiary and whether or not the person can receive a distribution from the trust in the current year. In addition, a U.S. beneficiary includes:

• A foreign corporation that is a controlled foreign corporation (as defined in section 957(a)),

• A foreign partnership if a U.S. person is a partner of the partnership, and

• A foreign estate or trust if the estate or trust has a U.S. beneficiary.

A foreign trust will be treated as having a U.S. beneficiary unless the terms of the trust instrument specifically prohibit any distribution of income or corpus to a U.S. person at any time, even after the death of the U.S. transferor, and the trust cannot be amended or revised to allow such a distribution.

A **U.S. person** is:

• A citizen or resident alien of the United States (see **Pub. 519,** U.S. Tax Guide for Aliens, for guidance on determining resident alien status),

• A domestic partnership,

• A domestic corporation,

• Any estate (other than a foreign estate, within the meaning of section 7701(a)(31)), and

• Any trust if it is not a **foreign trust** (defined on page 1).

Penalties

The U.S. owner is subject to a penalty of 5% of the gross value of the portion of the trust's assets treated as owned by that person at the close of that year if the foreign trust: **(a)** fails to file a timely Form 3520-A, or **(b)** does not furnish the information required by section 6048(b). See section 6677(b).

• Additional penalties may be imposed if noncompliance continues after the IRS mails a notice of failure to comply with the required reporting. See section 6677(a).

• Criminal penalties for failure to file on time and for filing a false or fraudulent return are provided by sections 7203, 7206, and 7207.

Reasonable cause. No penalties will be imposed if the taxpayer can demonstrate that the failure to comply was due to reasonable cause and not willful neglect.

Note: *The fact that a foreign country would impose penalties for disclosing the required information is not reasonable cause. Similarly, reluctance on the part of a foreign fiduciary or provisions in the trust instrument that prevent the disclosure of required information, is not reasonable cause.*

Who Must Sign

If the return is filed by:

• An individual or fiduciary, it must be signed by that individual or fiduciary.

• A partnership, it must be signed by a general partner or limited liability company member.

• A corporation, it must be signed by the president, vice president, treasurer, assistant treasurer, chief accounting officer, or other corporate officer (such as a tax officer) who is authorized to sign.

The paid preparer must complete the required preparer information and:

• Sign the return, by hand, in the space provided for the preparer's signature (signature stamps are not acceptable).

• Give a copy of the return to the filer.

Identification Numbers and Addresses

Identification numbers. Use social security numbers or individual taxpayer identification numbers to identify individuals. Use employer identification numbers to identify estates, trusts, partnerships, and corporations.

Address. Include the suite, room, or other unit number after the street address. If the Post Office does not deliver mail to the street address and the U.S. person has a P.O. box, show the box number instead of the street address.

Foreign address. Enter the information in the following order: city, province or state, and country. Follow the foreign country's pratice for entering the postal code, if any. Please do not abbreviate the country name.

Specific Instructions

Part I, General Information

Line 2. If the trust did not appoint a U.S. agent, attach the following documents to Form 3520-A:

• A summary of the terms of the trust that includes a summary of any oral agreements or understandings you have with the trustee, whether or not legally enforceable.

• A copy of all trust documents (and any revisions), including the trust instrument, any memoranda of wishes prepared by the trustees summarizing the settlor's wishes, any letter of wishes prepared by the settlor summarizing his/her wishes, and any similar documents.

Lines 3a through 3g, U.S. agent. If a foreign trust with a U.S. owner does not have a U.S. agent, the Secretary may determine the amounts required to be taken into account with respect to the foreign trust by the U.S. owner. See section 6048(b)(2). In order to avoid this result, a U.S. owner of a foreign trust should ensure that the foreign trust appoints a U.S. person to act as the foreign trust's limited agent for purposes of applying sections 7602, 7603, and 7604 with respect to a request by the Secretary to examine records or produce testimony, or a summons by the Secretary for such records or testimony. Any U.S. citizen, resident alien, or domestic corporation (including a U.S. grantor or U.S. beneficiary of a foreign trust) may act as the U.S. agent of the trust.

In order to authorize a U.S. person to act as an agent under section 6048(b), the trust and the agent must enter into a binding agreement substantially in the format that follows on page 3. Attach a copy of the authorization to Form 3520-A.

AUTHORIZATION OF AGENT

[Name of foreign trust] hereby expressly authorizes [name of U.S. agent] to act as its agent solely for purposes of sections 7602, 7603, and 7604 of the Internal Revenue Code with respect to any request to examine records or produce testimony related to the proper treatment of amounts required to be taken into account under the rules of section 6048(b)(1)(A) or to any summons for such records or testimony. I certify that I have the authority to execute this authorization of agent to act on behalf of [name of foreign trust].

Signature of trustee (or other authorized person)	(title)	(date)

Your Name (type or print)

Identification Number (if any)

Address

[Name of agent] accepts this appointment to act as agent for [name of foreign trust] for the above purpose. I certify that I have the authority to execute this authorization of agent to act on behalf of [name of foreign trust] and agree to accept service of process for the above purposes.

Signature of agent	(title)	(date)

Your Name (type or print)

Identification Number (if any)

Address

Line 5. Attach a statement that provides the following information concerning the transfer:

1. Name, U.S. taxpayer identification number (if any), and country of organization or residence of the person to whom the property was transferred.

2. A general description of the transfer, and any wider transaction of which it forms a part, including a chronology of the transfers involved and an identification of the other parties to the transaction to the extent known.

3. A description of the property transferred, including the estimated FMV and the adjusted basis of the property.

4. A description of the consideration received by the trust, including its estimated FMV, and in the case of stock or securities, the class or type, amount, and characteristics of the interest received. If no consideration was received by the trust, indicate whether the trust or a U.S. owner exercises any powers over the entity to which the property was transferred (including a description of such powers), and identify the name, U.S. taxpayer identification number (if any), and country of organization or residence of all beneficial owners of such entity.

5. To the extent known, a description of any subsequent transfer of the property, including the name, U.S. taxpayer identification number (if any), and country of organization or residence of the person to whom the property was subsequently transferred.

The statement must also contain a description of the trust ownership structure setting forth the name, U.S. taxpayer identification number (if any), and country of organization of all entities in which the trust has an ownership interest, including an ownership chart showing the trust's position in the chain of ownership and the percentages of ownership.

Part II, Foreign Trust Income Statement

Include all income from U.S. and non-U.S. sources. This financial statement must reasonably reflect the trust's accumulated income under U.S. income tax principles.

Line 1, Interest income. Report the trust's share of all taxable interest income that was received during the tax year. Examples of taxable interest include, but are not limited to, interest from:

- Accounts (including certificates of deposit and money market accounts) with banks, credit unions, and thrifts.
- Notes, loans, and mortgages.
- U.S. Treasury bills, notes, and bonds.
- U.S. savings bonds.
- Original issue discount.
- Income received as a regular interest holder of a real estate mortgage investment conduit (REMIC).

For taxable bonds acquired after 1987, amortizable bond premium is treated as an offset to the interest income instead of as a separate interest deduction. See **Pub. 550**, Investment Income and Expenses.

Line 2, Dividends. Report the trust's share of all ordinary dividends received during the tax year.

Note: *Report capital gains on line 5.*

Lines 3 and 4, Gross rents, royalties, partnership income, etc. If the trust received a Schedule K-1 from a partnership, S corporation, or other flow-through entity, use the corresponding lines on Form 3520-A to report the interest, dividends, capital gains, etc., from the flow-through entity.

Line 5, Capital gains (losses). Use Schedule D (corporate or individual, whichever applies) to compute any capital gains or (losses).

Line 6, Ordinary gains (losses). Enter the ordinary gain or (loss) from the sale or exchange of property other than capital assets and also from involuntary conversions (other than casualty or theft).

Line 7, Other income. Enter other items of income not included on lines 1 through 6. List the types and amounts on an attached schedule if the trust has more than one item.

Items to be reported on line 7 include any part of a total distribution shown on **Form 1099-R,** Distributions From Pensions, Annuities, Retirement or Profit-Sharing Plans, IRAs, Insurance Contracts, etc., that is treated as ordinary income. For more information, see the separate instructions for **Form 4972,** Tax on Lump-Sum Distributions.

Expenses

Line 9, Interest expense. Enter the amount of interest (subject to limitations) paid or incurred by the trust on amounts borrowed by the trust or on debt acquired by the trust.

If the proceeds of a loan were used for more than one purpose (e.g., to purchase a portfolio investment and to acquire an interest in a passive activity), the fiduciary must make an interest allocation according to the rules in Temporary Regulations section 1.163-8T.

Do not include interest paid on indebtedness incurred or continued to purchase or carry obligations on which the interest is wholly exempt from income tax.

Line 10a, Foreign taxes. A foreign tax includes only a tax imposed by the authority of a foreign country.

Line 10b, State and local taxes. Enter any deductible taxes paid or incurred during the tax year. Deductible taxes include:

- State and local income or real property taxes.
- The generation-skipping transfer (GST) tax imposed on income distributions.

Do not deduct:

- Federal income taxes.
- Estate, inheritance, legacy, succession, and gift taxes.

- Federal duties and excise taxes.
- State and local sales taxes. Instead, treat these taxes as part of the cost of the property.

Line 11, Amortization and depreciation (depletion). A reasonable allowance is allowed as a depreciation deduction for the exhaustion, wear, and tear of:

- Property used in the trade or business, or
- Property held for the production of income.

A trust is allowed a deduction for amortization, depletion, and depreciation only to the extent the deductions are attributable to the trust.

Line 12, Trustee and advisor fees. Enter the deductible fees paid or incurred to the fiduciary for administering the trust during the tax year.

Line 13, Charitable contributions. Generally, any part of the gross income of a trust (other than a simple trust) that, under the terms of the will or governing instrument, is paid (or treated as paid) during the tax year for a charitable purpose specified in section 170(c) is allowed as a deduction to the trust. It is not necessary that the charitable organization be created or organized in the United States.

Line 14, Other expenses. Enter other items of expense not listed on lines 9 through 13. List the type and amount on an attached schedule if the trust has more than one item.

Lines 17b and 17c, Distributions to U.S. owners and beneficiaries. Separately list the total amount of distributions to each U.S. owner and beneficiary. List the full name, identification number, date of distribution, and FMV (dollar amount) for each U.S. owner and beneficiary receiving a distribution. If more space is needed, attach a schedule.

Prepare a separate Foreign Grantor Trust Owner Statement or a Foreign Grantor Trust Beneficiary Statement for each U.S. owner or beneficiary who receives a distribution.

Part III, Foreign Trust Balance Sheet

List all assets and liabilities of the trust, including those assets and liabilities attributable to the portion(s) of the trust (if any) not treated as owned by a U.S. person.

The balance sheet should reflect FMV. Include certificates of deposit as cash on line 1.

Line 18, Accumulated trust income. Include on line 18 the total amount of trust income accumulated and not distributed.

Foreign Grantor Trust Owner Statement

A copy of this statement (page 3 of Form 3520-A) must be furnished to each U.S. person who is treated as an owner of the foreign trust under grantor trust rules. The statement must be furnished no later than the 15th day of the 3rd month following the end of the trust's tax year or later, if pursuant to an extension of time to file.

Line 8, Trust documents. If the trust did not appoint a U.S. agent, list the documents attached to a Form 3520-A filed within the last 3 years. See the instructions for line 2, Part I, for a list of documents the trust may have been required to attach to Form 3520-A.

Statement of Foreign Trust Income Attributable to U.S. Owner

A copy of this statement (page 3 of Form 3520-A) is required to be furnished to each U.S. person who is deemed to be an owner of a foreign grantor trust. The U.S. owner must include the income and expenses attributable to the owner on its U.S. income tax return. The statement must be furnished to the U.S. owner no later than the 15th day of the 3rd month after the end of the trust's tax year or later, if pursuant to an extension of time to file.

The amounts on the statement must include the portion of income reported by the foreign trust deemed attributable to the U.S. owner.

The foreign trust may need to furnish to the U.S. owner additional information, including applicable schedules, to ensure that the owner accurately reports income and expenses on the owner's U.S. income tax return.

Foreign Grantor Trust Beneficiary Statement

A copy of this statement (page 4 of Form 3520-A) must be furnished to each U.S. beneficiary who receives a distribution from the foreign trust during the tax year. The statement must be furnished to the U.S. beneficiary no later than the 15th day of the 3rd month following the end of the trust's tax year or later, if pursuant to an extension of time to file.

Paperwork Reduction Act Notice. We ask for the information on this form to carry out the Internal Revenue laws of the United States. You are required to give us the information. We need it to ensure that you are complying with these laws and to allow us to figure and collect the right amount of tax.

You are not required to provide the information requested on a form that is subject to the Paperwork Reduction Act unless the form displays a valid OMB control number. Books or records relating to a form or its instructions must be retained for as long as their contents may become material in the administration of any Internal Revenue law. Generally, tax returns and return information are confidential, as required by section 6103.

The time needed to complete and file the form will vary depending on individual circumstances. The estimated average time is:

Recordkeeping	36 hr., 21 min.
Learning about the law or the form	2 hr., 59 min.
Preparing and sending the form to the IRS	3 hr., 42 min.

If you have comments concerning the accuracy of these time estimates or suggestions for making this form simpler, we would be happy to hear from you. You can write to the Tax Forms Committee, Western Area Distribution Center, Rancho Cordova, CA 95743-0001. **DO NOT** send the form to this office. Instaed, see **When and Where To File** on page 1.

Form **1041** Department of the Treasury—Internal Revenue Service

U.S. Income Tax Return for Estates and Trusts **1998**

For calendar year 1998 or fiscal year beginning , 1998, and ending , 19

OMB No. 1545-0092

A Type of entity:
- ☐ Decedent's estate
- ☐ Simple trust
- ☐ Complex trust
- ☐ Grantor type trust
- ☐ Bankruptcy estate–Ch. 7
- ☐ Bankruptcy estate–Ch. 11
- ☐ Pooled income fund

B Number of Schedules K-1 attached (see instructions) ▶

Name of estate or trust (If a grantor type trust, see page 8 of the instructions.)

Name and title of fiduciary

Number, street, and room or suite no. (If a P.O. box, see page 8 of the instructions.)

City or town, state, and ZIP code

C Employer identification number

D Date entity created

E Nonexempt charitable and split-interest trusts, check applicable boxes (see page 10 of the instructions):
- ☐ Described in section 4947(a)(1)
- ☐ Not a private foundation
- ☐ Described in section 4947(a)(2)

F Check applicable boxes: ☐ Initial return ☐ Final return ☐ Amended return ☐ Change in fiduciary's name ☐ Change in fiduciary's address

G Pooled mortgage account (see page 10 of the instructions): ☐ Bought ☐ Sold Date:

Income

1	Interest income	1	
2	Ordinary dividends	2	
3	Business income or (loss) (attach Schedule C or C-EZ (Form 1040))	3	
4	Capital gain or (loss) (attach Schedule D (Form 1041))	4	
5	Rents, royalties, partnerships, other estates and trusts, etc. (attach Schedule E (Form 1040))	5	
6	Farm income or (loss) (attach Schedule F (Form 1040))	6	
7	Ordinary gain or (loss) (attach Form 4797)	7	
8	Other income. List type and amount	8	
9	Total income. Combine lines 1 through 8 ▶	9	

Deductions

10	Interest. Check if Form 4952 is attached ▶ ☐	10	
11	Taxes	11	
12	Fiduciary fees	12	
13	Charitable deduction (from Schedule A, line 7)	13	
14	Attorney, accountant, and return preparer fees	14	
15a	Other deductions NOT subject to the 2% floor (attach schedule)	15a	
b	Allowable miscellaneous itemized deductions subject to the 2% floor	15b	
16	Total. Add lines 10 through 15b	16	
17	Adjusted total income or (loss). Subtract line 16 from line 9. Enter here and on Schedule B, line 1	17	
18	Income distribution deduction (from Schedule B, line 15) (attach Schedules K-1 (Form 1041))	18	
19	Estate tax deduction (including certain generation-skipping taxes) (attach computation)	19	
20	Exemption	20	
21	Total deductions. Add lines 18 through 20 ▶	21	

Tax and Payments

22	Taxable income. Subtract line 21 from line 17. If a loss, see page 14 of the instructions	22	
23	Total tax (from Schedule G, line 8)	23	
24	Payments: a 1998 estimated tax payments and amount applied from 1997 return	24a	
b	Estimated tax payments allocated to beneficiaries (from Form 1041-T)	24b	
c	Subtract line 24b from line 24a	24c	
d	Tax paid with extension of time to file: ☐ Form 2758 ☐ Form 8736 ☐ Form 8800	24d	
e	Federal income tax withheld. If any is from Form(s) 1099, check ▶ ☐	24e	
	Other payments: f Form 2439 ; g Form 4136 ; Total ▶	24h	
25	Total payments. Add lines 24c through 24e, and 24h ▶	25	
26	Estimated tax penalty (see page 15 of the instructions)	26	
27	Tax due. If line 25 is smaller than the total of lines 23 and 26, enter amount owed	27	
28	Overpayment. If line 25 is larger than the total of lines 23 and 26, enter amount overpaid	28	
29	Amount of line 28 to be: a Credited to 1999 estimated tax ▶ ; b Refunded ▶	29	

Please Sign Here

Under penalties of perjury, I declare that I have examined this return, including accompanying schedules and statements, and to the best of my knowledge and belief, it is true, correct, and complete. Declaration of preparer (other than fiduciary) is based on all information of which preparer has any knowledge.

▶ Signature of fiduciary or officer representing fiduciary | Date | ▶ EIN of fiduciary if a financial institution (see page 5 of the instructions)

Paid Preparer's Use Only

Preparer's signature ▶ | Date | Check if self-employed ▶ ☐ | Preparer's social security no.

Firm's name (or yours if self-employed) and address ▶ | EIN ▶ | ZIP code ▶

For Paperwork Reduction Act Notice, see the separate instructions. Cat. No. 11370H Form **1041** (1998)

Schedule A Charitable Deduction. Do not complete for a simple trust or a pooled income fund.

1	Amounts paid or permanently set aside for charitable purposes from gross income (see page 15)	1	
2	Tax-exempt income allocable to charitable contributions (see page 16 of the instructions)	2	
3	Subtract line 2 from line 1	3	
4	Capital gains for the tax year allocated to corpus and paid or permanently set aside for charitable purposes	4	
5	Add lines 3 and 4	5	
6	Section 1202 exclusion allocable to capital gains paid or permanently set aside for charitable purposes (see page 16 of the instructions)	6	
7	Charitable deduction. Subtract line 6 from 5. Enter here and on page 1, line 13	7	

Schedule B Income Distribution Deduction

1	Adjusted total income (from page 1, line 17) (see page 16 of the instructions)	1	
2	Adjusted tax-exempt interest	2	
3	Total net gain from Schedule D (Form 1041), line 16, column (1) (see page 16 of the instructions)	3	
4	Enter amount from Schedule A, line 4 (reduced by any allocable section 1202 exclusion)	4	
5	Capital gains for the tax year included on Schedule A, line 1 (see page 16 of the instructions)	5	
6	Enter any gain from page 1, line 4, as a negative number. If page 1, line 4, is a loss, enter the loss as a positive number	6	
7	Distributable net income (DNI). Combine lines 1 through 6. If zero or less, enter -0-	7	
8	If a complex trust, enter accounting income for the tax year as determined under the governing instrument and applicable local law — 8		
9	Income required to be distributed currently	9	
10	Other amounts paid, credited, or otherwise required to be distributed	10	
11	Total distributions. Add lines 9 and 10. If greater than line 8, see page 17 of the instructions	11	
12	Enter the amount of tax-exempt income included on line 11	12	
13	Tentative income distribution deduction. Subtract line 12 from line 11	13	
14	Tentative income distribution deduction. Subtract line 2 from line 7. If zero or less, enter -0-	14	
15	Income distribution deduction. Enter the smaller of line 13 or line 14 here and on page 1, line 18	15	

Schedule G Tax Computation (see page 17 of the instructions)

1	Tax: a ☐ Tax rate schedule or ☐ Schedule D (Form 1041)	1a			
	b Tax on lump-sum distributions (attach Form 4972)	1b			
	c Total. Add lines 1a and 1b ▶			1c	
2a	Foreign tax credit (attach Form 1116)	2a			
b	Check: ☐ Nonconventional source fuel credit ☐ Form 8834	2b			
c	General business credit. Enter here and check which forms are attached: ☐ Form 3800 or ☐ Forms (specify) ▶	2c			
d	Credit for prior year minimum tax (attach Form 8801)	2d			
3	Total credits. Add lines 2a through 2d ▶			3	
4	Subtract line 3 from line 1c			4	
5	Recapture taxes. Check if from: ☐ Form 4255 ☐ Form 8611			5	
6	Alternative minimum tax (from Schedule I, line 39)			6	
7	Household employment taxes. Attach Schedule H (Form 1040)			7	
8	Total tax. Add lines 4 through 7. Enter here and on page 1, line 23 ▶			8	

Other Information

		Yes	No
1	Did the estate or trust receive tax-exempt income? If "Yes," attach a computation of the allocation of expenses. Enter the amount of tax-exempt interest income and exempt-interest dividends ▶ $		
2	Did the estate or trust receive all or any part of the earnings (salary, wages, and other compensation) of any individual by reason of a contract assignment or similar arrangement?		
3	At any time during calendar year 1998, did the estate or trust have an interest in or a signature or other authority over a bank, securities, or other financial account in a foreign country? See page 19 of the instructions for exceptions and filing requirements for Form TD F 90-22.1. If "Yes," enter the name of the foreign country ▶		
4	During the tax year, did the estate or trust receive a distribution from, or was it the grantor of, or transferor to, a foreign trust? If "Yes," the estate or trust may have to file Form 3520. See page 19 of the instructions		
5	Did the estate or trust receive, or pay, any seller-financed mortgage interest? If "Yes," see page 19 for required attachment		
6	If this is an estate or a complex trust making the section 663(b) election, check here (see page 19) ▶ ☐		
7	To make a section 643(e)(3) election, attach Schedule D (Form 1041), and check here (see page 19) ▶ ☐		
8	If the decedent's estate has been open for more than 2 years, attach an explanation for the delay in closing the estate, and check here ▶ ☐		
9	Are any present or future trust beneficiaries skip persons? See page 19 of the instructions		

Schedule I Alternative Minimum Tax (see pages 19 through 24 of the instructions)

Part I—Estate's or Trust's Share of Alternative Minimum Taxable Income

1	Adjusted total income or (loss) (from page 1, line 17)			1	
2	Net operating loss deduction. Enter as a positive amount			2	
3	Add lines 1 and 2			3	
4	Adjustments and tax preference items:				
a	Interest	4a			
b	Taxes	4b			
c	Miscellaneous itemized deductions (from page 1, line 15b)	4c			
d	Refund of taxes	4d	( )		
e	Depreciation of property placed in service after 1986	4e			
f	Circulation and research and experimental expenditures	4f			
g	Mining exploration and development costs	4g			
h	Long-term contracts entered into after February 28, 1986	4h			
i	Amortization of pollution control facilities	4i			
j	Installment sales of certain property	4j			
k	Adjusted gain or loss (including incentive stock options)	4k			
l	Certain loss limitations	4l			
m	Tax shelter farm activities	4m			
n	Passive activities	4n			
o	Beneficiaries of other trusts or decedent's estates	4o			
p	Tax-exempt interest from specified private activity bonds	4p			
q	Depletion	4q			
r	Accelerated depreciation of real property placed in service before 1987	4r			
s	Accelerated depreciation of leased personal property placed in service before 1987	4s			
t	Intangible drilling costs	4t			
u	Other adjustments	4u			
5	Combine lines 4a through 4u			5	
6	Add lines 3 and 5			6	
7	Alternative tax net operating loss deduction (see page 23 of the instructions for limitations)			7	
8	Adjusted alternative minimum taxable income. Subtract line 7 from line 6. Enter here and on line 13 Note: Complete Part II below before going to line 9.			8	
9	Income distribution deduction from line 27 below	9			
10	Estate tax deduction (from page 1, line 19)	10			
11	Add lines 9 and 10			11	
12	Estate's or trust's share of alternative minimum taxable income. Subtract line 11 from line 8			12	

If line 12 is:

- $22,500 or less, stop here and enter -0- on Schedule G, line 6. The estate or trust is not liable for the alternative minimum tax.
- Over $22,500, but less than $165,000, go to line 28.
- $165,000 or more, enter the amount from line 12 on line 34 and go to line 35.

Part II—Income Distribution Deduction on a Minimum Tax Basis

13	Adjusted alternative minimum taxable income (from line 8)	13	
14	Adjusted tax-exempt interest (other than amounts included on line 4p)	14	
15	Total net gain from Schedule D (Form 1041), line 16, column (1). If a loss, enter -0-	15	
16	Capital gains for the tax year allocated to corpus and paid or permanently set aside for charitable purposes (from Schedule A, line 4)	16	
17	Capital gains paid or permanently set aside for charitable purposes from gross income (see page 23 of the instructions)	17	
18	Capital gains computed on a minimum tax basis included on line 8	18	( )
19	Capital losses computed on a minimum tax basis included on line 8. Enter as a positive amount	19	
20	Distributable net alternative minimum taxable income (DNAMTI). Combine lines 13 through 19. If zero or less, enter -0-	20	
21	Income required to be distributed currently (from Schedule B, line 9)	21	
22	Other amounts paid, credited, or otherwise required to be distributed (from Schedule B, line 10)	22	
23	Total distributions. Add lines 21 and 22	23	
24	Tax-exempt income included on line 23 (other than amounts included on line 4p)	24	
25	Tentative income distribution deduction on a minimum tax basis. Subtract line 24 from line 23	25	
26	Tentative income distribution deduction on a minimum tax basis. Subtract line 14 from line 20. If zero or less, enter -0-	26	
27	Income distribution deduction on a minimum tax basis. Enter the smaller of line 25 or line 26. Enter here and on line 9	27	

Part III—Alternative Minimum Tax

Line	Description			Line	Amount
28	Exemption amount			28	$22,500
29	Enter the amount from line 12	29			
30	Phase-out of exemption amount	30	$75,000		
31	Subtract line 30 from line 29. If zero or less, enter -0-	31			
32	Multiply line 31 by 25% (.25)			32	
33	Subtract line 32 from line 28. If zero or less, enter -0-			33	
34	Subtract line 33 from line 29			34	
35	If the estate or trust completed Schedule D (Form 1041) and has an amount on line 24 or 26 (or would have had an amount on either line if Part V had been completed) (as refigured for the AMT, if necessary), go to Part IV below to figure line 35. All others: If line 34 is— • $175,000 or less, multiply line 34 by 26% (.26). • Over $175,000, multiply line 34 by 28% (.28) and subtract $3,500 from the result			35	
36	Alternative minimum foreign tax credit (see page 23 of instructions)			36	
37	Tentative minimum tax. Subtract line 36 from line 35			37	
38	Enter the tax from Schedule G, line 1a (minus any foreign tax credit from Schedule G, line 2a)			38	
39	Alternative minimum tax. Subtract line 38 from line 37. If zero or less, enter -0-. Enter here and on Schedule G, line 6			39	

Part IV—Line 35 Computation Using Maximum Capital Gains Rates

Caution: If the estate or trust did not complete Part V of Schedule D (Form 1041), complete lines 19 through 26 of Schedule D (as refigured for the AMT, if necessary) before completing this part.

Line	Description			Line	Amount
40	Enter the amount from line 34			40	
41	Enter the amount from Schedule D (Form 1041), line 26 (as refigured for AMT, if necessary)	41			
42	Enter the amount from Schedule D (Form 1041), line 24 (as refigured for AMT, if necessary)	42			
43	Add lines 41 and 42. If zero or less, enter -0-	43			
44	Enter the amount from Schedule D (Form 1041), line 21 (as refigured for AMT, if necessary)	44			
45	Enter the smaller of line 43 or line 44			45	
46	Subtract line 45 from line 40. If zero or less, enter -0-			46	
47	If line 46 is $175,000 or less, multiply line 46 by 26% (.26). Otherwise, multiply line 46 by 28% (.28) and subtract $3,500 from the result ▶			47	
48	Enter the amount from Schedule D (Form 1041), line 35 (as figured for the regular tax)			48	
49	Enter the smallest of line 40, line 41, or line 48			49	
50	Multiply line 49 by 10% (.10) ▶			50	
51	Enter the smaller of line 40 or line 41			51	
52	Enter the amount from line 49			52	
53	Subtract line 52 from line 51. If zero or less, enter -0-			53	
54	Multiply line 53 by 20% (.20) ▶			54	
55	Enter the amount from line 40			55	
56	Add lines 46, 49, and 53			56	
57	Subtract line 56 from line 55			57	
58	Multiply line 57 by 25% (.25) ▶			58	
59	Add lines 47, 50, 54, and 58			59	
60	If line 40 is $175,000 or less, multiply line 40 by 26% (.26). Otherwise, multiply line 40 by 28% (.28) and subtract $3,500 from the result			60	
61	Enter the smaller of line 59 or line 60 here and on line 35 ▶			61	

SCHEDULE J
(Form 1041)

Department of the Treasury
Internal Revenue Service

Accumulation Distribution for Certain Complex Trusts

▶ Attach to Form 1041.
▶ See the Instructions for Form 1041.

OMB No. 1545-0092

1998

Name of trust | Employer identification number

Part I Accumulation Distribution in 1998

Note: See the Form 4970 instructions for certain income that minors may exclude and special rules for multiple trusts.

1 Other amounts paid, credited, or otherwise required to be distributed for 1998 (from Schedule B of Form 1041, line 10) . . .			1
2 Distributable net income for 1998 (from Schedule B of Form 1041, line 7) . . .	2		
3 Income required to be distributed currently for 1998 (from Schedule B of Form 1041, line 9) . . .	3		
4 Subtract line 3 from line 2. If zero or less, enter -0- . . .			4
5 Accumulation distribution for 1998. Subtract line 4 from line 1 . . .			5

Part II Ordinary Income Accumulation Distribution (Enter the applicable throwback years below.)

Note: If the distribution is thrown back to more than five years (starting with the earliest applicable tax year beginning after 1968), attach additional schedules. (If the trust was a simple trust, see Regulations section 1.665(e)-1A(b).)		Throwback year ending 19	Throwback year ending 19	Throwback year ending 19	Throwback year ending 19	Throwback year ending 19 ....
6 Distributable net income (see page 28 of the instructions) .	6					
7 Distributions (see page 28 of the instructions)	7					
8 Subtract line 7 from line 6 .	8					
9 Enter amount from page 2, line 25 or line 31, as applicable	9					
10 Undistributed net income Subtract line 9 from line 8 .	10					
11 Enter amount of prior accumulation distributions thrown back to any of these years	11					
12 Subtract line 11 from line 10	12					
13 Allocate the amount on line 5 to the earliest applicable year first. Do not allocate an amount greater than line 12 for the same year (see page 28 of the instructions) . . .	13					
14 Divide line 13 by line 10 and multiply result by amount on line 9	14					
15 Add lines 13 and 14 . . .	15					
16 Tax-exempt interest included on line 13 (see page 29 of the instructions)	16					
17 Subtract line 16 from line 15	17					

Part III Taxes Imposed on Undistributed Net Income (Enter the applicable throwback years below.) (see page 29 of the instructions)

Note: If more than five throwback years are involved, attach additional schedules. If the trust received an accumulation distribution from another trust, see Regulations section 1.665(d)-1A.

If the trust elected the alternative tax on capital gains (repealed for tax years beginning after 1978), SKIP lines 18 through 25 and COMPLETE lines 26 through 31.		Throwback year ending 19	Throwback year ending 19	Throwback year ending 19	Throwback year ending 19	Throwback year ending 19 ....
18 Regular tax	18					
19 Trust's share of net short-term gain	19					
20 Trust's share of net long-term gain.	20					
21 Add lines 19 and 20. . . .	21					
22 Taxable income	22					
23 Enter percent. Divide line 21 by line 22, but do not enter more than 100%	23	%	%	%	%	%
24 Multiply line 18 by the percentage on line 23 . . .	24					
25 Tax on undistributed net income. Subtract line 24 from line 18. Enter here and on page 1, line 9.	25					
Do not complete lines 26 through 31 unless the trust elected the alternative tax on long-term capital gain.						
26 Tax on income other than long-term capital gain . .	26					
27 Trust's share of net short-term gain	27					
28 Trust's share of taxable income less section 1202 deduction	28					
29 Enter percent. Divide line 27 by line 28, but do not enter more than 100%	29	%	%	%	%	%
30 Multiply line 26 by the percentage on line 29 . . .	30					
31 Tax on undistributed net income. Subtract line 30 from line 26. Enter here and on page 1, line 9	31					

Part IV Allocation to Beneficiary

Note: Be sure to complete Form 4970, Tax on Accumulation Distribution of Trusts.

Beneficiary's name		Identifying number	
Beneficiary's address (number and street including apartment number or P.O. box)	(a) This beneficiary's share of line 13	(b) This beneficiary's share of line 14	(c) This beneficiary's share of line 16
City, state, and ZIP code			

		(a)	(b)	(c)
32 Throwback year 19	32			
33 Throwback year 19	33			
34 Throwback year 19	34			
35 Throwback year 19	35			
36 Throwback year 19	36			
37 Total. Add lines 32 through 36. Enter here and on the appropriate lines of Form 4970.	37			

1998

Department of the Treasury
Internal Revenue Service

Instructions for Form 1041 and Schedules A, B, D, G, I, J, and K-1

U.S. Income Tax Return for Estates and Trusts

Section references are to the Internal Revenue Code unless otherwise noted.

Paperwork Reduction Act Notice. We ask for the information on this form to carry out the Internal Revenue laws of the United States. You are required to give us the information. We need it to ensure that you are complying with these laws and to allow us to figure and collect the right amount of tax.

You are not required to provide the information requested on a form that is subject to the Paperwork Reduction Act unless the form displays a valid OMB control number. Books or records relating to a form or its instructions must be retained as long as their contents may become material in the administration of any Internal Revenue law. Generally, tax returns and return information are confidential, as required by Code section 6103.

The time needed to complete and file this form and related schedules will vary depending on individual circumstances. The estimated average times are:

	Form 1041	Schedule D	Schedule J	Schedule K-1
Recordkeeping	46 hr., 38 min.	27 hr., 31 min.	39 hr., 28 min.	8 hr., 51 min.
Learning about the law or the form	18 hr., 49 min.	2 hr., 11 min.	1 hr., 17 min.	1 hr., 17 min.
Preparing the form	35 hr., 17 min.	2 hr., 44 min.	1 hr., 59 min.	1 hr., 29 min.
Copying, assembling, and sending the form to the IRS	4 hr., 17 min.			

If you have comments concerning the accuracy of these time estimates or suggestions for making this form and related schedules simpler, we would be happy to hear from you. You can write to the Tax Forms Committee, Western Area Distribution Center, Rancho Cordova, CA 95743-0001. **DO NOT** send the tax form to this address. Instead, see **Where To File** on page 4.

Contents Page

A Change To Note

For tax years beginning in 1998, the requirement to file a return for a bankruptcy estate applies only if gross income is at least $6,250.

Unresolved Tax Problems

Most problems can be solved with one contact by calling, writing, or visiting an IRS office. But if the estate or trust has tried unsuccessfully to resolve a problem with the IRS, it should contact the Taxpayer Advocate's Problem Resolution Program (PRP). Someone at PRP will assign the estate or trust a personal advocate who is in the best position to try to resolve the problem. The Taxpayer Advocate can also offer special help if the estate or trust has a significant hardship as a result of a tax problem.

Contact the Taxpayer Advocate if:

- The estate or trust has tried unsuccessfully to resolve a problem with the IRS and has not been contacted by the date promised, or
- The estate or trust is on its second attempt to resolve a problem.

You may contact a Taxpayer Advocate by calling a new toll-free assistance number, **1-877-777-4778.** Persons who have access to TTY/TDD equipment may call 1-800-829-4059 and ask for the Taxpayer Advocate. If the estate or trust prefers, it may write to the Taxpayer Advocate at the IRS office that last contacted the estate or trust.

While Taxpayer Advocates cannot change the tax law or make a technical tax decision, they can clear up problems that resulted from previous contacts and ensure that the estate's or trust's case is given a complete and impartial review.

Cat. No. 11372D

Taxpayer Advocates are working to put service first. For more details, see **Pub. 1546,** The Problem Resolution Program of the Internal Revenue Service.

How To Get Forms and Publications

Personal Computer

Access the IRS's Internet web site at **www.irs.ustreas.gov** to do the following:

- Download forms, instructions, and publications.
- See answers to frequently asked tax questions.
- Search publications on-line by topic or keyword.
- Send us comments or request help via e-mail.
- Sign up to receive hot tax issues and news by e-mail from the IRS Digital Dispatch.

You can also reach us using:

- Telnet at **iris.irs.ustreas.gov**
- File transfer protocol at **ftp.irs.ustreas.gov**
- Direct dial (by modem) at **703-321-8020.**

CD-ROM

Order **Pub. 1796,** Federal Tax Products on CD-ROM, and get:

- Current year forms, instructions, and publications.
- Prior year forms and instructions.
- Popular forms that may be filled in electronically, printed out for submission, and saved for recordkeeping.

Buy the CD-ROM on the Internet at **www.irs.ustreas.gov/cdorders** from the National Technical Information Service (NTIS) for $13 (plus a $5 handling fee) and save 35%, or call **1-877-CDFORMS** (1-877-233-6767) toll-free to buy the CD-ROM for $20 (plus a $5 handling fee).

By Phone and In Person

You can order forms and publications 24 hours a day, 7 days a week, by calling **1-800-TAX-FORM** (1-800-829-3676). You can also get most forms and publications at your local IRS office.

General Instructions

Purpose of Form

The fiduciary of a domestic decedent's estate, trust, or bankruptcy estate uses Form 1041 to report:

- The income, deductions, gains, losses, etc. of the estate or trust;
- The income that is either accumulated or held for future distribution or distributed currently to the beneficiaries;
- Any income tax liability of the estate or trust; and
- Employment taxes on wages paid to household employees.

Income Taxation of Trusts and Decedents' Estates

A trust (except a grantor type trust) or a decedent's estate is a separate legal entity for Federal tax purposes. A decedent's estate comes into existence at the time of death of an individual. A trust may be created during an individual's life (inter vivos) or at the time of his or her death under a will (testamentary). If the trust instrument contains certain provisions, then the person creating the trust (the grantor) is treated as the owner of the trust's assets. Such a trust is a grantor type trust.

A trust or decedent's estate figures its gross income in much the same manner as an individual. Most deductions and credits allowed to individuals are also allowed to estates and trusts. However, there is one major distinction. A trust or decedent's estate is allowed an income distribution deduction for distributions to beneficiaries. To figure this deduction, the fiduciary must complete Schedule B. The income distribution deduction determines the amount of any distributions taxed to the beneficiaries.

For this reason, a trust or decedent's estate sometimes is referred to as a "pass-through" entity. The beneficiary, and not the trust or decedent's estate, pays income tax on his or her distributive share of income. Schedule K-1 (Form 1041) is used to notify the beneficiaries of the amounts to be included on their income tax returns.

Before preparing Form 1041, the fiduciary must figure the accounting income of the estate or trust under the will or trust instrument and applicable local law to determine the amount, if any, of income that is required to be distributed, because the income distribution deduction is based, in part, on that amount.

Abusive Trust Arrangements

Certain trust arrangements purport to reduce or eliminate Federal taxes in ways that are not permitted under the law. Abusive trust arrangements typically are promoted by the promise of tax benefits with no meaningful change in the taxpayer's control over or benefit from the taxpayer's income or assets. The promised benefits may include reduction or elimination of income subject to tax; deductions for personal expenses paid by the trust; depreciation deductions of an owner's personal residence and furnishings; a stepped-up basis for property transferred to the trust; the reduction or elimination of self-employment taxes; and the reduction or elimination of gift and estate taxes. These promised benefits are inconsistent with the tax rules applicable to abusive trust arrangements.

Abusive trust arrangements often use trusts to hide the true ownership of assets and income or to disguise the substance of transactions. These arrangements frequently involve more than one trust, each holding different assets of the taxpayer (e.g., the taxpayer's business, business equipment, home, automobile, etc.). Some trusts may hold interests in other trusts, purport to involve charities, or are foreign trusts. Funds may flow from one trust to another trust by way of rental agreements, fees for services, purchase agreements, and distributions.

Some of the abusive trust arrangements that have been identified include unincorporated business trusts (or organizations), equipment or service trusts, family residence trusts, charitable trusts, and final trusts. In each of these trusts, the original owner of the assets that are nominally subject to the trust effectively retains the authority to cause financial benefits of the trust to be directly or indirectly returned or made available to the owner. For example, the trustee may be the promoter, or a relative or friend of the owner who simply carries out the directions of the owner whether or not permitted by the terms of the trust.

When trusts are used for legitimate business, family, or estate planning purposes, either the trust, the beneficiary, or the transferor to the trust will pay the tax on income generated by the trust property. Trusts cannot be used to transform a taxpayer's personal, living, or educational expenses into deductible items, and will not seek to avoid tax liability by ignoring either the true ownership of income and assets or the true substance of transactions. Therefore, the tax results promised by the promoters of abusive trust arrangements are not allowable under the law, and the participants in and promoters of these arrangements may be subject to civil or criminal penalties in appropriate cases.

For more details, including the legal principles that control the proper tax treatment of these abusive trust arrangements, see Notice 97-24, 1997-1 C.B. 409.

Definitions

Beneficiary

A beneficiary includes an heir, a legatee, or a devisee.

Distributable Net Income (DNI)

The income distribution deduction allowable to estates and trusts for amounts paid, credited, or required to be distributed to beneficiaries is limited to distributable net income (DNI). This amount, which is figured on Schedule B, line 7, is also used to determine how much of an amount paid, credited, or required to be distributed to a beneficiary will be includible in his or her gross income.

Income, Deductions, and Credits in Respect of a Decedent

Income. When completing Form 1041, you must take into account any items that are income in respect of a decedent (IRD).

In general, income in respect of a decedent is income that a decedent was entitled to receive but that was not properly includible in the decedent's final income tax return under the decedent's method of accounting.

IRD includes:

- All accrued income of a decedent who reported his or her income on the cash method of accounting;
- Income accrued solely because of the decedent's death in the case of a decedent who reported his or her income on the accrual method of accounting; and
- Income to which the decedent had a contingent claim at the time of his or her death.

Some examples of IRD of a decedent who kept his or her books on the cash method are:

- Deferred salary payments that are payable to the decedent's estate.
- Uncollected interest on U.S. savings bonds.
- Proceeds from the completed sale of farm produce.
- The portion of a lump sum distribution to the beneficiary of a decedent's IRA that equals the balance in the IRA at the time of the owner's death. This includes unrealized appreciation and income accrued to that date, less the aggregate amount of the owner's nondeductible contributions to the IRA. Such amounts are included in the beneficiary's gross income in the tax year that the distribution is received.

The IRD has the same character it would have had if the decedent lived and received such amount.

Deductions and credits. The following deductions and credits, when paid by the decedent's estate, are allowed on Form 1041 even though they were not allowable on the decedent's final income tax return:

- Business expenses deductible under section 162.
- Interest deductible under section 163.
- Taxes deductible under section 164.
- Investment expenses described in section 212 (in excess of 2% of AGI).
- Percentage depletion allowed under section 611.
- Foreign tax credit.

For more information, see section 691.

Income Required To Be Distributed Currently

Income required to be distributed currently is income that is required under the terms of the governing instrument and applicable local law to be distributed in the year it is received. The fiduciary must be under a duty to distribute the income currently, even if the actual distribution is not made until after the close of the trust's tax year. See Regulations section 1.651(a)-2.

Fiduciary

A fiduciary is a trustee of a trust; or an executor, executrix, administrator, administratrix, personal representative, or person in possession of property of a decedent's estate.

Note: *Any reference in these instructions to "you" means the fiduciary of the estate or trust.*

Trust

A trust is an arrangement created either by a will or by an inter vivos declaration by which trustees take title to property for the purpose of protecting or conserving it for the beneficiaries under the ordinary rules applied in chancery or probate courts.

Who Must File

Decedent's Estate

The fiduciary (or one of the joint fiduciaries) must file Form 1041 for a domestic estate that has:

1. Gross income for the tax year of $600 or more, or

2. A beneficiary who is a nonresident alien.

An estate is a **domestic estate** if it is **not** a foreign estate. A **foreign estate** is one the income of which, from sources outside the United States that is not effectively connected with the conduct of a U.S. trade or business, is not includible in gross income. If you are the fiduciary of a foreign estate, file **Form 1040NR,** U.S. Nonresident Alien Income Tax Return, instead of Form 1041.

Trust

The fiduciary (or one of the joint fiduciaries) must file Form 1041 for a domestic trust taxable under section 641 that has:

1. Any taxable income for the tax year, or

2. Gross income of $600 or more (regardless of taxable income), or

3. A beneficiary who is a nonresident alien.

Two or more trusts are treated as one trust if such trusts have substantially the same grantor(s) and substantially the same primary beneficiary(ies), and a principal purpose of such trusts is avoidance of tax. This provision applies only to that portion of the trust that is attributable to contributions to corpus made after March 1, 1984.

A trust is a **domestic trust** if:

- A U.S. court is able to exercise primary supervision over the administration of the trust, and
- One or more U.S. persons have the authority to control all substantial decisions of the trust.

The above definition of a domestic trust generally applies to tax years beginning after 1996. However, a trust (other than a trust treated as wholly-owned by the grantor) in existence on August 20, 1996, that was treated as a domestic trust under prior law, may elect to continue to be treated as a domestic trust under the procedures set forth in Notice 98-25, 1998-18 I.R.B. 11. See also Notice 96-65, 1996-2 C.B. 232, under which a trust (including a wholly-owned grantor trust) may amend the provisions of the trust in order to meet the new statutory requirements.

A trust that is not a domestic trust is treated as a foreign trust. If you are the trustee of a foreign trust, file Form 1040NR instead of Form 1041. Also, a foreign trust with a U.S. owner generally must file **Form 3520-A,** Annual Information Return of Foreign Trust With a U.S. Owner.

If a domestic trust becomes a foreign trust, it is treated under section 684 as having transferred all of its assets to a foreign trust, except to the extent a grantor or another person is treated as the owner of the trust when the trust becomes a foreign trust.

Special Rule for Certain Revocable Trusts

Section 645 provides that the executor of an estate **and** the trustee of a qualified revocable trust can elect to treat the trust as part of the estate instead of filing a separate Form 1041 for the trust. The election applies to all tax years of the estate ending after the date of the decedent's death and before the applicable date, as defined below. Once made, the election is irrevocable.

Qualified revocable trusts. A qualified revocable trust for this purpose is any trust or portion of a trust that is treated under section 676 as owned by the decedent whose estate is making the election because of a power in the grantor of the trust to revoke the trust. For this purpose, a power does not include any power in the grantor that is treated as held by the grantor because it is held by his or her spouse.

Applicable date. The applicable date is either:

- If the estate is required to file a Federal estate tax return, the date that is 6 months after the date of the final determination of the Federal estate tax liability, or
- If the estate is not required to file a Federal estate tax return, the date that is 2 years after the date of the decedent's death.

Making the election. You make the election by attaching a statement to Form 1041. The original statement must be attached to Form 1041 filed by the due date (including extensions) for the estate for its first tax year. If the revocable trust must file a Form 1041 for the tax year ending after the date of the decedent's death, you must attach a copy of the statement to that return.

See Rev. Proc. 98-13, 1998-4 I.R.B. 21 for details of what you must include in the statement and for additional information on the election.

Bankruptcy Estate

The bankruptcy trustee or debtor-in-possession must file Form 1041 for the estate of an individual involved in bankruptcy proceedings under chapter 7 or 11 of title 11 of the United States Code if the estate has gross income for the tax year of $6,250 or more. See **Of Special Interest To Bankruptcy Trustees and Debtors-In-Possession** on page 7 for other details.

Common Trust Funds

Do not file Form 1041 for a common trust fund maintained by a bank. Instead, the fund may use **Form 1065,** U.S. Partnership Return of Income, for its return. For more details, see section 584 and Regulations section 1.6032-1.

Qualified Settlement Funds

The trustee of a designated or qualified settlement fund must file **Form 1120-SF,** U.S. Income Tax Return for Settlement Funds, rather than Form 1041. See Regulations section 1.468B-5.

Electronic and Magnetic Media Filing

Qualified fiduciaries or transmitters may be able to file Form 1041 and related schedules electronically or on magnetic media. Tax return data may be filed electronically using telephone lines or on magnetic media using magnetic tape or floppy diskette.

If you wish to do this, you must file **Form 9041,** Application for Electronic/Magnetic Media Filing of Business and Employee Benefit Plan Returns. If you file Form 1041 electronically or on magnetic media, you must also file **Form 8453-F,** U.S. Estate or Trust Income Tax Declaration and Signature for Electronic and Magnetic Media Filing. For more details, get **Pub. 1437,** Procedures for Electronic and Magnetic Media Filing of U.S. Income Tax Returns for Estates and Trusts, Form 1041 for 1998, and **Pub. 1438,** File Specifications, Validation Criteria, and Record Layouts for Electronic and Magnetic Media Filing of Estate and Trust Returns, Form 1041. To order these forms and publications, or for more information on electronic and magnetic media filing of Form 1041, call the Magnetic Media Unit at the Philadelphia Service Center at (215) 516-7533 (not a toll-free number), or write to:

Internal Revenue Service Center
Attention: Magnetic Media Unit–DP 115
11601 Roosevelt Blvd.
Philadelphia, PA 19154

When To File

For calendar year estates and trusts, file Form 1041 and Schedules K-1 on or before April 15, 1999. For fiscal year estates and trusts, file Form 1041 by the 15th day of the 4th month following the close of the tax year. If the due date falls on a Saturday, Sunday, or legal holiday, file on the next business day. For example, an estate that has a tax year that ends on June 30, 1999, must file Form 1041 by October 15, 1999.

Private Delivery Services

You can use certain private delivery services designated by the IRS to meet the "timely mailing as timely filing/paying" rule for tax returns and payments. The IRS publishes a list of the designated private delivery services in September of each year. The list published in September 1998 includes only the following:

- Airborne Express (Airborne): Overnight Air Express Service, Next Afternoon Service, Second Day Service.
- DHL Worldwide Express (DHL): DHL "Same Day" Service, DHL USA Overnight.
- Federal Express (FedEx): FedEx Priority Overnight, FedEx Standard Overnight, FedEx 2 Day.
- United Parcel Service (UPS): UPS Next Day Air, Next Day Air Saver, UPS 2nd Day Air, UPS 2nd Day Air A.M.

The private delivery service can tell you how to get written proof of the mailing date.

Extension of Time To File

Estates. Use **Form 2758,** Application for Extension of Time To File Certain Excise, Income, Information, and Other Returns, to apply for an extension of time to file.

Trusts. Use **Form 8736,** Application for Automatic Extension of Time To File U.S. Return for a Partnership, REMIC, or for Certain Trusts, to request an automatic 3-month extension of time to file.

If more time is needed, file **Form 8800,** Application for Additional Extension of Time To File U.S. Return for a Partnership, REMIC, or for Certain Trusts, for an additional extension of up to 3 months. To obtain this additional extension of time to file, you must show reasonable cause for the additional time you are requesting. Form 8800 must be filed by the extended due date for Form 1041.

Period Covered

File the 1998 return for calendar year 1998 and fiscal years beginning in 1998 and ending in 1999. If the return is for a fiscal year or a short tax year, fill in the tax year space at the top of the form.

The 1998 Form 1041 may also be used for a tax year beginning in 1999 if:

1. The estate or trust has a tax year of less than 12 months that begins and ends in 1999; and

2. The 1999 Form 1041 is not available by the time the estate or trust is required to file its tax return. However, the estate or trust must show its 1999 tax year on the 1998 Form 1041 and incorporate any tax law changes that are effective for tax years beginning after December 31, 1998.

Where To File

For all estates and trusts, **except** charitable and split-interest trusts and pooled income funds:

If you are located in	Please mail to the following Internal Revenue Service Center
New Jersey, New York (New York City and counties of Nassau, Rockland, Suffolk, and Westchester)	Holtsville, NY 00501
New York (all other counties), Connecticut, Maine, Massachusetts, New Hampshire, Rhode Island, Vermont	Andover, MA 05501
Florida, Georgia, South Carolina	Atlanta, GA 39901
Indiana, Kentucky, Michigan, Ohio, West Virginia	Cincinnati, OH 45999
Kansas, New Mexico, Oklahoma, Texas	Austin, TX 73301
Alaska, Arizona, California (counties of Alpine, Amador, Butte, Calaveras, Colusa, Contra Costa, Del Norte, El Dorado, Glenn, Humboldt, Lake, Lassen, Marin, Mendocino, Modoc, Napa, Nevada, Placer, Plumas, Sacramento, San Joaquin, Shasta, Sierra, Siskiyou, Solano, Sonoma, Sutter, Tehama, Trinity, Yolo, and Yuba), Colorado, Idaho, Montana, Nebraska, Nevada, North Dakota, Oregon, South Dakota, Utah, Washington, Wyoming	Ogden, UT 84201
California (all other counties), Hawaii	Fresno, CA 93888
Illinois, Iowa, Minnesota, Missouri, Wisconsin	Kansas City, MO 64999
Alabama, Arkansas, Louisiana, Mississippi, North Carolina, Tennessee	Memphis, TN 37501
Delaware, District of Columbia, Maryland, Pennsylvania, Virginia, any U.S. possession, or foreign country	Philadelphia, PA 19255

For a charitable or split-interest trust described in section 4947(a) and a pooled income fund defined in section 642(c)(5):

If you are located in	Please mail to the following Internal Revenue Service Center
Alabama, Arkansas, Florida, Georgia, Louisiana, Mississippi, North Carolina, South Carolina, Tennessee	Atlanta, GA 39901

Arizona, Colorado, Kansas, New Mexico, Oklahoma, Texas, Utah, Wyoming	Austin, TX 73301
Indiana, Kentucky, Michigan, Ohio, West Virginia	Cincinnati, OH 45999
Alaska, California, Hawaii, Idaho, Nevada, Oregon, Washington	Fresno, CA 93888
Connecticut, Maine, Massachusetts, New Hampshire, New York, Rhode Island, Vermont	Holtsville, NY 00501
Illinois, Iowa, Minnesota, Missouri, Montana, Nebraska, North Dakota, South Dakota, Wisconsin	Kansas City, MO 64999
Delaware, District of Columbia, Maryland, New Jersey, Pennsylvania, Virginia, any U.S. possession, or foreign country	Philadelphia, PA 19255

Who Must Sign

Fiduciary

The fiduciary, or an authorized representative, must sign Form 1041.

A financial institution that submitted estimated tax payments for trusts for which it is the trustee must enter its EIN in the space provided for the EIN of the fiduciary. Do not enter the EIN of the trust. For this purpose, a financial institution is one that maintains a Treasury Tax and Loan account. If you are an attorney or other individual functioning in a fiduciary capacity, leave this space blank. DO NOT enter your individual social security number (SSN).

If you, as fiduciary, fill in Form 1041, leave the Paid Preparer's space blank. If someone prepares this return and does not charge you, that person should not sign the return.

Paid Preparer

Generally, anyone who is paid to prepare a tax return must sign the return and fill in the other blanks in the Paid Preparer's Use Only area of the return.

The person required to sign the return must complete the required preparer information and:

- Sign it in the space provided for the preparer's signature. A facsimile signature is acceptable if certain conditions are met. See Regulations section 1.6695-1(b)(4)(iv) for details.
- Give you a copy of the return in addition to the copy to be filed with the IRS.

Accounting Methods

Figure taxable income using the method of accounting regularly used in keeping the estate's or trust's books and records. Generally, permissible methods include the cash method, the accrual method, or any other method authorized by the Internal Revenue Code. In all cases, the method used must clearly reflect income.

Generally, the estate or trust may change its accounting method (for income as a whole or for any material item) only by getting consent on **Form 3115,** Application for Change in Accounting Method. For more information, see **Pub. 538,** Accounting Periods and Methods.

Accounting Periods

For a decedent's estate, the moment of death determines the end of the decedent's tax year and the beginning of the estate's tax year. As executor or administrator, you choose the estate's tax period when you file its first income tax return. The estate's first tax year may be any period of 12 months or less that ends on the last day of a month. If you select the last day of any month other than December, you are adopting a fiscal tax year.

To change the accounting period of an estate, get **Form 1128,** Application To Adopt, Change, or Retain a Tax Year.

Generally, a trust must adopt a calendar year. The following trusts are exempt from this requirement:

- A trust that is exempt from tax under section 501(a);
- A charitable trust described in section 4947(a)(1); and
- A trust that is treated as wholly owned by a grantor under the rules of sections 671 through 679.

Rounding Off to Whole Dollars

You may show the money items on the return and accompanying schedules as whole-dollar amounts. To do so, drop amounts less than 50 cents and increase any amounts from 50 to 99 cents to the next dollar.

Estimated Tax

Generally, an estate or trust must pay estimated income tax for 1999 if it expects to owe, after subtracting any withholding and credits, at least $1,000 in tax, and it expects the withholding and credits to be less than the smaller of:

1. 90% of the tax shown on the 1999 tax return, or

2. 100% of the tax shown on the 1998 tax return (105% of that amount if the estate's or trust's adjusted gross income on that return is more than $150,000, and less than ⅔ of gross income for 1998 or 1999 is from farming or fishing).

However, if a return was not filed for 1998 or that return did not cover a full 12 months, item **2** does not apply.

For this purpose, include household employment taxes in the tax shown on the tax return, but **only** if **either** of the following is true:

- The estate or trust will have Federal income tax withheld for 1999 (see the instructions on page 15 for line 24e), or
- The estate or trust would be required to make estimated tax payments for 1999 even if it **did not** include household employment taxes when figuring estimated tax.

Exceptions

Estimated tax payments are not required from:

1. An estate of a domestic decedent or a domestic trust that had no tax liability for the full 12-month 1998 tax year;

2. A decedent's estate for any tax year ending before the date that is 2 years after the decedent's death; or

3. A trust that was treated as owned by the decedent if the trust will receive the residue of the decedent's estate under the will (or if no will is admitted to probate, the trust primarily responsible for paying debts, taxes, and expenses of administration) for any tax year ending before the date that is 2 years after the decedent's death.

For more information, see **Form 1041-ES,** Estimated Income Tax for Estates and Trusts.

Section 643(g) Election

Fiduciaries of trusts that pay estimated tax may elect under section 643(g) to have any portion of their estimated tax payments allocated to any of the beneficiaries.

The fiduciary of a decedent's estate may make a section 643(g) election only for the final year of the estate.

See the instructions on page 15 for line 24b for more details.

Interest and Penalties

Interest

Interest is charged on taxes not paid by the due date, even if an extension of time to file is granted.

Interest is also charged on the failure-to-file penalty, the accuracy-related penalty, and the fraud penalty. The interest charge is figured at a rate determined under section 6621.

Late Filing of Return

The law provides a penalty of 5% a month, or part of a month, up to a maximum of 25%, for each month the return is not filed. The penalty is imposed on the net amount due. If the return is more than 60 days late, the minimum penalty is the smaller of $100 or the tax due. The penalty will not be imposed if you can show that the failure to file on time was due to reasonable cause. If the failure is due to reasonable cause, attach an explanation to the return.

Late Payment of Tax

Generally, the penalty for not paying tax when due is ½ of 1% of the unpaid amount for each month or part of a month it remains unpaid. The maximum penalty is 25% of the unpaid amount. The penalty is imposed on the net amount due. Any penalty is in addition to interest charges on late payments.

Note: *If you include interest or either of these penalties with your payment, identify and enter these amounts in the bottom margin of Form 1041, page 1. Do not include the interest or penalty amount in the balance of tax due on line 27.*

Failure To Provide Information Timely

You must provide Schedule K-1 (Form 1041), on or before the day you are required to file Form 1041, to each beneficiary who receives a distribution of property or an allocation of an item of the estate.

For each failure to provide Schedule K-1 to a beneficiary when due and each failure to include on Schedule K-1 all the information required to be shown (or the inclusion of incorrect information), a $50 penalty may be imposed with regard to each Schedule K-1 for which a failure occurs. The maximum penalty is $100,000 for all such failures during a calendar year. If the requirement to report information is intentionally disregarded, each $50 penalty is increased to $100 or, if greater, 10% of the aggregate amount of items required to be reported, and the $100,000 maximum does not apply.

The penalty will not be imposed if the fiduciary can show that not providing information timely was due to reasonable cause and not due to willful neglect.

Underpaid Estimated Tax

If the fiduciary underpaid estimated tax, use **Form 2210,** Underpayment of Estimated Tax by Individuals, Estates, and Trusts, to figure any penalty. Enter the amount of any penalty on line 26, Form 1041.

Trust Fund Recovery Penalty

This penalty may apply if certain excise, income, social security, and Medicare taxes that must be collected or withheld are not collected or withheld, or these taxes are not paid. These taxes are generally reported on Forms 720, 941, 943, or 945. The trust fund recovery penalty may be imposed on all persons who are determined by the IRS to have been **responsible** for collecting, accounting for, and paying over these taxes, and who acted willfully in not doing so. The penalty is equal to the unpaid trust fund tax. See the instructions for Form 720, **Pub. 15 (Circular E),** Employer's Tax Guide, or **Pub. 51 (Circular A),** Agricultural Employer's Tax Guide, for more details, including the definition of responsible persons.

Other Penalties

Other penalties can be imposed for negligence, substantial understatement of tax, and fraud. See **Pub. 17,** Your Federal Income Tax, for details on these penalties.

Other Forms That May Be Required

Forms W-2 and **W-3,** Wage and Tax Statement; and Transmittal of Wage and Tax Statements.

Form 56, Notice Concerning Fiduciary Relationship.

Form 706, United States Estate (and Generation-Skipping Transfer) Tax Return; or **Form 706-NA,** United States Estate (and Generation-Skipping Transfer) Tax Return, Estate of nonresident not a citizen of the United States.

Form 706-GS(D), Generation-Skipping Transfer Tax Return For Distributions.

Form 706-GS(D-1), Notification of Distribution From a Generation-Skipping Trust.

Form 706-GS(T), Generation-Skipping Transfer Tax Return for Terminations.

Form 720, Quarterly Federal Excise Tax Return. Use Form 720 to report environmental excise taxes, communications and air transportation taxes, fuel taxes, luxury tax on passenger vehicles, manufacturers' taxes, ship passenger tax, and certain other excise taxes.

Caution: *See* ***Trust Fund Recovery Penalty*** *above.*

Form 926, Return by a U.S. Transferor of Property to a Foreign Corporation. Use this form to report certain information required under section 6038B.

Form 940 or **Form 940-EZ,** Employer's Annual Federal Unemployment (FUTA) Tax Return. The estate or trust may be liable for FUTA tax and may have to file Form 940 or 940-EZ if it paid wages of $1,500 or more in any calendar quarter during the calendar year (or the preceding calendar year) or one or more employees worked for the estate or trust for some part of a day in any 20 different weeks during the calendar year (or the preceding calendar year).

Form 941, Employer's Quarterly Federal Tax Return. Employers must file this form quarterly to report income tax withheld on wages and employer and employee social security and Medicare taxes. Agricultural employers must file **Form 943,** Employer's Annual Tax Return for Agricultural Employees, instead of Form 941, to report income tax withheld and employer and employee social security and Medicare taxes on farmworkers.

Caution: *See* ***Trust Fund Recovery Penalty*** *above.*

Form 945, Annual Return of Withheld Federal Income Tax. Use this form to report income tax withheld from nonpayroll payments, including pensions, annuities, IRAs, gambling winnings, and backup withholding.

Caution: *See* ***Trust Fund Recovery Penalty*** *above.*

Form 1040, U.S. Individual Income Tax Return.

Form 1040NR, U.S. Nonresident Alien Income Tax Return.

Form 1041-A, U.S. Information Return—Trust Accumulation of Charitable Amounts.

Forms 1042 and **1042-S,** Annual Withholding Tax Return for U.S. Source Income of Foreign Persons; and Foreign Person's U.S. Source Income Subject to Withholding. Use these forms to report and transmit withheld tax on payments or distributions made to nonresident alien individuals, foreign partnerships, or foreign corporations to the extent such payments or distributions constitute gross income from sources within the United States that is not effectively connected with a U.S. trade or business. For more information, see sections 1441 and 1442, and **Pub. 515,** Withholding of Tax on Nonresident Aliens and Foreign Corporations.

Forms 1099-A, B, INT, LTC, MISC, MSA, OID, R, and S. You may have to file these information returns to report acquisitions or abandonments of secured property; proceeds from broker and barter exchange transactions; interest payments; payments of long-term care and accelerated death benefits; miscellaneous income payments; distributions from a medical savings account; original issue discount; distributions from pensions, annuities, retirement or profit-sharing plans, IRAs, insurance contracts, etc.; and proceeds from real estate transactions.

Also, use certain of these returns to report amounts received as a nominee on behalf of another person, except amounts reported to beneficiaries on Schedule K-1 (Form 1041).

Form 8275, Disclosure Statement. File Form 8275 to disclose items or positions, except those contrary to a regulation, that are not otherwise adequately disclosed on a tax return. The disclosure is made to avoid parts of the accuracy-related penalty imposed for disregard of rules or substantial understatement of tax. Form 8275 is also used for disclosures relating to preparer penalties for understatements due to unrealistic positions or disregard of rules.

Form 8275-R, Regulation Disclosure Statement, is used to disclose any item on a tax return for which a position has been taken that is contrary to Treasury regulations.

Forms 8288 and **8288-A,** U.S. Withholding Tax Return for Dispositions by Foreign Persons of U.S. Real Property Interests; and Statement of Withholding on Dispositions by Foreign Persons of U.S. Real Property Interests. Use these forms to report and transmit withheld tax on the sale of U.S. real property by a foreign person. Also, use these forms to report and transmit tax withheld from amounts distributed to a foreign beneficiary from a "U.S. real property interest account" that a domestic estate or trust is required to establish under Regulations section 1.1445-5(c)(1)(iii).

Form 8300, Report of Cash Payments Over $10,000 Received in a Trade or Business. Generally, this form is used to report the receipt of more than $10,000 in cash or foreign currency in one transaction (or a series of related transactions).

Attachments

If you need more space on the forms or schedules, attach separate sheets. Use the same size and format as on the printed forms. **But show the totals on the printed forms.**

Attach these separate sheets after all the schedules and forms. Enter the estate's or trust's EIN on each sheet.

Do not file a copy of the decedent's will or the trust instrument unless the IRS requests it.

Additional Information

The following publications may assist you in preparing Form 1041.

Pub. 550, Investment Income and Expenses; and

Pub. 559, Survivors, Executors, and Administrators.

Of Special Interest to Bankruptcy Trustees and Debtors-in-Possession

Taxation of Bankruptcy Estates of an Individual

A bankruptcy estate is a separate taxable entity created when an individual debtor files a petition under either chapter 7 or 11 of title 11 of the U.S. Code. The estate is administered by a trustee or a debtor-in-possession. If the case is later dismissed by the bankruptcy court, the debtor is treated as if the bankruptcy petition had never been filed. This provision does NOT apply to partnerships or corporations.

Who Must File

Every trustee (or debtor-in-possession) for an individual's bankruptcy estate under chapter 7 or 11 of title 11 of the U.S. Code must file a return if the bankruptcy estate has gross income of $6,250 or more for tax years beginning in 1998.

Failure to do so may result in an estimated Request for Administrative Expenses being filed by the IRS in the bankruptcy proceeding or a motion to compel filing of the return.

Important: *The filing of a tax return for the bankruptcy estate does not relieve the individual debtor of his or her (or their) individual tax obligations.*

Employer Identification Number

Every bankruptcy estate of an individual required to file a return must have its own employer identification number (EIN). The social security number (SSN) of the individual debtor cannot be used as the EIN for the bankruptcy estate.

Accounting Period

A bankruptcy estate is allowed to have a fiscal year. The period can be no longer than 12 months.

When To File

File Form 1041 on or before the 15th day of the 4th month following the close of the tax year. Use Form 2758 to apply for an extension of time to file.

Disclosure of Return Information

Under section 6103(e)(5), tax returns of individual debtors who have filed for bankruptcy under chapters 7 or 11 of title 11 are, upon written request, open to inspection by or disclosure to the trustee.

The returns subject to disclosure to the trustee are those for the year the bankruptcy begins and prior years. Use **Form 4506,** Request for Copy or Transcript of Tax Form, to request copies of the individual debtor's tax returns.

If the bankruptcy case was not voluntary, disclosure cannot be made before the bankruptcy court has entered an order for relief, unless the court rules that the disclosure is needed for determining whether relief should be ordered.

Transfer of Tax Attributes From the Individual Debtor to the Bankruptcy Estate

The bankruptcy estate succeeds to the following tax attributes of the individual debtor:

1. Net operating loss (NOL) carryovers;
2. Charitable contributions carryovers;
3. Recovery of tax benefit items;
4. Credit carryovers;
5. Capital loss carryovers;
6. Basis, holding period, and character of assets;
7. Method of accounting;
8. Unused passive activity losses;
9. Unused passive activity credits; and
10. Unused section 465 losses.

Income, Deductions, and Credits

Under section 1398(c), the taxable income of the bankruptcy estate generally is figured in the same manner as an individual. The gross income of the bankruptcy estate includes any income included in property of the estate as defined in Bankruptcy Code section 541. Also included is gain from the sale of property. To figure gain, the trustee or debtor-in-possession must determine the correct basis of the property.

To determine whether any amount paid or incurred by the bankruptcy estate is allowable as a deduction or credit, or is treated as wages for employment tax purposes, treat the amount as if it were paid or incurred by the individual debtor in the same trade or business or other activity the debtor engaged in before the bankruptcy proceedings began.

Administrative expenses. The bankruptcy estate is allowed a deduction for any administrative expense allowed under section 503 of title 11 of the U.S. Code, and any fee or charge assessed under chapter 123 of title 28 of the U.S. Code, to the extent not disallowed under an Internal Revenue Code provision (e.g., section 263, 265, or 275).

Administrative expense loss. When figuring a net operating loss, nonbusiness deductions (including administrative expenses) are limited under section 172(d)(4) to the bankruptcy estate's nonbusiness income. The excess nonbusiness deductions are an administrative expense loss that may be carried back to each of the 3 preceding tax years and forward to each of the 7 succeeding tax years of the bankruptcy estate. The amount of an administrative expense loss that may be carried to any tax year is determined after the net operating loss deductions allowed for that year. An administrative expense loss is allowed only to the bankruptcy estate and cannot be carried to any tax year of the individual debtor.

Carryback of net operating losses and credits. If the bankruptcy estate itself incurs a net operating loss (apart from losses carried forward to the estate from the individual debtor), it can carry back its net operating losses not only to previous tax years of the bankruptcy estate, but also to tax years of the individual debtor prior to the year in which the bankruptcy proceedings began. Excess credits, such as the foreign tax credit, also may be carried back to pre-bankruptcy years of the individual debtor.

Exemption. For tax years beginning in 1998, a bankruptcy estate is allowed a personal exemption of $2,700.

Standard deduction. For tax years beginning in 1998, a bankruptcy estate that does not itemize deductions is allowed a standard deduction of $3,550.

Discharge of Indebtedness. In a title 11 case, gross income does not include amounts that normally would be included in gross income resulting from the discharge of indebtedness. However, any amounts excluded from gross income must be applied to reduce certain tax attributes in a certain order. Attach **Form 982,** Reduction of Tax Attributes Due to Discharge of Indebtedness, to show the reduction of tax attributes.

Tax Rate Schedule

Figure the tax for the bankruptcy estate using the tax rate schedule on page 8. Enter the tax on Form 1040, line 40.

If taxable income is:

Over—	But not over—	The tax is:	Of the amount over—
$0	$21,175	15%	$0
21,175	51,150	$3,176.25 + 28%	21,175
51,150	77,975	11,569.25 + 31%	51,150
77,975	139,225	19,885.00 + 36%	77,975
139,225	------	41,935.00 + 39.6%	139,225

Prompt Determination of Tax Liability

To request a prompt determination of the tax liability of the bankruptcy estate, the trustee or debtor-in-possession must file a written application for the determination with the IRS District Director for the district in which the bankruptcy case is pending. The application must be submitted in duplicate and executed under the penalties of perjury. The trustee or debtor-in-possession must submit with the application an **exact copy** of the return (or returns) filed by the trustee with the IRS for a completed tax period, and a statement of the name and location of the office where the return was filed. The envelope should be marked, "Personal Attention of the Special Procedures Function (Bankruptcy Section). DO NOT OPEN IN MAILROOM."

The IRS will notify the trustee or debtor-in-possession within 60 days from receipt of the application whether the return filed by the trustee or debtor-in-possession has been selected for examination or has been accepted as filed. If the return is selected for examination, it will be examined as soon as possible. The IRS will notify the trustee or debtor-in-possession of any tax due within 180 days from receipt of the application or within any additional time permitted by the bankruptcy court.

See Rev. Proc. 81-17, 1981-1 C.B. 688.

Special Filing Instructions for Bankruptcy Estates

Use Form 1041 only as a transmittal for Form 1040. In the top margin of Form 1040 write "Attachment to Form 1041. DO NOT DETACH." Attach Form 1040 to Form 1041. Complete only the identification area at the top of Form 1041. Enter the name of the individual debtor in the following format: "John Q. Public Bankruptcy Estate." Beneath, enter the name of the trustee in the following format: "Avery Snow, Trustee." In item D, enter the date the petition was filed or the date of conversion to a chapter 7 or 11 case.

Enter on Form 1041, line 23, any tax due from line 56 of Form 1040. Complete lines 24 through 29 of Form 1041, and sign and date it.

Specific Instructions

Name of Estate or Trust

Copy the exact name of the estate or trust from the **Form SS-4,** Application for Employer Identification Number, that you used to apply for the employer identification number (EIN).

If a grantor type trust (discussed below), write the name, identification number, and address of the grantor(s) or other owner(s) in parentheses after the name of the trust.

Address

Include the suite, room, or other unit number after the street address.

If the Post Office does not deliver mail to the street address and the fiduciary has a P.O. box, show the box number instead of the street address.

If you change your address after filing Form 1041, use **Form 8822,** Change of Address, to notify the IRS.

A. Type of Entity

Check the appropriate box that describes the entity for which you are filing the return.

Note: *There are special filing requirements for grantor type trusts and bankruptcy estates (discussed below).*

Decedent's Estate

An estate of a deceased person is a taxable entity separate from the decedent. It generally continues to exist until the final distribution of the assets of the estate is made to the heirs and other beneficiaries. The income earned from the property of the estate during the period of administration or settlement must be accounted for and reported by the estate.

Simple Trust

A trust may qualify as a simple trust if:

1. The trust instrument requires that all income must be distributed currently;

2. The trust instrument does not provide that any amounts are to be paid, permanently set aside, or used for charitable purposes; and

3. The trust does not distribute amounts allocated to the corpus of the trust.

Complex Trust

A complex trust is any trust that does not qualify as a simple trust as explained above.

Grantor Type Trust

A grantor type trust is a legal trust under applicable state law that is not recognized as a separate taxable entity for income tax purposes because the grantor or other substantial owners have not relinquished complete dominion and control over the trust.

Generally, for transfers made in trust after March 1, 1986, the grantor is treated as the owner of any portion of a trust in which he or she has a reversionary interest in either the income or corpus therefrom, if, as of the inception of that portion of the trust, the value of the reversionary interest is more than 5% of the value of that portion. Also, the grantor is treated as holding any power or interest that was held by either the grantor's spouse at the time that the power or interest was created or who became the grantor's spouse after the creation of that power or interest.

Caution: *The following instructions apply **only** to grantor type trusts that are not using an optional filing method, explained later.*

Report on Form 1041 **only** the part of the income that is taxable to the trust. Do not report on Form 1041 the income that is taxable to the grantor or another person. Instead, attach a separate sheet to report:

- The income of the trust that is taxable to the grantor or another person under sections 671 through 678;
- The name, identifying number, and address of the person(s) to whom the income is taxable; and
- Any deductions or credits applied to this income.

The income taxable to the grantor or another person under sections 671 through 678 and the deductions and credits applied to the income must be reported by that person on his or her own income tax return.

Mortgage pools. The trustee of a mortgage pool, such as the Federal National Mortgage Association, collects principal and interest payments on each mortgage and makes distributions to the certificate holders. Each pool is considered a grantor type trust, and each certificate holder is treated as the owner of an undivided interest in the entire trust under the grantor trust rules. Certificate holders must report their proportionate share of the mortgage interest and other items of income on their individual tax returns.

Pre-need funeral trusts. The purchasers of pre-need funeral services are the grantors and the owners of pre-need funeral trusts established under state laws. See Rev. Rul. 87-127, 1987-2 C.B. 156. However, the trustees of pre-need funeral trusts can elect to file the return and pay the tax for qualified funeral trusts. For more information, see **Form 1041-QFT,** U.S. Income Tax Return for Qualified Funeral Trusts.

Nonqualified deferred compensation plans. Taxpayers may adopt and maintain grantor trusts in connection with nonqualified deferred compensation plans (sometimes referred to as "rabbi trusts"). Rev. Proc. 92-64, 1992-2 C.B. 422, provides a "model grantor trust" for use in rabbi trust arrangements. The procedure also provides guidance for requesting rulings on the plans that use these trusts.

Optional Filing Methods for Certain Grantor Type Trusts

Generally, for a trust all of which is treated as owned by one or more grantors or other persons, the trustee may use one of the following 3 optional methods to report instead of filing Form 1041.

Method 1. For a trust treated as owned by one grantor or by one other person, the trustee must give all payers of income during the tax year the name and taxpayer identification number (TIN) of the grantor or other person treated as the owner of the trust and the address of the trust. This method may be used only if the owner of the trust provides the trustee with a signed **Form W-9,** Request for Taxpayer Identification Number and Certification. In addition, unless the grantor or other person treated as owner of the trust is the trustee or a co-trustee of the trust, the trustee must give the grantor or other person treated as owner of the trust a statement that:

- Shows all items of income, deduction, and credit of the trust;
- Identifies the payer of each item of income;
- Explains how the grantor or other person treated as owner of the trust takes those items into account when figuring the grantor's or other person's taxable income or tax; and
- Informs the grantor or other person treated as the owner of the trust that those items must be included when figuring taxable income and credits on his or her income tax return.

Important: *Grantor trusts that have not applied for an EIN and are going to file under **Method 1** do not need an EIN for the trust as long as they continue to report under that method.*

Method 2. For a trust treated as owned by one grantor or by one other person, the trustee must give all payers of income during the tax year the name, address, and TIN of the trust. The trustee also must file with the IRS the appropriate Forms 1099 to report the income or gross proceeds paid to the trust during the tax year that shows the trust as the payer and the grantor or other person treated as owner as the payee. The trustee must report each type of income in the aggregate and each item of gross proceeds separately. The due date for any Forms 1099 required to be filed with the IRS by a trustee under this method is March 1, 1999.

In addition, unless the grantor or other person treated as owner of the trust is the trustee or a co-trustee of the trust, the trustee must give the grantor or other person treated as owner of the trust a statement that:

- Shows all items of income, deduction, and credit of the trust;
- Explains how the grantor or other person treated as owner of the trust takes those items into account when figuring the grantor's or other person's taxable income or tax; and
- Informs the grantor or other person treated as the owner of the trust that those items must be included when figuring taxable income and credits on his or her income tax return. This statement satisfies the requirement to give the recipient copies of the Forms 1099 filed by the trustee.

Method 3. For a trust treated as owned by two or more grantors or other persons, the trustee must give all payers of income during the tax year the name, address, and TIN of the trust. The trustee also must file with the IRS the appropriate Forms 1099 to report the income or gross proceeds paid to the trust by all payers during the tax year attributable to the part of the trust treated as owned by each grantor or other person, showing the trust as the payer and each grantor or other person treated as owner of the trust as the payee. The trustee must report each type of income in the aggregate and each item of gross proceeds separately. The due date for any Forms 1099 required to be filed with the IRS by a trustee under this method is March 1, 1999.

In addition, the trustee must give each grantor or other person treated as owner of the trust a statement that:

- Shows all items of income, deduction, and credit of the trust attributable to the part of the trust treated as owned by the grantor or other person;
- Explains how the grantor or other person treated as owner of the trust takes those items into account when figuring the grantor's or other person's taxable income or tax; and
- Informs the grantor or other person treated as the owner of the trust that those items must be included when figuring taxable income and credits on his or her income tax return. This statement satisfies the requirement to give the recipient copies of the Forms 1099 filed by the trustee.

Exceptions. The following trusts cannot report using the optional filing methods:

1. A common trust fund (as defined in section 584(a)).

2. A foreign trust or a trust that has any of its assets located outside the United States.

3. A qualified subchapter S trust (as defined in section 1361(d)(3)).

4. A trust all of which is treated as owned by one grantor or one other person whose tax year is other than a calendar year.

5. A trust all of which is treated as owned by one or more grantors or other persons, one of which is not a U.S. person.

6. A trust all of which is treated as owned by one or more grantors or other persons if at least one grantor or other person is an exempt recipient for information reporting purposes, unless at least one grantor or other person is not an exempt recipient and the trustee reports without treating any of the grantors or other persons as exempt recipients.

Changing filing methods. A trustee who previously had filed Form 1041 can change to one of the optional methods by filing a final Form 1041 for the tax year that immediately precedes the first tax year for which the trustee elects to report under one of the optional methods. On the front of the final Form 1041, the trustee must write "Pursuant to section 1.671-4(g), this is the final Form 1041 for this grantor trust," and check the "Final return" box in item F.

For more details on changing reporting methods, including changes from one optional method to another, see Regulations section 1.671-4(g).

Backup withholding. Generally, a grantor trust is considered a payor of reportable payments received by the trust for purposes of backup withholding. If the trust has 10 or fewer grantors, a reportable payment made to the trust is treated as a reportable payment of the same kind made to the grantors on the date the trust received the payment. If the trust has more than 10 grantors, a reportable payment made to the trust is treated as a payment of the same kind made by the trust to each grantor in an amount equal to the distribution made to each grantor on the date the grantor is paid or credited. The trustee must withhold 31% of reportable payments made to any grantor who is subject to backup withholding. For more information, see section 3406 and Temporary Regulations section 35a.9999-2, Q&A 20.

Bankruptcy Estate

A chapter 7 or 11 bankruptcy estate is a separate and distinct taxable entity from the individual debtor for Federal income tax purposes. See **Of Special Interest to Bankruptcy Trustees and Debtors-in-Possession** on page 7.

For more information, see section 1398 and **Pub. 908,** Bankruptcy Tax Guide.

Pooled Income Fund

A pooled income fund is a split-interest trust with a remainder interest for a public charity and a life income interest retained by the donor or for another person. The property is held in a pool with other pooled income fund property and does not include any tax-exempt securities. The income for a retained life interest is figured using the yearly rate of return earned by the trust. See section 642(c) and the related regulations for more information.

If you are filing for a pooled income fund, attach a statement to support the following:

- The calculation of the yearly rate of return.
- The computation of the deduction for distributions to the beneficiaries.

• The computation of any charitable deduction.

You do not have to complete Schedules A or B of Form 1041.

If the fund has accumulations of income, file Form 1041-A unless the fund is required to distribute all of its net income to beneficiaries currently.

You must also file **Form 5227,** Split-Interest Trust Information Return, for the pooled income fund.

B. Number of Schedules K-1 Attached

Every trust or decedent's estate claiming an income distribution deduction on page 1, line 18, must enter the number of Schedules K-1 (Form 1041) that are attached to Form 1041.

C. Employer Identification Number

Every estate or trust that is required to file Form 1041 must have an EIN. To apply for one, use Form SS-4. Form SS-4 has information on how to apply for an EIN by mail or by telephone. If the estate or trust has not received its EIN by the time the return is due, write "Applied for" in the space for the EIN. See **Pub. 583,** Starting a Business and Keeping Records, for more information.

If you are filing a return for a mortgage pool, such as one created under the mortgage-backed security programs administered by the Federal National Mortgage Association ("Fannie Mae") or the Government National Mortgage Association ("Ginnie Mae"), the EIN stays with the pool if that pool is traded from one financial institution to another.

D. Date Entity Created

Enter the date the trust was created, or, if a decedent's estate, the date of the decedent's death.

E. Nonexempt Charitable and Split-Interest Trusts

Section 4947(a)(1) Trust

Check this box if the trust is a nonexempt charitable trust within the meaning of section 4947(a)(1). A nonexempt charitable trust is a trust that is not exempt from tax under section 501(a); all of the unexpired interests are devoted to one or more charitable purposes described in section 170(c)(2)(B); and for which a deduction was allowed under section 170 (for individual taxpayers) or similar Code section for personal holding companies, foreign personal holding companies, or estates or trusts (including a deduction for estate or gift tax purposes).

Not a Private Foundation

Check this box if the charitable trust is not treated as a private foundation under section 509. For more information, see Regulations section 53.4947-1.

If a nonexempt charitable trust is not treated as though it were a private foundation, the fiduciary must file, in addition to Form 1041, **Form 990** (or **Form 990-EZ**), Return of Organization Exempt From Income Tax, and **Schedule A (Form 990),** Organization Exempt Under Section 501(c)(3), if the trust's gross receipts are normally more than $25,000.

If a nonexempt charitable trust is not treated as though it were a private foundation, and it has no taxable income under Subtitle A, it can file either Form 990 or Form 990-EZ instead of Form 1041 to meet its section 6012 filing requirement.

Section 4947(a)(2) Trust

Check this box if the trust is a split-interest trust described in section 4947(a)(2). A split-interest trust is a trust that is not exempt from tax under section 501(a); has some unexpired interests that are devoted to purposes other than religious, charitable, or similar purposes described in section 170(c)(2)(B); and has amounts transferred in trust after May 26, 1969, for which a deduction was allowed under section 170 (for individual taxpayers) or similar Code section for personal holding companies, foreign personal holding companies, or estates or trusts (including a deduction for estate or gift tax purposes).

The fiduciary of a split-interest trust must also file Form 5227 (for amounts transferred in trust after May 26, 1969); and Form 1041-A if the trust's governing instrument does not require that all of the trust's income be distributed currently.

If a split-interest trust has any unrelated business taxable income, however, it must file Form 1041 to report **all** of its income and to pay any tax due.

Nonexempt Charitable Trust Treated as a Private Foundation

If a nonexempt charitable trust is treated as though it were a private foundation under section 509, then the fiduciary must file **Form 990-PF,** Return of Private Foundation, in addition to Form 1041.

If a nonexempt charitable trust is subject to any of the private foundation excise taxes, then it must also file **Form 4720,** Return of Certain Excise Taxes on Charities and Other Persons Under Chapters 41 and 42 of the Internal Revenue Code. None of the private foundation taxes paid by the trust can be taken as a deduction on Form 1041.

If a nonexempt charitable trust is treated as though it were a private foundation, and it has no taxable income under Subtitle A, it may file Form 990-PF instead of Form 1041 to meet its section 6012 filing requirement.

F. Initial Return, Amended Return, Final Return; or Change in Fiduciary's Name or Address

Amended Return

If you are filing an amended Form 1041, check the "Amended return" box. Complete the entire return, correct the appropriate lines with the new information, and refigure the estate's or trust's tax liability. If the total tax on line 23 is larger on the amended return than on the original return, you generally should pay the difference with the amended return. However, you should adjust this amount if there is any increase or decrease in the total payments shown on line 25.

On an attached sheet explain the reason for the amendments and identify the lines and amounts being changed on the amended return.

If the amended return results in a change to income, or a change in distribution of any income or other information provided to a beneficiary, an amended Schedule K-1 (Form 1041) must also be filed with the amended Form 1041 and given to each beneficiary. Check the "Amended K-1" box at the top of the amended Schedule K-1.

Final Return

Check this box if this is a final return because the estate or trust has terminated. Also, check the "Final K-1" box at the top of Schedule K-1.

If, on the final return, there are excess deductions, an unused capital loss carryover, or a net operating loss carryover, see the instructions for Schedule K-1, lines 13a through 13e, on page 31.

G. Pooled Mortgage Account

If you bought a pooled mortgage account during the year, and still have that pool at the end of the tax year, check the "Bought" box and enter the date of purchase. If you sold a pooled mortgage account that was purchased during this, or a previous, tax year, check the "Sold" box and enter the date of sale. If you neither bought nor sold a pooled mortgage account, skip this item.

Income

Special Rule for Blind Trust

If you are reporting income from a qualified blind trust (under the Ethics in Government Act of 1978), do not identify the payer of any income to the trust but complete the rest of the return as provided in the instructions. Also write "Blind Trust" at the top of page 1.

Line 1—Interest Income

Report the estate's or trust's share of all taxable interest income that was received during the tax year. Examples of taxable interest include interest from:

- Accounts (including certificates of deposit and money market accounts) with banks, credit unions, and thrifts.
- Notes, loans, and mortgages.
- U.S. Treasury bills, notes, and bonds.
- U.S. savings bonds.
- Original issue discount.
- Income received as a regular interest holder of a real estate mortgage investment conduit (REMIC).

For taxable bonds acquired after 1987, amortizable bond premium is treated as an offset to the interest income instead of as a separate interest deduction. See Pub. 550.

For the year of the decedent's death, Forms 1099-INT issued in the decedent's name may include interest income earned after the date of death that should be reported on the income tax return of the decedent's estate. When preparing the decedent's final income tax return, report on line 1 of Schedule B (Form 1040) or Schedule 1 (Form 1040A) the total interest shown on Form 1099-INT. Under the last entry on line 1, subtotal all the interest reported on line 1. Below the subtotal, write "Form 1041" and the name and address shown on Form 1041 for the decedent's estate. Also, show the part of the interest reported on Form 1041 and subtract it from the subtotal.

Line 2—Ordinary Dividends

Report the estate's or trust's share of all ordinary dividends received during the tax year.

For the year of the decedent's death, Forms 1099-DIV issued in the decedent's name may include dividends earned after the date of death that should be reported on the income tax return of the decedent's estate. When preparing the decedent's final income tax return, report on line 5 of Schedule B (Form 1040) or Schedule 1 (Form 1040A) the ordinary dividends shown on Form 1099-DIV. Under the last entry on line 5, subtotal all the dividends reported on line 5. Below the subtotal, write "Form 1041" and the name and address shown on Form 1041 for the decedent's estate. Also, show the part of the ordinary dividends reported on Form 1041 and subtract it from the subtotal.

Note: *Report capital gain distributions on Schedule D (Form 1041), line 9.*

Line 3—Business Income or (Loss)

If the estate or trust operated a business, report the income and expenses on **Schedule C (Form 1040),** Profit or Loss From Business (or **Schedule C-EZ (Form 1040),** Net Profit From Business). Enter the net profit or (loss) from Schedule C (or Schedule C-EZ) on line 3.

Line 4—Capital Gain or (Loss)

Enter the gain from Schedule D (Form 1041), Part III, line 16, column (3); or the loss from Part IV, line 17.

Note: ***Do not*** *substitute Schedule D (Form 1040) for Schedule D (Form 1041).*

Line 5—Rents, Royalties, Partnerships, Other Estates and Trusts, etc.

Use **Schedule E (Form 1040),** Supplemental Income and Loss, to report the estate's or trust's share of income or (losses) from rents, royalties, partnerships, S corporations, other estates and trusts, and REMICs. Enter the net profit or (loss) from Schedule E on line 5. See the instructions for Schedule E (Form 1040) for reporting requirements.

If the estate or trust received a Schedule K-1 from a partnership, S corporation, or other flow-through entity, use the corresponding lines on Form 1041 to report the interest, dividends, capital gains, etc., from the flow-through entity.

Line 6—Farm Income or (Loss)

If the estate or trust operated a farm, use **Schedule F (Form 1040),** Profit or Loss From Farming, to report farm income and expenses. Enter the net profit or (loss) from Schedule F on line 6.

Line 7—Ordinary Gain or (Loss)

Enter from line 18, **Form 4797,** Sales of Business Property, the ordinary gain or loss from the sale or exchange of property other than capital assets and also from involuntary conversions (other than casualty or theft).

Line 8—Other Income

Enter other items of income not included on lines 1 through 7. List the type and amount on an attached schedule if the estate or trust has more than one item.

Items to be reported on line 8 include:

- Unpaid compensation received by the decedent's estate that is income in respect of a decedent.
- Any part of a total distribution shown on **Form 1099-R,** Distributions From Pensions, Annuities, Retirement or Profit-Sharing Plans, IRAs, Insurance Contracts, etc., that is treated as ordinary income. For more information, see the separate instructions for **Form 4972,** Tax on Lump-Sum Distributions.

Deductions

Depreciation, Depletion, and Amortization

A trust or decedent's estate is allowed a deduction for depreciation, depletion, and amortization only to the extent the deductions are not apportioned to the beneficiaries. An estate or trust is not allowed to make an election under section 179 to expense certain tangible property.

The estate's or trust's share of depreciation, depletion, and amortization should be reported on the appropriate lines of Schedule C (or C-EZ), E, or F (Form 1040), the net income or loss from which is shown on line 3, 5, or 6 of Form 1041. If the deduction is not related to a specific business or activity, then report it on line 15a.

Depreciation. For a decedent's estate, the depreciation deduction is apportioned between the estate and the heirs, legatees, and devisees on the basis of the estate's income allocable to each.

For a trust, the depreciation deduction is apportioned between the income beneficiaries and the trust on the basis of the trust income allocable to each, unless the governing instrument (or local law) requires or permits the trustee to maintain a depreciation reserve. If the trustee is required to maintain a reserve, the deduction is first allocated to the trust, up to the amount of the reserve. Any excess is allocated among the beneficiaries in the same manner as the trust's accounting income. See Regulations section 1.167(h)-1(b).

Depletion. For mineral or timber property held by a decedent's estate, the depletion deduction is apportioned between the estate and the heirs, legatees, and devisees on the basis of the estate's income from such property allocable to each.

For mineral or timber property held in trust, the depletion deduction is apportioned between the income beneficiaries and the trust based on the trust income from such property allocable to each, unless the governing instrument (or local law) requires or permits the trustee to maintain a reserve for depletion. If the trustee is required to maintain a reserve, the deduction is first allocated to the trust, up to the amount of the reserve. Any excess is allocated among the beneficiaries in the same manner as the trust's accounting income. See Regulations section 1.611-1(c)(4).

Amortization. The deduction for amortization is apportioned between an estate or trust and its beneficiaries under the same principles for apportioning the deductions for depreciation and depletion.

The deduction for the amortization of reforestation expenditures under section 194 is allowed only to an estate.

Allocation of Deductions for Tax-Exempt Income

Generally, no deduction that would otherwise be allowable is allowed for any expense (whether for business or for the production of income) that is allocable to tax-exempt income. Examples of tax-exempt income include:

- Certain death benefits (section 101);
- Interest on state or local bonds (section 103);
- Compensation for injuries or sickness (section 104); and

• Income from discharge of indebtedness in a title 11 case (section 108).

Exception. State income taxes and business expenses that are allocable to tax-exempt interest are deductible.

Expenses that are directly allocable to tax-exempt income are allocated only to tax-exempt income. A reasonable proportion of expenses indirectly allocable to both tax-exempt income and other income must be allocated to each class of income.

Deductions That May Be Allowable for Estate Tax Purposes

Administration expenses and casualty and theft losses deductible on Form 706 may be deducted, to the extent otherwise deductible for income tax purposes, on Form 1041 if the fiduciary files a statement waiving the right to deduct the expenses and losses on Form 706. The statement must be filed before the expiration of the statutory period of limitations for the tax year the deduction is claimed. See Pub. 559 for more information.

Accrued Expenses

Generally, an accrual basis taxpayer can deduct accrued expenses in the tax year that: **(a)** all events have occurred that determine the liability; and **(b)** the amount of the liability can be figured with reasonable accuracy. However, all the events that establish liability are treated as occurring only when economic performance takes place. There are exceptions for recurring items. See section 461(h).

Limitations on Deductions

At-Risk Loss Limitations

Generally, the amount the estate or trust has "at risk" limits the loss it can deduct for any tax year. Use **Form 6198,** At-Risk Limitations, to figure the deductible loss for the year and file it with Form 1041. For more information, see **Pub. 925,** Passive Activity and At-Risk Rules.

Passive Activity Loss and Credit Limitations

In general. Section 469 and the regulations thereunder generally limit losses from passive activities to the amount of income derived from all passive activities. Similarly, credits from passive activities are generally limited to the tax attributable to such activities. These limitations are first applied at the estate or trust level.

Generally, an activity is a passive activity if it involves the conduct of any trade or business, and the taxpayer does not materially participate in the activity. Passive activities do not include working interests in oil and gas properties. See section 469(c)(3).

Note: *Material participation standards for estates and trusts had not been established by regulations at the time these instructions went to print.*

For a grantor trust, material participation is determined at the grantor level.

If the estate or trust distributes an interest in a passive activity, the basis of the property immediately before the distribution is increased by the passive activity losses allocable to the interest, and such losses cannot be deducted. See section 469(j)(12).

Note: *Losses from passive activities are first subject to the at-risk rules. When the losses are deductible under the at-risk rules, the passive activity rules then apply.*

Rental activities. Generally, rental activities are passive activities, whether or not the taxpayer materially participates. However, certain taxpayers who materially participate in real property trades or businesses are not subject to the passive activity limitations on losses from rental real estate activities in which they materially participate. For more details, see section 469(c)(7).

For tax years of an estate ending less than 2 years after the decedent's date of death, up to $25,000 of deductions and deduction equivalents of credits from rental real estate activities in which the decedent actively participated are allowed. Any excess losses and/or credits are suspended for the year and carried forward.

Portfolio income. Portfolio income is not treated as income from a passive activity, and passive losses and credits generally may not be applied to offset it. Portfolio income generally includes interest, dividends, royalties, and income from annuities. Portfolio income of an estate or trust must be accounted for separately.

Forms to file. See **Form 8582,** Passive Activity Loss Limitations, to figure the amount of losses allowed from passive activities. See **Form 8582-CR,** Passive Activity Credit Limitations, to figure the amount of credit allowed for the current year.

Transactions Between Related Taxpayers

Under section 267, a trust that uses the accrual method of accounting may only deduct business expenses and interest owed to a related party in the year the payment is included in the income of the related party. For this purpose, a related party includes:

1. A grantor and a fiduciary of any trust;

2. A fiduciary of a trust and a fiduciary of another trust, if the same person is a grantor of both trusts;

3. A fiduciary of a trust and a beneficiary of such trust;

4. A fiduciary of a trust and a beneficiary of another trust, if the same person is a grantor of both trusts;

5. A fiduciary of a trust and a corporation more than 50% in value of the outstanding stock of which is owned, directly or indirectly, by or for the trust or by or for a person who is a grantor of the trust; and

6. An executor of an estate and a beneficiary of that estate, except for a sale or exchange to satisfy a pecuniary bequest (i.e., a bequest of a sum of money).

Line 10—Interest

Enter the amount of interest (subject to limitations) paid or incurred by the estate or trust on amounts borrowed by the estate or trust, or on debt acquired by the estate or trust (e.g., outstanding obligations from the decedent) that is not claimed elsewhere on the return.

If the proceeds of a loan were used for more than one purpose (e.g., to purchase a portfolio investment and to acquire an interest in a passive activity), the fiduciary must make an interest allocation according to the rules in Temporary Regulations section 1.163-8T.

Do not include interest paid on indebtedness incurred or continued to purchase or carry obligations on which the interest is wholly exempt from income tax.

Personal interest is not deductible. Examples of personal interest include interest paid on:

• Revolving charge accounts used to purchase personal use property.

• Personal notes for money borrowed from a bank, credit union, or other person.

• Installment loans on personal use property.

• Underpayments of Federal, state, or local income taxes.

Interest that is paid or incurred on indebtedness allocable to a trade or business (including a rental activity) should be deducted on the appropriate line of Schedule C (or C-EZ), E, or F (Form 1040), the net income or loss from which is shown on line 3, 5, or 6 of Form 1041.

Types of interest to include on line 10 are:

1. Any investment interest (subject to limitations—see below);

2. Any qualified residence interest (see page 13); and

3. Any interest payable under section 6601 on any unpaid portion of the estate tax attributable to the value of a reversionary or remainder interest in property for the period during which an extension of time for payment of such tax is in effect.

Investment interest. Generally, investment interest is interest (including amortizable bond premium on taxable bonds acquired after October 22, 1986, but before January 1, 1988) that is paid or incurred on indebtedness that is properly allocable to property held for investment. Investment interest does not include any qualified residence interest, or interest that is taken into account under section 469 in figuring income or loss from a passive activity.

Generally, net investment income is the excess of investment income over investment expenses. Investment expenses are those expenses (other than interest) allowable after application of the 2% floor on miscellaneous itemized deductions.

The amount of the investment interest deduction may be limited. Use **Form 4952,** Investment Interest Expense Deduction, to figure the allowable investment interest deduction.

If you must complete Form 4952, check the box on line 10 and attach Form 4952. Then, add the deductible investment interest to the other types of deductible interest and enter the total on line 10.

Qualified residence interest. Interest paid or incurred by an estate or trust on indebtedness secured by a qualified residence of a beneficiary of an estate or trust is treated as qualified residence interest if the residence would be a qualified residence (i.e., the principal residence or the second residence selected by the beneficiary) if owned by the beneficiary. The beneficiary must have a present interest in the estate or trust or an interest in the residuary of the estate or trust. See **Pub. 936,** Home Mortgage Interest Deduction, for an explanation of the general rules for deducting home mortgage interest.

See section 163(h)(3) for a definition of qualified residence interest and for limitations on indebtedness.

Line 11—Taxes

Enter any deductible taxes paid or incurred during the tax year that are not deductible elsewhere on Form 1041.

Deductible taxes include:

- State and local income or real property taxes.
- The generation-skipping transfer (GST) tax imposed on income distributions.

Do not deduct:

- Federal income taxes.
- Estate, inheritance, legacy, succession, and gift taxes.
- Federal duties and excise taxes.
- State and local sales taxes. Instead, treat these taxes as part of the cost of the property.

Line 12—Fiduciary Fees

Enter the deductible fees paid or incurred to the fiduciary for administering the estate or trust during the tax year.

Note: *Fiduciary fees deducted on Form 706 cannot be deducted on Form 1041.*

Line 15a—Other Deductions NOT Subject to the 2% Floor

Attach your own schedule, listing by type and amount, all allowable deductions that are not deductible elsewhere on Form 1041.

Do not include any losses on worthless bonds and similar obligations and nonbusiness bad debts. Report these losses on Schedule D (Form 1041).

Do not deduct medical or funeral expenses on Form 1041. Medical expenses of the decedent paid by the estate may be deductible on the decedent's income tax return for the year incurred. See section 213(c). Funeral expenses are deductible ONLY on Form 706.

The following are examples of deductions that are reported on line 15a.

Bond premium(s). For taxable bonds acquired before October 23, 1986, if the fiduciary elected to amortize the premium, report the amortization on this line. You cannot deduct the amortization for tax-exempt bonds. In all cases where the fiduciary has made an election to amortize the premium, the basis must be reduced by the amount of amortization.

For more information, see section 171 and Pub. 550.

If you claim a bond premium deduction for the estate or trust, figure the deduction on a separate sheet and attach it to Form 1041.

Casualty and theft losses. Use **Form 4684,** Casualties and Thefts, to figure any deductible casualty and theft losses.

Deduction for clean-fuel vehicles. Section 179A allows a deduction for part of the cost of qualified clean-fuel vehicle property. See **Pub. 535,** Business Expenses, for more details.

Net operating loss deduction (NOLD). An estate or trust is allowed the net operating loss deduction (NOLD) under section 172.

If you claim an NOLD for the estate or trust, figure the deduction on a separate sheet and attach it to this return.

Estate's or trust's share of amortization, depreciation, and depletion not claimed elsewhere. If you cannot deduct the amortization, depreciation, and depletion as rent or royalty expenses on Schedule E (Form 1040), or as business or farm expenses on Schedule C, C-EZ, or F (Form 1040), itemize the fiduciary's share of the deductions on an attached sheet and include them on line 15a. Itemize each beneficiary's share of the deductions and report them on the appropriate line of Schedule K-1 (Form 1041).

Line 15b—Allowable Miscellaneous Itemized Deductions Subject to the 2% Floor

Miscellaneous itemized deductions are deductible only to the extent that the aggregate amount of such deductions exceeds 2% of adjusted gross income (AGI).

Among the miscellaneous itemized deductions that must be included on line 15b are expenses for the production or collection of income under section 212, such as investment advisory fees, subscriptions to investment advisory publications, and the cost of safe deposit boxes.

Miscellaneous itemized deductions **do not** include deductions for:

- Interest under section 163.
- Taxes under section 164.
- The amortization of bond premium under section 171.
- Estate taxes attributable to income in respect of a decedent under section 691(c).
- Expenses paid or incurred in connection with the administration of the estate or trust that would not have been incurred if the property were NOT held in the estate or trust.

For other exceptions, see section 67(b).

For estates and trusts, the AGI is figured by subtracting the following from total income on line 9 of page 1:

1. The administration costs of the estate or trust (the total of lines 12, 14, and 15a to the extent they are costs incurred in the administration of the estate or trust) that would not have been incurred if the property were NOT held by the estate or trust;

2. The income distribution deduction (line 18);

3. The amount of the exemption (line 20);

4. The deduction for clean-fuel vehicles claimed on line 15a; and

5. The net operating loss deduction claimed on line 15a.

For those estates and trusts whose income distribution deduction is limited to the actual distribution, and NOT the DNI (i.e., the income distribution is less than the DNI), when computing the AGI, use the amount of the actual distribution.

For those estates and trusts whose income distribution deduction is limited to the DNI (i.e., the actual distribution exceeds the DNI), the DNI must be figured taking into account the allowable miscellaneous itemized deductions (AMID) after application of the 2% floor. In this situation there are two unknown amounts: **(a)** the AMID; and **(b)** the DNI.

The following example illustrates how an algebraic equation can be used to solve for these unknown amounts:

The Malcolm Smith Trust, a complex trust, earned $20,000 of dividend income, $20,000 of capital gains, and a fully deductible $5,000 loss from XYZ partnership (chargeable to corpus) in 1998. The trust instrument provides that capital gains are added to corpus. 50% of the fiduciary fees are allocated to income and 50% to corpus. The trust claimed a $2,000 deduction on line 12 of Form 1041. The trust incurred $1,500 of miscellaneous itemized deductions (chargeable to income), which are subject to the 2% floor. There are no other deductions. The trustee made a discretionary distribution of the accounting income of $17,500 to the trust's sole beneficiary.

Because the actual distribution can reasonably be expected to exceed the DNI, the trust must figure the DNI, taking into account the allowable miscellaneous itemized deductions, to determine the amount to enter on line 15b.

The trust also claims an exemption of $100 on line 20.

To compute line 15b, use the equation below:

AMID = total miscellaneous itemized deductions – (.02(AGI))

In the above example:

AMID = 1,500 – (.02(AGI))

In all situations, use the following equation to compute the AGI:

AGI = (line 9) – (the total of lines 12, 14, and 15a to the extent they are costs incurred in the administration of the estate or trust that would not have been incurred if the property were NOT held by the estate or trust) – (line 18) – (line 20).

Note: *There are no other deductions claimed by the trust on line 15a that are deductible in arriving at AGI.*

In the above example:

AGI = 35,000 – 2,000 – DNI – 100

Since the value of line 18 is not known because it is limited to the DNI, you are left with the following:

AGI = 32,900 – DNI

Substitute the value of AGI in the equation:

AMID = 1,500 – (.02(32,900 – DNI))

The equation cannot be solved until the value of DNI is known. The DNI can be expressed in terms of the AMID. To do this, compute the DNI using the known values. In this example, the DNI is equal to the total income of the trust (less any capital gains allocated to corpus; or plus any capital loss from line 4); less total deductions from line 16 (excluding any miscellaneous itemized deductions); less the AMID.

Thus, DNI = (line 9) – (line 16, column (2) of Schedule D (Form 1041)) – (line 16) – (AMID)

Substitute the known values:

DNI = 35,000 – 20,000 – 2,000 – AMID

DNI = 13,000 – AMID

Substitute the value of DNI in the equation to solve for AMID:

AMID = 1,500 – (.02(32,900 – (13,000 – AMID)))

AMID = 1,500 – (.02(32,900 – 13,000 + AMID))

AMID = 1,500 – (658 – 260 + .02 AMID)

AMID = 1,102 – .02AMID

1.02AMID = 1,102

AMID = 1,080

DNI = 11,920 (i.e., 13,000 – 1,080)

AGI = 20,980 (i.e., 32,900 – 11,920)

Note: *The income distribution deduction is equal to the smaller of the distribution ($17,500) or the DNI ($11,920).*

Enter the value of AMID on line 15b (the DNI should equal line 7 of Schedule B) and complete the rest of Form 1041 according to the instructions.

If the 2% floor is more than the deductions subject to the 2% floor, no deductions are allowed.

Line 18—Income Distribution Deduction

If the estate or trust was required to distribute income currently or if it paid, credited, or was required to distribute any other amounts to beneficiaries during the tax year, complete Schedule B to determine the estate's or trust's income distribution deduction. However, if you are filing for a pooled income fund, do not complete Schedule B. Instead, attach a statement to support the computation of the income distribution deduction. If the estate or trust claims an income distribution deduction, complete and attach:

- Part I (through line 9) and Part II of Schedule I to refigure the deduction on a minimum tax basis; AND
- Schedule K-1 (Form 1041) for each beneficiary to which a distribution was made or required to be made.

Cemetery perpetual care fund. On line 18, deduct the amount, not more than $5 per gravesite, paid for maintenance of cemetery property. To the right of the entry space for line 18, enter the number of gravesites. Also write "Section 642(i) trust" in parentheses after the trust's name at the top of Form 1041. You do not have to complete Schedules B of Form 1041 and K-1 (Form 1041).

Line 19—Estate Tax Deduction (Including Certain Generation-Skipping Transfer Taxes)

If the estate or trust includes income in respect of a decedent (IRD) in its gross income, and such amount was included in the decedent's gross estate for estate tax purposes, the estate or trust is allowed to deduct in the same tax year the income is included, that portion of the estate tax imposed on the decedent's estate that is attributable to the inclusion of the IRD in the decedent's estate. For an example of the computation, see Regulations section 1.691(c)-1 and Pub. 559.

If any amount properly paid, credited, or required to be distributed by an estate or trust to a beneficiary consists of IRD received by the estate or trust, do not include such amounts in determining the estate tax deduction for the estate or trust. Figure the deduction on a separate sheet. Attach the sheet to your return.

Also, a deduction is allowed for the GST tax imposed as a result of a taxable termination or a direct skip occurring as a result of the death of the transferor. See section 691(c)(3). Enter the estate's or trust's share of these deductions on line 19.

Line 20—Exemption

Decedents' estates. A decedent's estate is allowed a $600 exemption.

Trusts. A trust whose governing instrument requires that all income be distributed currently is allowed a $300 exemption, even if it distributed amounts other than income during the tax year. All other trusts are allowed a $100 exemption. See Regulations section 1.642(b)-1.

Tax and Payments

Line 22—Taxable Income

Net operating loss. If line 22 is a loss, the estate or trust may have a net operating loss (NOL). Do not include the deductions claimed on lines 13, 18, and 20 when figuring the amount of the NOL. An NOL generally may be carried back to the 2 prior tax years and forward to the 20 following tax years. However, if the estate or trust has:

- A casualty or theft loss for the tax year, the part of the NOL attributable to casualty or theft losses may be carried back to the 3 prior tax years and forward to the 20 following tax years.
- A farming loss for the tax year, the part of the NOL attributable to the farming loss may be carried back to the 5 prior tax years and forward to the 20 following tax years.

Complete Schedule A of **Form 1045,** Application for Tentative Refund, to figure the amount of the NOL that is available for carryback or carryover. Use Form 1045 or file an amended return to apply for a refund based on an NOL carryback. For more details, see **Pub. 536,** Net Operating Losses.

On the termination of the estate or trust, any unused NOL carryover that would be allowable to the estate or trust in a later tax year, but for the termination, is allowed to the beneficiaries succeeding to the property of the estate or trust. See the instructions for Schedule K-1, lines 13d and 13e.

Excess deductions on termination. If the estate or trust has for its final year deductions (excluding the charitable deduction and exemption) in excess of its gross income, the excess is allowed as an itemized deduction to the beneficiaries succeeding to the property of the estate or trust.

In general, an unused NOL carryover that is allowed to beneficiaries (as explained above) cannot also be treated as an excess deduction. However, if the final year of the estate or trust is also the last year of the NOL carryover period, the NOL carryover not absorbed in that tax year by the estate or trust is included as an excess deduction. See the instructions for Schedule K-1, line 13a.

Line 24a—1998 Estimated Tax Payments and Amount Applied From 1997 Return

Enter the amount of any estimated tax payment you made with Form 1041-ES for 1998 plus the amount of any overpayment from the 1997 return that was applied to the 1998 estimated tax.

If the estate or trust is the beneficiary of another trust and received a payment of estimated tax that was credited to the trust (as reflected on the Schedule K-1 issued to the trust), then report this amount separately with the notation "section 643(g)" in the space next to line 24a.

Caution: *Do not include on Form 1041 estimated tax paid by an individual before death. Instead, include the payments on the decedent's final income tax return.*

Line 24b—Estimated Tax Payments Allocated to Beneficiaries

The trustee (or executor, for the final year of the estate) may elect under section 643(g) to have any portion of its estimated tax treated as a payment of estimated tax made by a beneficiary or beneficiaries. The election is made on **Form 1041-T,** Allocation of Estimated Tax Payments to Beneficiaries, which must be filed by the 65th day after the close of the trust's tax year. Form 1041-T shows the amounts to be allocated to each beneficiary. This amount is reported on the beneficiary's Schedule K-1, line 14a.

Failure to file Form 1041-T by the due date (March 8, 1999, for calendar year estates and trusts) will result in an invalid election. An invalid election will require the filing of amended Schedules K-1 for each beneficiary who was allocated a payment of estimated tax.

Attach Form 1041-T to your return ONLY if you have not yet filed it. If you have already filed Form 1041-T, do not attach a copy to your return.

Line 24d—Tax Paid With Extension of Time To File

If you filed either Form 2758 (for estates only), Form 8736, or Form 8800 to request an extension of time to file Form 1041, enter the amount that you paid with the extension request and check the appropriate box(es).

Line 24e—Federal Income Tax Withheld

Use line 24e to claim a credit for any Federal income tax withheld (and not repaid) by: **(a)** an employer on wages and salaries of a decedent received by the decedent's estate; **(b)** a payer of certain gambling winnings (e.g., state lottery winnings); or **(c)** a payer of distributions from pensions, annuities, retirement or profit-sharing plans, IRAs, insurance contracts, etc., received by a decedent's estate or trust. Attach a copy of **Form W-2, Form W-2G,** or **Form 1099-R.**

Backup withholding. If the estate or trust received a 1998 Form 1099 showing Federal income tax withheld (i.e., backup withholding) on interest income, dividends, or other income, check the box and include the amount withheld on income retained by the estate or trust in the total for line 24e.

Report on Schedule K-1 (Form 1041), line 14, any credit for backup withholding on income distributed to the beneficiary.

Line 24f—Credit For Tax Paid on Undistributed Capital Gains

Attach copy B of **Form 2439,** Notice to Shareholder of Undistributed Long-Term Capital Gains.

Line 24g—Credit for Federal Tax on Fuels

Enter any credit for Federal excise taxes paid on fuels that are ultimately used for nontaxable purposes (e.g., an off-highway business use). Attach **Form 4136,** Credit for Federal Tax Paid on Fuels. See **Pub. 378,** Fuel Tax Credits and Refunds, for more information.

Line 26—Underpayment of Estimated Tax

If line 27 is at least $1,000 and more than 10% of the tax shown on Form 1041, or the estate or trust underpaid its 1998 estimated tax liability for any payment period, it may owe a penalty. See Form 2210 to determine whether the estate or trust owes a penalty and to figure the amount of the penalty.

Note: *The penalty may be waived under certain conditions. See* ***Pub. 505,*** *Tax Withholding and Estimated Tax, for details.*

Line 27—Tax Due

You must pay the tax in full when the return is filed. Make the check or money order payable to the "United States Treasury." Write the EIN and "1998 Form 1041" on the payment. Enclose, but do not attach, the payment with Form 1041.

Line 29a—Credit to 1999 Estimated Tax

Enter the amount from line 28 that you want applied to the estate's or trust's 1999 estimated tax.

Schedule A—Charitable Deduction

General Instructions

Generally, any part of the gross income of an estate or trust (other than a simple trust) that, under the terms of the will or governing instrument, is paid (or treated as paid) during the tax year for a charitable purpose specified in section 170(c) is allowed as a deduction to the estate or trust. It is not necessary that the charitable organization be created or organized in the United States.

Trusts that claim a charitable deduction must also file Form 1041-A. See Form 1041-A for exceptions.

A pooled income fund, nonexempt private foundation, or trust with unrelated business income should attach a separate sheet to Form 1041 instead of using Schedule A of Form 1041 to figure the charitable deduction.

Election to treat contributions as paid in the prior tax year. The fiduciary of an estate or trust may elect to treat as paid during the tax year any amount of gross income received during that tax year or any prior tax year that was paid in the next tax year for a charitable purpose.

For example, if a calendar year estate or trust makes a qualified charitable contribution on February 10, 1999, from income earned in 1998 or prior, then the fiduciary can elect to treat the contribution as paid in 1998.

To make the election, the fiduciary must file a statement with Form 1041 for the tax year in which the contribution is treated as paid. This statement must include:

1. The name and address of the fiduciary;

2. The name of the estate or trust;

3. An indication that the fiduciary is making an election under section 642(c)(1) for contributions treated as paid during such tax year;

4. The name and address of each organization to which any such contribution is paid; and

5. The amount of each contribution and date of actual payment or, if applicable, the total amount of contributions paid to each organization during the next tax year, to be treated as paid in the prior tax year.

The election must be filed by the due date (including extensions) for Form 1041 for the next tax year.

For more information about the charitable deduction, see section 642(c) and related regulations.

Specific Instructions

Line 1—Amounts Paid or Permanently Set Aside for Charitable Purposes From Gross Income

Enter amounts that were paid for a charitable purpose out of the estate's or trust's gross income, including any capital gains that are attributable to income under the governing instrument or local law. Include amounts paid during the tax year from gross income received in a prior tax year, but only if no deduction was allowed for any prior tax year for these amounts.

Estates, and certain trusts, may claim a deduction for amounts permanently set aside for a charitable purpose from gross income. Such amounts must be permanently set aside during the tax year to be used exclusively for religious, charitable, scientific, literary, or educational purposes, or for the prevention of cruelty to children or animals, or for the establishment, acquisition, maintenance, or operation of a public cemetery not operated for profit.

For a trust to qualify, the trust may not be a simple trust, and the set aside amounts must be required by the terms of a trust instrument that was created on or before October 9, 1969.

Further, the trust instrument must provide for an irrevocable remainder interest to be transferred to or for the use of an organization described in section 170(c); OR the trust must have been created by a grantor who was at all times after October 9, 1969, under a mental disability to change the terms of the trust.

Also, certain testamentary trusts that were established by a will that was executed on or before October 9, 1969, may qualify. See Regulations section 1.642(c)-2(b).

Do not include any capital gains for the tax year allocated to corpus and paid or permanently set aside for charitable purposes. Instead, enter these amounts on line 4.

Line 2—Tax-Exempt Income Allocable to Charitable Contributions

Any estate or trust that pays or sets aside any part of its income for a charitable purpose must reduce the deduction by the portion allocable to any tax-exempt income. If the governing instrument specifically provides as to the source from which amounts are paid, permanently set aside, or to be used for charitable purposes, the specific provisions control. In all other cases, determine the amount of tax-exempt income allocable to charitable contributions by multiplying line 1 by a fraction, the numerator of which is the total tax-exempt income of the estate or trust, and the denominator of which is the gross income of the estate or trust. Do not include in the denominator any losses allocated to corpus.

Line 4—Capital Gains for the Tax Year Allocated to Corpus and Paid or Permanently Set Aside for Charitable Purposes

Enter the total of all capital gains for the tax year that are:

- Allocated to corpus; and
- Paid or permanently set aside for charitable purposes.

Line 6—Section 1202 Exclusion Allocable to Capital Gains Paid or Permanently Set Aside for Charitable Purposes

If the exclusion of gain from the sale or exchange of qualified small business stock was claimed, enter the part of the gain included on Schedule A, lines 1 and 4, that was excluded under section 1202.

Schedule B—Income Distribution Deduction

General Instructions

If the estate or trust was required to distribute income currently or if it paid, credited, or was required to distribute any other amounts to beneficiaries during the tax year, complete Schedule B to determine the estate's or trust's income distribution deduction. However, if you are filing for a pooled income fund, do not complete Schedule B. Instead, attach a statement to support the computation of the income distribution deduction.

Note: *Use Schedule I to compute the DNI and income distribution deduction on a minimum tax basis.*

Separate share rule. If a single trust has more than one beneficiary, and if different beneficiaries have substantially separate and independent shares, their shares are treated as separate trusts for the sole purpose of determining the DNI allocable to the respective beneficiaries. For the estates of decedents dying after August 5, 1997, a similar rule applies to treat substantially separate and independent shares of different beneficiaries of an estate as separate estates.

If the separate share rule applies, figure the DNI allocable to each beneficiary on a separate sheet and attach the sheet to this return. Any deduction or loss that is applicable solely to one separate share of the trust or estate is not available to any other share of the same trust or estate.

For more information, see section 663(c) and related regulations.

Specific Instructions

Line 1—Adjusted Total Income

If the amount on line 17 of page 1 is a loss that is attributable wholly or in part to the capital loss limitation rules under section 1211(b) (line 4), then enter as a negative amount on line 1, Schedule B, the smaller of the loss from line 17 on page 1, or the loss from line 4 on page 1. If the line 17 loss is not attributable to the capital loss on line 4, enter zero.

If you are filing for a simple trust, subtract from adjusted total income any extraordinary dividends or taxable stock dividends included on page 1, line 2, and determined under the governing instrument and applicable local law to be allocable to corpus.

Line 2—Adjusted Tax-Exempt Interest

To figure the adjusted tax-exempt interest:

Step 1. Add tax-exempt interest income on line 2 of Schedule A, any expenses allowable under section 212 allocable to tax-exempt interest, and any interest expense allocable to tax-exempt interest.

Step 2. Subtract the Step 1 total from the amount of tax-exempt interest (including exempt-interest dividends) received.

Section 212 expenses that are directly allocable to tax-exempt interest are allocated only to tax-exempt interest. A reasonable proportion of section 212 expenses that are indirectly allocable to both tax-exempt interest and other income must be allocated to each class of income.

Figure the interest expense allocable to tax-exempt interest according to the guidelines in Rev. Proc. 72-18, 1972-1 C.B. 740.

See Regulations sections 1.643(a)-5 and 1.265-1 for more information.

Line 3

Include all capital gains, whether or not distributed, that are attributable to income under the governing instrument or local law. For example, if the trustee distributed 50% of the current year's capital gains to the income beneficiaries (and reflects this amount in column (1), line 16 of Schedule D (Form 1041)), but under the governing instrument all capital gains are attributable to income, then include 100% of the capital gains on line 3. If the amount on Schedule D (Form 1041), line 16, column (1) is a net loss, enter zero.

If the exclusion of gain from the sale or exchange of qualified small business stock was claimed, **do not** reduce the gain on line 3 by any amount excluded under section 1202.

Line 5

In figuring the amount of long-term and short-term capital gain for the tax year included on Schedule A, line 1, the specific provisions of the governing instrument control if the instrument specifically provides as to the source from which amounts are paid, permanently set aside, or to be used for charitable purposes.

In all other cases, determine the amount to enter by multiplying line 1 of Schedule A by a fraction, the numerator of which is the amount of net capital gains that are included in the accounting income of the estate or trust (i.e., not allocated to corpus) AND are distributed to charities, and the denominator of which is all items of income (including the amount of such net capital gains) included in the DNI.

Reduce the amount on line 5 by any allocable section 1202 exclusion.

Line 8—Accounting Income

If you are filing for a decedent's estate or a simple trust, skip this line. If you are filing for a complex trust, enter the income for the tax year determined under the terms of the governing instrument and applicable local law. Do not include extraordinary dividends or taxable stock dividends determined under the governing instrument and applicable local law to be allocable to corpus.

Lines 9 and 10

Do not include any:

- Amounts deducted on prior year's return that were required to be distributed in the prior year.
- Amount that is properly paid or credited as a gift or bequest of a specific amount of money or specific property. (To qualify as a gift or bequest, the amount must be paid in three or fewer installments.) An amount that can be paid or credited only from income is not considered a gift or bequest.
- Amount paid or permanently set aside for charitable purposes or otherwise qualifying for the charitable deduction.

Line 9—Income Required To Be Distributed Currently

Line 9 is to be completed by all simple trusts as well as complex trusts and decedent's estates, that are required to distribute income currently, whether it is distributed or not. The determination of whether trust income is required to be distributed currently depends on the terms of the governing instrument and the applicable local law.

The line 9 distributions are referred to as first tier distributions and are deductible by the estate or trust to the extent of the DNI. The beneficiary includes such amounts in his or her income to the extent of his or her proportionate share of the DNI.

Line 10—Other Amounts Paid, Credited, or Otherwise Required To Be Distributed

Line 10 is to be completed ONLY by a decedent's estate or complex trust. These distributions consist of any other amounts paid, credited, or required to be distributed and are referred to as second tier distributions. Such amounts include annuities to the extent not paid out of income, mandatory and discretionary distributions of corpus, and distributions of property in kind.

If Form 1041-T was filed to elect to treat estimated tax payments as made by a beneficiary, the payments are treated as paid or credited to the beneficiary on the last day of the tax year and must be included on line 10.

Unless a section 643(e)(3) election is made, the value of all noncash property actually paid, credited, or required to be distributed to any beneficiaries is the smaller of:

1. The estate's or trust's adjusted basis in the property immediately before distribution, plus any gain or minus any loss recognized by the estate or trust on the distribution (basis of beneficiary), or

2. The fair market value (FMV) of such property.

If a section 643(e)(3) election is made by the fiduciary, then the amount entered on line 10 will be the FMV of the property.

A fiduciary of a complex trust or a decedent's estate may elect to treat any amount paid or credited to a beneficiary within 65 days following the close of the tax year as being paid or credited on the last day of that tax year. To make this election, see the instructions for Question 6 on page 19.

The beneficiary includes the amounts on line 10 in his or her income only to the extent of his or her proportionate share of the DNI.

Complex trusts. If the second tier distributions exceed the DNI allocable to the second tier, the trust may have an accumulation distribution. See the line 11 instructions below.

Line 11—Total Distributions

If line 11 is more than line 8, and you are filing for a complex trust that has previously accumulated income, see the instructions on page 28 to see if you must complete **Schedule J (Form 1041).**

Line 12—Adjustment for Tax-Exempt Income

In figuring the income distribution deduction, the estate or trust is not allowed a deduction for any item of the DNI that is not included in the gross income of the estate or trust. Thus, for purposes of figuring the allowable income distribution deduction, the DNI (line 7) is figured without regard to any tax-exempt interest.

If tax-exempt interest is the only tax-exempt income included in the total distributions (line 11), and the DNI (line 7) is less than or equal to line 11, then enter on line 12 the amount from line 2.

If tax-exempt interest is the only tax-exempt income included in the total distributions (line 11), and the DNI is more than line 11 (i.e., the estate or trust made a distribution that is less than the DNI), then figure the adjustment by multiplying line 2 by a fraction, the numerator of which is the total distributions (line 11), and the denominator of which is the DNI (line 7). Enter the result on line 12.

If line 11 includes tax-exempt income other than tax-exempt interest, figure line 12 by subtracting the total of the following from tax-exempt income included on line 11:

1. The charitable contribution deduction allocable to such tax-exempt income, and

2. Expenses allocable to tax-exempt income.

Expenses that are directly allocable to tax-exempt income are allocated only to tax-exempt income. A reasonable proportion of expenses indirectly allocable to both tax-exempt income and other income must be allocated to each class of income.

Schedule G—Tax Computation

Line 1a

Tax rate schedule. For tax years beginning in 1998, figure the tax using the Tax Rate Schedule below. Enter the tax on line 1a and check the "Tax rate schedule" box.

1998 Tax Rate Schedule

If taxable income is: Over—	But not over—	Its tax is:	Of the amount over—
$0	$1,700	15%	$0
1,700	4,000	$255.00 + 28%	1,700
4,000	6,100	899.00 + 31%	4,000
6,100	8,350	1,550.00 + 36%	6,100
8,350	-----	2,360.00 + 39.6%	8,350

Schedule D. If the estate or trust had both net capital gain and any taxable income, complete Part V of Schedule D (Form 1041), enter the tax from line 53 of Schedule D, and check the "Schedule D" box.

Line 2a—Foreign Tax Credit

Attach **Form 1116,** Foreign Tax Credit (Individual, Estate, Trust, or Nonresident Alien Individual), if you elect to claim credit for income or profits taxes paid or accrued to a foreign country or a U.S. possession. The estate or trust may claim credit for that part of the foreign taxes not allocable to the beneficiaries (including charitable beneficiaries). Enter the estate's or trust's share of the credit on line 2a. See **Pub. 514,** Foreign Tax Credit for Individuals, for details.

Line 2b

Nonconventional Source Fuel Credit

If the estate or trust can claim any section 29 credit for producing fuel from a nonconventional source, figure the credit on a separate sheet and attach it to the return. Include the credit on line 2b.

Qualified Electric Vehicle Credit

Use **Form 8834,** Qualified Electric Vehicle Credit, if the estate or trust can claim a credit for the purchase of a new qualified electric vehicle. Include the credit on line 2b.

Line 2c—General Business Credit

Complete this line if the estate or trust is claiming any of the credits listed below. Use the appropriate credit form to figure the credit. If the estate or trust is claiming only one credit, enter the form number and the amount of the credit in the space provided.

If the estate or trust is claiming more than one credit (not including the empowerment zone employment credit), a credit from a passive activity (other than the low-income housing credit or the empowerment zone employment credit), or a credit carryforward, also complete **Form 3800,** General Business Credit, to figure the total credit and enter the amount from Form 3800 on line 2c. Also, be sure to check the box for Form 3800.

Do not include any amounts that are allocated to a beneficiary. Credits that are allocated between the estate or trust and the beneficiaries are listed in the instructions for Schedule K-1, line 14, on page 31. Generally, these credits are apportioned on the basis of the income allocable to the estate or trust and the beneficiaries.

- Investment credit (Form 3468).
- Work opportunity credit (Form 5884).
- Welfare-to-work credit (Form 8861).
- Credit for alcohol used as fuel (Form 6478).
- Credit for increasing research activities (Form 6765).
- Low-income housing credit (Form 8586).
- Enhanced oil recovery credit (Form 8830).
- Disabled access credit (Form 8826).
- Renewable electricity production credit (Form 8835).
- Empowerment zone employment credit (Form 8844).
- Indian employment credit (Form 8845).
- Credit for employer social security and Medicare taxes paid on certain employee tips (Form 8846).
- Orphan drug credit (Form 8820).
- Credit for contributions to selected community development corporations (Form 8847).
- General credits from an electing large partnership. Report these credits on Form 3800, line 1o.

Line 2d—Credit for Prior Year Minimum Tax

An estate or trust that paid alternative minimum tax in a previous year may be eligible for a minimum tax credit in 1998. See **Form 8801,** Credit for Prior Year Minimum Tax—Individuals, Estates, and Trusts.

Line 5—Recapture Taxes

Recapture of investment credit. If the estate or trust disposed of investment credit property or changed its use before the end of the recapture period, see **Form 4255,** Recapture of Investment Credit, to figure the recapture tax allocable to the estate or trust.

Recapture of low-income housing credit. If the estate or trust disposed of property (or there was a reduction in the qualified basis of the property) on which the low-income housing credit was claimed, see **Form 8611,** Recapture of Low-Income Housing Credit, to figure any recapture tax allocable to the estate or trust.

Recapture of qualified electric vehicle credit. If the estate or trust claimed the qualified electric vehicle credit in a prior tax year for a vehicle that ceased to qualify for the credit, part or all of the credit may have to be recaptured. See Pub. 535 for details. If the estate or trust owes any recapture tax, include it on line 5 and write "QEV" on the dotted line to the left of the entry space.

Recapture of the Indian employment credit. Generally, if the estate or trust terminates a qualified employee less than 1 year after the date of initial employment, any Indian employment credit allowed for a prior tax year by reason of wages paid or incurred to that employee must be recaptured. See Form 8845 for details. If the estate or trust owes any recapture tax, include it on line 5 and write "45A" on the dotted line to the left of the entry space.

Line 7—Household Employment Taxes

If any of the following apply, get **Schedule H (Form 1040),** Household Employment Taxes, and its instructions, to see if the estate or trust owes these taxes.

1. The estate or trust paid **any one** household employee cash wages of $1,000 or more in 1998. When figuring the amount of cash wages paid, combine cash wages paid by the estate or trust with cash wages paid to the household employee in the same calendar year by the household of the decedent or beneficiary for whom the administrator, executor, or trustee of the estate or trust is acting.

2. The estate or trust withheld Federal income tax during 1998 at the request of any household employee.

3. The estate or trust paid **total** cash wages of $1,000 or more in **any** calendar **quarter** of 1997 or 1998 to household employees.

Line 8—Total Tax

Interest on tax deferred under the installment method for certain nondealer real property installment obligations. If an obligation arising from the disposition of real property to which section 453A applies is outstanding at the close of the year, the estate or trust must include the interest due under section 453A(c) in the amount to be entered on line 8 of Schedule G, Form 1041, with the notation "Section 453A(c) interest." Attach a schedule showing the computation.

Form 4970, Tax on Accumulation Distribution of Trusts. Include on this line any tax due on an accumulation distribution from a trust. To the left of the entry space, write "From Form 4970" and the amount of the tax.

Form 8697, Interest Computation Under the Look-Back Method for Completed Long-Term Contracts. Include the interest due under the look-back method of section 460(b)(2). To the left of the entry space, write "From Form 8697" and the amount of interest due.

Form 8866, Interest Computation Under the Look-Back Method for Property Depreciated Under the Income Forecast Method. Include the interest due under the look-back method of section 167(g)(2). To the left of the entry space, write "From Form 8866" and the amount of interest due.

Form 5329, Additional Taxes Attributable to IRAs, Other Qualified Retirement Plans, Annuities, Modified Endowment Contracts, and MSAs. If the estate or trust fails to receive the minimum distribution under section 4974, use Form 5329 to pay the excise tax. To the left of the entry space, write "From Form 5329" and the amount of the tax.

Tax on electing small business trusts (ESBTs). Special rules apply when figuring the tax on the portion of an ESBT consisting of stock in 1 or more S corporations. This tax must be figured separately from the tax on the remainder of the ESBT and is included in the total tax on Schedule G, line 8. The tax on the remainder of the ESBT is figured in the normal manner on Form 1041.

The tax on the S corporation items is figured as if that portion of the ESBT were a separate trust with the following modifications:

- Take into account only the income, losses, deductions, and credits allocated to the ESBT as an S corporation shareholder and gain or loss from the disposition of S corporation stock.
- You may not claim a deduction for capital losses in excess of capital gains.
- You may not claim an income distribution deduction or an exemption amount.
- Except in figuring the maximum tax on capital gains, the tax is 39.6% of the separate trust's taxable income.
- You may not claim an exemption amount in figuring the alternative minimum tax.

When figuring the tax and DNI on the remaining portion of the trust, disregard the S corporation items.

Do not apportion to the beneficiaries any of the S corporation items.

Attach the tax computation to the return. To the left of the entry space, write "Sec. 641(c)" and the amount of tax on the S corporation items.

If the ESBT consists entirely of stock in 1 or more S corporations, you do not need to make any entries on lines 1–22 of page 1. Complete the entity portion; follow the instructions above for figuring the tax on the S corporation items; carry the tax from line 8 of Schedule G to line 23 on page 1; and complete the rest of the return.

Other Information

Question 1

If the estate or trust received tax-exempt income, figure the allocation of expenses between tax-exempt and taxable income on a separate sheet and attach it to the return. Enter only the deductible amounts on the return. Do not figure the allocation on the return itself. For more information, see the instructions for **Allocation of Deductions for Tax-Exempt Income** on page 11.

Report the amount of tax-exempt interest income received or accrued in the space provided below Question 1.

Also, include any exempt-interest dividends the estate or trust received as a shareholder in a mutual fund or other regulated investment company.

Question 2

All salaries, wages, and other compensation for personal services must be included on the return of the person who earned the income, even if the income was irrevocably assigned to a trust by a contract assignment or similar arrangement.

The grantor or person creating the trust is considered the owner if he or she keeps "beneficial enjoyment" of or substantial control over the trust property. The trust's income, deductions, and credits are allocable to the owner.

If you checked "Yes" for Question 2, see the **Grantor Type Trust** instructions on page 8.

Question 3

Check the "Yes" box and enter the name of the foreign country if either **1** or **2** below applies.

1. At any time during the year the estate or trust had an interest in or signature or other authority over a bank, securities, or other financial account in a foreign country.

Exception. Check "No" if either of the following applies to the estate or trust:

- The combined value of the accounts was $10,000 or less during the whole year; OR
- The accounts were with a U.S. military banking facility operated by a U.S. financial institution.

2. The estate or trust owns more than 50% of the stock in any corporation that owns one or more foreign bank accounts.

Get **Form TD F 90-22.1,** Report of Foreign Bank and Financial Accounts, to see if the estate or trust is considered to have an interest in or signature or other authority over a bank, securities, or other financial account in a foreign country.

If you checked "Yes" for Question 3, file Form TD F 90-22.1 by June 30, 1999, with the Department of the Treasury at the address shown on the form.

Form TD F 90-22.1 is not a tax return, so do not file it with Form 1041.

You may order Form TD F 90-22.1 by calling 1-800-829-3676 (1-800-TAX-FORM).

Question 4

The estate or trust may be required to file **Form 3520,** Annual Return To Report Transactions With Foreign Trusts and Receipt of Certain Foreign Gifts, if:

- It directly or indirectly transferred property or money to a foreign trust. For this purpose, any U.S. person who created a foreign trust is considered a transferor.
- It is treated as the owner of any part of the assets of a foreign trust under the grantor trust rules.
- It received a distribution from a foreign trust.

Note: *An owner of a foreign trust must ensure that the trust files an annual information return on Form 3520-A.*

Question 5

An estate or trust claiming an interest deduction for qualified residence interest (as defined in section 163(h)(3)) on seller-provided financing, must include on an attachment to the 1998 Form 1041 the name, address, and taxpayer identifying number of the person to whom the interest was paid or accrued (i.e., the seller).

If the estate or trust received or accrued such interest, it must provide identical information on the person liable for such interest (i.e., the buyer). This information does not need to be reported if it duplicates information already reported on Form 1098.

Question 6

To make the section 663(b) election to treat any amount paid or credited to a beneficiary within 65 days following the close of the tax year as being paid or credited on the last day of that tax year, check the box. This election can be made by the fiduciary of a complex trust or the executor of a decedent's estate. For the election to be valid, you must file Form 1041 by the due date (including extensions). Once made, the election is irrevocable.

Question 7

To make the section 643(e)(3) election to recognize gain on property distributed in kind, check the box and see the instructions for Schedule D (Form 1041).

Question 9

A beneficiary is a skip person if the beneficiary is in a generation that is two or more generations below the generation of the transferor to the trust.

To determine if a beneficiary that is a trust is a skip person, and for exceptions to the general rules, see the definition of a skip person in the Instructions for Schedule R of Form 706.

Schedule I—Alternative Minimum Tax

Changes To Note

- For property placed in service after 1998, the same recovery period that was used for the regular tax is used to figure any AMT depreciation adjustment.
- For certified pollution control facilities placed in service after 1998, the amortization deduction for the AMT is figured under the modified accelerated cost recovery system (MACRS) using the straight line method.
- The estate or trust may elect to use a simplified foreign tax credit limitation for the AMT. See page 24.
- Partners in an electing large partnership must take into account amounts from Schedule K-1 (Form 1065-B) as an adjustment on line 4n or line 4u. See page 22.

General Instructions

Use Schedule I to compute:

1. The estate's or trust's alternative minimum taxable income;

2. The income distribution deduction on a minimum tax basis; and

3. The estate's or trust's alternative minimum tax (AMT).

Who Must Complete

- Complete Schedule I, Parts I and II, if the decedent's estate or trust is required to complete Schedule B.
- Complete Schedule I, Parts I and III (and IV, if applicable), if the decedent's estate's or trust's share of alternative minimum taxable income (Part I, line 13) exceeds $22,500.

Recordkeeping

Schedule I contains adjustments and tax preference items that are treated differently for regular tax and AMT purposes. If you, as fiduciary for the estate or trust, completed a form to figure an item for regular tax purposes, you may have to complete it a second time for AMT purposes. Generally, the difference between the amounts on the two forms is the AMT adjustment or tax preference item to enter on Schedule I. Except for Form 1116, any additional form completed for AMT purposes does not have to be filed with Form 1041.

For regular tax purposes, some deductions and credits may result in carrybacks or carryforwards to other tax years. Examples are: investment interest expense; a net operating loss deduction; a capital loss; and the foreign tax credit. Because these items may be refigured for the AMT, the carryback or carryforward amount may be different for regular and AMT purposes. Therefore, you should keep records of these different carryforward and carryback amounts for the AMT and regular tax. The AMT carryforward will be important in completing Schedule I for 1999.

Credit for Prior Year Minimum Tax

Estates and trusts that paid alternative minimum tax in 1997, or had a minimum tax credit carryforward, may be eligible for a minimum tax credit in 1998. See Form 8801.

Partners, Shareholders, etc.

An estate or trust that is a partner in a partnership or a shareholder in an S corporation must take into account its share of items of income and deductions that enter into the computation of its adjustments and tax preference items.

Allocation of Deductions to Beneficiaries

The distributable net alternative minimum taxable income (DNAMTI) of the estate or trust does not include amounts of depreciation, depletion, and amortization that are allocated to the beneficiaries, just as the distributable net income (DNI) of the estate or trust does not include these items for regular tax purposes.

Report separately on line 12 of Schedule K-1 (Form 1041) any adjustments or tax preference items attributable to depreciation, depletion, and amortization that were allocated to the beneficiaries.

Optional Write-Off for Certain Expenditures

There is no AMT adjustment for the following items if the estate or trust elects to deduct them ratably over the period of time shown for the regular tax:

- Circulation expenditures—3 years (section 173).
- Research and experimental expenditures—10 years (section 174).
- Intangible drilling costs—60 months (section 263(c)).
- Mining exploration and development costs—10 years (sections 616(a) and 617(a)).

The election must be made in the year the expenditure was made and may be revoked only with IRS consent. See section 59(e) for more details.

Specific Instructions

Part I—Estate's or Trust's Share of Alternative Minimum Taxable Income

Line 1—Adjusted Total Income or (Loss)

Enter the amount from line 17 of page 1. If the adjusted total income includes the amount of the alcohol fuel credit as required under section 87, reduce the adjusted total income by the credit included in income.

Line 2—Net Operating Loss Deduction

Enter any net operating loss deduction (NOLD) from line 15a of page 1 as a positive amount.

Line 4a—Interest

In determining the alternative minimum taxable income, qualified residence interest (other than qualified housing interest defined in section 56(e)) is not allowed.

If you completed Form 4952 for regular tax purposes, you may have an adjustment on this line. Refigure your investment interest expense on another Form 4952 as follows:

Step 1. On line 1 of Form 4952, add any interest expense allocable to specified private activity bonds issued after August 7, 1986, to the other interest expense. For a definition of "specified private activity bonds," see the instructions for line 4p.

Step 2. On line 2, enter the AMT disallowed investment interest expense from 1997.

Step 3. When completing Part II of Form 4952, refigure gross income from property held for investment, any net gain from the disposition of property held for investment, and any investment expenses, taking into account all AMT adjustments and tax preference items that apply. Include any interest income and investment expenses from private activity bonds issued after August 7, 1986.

To figure the adjustment for line 4a, subtract the total interest allowable for AMT purposes from the interest deduction claimed on line 10 of page 1. If the total interest expense allowed for AMT purposes is more than that allowed for regular tax purposes, enter the difference as a negative amount on line 4a.

Line 4b—Taxes

Enter any state, local, or foreign real property taxes; state or local personal property taxes; and state, local, or foreign income taxes that were included on line 11 of page 1.

Line 4d—Refund of Taxes

Enter any refunds received in 1998 of taxes described for line 4b above that were deducted in a tax year after 1986.

Line 4e—Depreciation of Property Placed in Service After 1986

Do not include on this line any depreciation adjustment from: **(a)** an activity for which you are not at risk; **(b)** a partnership or an S corporation if the basis limitations under section 704(d) or 1366(d) apply; **(c)** a tax shelter farm activity; or **(d)** a passive activity. Instead, take these depreciation adjustments into account when figuring the adjustments on line 4l, 4m, or 4n, whichever applies.

For AMT purposes, the depreciation deduction for tangible property placed in service after 1986 (or after July 31, 1986, if an election was made) and before 1999 must be refigured under the alternative depreciation system (ADS) described in section 168(g).

Generally, ADS depreciation is figured over the class life of the property. For tangible personal property not assigned a class life, use 12 years. See **Pub. 946,** How To Depreciate Property, for a discussion of class lives. For residential rental and nonresidential real property, use the straight line method over 40 years. Use the same convention that was used for regular tax purposes.

For property, other than residential rental and nonresidential real property, use the 150% declining balance method (switching to the straight line method in the first tax year when that method gives a better result). However, use the straight line method if that method was used for the regular tax.

See Rev. Proc. 87-57, 1987-2 C.B. 687, or Pub. 946 for the optional tables for the alternative minimum tax using the 150% declining balance method.

For property placed in service after 1998, do not make a depreciation adjustment for residential rental property, nonresidential real property, or any other property depreciated using the straight line or 150% declining balance method for the regular tax. For property placed in service after 1998 and depreciated using the 200% declining balance method for the regular tax, figure AMT depreciation using the 150% declining balance method, switching to straight line for the first tax year that method gives a better result. Use the regular tax recovery period and convention.

Do not make an adjustment for motion picture films, videotapes, sound recordings, or property depreciated under the unit-of-production method or any other method not expressed in a term of years. (See section 168(f)(1), (2), (3), or (4).)

When refiguring the depreciation deduction, be sure to report any adjustment from depreciation that was allocated to the beneficiary for regular tax purposes separately on line 12 of Schedule K-1 (Form 1041).

To figure the adjustment, subtract the depreciation for AMT purposes from the depreciation for regular tax purposes.

If the depreciation figured for AMT purposes exceeds the depreciation allowed for regular tax purposes, enter the adjustment as a negative amount.

Line 4f—Circulation and Research and Experimental Expenditures

Caution: *Do not make this adjustment for expenditures for which you elected the optional 3-year write-off period (10-year for research and experimental expenditures) under section 59(e) for regular tax purposes.*

Circulation expenditures. Circulation expenditures deducted under section 173(a) for regular tax purposes must be amortized for AMT purposes over 3 years beginning with the year the expenditures were paid or incurred.

Research and experimental expenditures. Research and experimental expenditures deducted under section 174(a) for regular tax purposes generally must be amortized for AMT purposes over 10 years beginning with the year the expenditures were paid or incurred. However, do not make an adjustment for expenditures paid or incurred in connection with an activity in which the estate or trust materially participated under the passive activity rules.

Enter the difference between the amount allowed for AMT purposes and the amount allowed for regular tax purposes. If the amount for AMT purposes exceeds the amount allowed for regular tax purposes, enter the difference as a negative amount.

See section 56(b)(2)(B) for a discussion of the rules for losses on properties for which a deduction was allowed under section 173(a) or 174(a).

Line 4g—Mining Exploration and Development Costs

Caution: *Do not make this adjustment for costs for which you elected the optional 10-year write-off period under section 59(e) for regular tax purposes.*

Expenditures for the development or exploration of a mine or certain other mineral deposits (other than an oil, gas, or geothermal well) deducted under sections 616(a) and 617(a) for regular tax purposes must be amortized for AMT purposes over 10 years beginning with the year the expenditures were paid or incurred.

Enter the difference between the amount allowed for AMT purposes and the amount allowed for regular tax purposes. If the amount allowed for AMT purposes exceeds the amount deducted for regular tax purposes, enter the difference as a negative amount.

See section 56(a)(2)(B) for a discussion of the rules for losses sustained on properties for which a deduction was allowed under section 616(a) or 617(a).

Line 4h—Long-Term Contracts Entered Into After February 28, 1986

For AMT purposes, the percentage of completion method of accounting described in section 460(b) generally must be used. However, this rule does not apply to any home construction contract (as defined in section 460(e)(6)).

Note: *Contracts described in section 460(e)(1) are subject to the simplified method of cost allocation of section 460(b)(4).*

Enter the difference between the amount reported for regular tax purposes and the AMT amount. If the AMT amount is less than the amount figured for regular tax purposes, enter the difference as a negative amount.

Line 4i—Amortization of Pollution Control Facilities

The amortization deduction under section 169 must be refigured for the AMT. For facilities placed in service after 1986 and before 1999, figure the amortization deduction for the AMT using the ADS described in section 168(g) (i.e., the straight line method over the facility's class life). For facilities placed in service after 1998, figure the amortization deduction for the AMT under the modified accelerated cost recovery system (MACRS) using the straight line method. Enter the difference between the regular tax and AMT deduction. If the AMT amount is greater, enter the difference as a negative amount.

Line 4j—Installment Sales of Certain Property

The installment method does not apply for AMT purposes to any nondealer disposition of property that occurred after August 16, 1986, but before the first day of your tax year that began in 1987, if an installment obligation to which the proportionate disallowance rule applied arose from the disposition. Enter as a negative adjustment on line 4j the amount of installment sale income that was reported for regular tax purposes.

If the estate or trust disposed of property during the tax year that was used or produced in a farming business and held primarily for sale to customers, **do not** make an adjustment on this line. If the estate or trust reported income for the regular tax on an installment sale of such property disposed of in a prior year **and** also reported the sale for the AMT in the year of the disposition, enter as a negative amount on line 4j the amount of installment sale income reported for the regular tax. Instead of making this adjustment, the estate or trust may be able to apply the installment method for the AMT in a prior year by filing an amended Form 1041. For more details, see **Pub. 225,** Farmer's Tax Guide.

Line 4k—Adjusted Gain or Loss (Including Incentive Stock Options)

Adjusted gain or loss. If the estate or trust sold or exchanged property during the year, or had a casualty gain or loss to business or income-producing property, it may have an adjustment. The gain or loss on the disposition of certain assets is refigured for AMT purposes. Use this line if the estate or trust reported a gain or loss on Form 4797, Schedule D (Form 1041), or Form 4684 (Section B). When figuring the adjusted basis for those forms, take into account any AMT adjustments made this year, or in previous years, for items related to lines 4e, 4f, 4g, and 4i of Schedule I. For example, to figure the adjusted basis for AMT purposes, reduce the cost of an asset only by the depreciation allowed for AMT purposes.

Enter the difference between the gain or loss reported for regular tax purposes, and that figured for AMT purposes. If the AMT gain is less than the gain reported for regular tax purposes, enter the adjustment as a negative amount. If the AMT loss is more than the loss allowed for regular tax purposes, enter the adjustment as a negative amount.

Incentive stock options (ISOs). For regular tax purposes, no income is recognized when an incentive stock option (as defined in section 422(b)) is exercised. However, this rule does not apply for AMT purposes. Instead, the estate or trust must generally include on line 4k the excess, if any, of:

1. The fair market value of the stock acquired through exercise of the option (determined without regard to any lapse restriction) when its rights in the stock first become transferable or when these rights are no longer subject to a substantial risk of forfeiture, over

2. The amount paid for the stock, including any amount paid for the option used to acquire the stock.

Note: *Even if the estate's or trust's rights in the stock are not transferable and are subject to a substantial risk of forfeiture, you may elect to include in AMT income the excess of the stock's fair market value (determined without regard to any lapse restriction) over the exercise price upon the transfer to the estate or trust of the stock acquired through exercise of the option. See section 83(b) for more details. The election must be made no later than 30 days after the date of transfer.*

Increase the AMT basis of any stock acquired through the exercise of an incentive stock option by the amount of the adjustment.

Line 4l—Certain Loss Limitations

Caution: *If the loss is from a passive activity, use line 4n instead. If the loss is from a tax shelter farm activity (that is not passive), use line 4m.*

Refigure your allowable losses for AMT purposes from activities for which you are not at risk and basis limitations applicable to interests in partnerships and stock in S corporations, by taking into account your AMT adjustments and tax preference items. See sections 59(h), 465, 704(d), and 1366(d).

Enter the difference between the loss reported for regular tax purposes and the AMT loss. If the AMT loss is more than the loss reported for regular tax purposes, enter the adjustment as a negative amount.

Line 4m—Tax Shelter Farm Activities

Note: *Use this line only if the tax shelter farm activity is not a passive activity. Otherwise, use line 4n.*

For AMT purposes, no loss is allowed from any tax shelter farm activity as defined in section 58(a)(2).

An excess farm loss from one farm activity cannot be netted against income from another farm activity. Any disallowed loss (for AMT purposes) is carried forward until offset by income from the same activity or when the entire activity is sold.

Include any other adjustment or tax preference item and your prior year AMT unallowed loss when refiguring the farm loss. For example, if depreciation must be refigured for AMT purposes, include the adjustment on this line. DO NOT include it again on line 4e, 4r, or 4s.

Determine your tax shelter farm activity gain or loss for AMT purposes using the same rules you used for regular tax purposes except that any AMT loss is allowed only to the extent that a taxpayer is insolvent (see section 58(c)(1)). An AMT loss may not be used in the current tax year to offset gains from other tax shelter farm activities. Instead, it must be suspended and carried forward indefinitely until either you have a gain in a subsequent tax year from that same tax shelter farm activity or the activity is disposed of.

Line 4n—Passive Activities

For AMT purposes, the rules described in section 469 apply, except that in applying the limitations, minimum tax rules apply.

Refigure passive activity gains and losses on an AMT basis. Refigure a passive activity gain or loss by taking into account all AMT adjustments or tax preference items that pertain to that activity.

You may complete a second Form 8582 to determine the passive activity losses allowed for AMT purposes, but do not send this AMT Form 8582 to the IRS.

Note: *The amount of any passive activity loss that is not deductible (and is therefore carried forward) for AMT purposes is likely to differ from the amount (if any) that is carried forward for regular tax purposes. Therefore, it is essential that you retain adequate records for both AMT and regular tax purposes.*

Enter the difference between the loss reported on page 1, and the AMT loss, if any.

Caution: *Do not enter again elsewhere on this schedule any AMT adjustment or tax preference item included on this line.*

Publicly traded partnerships (PTPs). If the estate or trust had a loss from a PTP, refigure the loss using any AMT adjustments and tax preference items.

Line 4o—Beneficiaries of Other Trusts or Decedent's Estates

If the estate or trust is the beneficiary of another estate or trust, enter the adjustment for minimum tax purposes from line 9, Schedule K-1 (Form 1041).

Line 4p—Tax-Exempt Interest From Specified Private Activity Bonds

Enter the interest earned from specified private activity bonds reduced (but not below zero) by any deduction that would have been allowable if the interest were includible in gross income for regular tax purposes. Specified private activity bonds are any qualified bonds (as defined in section 141) issued after August 7, 1986. See section 57(a)(5) for more information.

Exempt-interest dividends paid by a regulated investment company are treated as interest from specified private activity bonds to the extent the dividends are attributable to interest received by the company on the bonds, minus an allocable share of the expenses paid or incurred by the company in earning the interest.

Line 4q—Depletion

Refigure the depletion deduction for AMT purposes by using only the income and deductions allowed for the AMT when refiguring the limit based on taxable income from the property under section 613(a) and the limit based on taxable income, with certain adjustments, under section 613A(d)(1). Also, the depletion deduction for mines, wells, and other natural deposits under section 611 is limited to the property's adjusted basis at the end of the year, as refigured for the AMT, unless the estate or trust is an independent producer or royalty owner claiming percentage depletion for oil and gas wells. Figure this limit separately for each property. When refiguring the property's adjusted basis, take into account any AMT adjustments made this year or in previous years that affect basis (other than the current year's depletion).

Enter on line 4q the difference between the regular tax and AMT deduction. If the AMT deduction is more than the regular tax deduction, enter the difference as a negative amount.

Line 4r—Accelerated Depreciation of Real Property Placed in Service Before 1987

For AMT purposes, use the straight line method to figure depreciation. Use a recovery period of 19 years for 19-year real property and 15 years for low-income housing. Enter the excess of depreciation claimed for regular tax purposes over depreciation refigured using the straight line method. Figure this amount separately for each property and include on line 4r only positive amounts.

Line 4s—Accelerated Depreciation of Leased Personal Property Placed in Service Before 1987

For leased personal property other than recovery property, enter the amount by which the regular tax depreciation using the pre-1987 rules exceeds the depreciation allowable using the straight line method.

For leased 10-year recovery property and leased 15-year public utility property, enter the amount by which the depreciation deduction determined for regular tax purposes is more than the deduction allowable using the straight line method with a half-year convention, no salvage value, and the following recovery period:

10-year property	15 years
15-year public utility property	22 years

Figure this amount separately for each property and include on line 4s only positive amounts.

Line 4t—Intangible Drilling Costs

Caution: *Do not make this adjustment for costs for which you elected the optional 60-month write-off under section 59(e) for regular tax purposes.*

Except as provided below, intangible drilling costs (IDCs) from oil, gas, and geothermal wells are a tax preference item to the extent that the excess IDCs exceed 65% of the net income from the wells. Figure the tax preference item for all geothermal properties separately from the preference for all oil and gas properties.

Excess IDCs are figured by taking the amount of your IDCs allowed for regular tax purposes under section 263(c) (not including any section 263(c) deduction for nonproductive wells) minus the amount that would have been allowed if that amount had been amortized over a 120-month period starting with the month the well was placed in production.

Note: *Cost depletion can be substituted for the amount allowed using amortization over 120 months.*

Net income is determined by taking the gross income from all oil, gas, and geothermal wells reduced by the deductions allocable to those properties (determined without regard to excess IDCs). When figuring net income, use only income and deductions allowed for the AMT.

Exception. The preference for IDCs from oil and gas wells does not apply to taxpayers who are independent producers (i.e., not integrated oil companies as defined in section 291(b)(4)). However, this benefit may be limited. First, figure the IDC preference as if this exception did not apply. Then, for purposes of this exception, complete Schedule I through line 6, including the IDC preference. If the amount of the IDC preference exceeds 40% of the amount figured for line 6, enter the excess on line 4t (the benefit of this exception is limited). If the amount of the IDC preference is equal to or less than 40% of the amount figured for line 6, do not enter an amount on line 4t (the benefit of this exception is not limited).

Line 4u—Other Adjustments

Include on this line:

- **Net AMT adjustment from an electing large partnership.** If the estate or trust is a partner in an electing large partnership, include on line 4u the amount from Schedule K-1 (Form 1065-B), box 6. Take into account any amount from Schedule K-1 (Form 1065-B), box 5, when figuring the amount to enter on line 4n.
- **Patron's adjustment.** Distributions the estate or trust received from a cooperative may be includible in income. Unless the distributions are nontaxable, include on

line 4u the total AMT patronage dividend adjustment reported to the estate or trust from the cooperative.

• **Section 1202 exclusion.** If the estate or trust claimed the exclusion under section 1202 for gain on qualified small business stock, multiply the amount of the gain excluded from income (as shown on line 6 of Schedule D (Form 1041)) by 42% (.42). Enter the result as a positive number.

• **Related adjustments.** AMT adjustments and tax preference items may affect deductions that are based on an income limit other than AGI or modified AGI (e.g., farm conservation expenses). Refigure these deductions using the income limit as modified for the AMT. Include the difference between the regular tax and AMT deduction on line 4u. If the AMT deduction is more than the regular tax deduction, include the difference as a negative amount.

Note: *Do not make an adjustment on line 4u for an item you refigured on another line of Schedule I (e.g., line 4q).*

Line 7—Alternative Tax Net Operating Loss Deduction (ATNOLD)

For tax years beginning after 1986, the net operating loss (NOL) under section 172(c) is modified for alternative tax purposes by **(a)** adding the adjustments made under sections 56 and 58 (subtracting if the adjustments are negative); and **(b)** reducing the NOL by any item of tax preference under section 57 (except the appreciated charitable contribution preference item). For an estate or trust that held a residual interest in a real estate mortgage investment conduit (REMIC), figure the ATNOLD without regard to any excess inclusion.

When figuring an NOL from a loss year prior to 1987, the rules in effect before enactment of the Tax Reform Act (TRA) of 1986 apply. The NOL under section 172(c) is reduced by the amount of the tax preference items that were taken into account in figuring the NOL. In addition, the NOL is figured by taking into account only itemized deductions that were alternative tax itemized deductions for the tax year and that were a modification to the NOL under section 172(d). See sections 55(d) and 172 as in effect before the TRA of 1986.

If this estate or trust is the beneficiary of another estate or trust that terminated in 1998, include any AMT NOL carryover that was reported on line 13e of Schedule K-1 (Form 1041).

The ATNOLD may be limited. To figure the ATNOLD limitation, first figure AMTI without regard to the ATNOLD. For this purpose, figure a tentative amount for line 4q of Schedule I by treating line 7 as if it were zero. Then, figure a tentative amount for line 6 of Schedule I. The ATNOLD limitation is 90% of the tentative line 6 amount. Enter on line 7 the smaller of the ATNOLD or the ATNOLD limitation. Any alternative tax NOL not used because of the ATNOLD limitation can be carried back or forward. See section 172(b) for details. The treatment of alternative tax NOLs does not affect your regular tax NOL.

Note: *If you elected under section 172(b)(3) to forego the carryback period for regular tax purposes, the election will also apply for the AMT.*

Line 12—Estate's or Trust's Share of Alternative Minimum Taxable Income

For an estate or trust that held a residual interest in a REMIC, line 12 may not be less than the estate's or trust's share of the amount on Schedule E (Form 1040), line 37, column (c). If that amount is larger than the amount you would otherwise enter on line 12, enter that amount instead and write "Sch. Q" on the dotted line next to line 12.

Part II—Income Distribution Deduction on a Minimum Tax Basis

Line 13—Adjusted Alternative Minimum Taxable Income

If the amount on line 8 of Schedule I is less than zero, and the negative number is attributable wholly or in part to the capital loss limitation rules under section 1211(b), then enter as a negative number the smaller of **(a)** the loss from line 8; or **(b)** the loss from line 4 on page 1.

Line 14—Adjusted Tax-Exempt Interest

To figure the adjusted tax-exempt interest (including exempt-interest dividends received as a shareholder in a mutual fund or other regulated investment company), subtract the total of **(a)** any tax-exempt interest from line 2 of Schedule A of Form 1041 figured for AMT purposes; and **(b)** any section 212 expenses allowable for AMT purposes allocable to tax-exempt interest, from the amount of tax-exempt interest received. DO NOT subtract any deductions reported on lines 4a through 4c. Section 212 expenses that are directly allocable to tax-exempt interest are allocated only to tax-exempt interest. A reasonable proportion of section 212 expenses that are indirectly allocable to both tax-exempt interest and other income must be allocated to each class of income.

Line 16

Reduce the amount on line 16 by any allocable section 1202 exclusion (as refigured for AMT purposes).

Line 17

Enter any capital gains that were paid or permanently set aside for charitable purposes from the current year's income included on line 1 of Schedule A. Reduce the amount on line 17 by any allocable section 1202 exclusion (as refigured for AMT purposes).

Lines 18 and 19

Capital gains and losses must take into account any basis adjustments from line 4k, Part I.

Line 24—Adjustment for Tax-Exempt Income

In figuring the income distribution deduction on a minimum tax basis, the estate or trust is not allowed a deduction for any item of DNAMTI (line 20) that is not included in the gross income of the estate or trust figured on an AMT basis. Thus, for purposes of figuring the allowable income distribution deduction on a minimum tax basis, the DNAMTI is figured without regard to any tax-exempt interest (except for amounts from line 4p).

If tax-exempt interest is the only tax-exempt income included in the total distributions (line 23), and the DNAMTI (line 20) is less than or equal to line 23, then enter on line 24 the amount from line 14.

If tax-exempt interest is the only tax-exempt income included in the total distributions (line 23), and the DNAMTI is more than line 23 (i.e., the estate or trust made a distribution that is less than the DNAMTI), then figure the adjustment by multiplying line 14 by a fraction, the numerator of which is the total distributions (line 23), and the denominator of which is the DNAMTI (line 20). Enter the result on line 24.

If line 23 includes tax-exempt income other than tax-exempt interest (except for amounts from line 4p), figure line 24 by subtracting the total expenses allocable to tax-exempt income that are allowable for AMT purposes from tax-exempt income included on line 23.

Expenses that are directly allocable to tax-exempt income are allocated only to tax-exempt income. A reasonable proportion of expenses indirectly allocable to both tax-exempt income and other income must be allocated to each class of income.

Line 27—Income Distribution Deduction on a Minimum Tax Basis

Allocate the income distribution deduction figured on a minimum tax basis among the beneficiaries in the same manner as income was allocated for regular tax purposes. Report each beneficiary's share on line 7 of Schedule K-1 (Form 1041).

Part III—Alternative Minimum Tax Computation

Line 36—Alternative Minimum Foreign Tax Credit

To figure the AMT foreign tax credit:

1. Complete and attach a separate AMT Form 1116, with the notation at the top, "Alt Min Tax" for each type of income specified at the top of Form 1116.

2. If you are making the **simplified limitation election** (see page 24), skip Part I and enter on the AMT Form 1116, line 16, the same amount you entered on that line for the regular tax. Otherwise, complete Part I, using only income and deductions allowed for the AMT that are attributable to sources outside the United States.

3. Complete Part III of the AMT Form 1116. Enter the AMT foreign tax credit carryover on the AMT Form 1116, line 10. Enter the AMTI from Schedule I, line 12, on the AMT Form 1116, line 17. Enter the amount from Schedule I, line 35, on the AMT Form 1116, line 19.

4. Complete Part IV of the AMT Form 1116. The foreign tax credit from line 32 of the AMT Form 1116 is limited to the tax on line 35 of Schedule I, less 10% of what would have been the tax on line 35 of Schedule I, if line 7 of Schedule I had been zero and the exception for intangible drilling costs does not apply (see the instructions for line 4t on page 22). If Schedule I, line 7, is zero or blank, and the estate or trust has no intangible drilling costs (or the exception does not apply), enter on Schedule I, line 36, the smaller of Form 1116, line 32; or 90% of Schedule I, line 35. If line 7 has an entry (other than zero), or the exception for intangible drilling costs applies, for purposes of this line refigure what the tax would have been on Schedule I, line 35, if line 7 were zero and the exception did not apply. Multiply that amount by 10% and subtract the result from line 35. Enter on Schedule I, line 36, the smaller of that amount or the amount from Form 1116, line 32.

If the AMT foreign tax credit is limited, any unused amount can be carried back or forward in accordance with section 904(c).

Note: *The election to forego the carryback period for regular tax purposes also applies for the AMT.*

Simplified limitation election. The estate or trust may elect to use a simplified section 904 limitation for tax years after 1997. To do so, use the estate's or trust's regular tax income for Form 1116, Part I, instead of refiguring the estate's or trust's foreign source income for the AMT, as described in **2** on page 23. The estate or trust must make the election for the first tax year after 1997 for which it claims an alternative minimum tax foreign tax credit. If it does not make the election for that year, it cannot make it for a later year. Once made, the election applies to all later tax years and can only be revoked with IRS consent.

Part IV—Line 35 Computation Using Maximum Capital Gains Rates

Lines 41, 42, and 44. You generally may enter the amounts from Schedule D (Form 1041), lines 26, 24, and 21, on Schedule I, lines 41, 42, and 44, respectively. But if the gain or loss for any asset disposition on Schedule D is different for the AMT than for the regular tax (e.g., because of a different basis for the AMT from depreciation adjustments or an incentive stock option adjustment), or you completed Schedule D but did not complete Part V you must refigure the amounts from Schedule D, lines 26, 24, and 21 for the AMT. You should complete a second Schedule D using amounts for the AMT. Keep that Schedule D for your records, but **do not** attach it to Form 1041. Enter the amounts from lines 26, 24, and 21 of the AMT Schedule D on Schedule I, lines 41, 42, and 44 respectively.

Note: ***Do not*** *refigure the amount from Schedule D, line 35, when completing Schedule I, line 48. If you did not complete Part V of Schedule D for the regular tax, enter zero on Schedule I, line 48.*

Schedule D (Form 1041)—Capital Gains and Losses

A Change To Note

For sales, exchanges, and conversions after 1997, property held more than 1 year (instead of more than 18 months) generally is eligible for the 10%, 20%, and 25% maximum capital gains rates. This rule also applies to installment payments received after 1997. The 28% rate will now apply only to pre-1998 gains (e.g., from fiscal year partnerships and mutual funds), collectibles gains, and part or all of the gain from the sale or exchange of qualified small business stock.

General Instructions

Purpose of Form

Use Schedule D (Form 1041) to report gains and losses from the sale or exchange of capital assets by an estate or trust.

To report sales or exchanges of property other than capital assets, including the sale or exchange of property used in a trade or business and involuntary conversions (other than casualties and thefts), see Form 4797 and related instructions.

If property is involuntarily converted because of a casualty or theft, use Form 4684.

Section 1256 contracts and straddles are reported on **Form 6781,** Gains and Losses From Section 1256 Contracts and Straddles.

Capital Asset

Each item of property held by the estate or trust (whether or not connected with its trade or business) is a capital asset except:

- Inventoriable assets or property held primarily for sale to customers;
- Depreciable or real property used in a trade or business;
- Certain copyrights, literary, musical, or artistic compositions, letters or memoranda, or similar property;
- Accounts or notes receivable acquired in the ordinary course of a trade or business for services rendered or from the sale of inventoriable assets or property held primarily for sale to customers; and
- Certain U.S. Government publications not purchased at the public sale price.

You may find additional helpful information in the following publications:

- **Pub. 544,** Sales and Other Dispositions of Assets; and
- **Pub. 551,** Basis of Assets.

Short-Term or Long-Term

Separate the capital gains and losses according to how long the estate or trust held or owned the property. The holding period for short-term capital gains and losses is 1 year or less. The holding period for long-term capital gains and losses is more than 1 year. Property acquired by a decedent's estate from the decedent is considered as held for more than 1 year.

When you figure the length of the period the estate or trust held property, begin counting on the day after the estate or trust acquired the property and include the day the estate or trust disposed of it. Use the trade dates for the date of acquisition and sale of stocks and bonds traded on an exchange or over-the-counter market.

Section 643(e)(3) Election

For noncash property distributions, a fiduciary may elect to have the estate or trust recognize gain or loss in the same manner as if the distributed property had been sold to the beneficiary at its fair market value (FMV). The distribution deduction is the property's FMV. This election applies to all distributions made by the estate or trust during the tax year and, once made, may be revoked only with IRS consent.

Note that section 267 does not allow a trust or a decedent's estate to claim a deduction for any loss on property to which a section 643(e)(3) election applies. In addition, when a trust or a decedent's estate distributes depreciable property, section 1239 applies to deny capital gains treatment for any gain on property to which a section 643(e)(3) election applies.

Related Persons

A trust cannot deduct a loss from the sale or exchange of property directly or indirectly between any of the following:

- A grantor and a fiduciary of a trust;
- A fiduciary and a fiduciary or beneficiary of another trust created by the same grantor;
- A fiduciary and a beneficiary of the same trust;
- A trust fiduciary and a corporation of which more than 50% in value of the outstanding stock is owned directly or indirectly by or for the trust or by or for the grantor of the trust; or
- An executor of an estate and a beneficiary of that estate, except when the sale or exchange is to satisfy a pecuniary bequest (i.e., a bequest of a sum of money).

Items for Special Treatment

The following items may require special treatment:

• Exchange of "like-kind" property.

• Wash sales of stock or securities (including contracts or options to acquire or sell stock or securities) (section 1091).

• Gain or loss on options to buy or sell (section 1234).

• Certain real estate subdivided for sale that may be considered a capital asset (section 1237).

• Gain on disposition of stock in an interest charge domestic international sales corporation (section 995(c)).

• Gain on the sale or exchange of stock in certain foreign corporations (section 1248).

• Sales of stock received under a qualified public utility dividend reinvestment plan. See Pub. 550 for details.

• Transfer of appreciated property to a political organization (section 84).

• Distributions received from an employee pension, profit sharing, or stock bonus plan. See Form 4972.

• Disposition of market discount bonds (section 1276).

Constructive Sales Treatment for Certain Appreciated Positions

Generally, the estate or trust must recognize gain (but not loss) on the date it enters into a constructive sale of any appreciated position in stock, a partnership interest, or certain debt instruments as if the position were disposed of at fair market value on that date.

The estate or trust is treated as making a constructive sale of an appreciated position when it (or a related person, in some cases) does one of the following:

• Enters into a short sale of the same or substantially identical property (i.e., a "short sale against the box").

• Enters into an offsetting notional principal contract relating to the same or substantially identical property.

• Enters into a futures or forward contract to deliver the same or substantially identical property.

• Acquires the same or substantially identical property (if the appreciated position is a short sale, offsetting notional principal contract, or a futures or forward contract).

Exception. Generally, constructive sale treatment **does not** apply if:

• The estate or trust closed the transaction before the end of the 30th day after the end of the year in which it was entered into,

• The estate or trust held the appreciated position to which the transaction relates throughout the 60-day period starting on the date the transaction was closed, **and**

• At no time during that 60-day period was the estate's or trust's risk of loss reduced by holding certain other positions.

For details and other exceptions to these rules, see Pub. 550.

Exclusion of Gain on Qualified Small Business Stock (Section 1202)

Section 1202 provides for an exclusion of 50% of the gain on the sale or exchange of qualified small business stock. The section 1202 exclusion applies **only** to qualified small business stock issued after August 10, 1993, and held for more than 5 years. To be **qualified small business stock,** the stock must meet **all** of the following tests:

• It must be stock in a C corporation (i.e., not S corporation stock).

• It must have been originally issued after August 10, 1993.

• As of the date the stock was issued, the corporation was a qualified small business. A qualified small business is a domestic C corporation with total gross assets of $50 million or less **(a)** at all times after August 9, 1993, and before the stock was issued, and **(b)** immediately after the stock was issued. Gross assets include those of any predecessor of the corporation. All corporations that are members of the same parent-subsidiary controlled group are treated as one corporation.

• The estate or trust acquired the stock at its original issue (either directly or through an underwriter), either in exchange for money or other property or as pay for services (other than as an underwriter) to the corporation. In certain cases, the estate or trust may meet the test if it acquired the stock from another person who met this test (such as by gift or at death) or through a conversion or exchange of qualified small business stock the estate or trust held.

• During substantially all the time the estate or trust held the stock:

1. The corporation was a C corporation,

2. At least 80% of the value of the corporation's assets were used in the active conduct of 1 or more qualified businesses (defined below), and

3. The corporation **was not** a foreign corporation, DISC, former DISC, corporation that has made (or that has a subsidiary that has made) a section 936 election, regulated investment company, real estate investment trust, REMIC, FASIT, or cooperative.

Note: *A specialized small business investment company (SSBIC) is treated as having met tests 2 and 3 above.*

A **qualified business** is any business **other than** the following:

• One involving services performed in the fields of health, law, engineering, architecture, accounting, actuarial science, performing arts, consulting, athletics, financial services, or brokerage services.

• One whose principal asset is the reputation or skill of one or more employees.

• Any banking, insurance, financing, leasing, investing, or similar business.

• Any farming business (including the raising or harvesting of trees).

• Any business involving the production of products for which percentage depletion can be claimed.

• Any business of operating a hotel, motel, restaurant, or similar business.

For more details about limits and additional requirements that may apply, see section 1202.

Pass-through entities. If the estate or trust held an interest in a pass-through entity (a partnership, S corporation, mutual fund, or other regulated investment company) that sold qualified small business stock, the estate or trust generally must have held the interest on the date the pass-through entity acquired the qualified small business stock and at all times thereafter until the stock was sold to qualify for the exclusion.

How to report. Report in column (f) of line 6 the entire gain realized on the sale of qualified small business stock. In column (g) of line 6, report as 28% rate gain an amount equal to the section 1202 exclusion. Directly below the line on which you reported the gain, enter in column (a) "Section 1202 exclusion," and enter as a (loss) in column (f) the amount of the allowable exclusion. Also include 42% of the exclusion as a positive amount on Schedule I, line 4u.

Gain from Form 1099-DIV. If the estate or trust received a Form 1099-DIV with a gain in box 2d, part or all of that gain (which is also included in box 2a) may be eligible for the section 1202 exclusion. In column (a) of line 6, enter the name of the corporation whose stock was sold. In column (f), enter the amount of the allowable exclusion as a (loss). In column (g), enter the amount of the allowable exclusion as a gain.

Gain from Form 2439. If the estate or trust received a Form 2439 with a gain in box 1d, part or all of that gain (which is also included in box 1a) may be eligible for the section 1202 exclusion. In column (a) of line 6, enter the name of the corporation whose stock was sold. In column (f), enter the amount of the allowable exclusion as a (loss). In column (g), enter the amount of the allowable exclusion as a gain.

Rollover of Gain From Qualified Stock

If the estate or trust held qualified small business stock (as defined above) for more than 6 months, it may postpone gain if it purchased other qualified small business stock during the 60-day period that began on the date of the sale. The estate or trust must recognize gain to the extent the sale proceeds exceed the cost of the replacement stock. Reduce the basis of the replacement stock by any postponed gain.

If the estate or trust chooses to postpone gain, report the entire gain realized on the sale on line 1 or 6. Directly below the line on which you reported the gain, enter in column (a) "Section 1045 Rollover" and enter as a (loss) in column (f) the amount of the postponed gain.

Specific Instructions

Lines 1 and 6

Short-term and long-term capital gains and losses. Enter all sales of stocks, bonds, etc.

Redemption of stock to pay death taxes. If stock is redeemed under the provisions of section 303, list and identify it on line 6 and give the name of the decedent and the IRS office where the estate tax or generation-skipping transfer tax return was filed.

If you are reporting capital gain from a lump-sum distribution, see the instructions for Form 4972 for information about the Federal estate tax.

Column (d)—Sales Price

Enter either the gross sales price or the net sales price from the sale. On sales of stocks and bonds, report the gross amount as reported to the estate or trust on Form 1099-B or similar statement. However, if the estate or trust was advised that gross proceeds less commissions and option premiums were reported to the IRS, enter that net amount in column (d).

Column (e)—Cost or Other Basis

Basis of trust property. Generally, the basis of property acquired by gift is the same as the basis in the hands of the donor. If the fair market value (FMV) of the property at the time it was transferred to the trust is less than the transferor's basis, then the FMV is used for determining any loss on disposition.

If the property was transferred to the trust after 1976, and a gift tax was paid under Chapter 12, then increase the donor's basis as follows:

Multiply the amount of the gift tax paid by a fraction, the numerator of which is the net appreciation in value of the gift (discussed below), and the denominator of which is the amount of the gift. For this purpose, the **net appreciation in value of the gift** is the amount by which the FMV of the gift exceeds the donor's adjusted basis.

Basis of decedent's estate property. Generally, the basis of property acquired by a decedent's estate is the FMV of the property at the date of the decedent's death, or the alternate valuation date if the executor elected to use an alternate valuation under section 2032.

See Pub. 551 for a discussion of the valuation of qualified real property under section 2032A.

Basis of property for bankruptcy estates. Generally, the basis of property held by the bankruptcy estate is the same as the basis in the hands of the individual debtor.

Adjustments to basis. Before figuring any gain or loss on the sale, exchange, or other disposition of property owned by the estate or trust, adjustments to the property's basis may be required.

Some items that may increase the basis include:

1. Broker's fees and commissions.

2. Reinvested dividends that were previously reported as income.

3. Reinvested capital gains that were previously reported as income.

4. Costs that were capitalized.

5. Original issue discount that has been previously included in income.

Some items that may decrease the basis include:

1. Nontaxable distributions that consist of return of capital.

2. Deductions previously allowed or allowable for depreciation.

3. Casualty or theft loss deductions.

Unrecaptured Section 1250 Gain Worksheet—Line 15b (keep for your records)

Note: **For each section 1250 property in Part III of Form 4797 for which the estate or trust had an entry in column (g), but not in column (h), of Part I of Form 4797, complete lines 1 through 3. If the estate or trust had more than one such property, complete lines 1 through 3 for each property on a separate worksheet. Enter the total of the line 3 amounts for all properties on line 3 and go to line 4.**

If the estate's or trust's only unrecaptured section 1250 gain was from:

- A partnership or an S corporation, go to line 4.
- An estate, trust, real estate investment trust, or mutual fund (or other regulated investment company), go to line 11.

1. If the estate or trust had a section 1250 property in Part III of Form 4797 for which there was an entry in column (g), but not in column (h), of Part I of Form 4797, enter the smaller of line 22 or line 24 of Form 4797 for that property . . . . . . 1. ______
2. Enter the amount from Form 4797, line 26g, for the property for which you made an entry on line 1 . . . 2. ______
3. Subtract line 2 from line 1 . . . . . . 3. ______
4. Enter the total of any amounts reported to the estate or trust on Schedules K-1 from a partnership or an S corporation as "unrecaptured section 1250 gain." Also include gain from the sale of an interest in a partnership attributable to unrecaptured section 1250 gain . . . . 4. ______
5. Add lines 3 and 4 . . . . . . 5. ______
6. Enter the smaller of line 5 or the gain, if any, from Form 4797, line 7, column (g) . . . . . . 6. ______

   Note: **If the estate or trust did not have an entry on Form 4797, line 8, enter the amount from line 6 above on line 10 below and go to line 11 below.**
7. Enter the amount from Form 4797, line 8, column (g) . . . . . . 7. ______
8. Enter the amount from Form 4797, line 8, column (h) . . . . . . 8. ______
9. Subtract line 8 from line 7 . . . . . . 9. ______
10. Subtract line 9 from line 6 . . . . . . 10. ______
11. Enter the total of any amounts reported to the estate or trust on Schedules K-1 and Forms 1099-DIV and 2439 as "unrecaptured section 1250 gain" from an estate, trust, real estate investment trust, or mutual fund (or other regulated investment company) . . . . . . 11. ______
12. Add lines 10 and 11 . . . . . . 12. ______
13. Enter the gain or (loss) from Schedule D, line 12 . . . . . . 13. ______
14. Enter the (loss), if any, from Schedule D, line 5. If Schedule D, line 5, is zero or a gain, enter -0- . . . . . . 14. ______
15. Combine lines 13 and 14.
    - If the result is zero or a gain, enter -0-.
    - If the result is a (loss), enter it as a positive amount 15. ______
16. Subtract line 15 from line 12. If zero or less, enter -0-. Enter the result in the appropriate columns of Schedule D, line 15b . . . . . . 16. ______

See Pub. 551 for additional information.

See section 852(f) for treatment of load charges incurred in acquiring stock in a regulated investment company.

Carryover basis. Carryover basis determined under repealed section 1023 applies to property acquired from a decedent who died after December 31, 1976, and before November 7, 1978, only if the executor elected it on a **Form 5970-A,** Election of Carryover Basis, that was filed on time.

Column (f)—Gain or (Loss)

Make a separate entry in this column for each transaction reported on lines 1 and 6 and any other lines that apply to the estate or trust. For lines 1 and 6, subtract the amount in column (e) from the amount in column (d). Enter negative amounts in parentheses.

Column (g)—28% Rate Gain or (Loss)

Enter in column (g) **only** the amount, if any, from Part II, column (f), that is equal to the amount of the estate's or trust's section 1202 exclusion from the eligible gain on qualified small business stock (see page 25) or from collectibles gains and losses. A **collectibles gain or loss** is any long-term gain or loss from the sale or exchange of a collectible that is a capital asset.

Collectibles includes works of art, rugs, antiques, metals (such as gold, silver, and platinum bullion), gems, stamps, coins, alcoholic beverages, and certain other tangible property.

Also include gain from the sale of an interest in a partnership, S corporation, or trust attributable to unrealized appreciation of collectibles.

Lines 2 and 7

Undistributed capital gains. Include on line 7, column (f), the amount from box 1a of **Form 2439.** This represents the estate's or trust's share of the undistributed long-term capital gains of the regulated investment company (mutual fund) or real estate investment trust.

Include on line 7, column (g), the amount, if any, from box 1b of Form 2439. If there is an amount in box 1c of Form 2439, see the worksheet for line 15b on page 26. If there is an amount in box 1d of Form 2439, see **Exclusion of Gain on Qualified Small Business Stock (Section 1202)** on page 25.

Enter on Form 1041, line 24f, the tax paid as shown in box 2 of Form 2439. Add to the basis of your stock the excess of the amount included in income over the amount of the credit for tax paid. See Pub. 550 for more details.

Installment sales. If the estate or trust sold property at a gain during the tax year, and will receive a payment in a later tax year, report the sale on the installment method and file **Form 6252,** Installment Sale Income, unless you elect not to do so.

Also, use Form 6252 to report any payment received in 1998 from a sale made in an earlier tax year that was reported on the installment method.

To elect out of the installment method, report the full amount of the gain on a timely filed return (including extensions).

Exchange of "like-kind" property. Generally, no gain or loss is recognized when property held for productive use in a trade or business or for investment is exchanged solely for property of a like-kind to be held either for productive use in a trade or business or for investment. However, if a trust exchanges like-kind property with a related person (see **Related Persons** on page 24), and before 2 years after the date of the last transfer that was part of the exchange the related person disposes of the property, or the trust disposes of the property received in exchange from the related person, then the original exchange will not qualify for nonrecognition. See section 1031(f) for exceptions.

Complete and attach **Form 8824,** Like-Kind Exchanges, to Form 1041 for each exchange.

Line 9—Capital Gain Distributions

Enter as a long-term capital gain on line 9, column (f), the **total** capital gain distributions paid during the year, regardless of how long the estate or trust held its investment. Enter on line 9, column (g), the total of the amounts reported as the 28% rate gain portion of total capital gain distributions.

Line 14, Column (1)—Beneficiaries' Net Short-Term Capital Gain or Loss

Enter the amount of net short-term capital gain or loss allocable to the beneficiary or beneficiaries. Except in the final year, include only those short-term capital losses that are taken into account in determining the amount of gain from the sale or exchange of capital assets that is paid, credited, or required to be distributed to any beneficiary during the tax year. See Regulations section 1.643(a)-3 for more information about allocation of capital gains and losses.

Except in the final year, if the losses from the sale or exchange of capital assets are more than the gains, all of the losses must be allocated to the estate or trust and none are allocated to the beneficiaries.

Line 14, Column (2)—Estate's or Trust's Net Short-Term Capital Gain or Loss

Enter the amount of the net short-term capital gain or loss allocable to the estate or trust. Include any capital gain paid or permanently set aside for a charitable purpose specified in section 642(c).

Capital Loss Carryover Worksheet (keep for your records)

Use this worksheet to figure your capital loss carryovers from 1998 to 1999 if Schedule D, line 17, is a loss and (a) the loss on Schedule D, line 16, column (3), is more than $3,000, OR (b) Form 1041, line 22 is a loss.

1. Enter taxable income (or loss) from Form 1041, line 22 . . . 1. ______
2. Enter loss from line 17 of Schedule D as a positive amount . . . 2. ______
3. Enter amount from Form 1041, line 20 . . . . 3. ______
4. Adjusted taxable income. Combine lines 1, 2, and 3, but do not enter less than zero . . . . 4. ______
5. Enter the smaller of line 2 or line 4 . . . . 5. ______
   Note: If line 5 of Schedule D is a loss, go to line 6; otherwise, enter -0- on line 6 and go to line 10.
6. Enter loss from Schedule D, line 5, as a positive amount . 6. ______
7. Enter gain, if any, from Schedule D, line 13. If that line is blank or shows a loss, enter -0- . . . . 7. ______
8. Add lines 5 and 7 . . . . 8. ______
9. Short-term capital loss carryover to 1999. Subtract line 8 from line 6. If zero or less, enter -0-. If this is the final return of the estate or trust, also enter on Schedule K-1 (Form 1041), line 13b . . . . 9. ______
   Note: If line 13 of Schedule D is a loss, go to line 10; otherwise, skip lines 10 through 14.
10. Enter loss from Schedule D, line 13, as a positive amount . 10. ______
11. Enter gain, if any, from Schedule D, line 5. If that line is blank or shows a loss, enter -0- . 11. ______
12. Subtract line 6 from line 5. If zero or less, enter -0- . . . . 12. ______
13. Add lines 11 and 12 . . . . 13. ______
14. Long-term capital loss carryover to 1999. Subtract line 13 from line 10. If zero or less, enter -0-. If this is the final return of the estate or trust, also enter on Schedule K-1 (Form 1041), line 13c . . . . 14. ______

Line 14, Column (3)—Total

Enter the total of the amounts entered in columns (1) and (2). The amount in column (3) should be the same as the amount on line 5.

Line 15—Net Long-Term Capital Gain or Loss

Allocate the net long-term capital gain or loss on line 15 in the same manner as the net short-term capital gain or loss on line 14. However, **do not** take the section 1202 exclusion on gain from the sale or exchange of qualified small business stock into account when figuring net long-term capital gain or loss allocable to the beneficiaries.

Part IV—Capital Loss Limitation

If the sum of all the capital losses is more than the sum of all the capital gains, then these capital losses are allowed as a deduction only to the extent of the smaller of the net loss or $3,000.

For any year (including the final year) in which capital losses exceed capital gains, the estate or trust may have a capital loss carryover. Use the **Capital Loss Carryover Worksheet** on page 27 to figure any capital loss carryover. A capital loss carryover may be carried forward indefinitely. Capital losses keep their character as either short-term or long-term when carried over to the following year.

Part V—Tax Computation Using Maximum Capital Gains Rate

Line 21

If the estate or trust received capital gains that were derived from income in respect of a decedent, and a section 691(c)(4) deduction was claimed, then line 21 must be reduced by the portion of the section 691(c)(4) deduction claimed on Form 1041, page 1, line 19.

Line 53

If the tax using the maximum capital gains rate (line 51) is less than the regular tax (line 52), enter the amount from line 53 on line 1a of Schedule G, Form 1041, and check the "Schedule D" box.

Schedule J (Form 1041) — Accumulation Distribution for Certain Complex Trusts

A Change To Note

For distributions made in tax years beginning after August 5, 1997, the Taxpayer Relief Act of 1997 generally repealed the throwback rules for domestic trusts. However, the throwback rules continue to apply to any domestic trust that was:

- Previously treated at any time as a foreign trust (unless an exception is provided in future regulations), or
- Created before March 1, 1984, unless that trust would not be aggregated with other trusts under the rules of section 643(f) if that section applied to the trust.

General Instructions

Use Schedule J (Form 1041) to report an accumulation distribution for a complex trust to which the throwback rules continue to apply (as explained above). An accumulation distribution is the excess of amounts properly paid, credited, or required to be distributed (other than income required to be distributed currently) over the DNI of the trust reduced by income required to be distributed currently. To have an accumulation distribution, the distribution must exceed the accounting income of the trust.

Specific Instructions

Part I—Accumulation Distribution in 1998

Line 1—Distribution Under Section 661(a)(2)

Enter the amount from Schedule B of Form 1041, line 10, for 1998. This is the amount properly paid, credited, or required to be distributed other than the amount of income for the current tax year required to be distributed currently.

Line 2—Distributable Net Income

Enter the amount from Schedule B of Form 1041, line 7, for 1998. This is the amount of distributable net income (DNI) for the current tax year determined under section 643(a).

Line 3—Distribution Under Section 661(a)(1)

Enter the amount from Schedule B of Form 1041, line 9, for 1998. This is the amount of income for the current tax year required to be distributed currently.

Line 5—Accumulation Distribution

If line 11, Schedule B of Form 1041 is more than line 8, Schedule B of Form 1041, complete the rest of Schedule J and file it with Form 1041, unless the trust has no previously accumulated income.

Generally, amounts accumulated before a beneficiary reaches age 21 may be excluded by the beneficiary. See sections 665 and 667(c) for exceptions relating to multiple trusts. The trustee reports to the IRS the total amount of the accumulation distribution before any reduction for income accumulated before the beneficiary reaches age 21. If the multiple trust rules do not apply, the beneficiary claims the exclusion when filing **Form 4970,** Tax on Accumulation Distribution of Trusts, as you may not be aware that the beneficiary may be a beneficiary of other trusts with other trustees.

For examples of accumulation distributions that include payments from one trust to another trust, and amounts distributed for a dependent's support, see Regulations section 1.665(b)-1A(b).

Part II—Ordinary Income Accumulation Distribution

Line 6—Distributable Net Income for Earlier Years

Enter the applicable amounts as follows:

Throwback year(s)	Amount from line
1969–1977	Schedule C, Form 1041, line 5
1978–1979	Form 1041, line 61
1980	Form 1041, line 60
1981–1982	Form 1041, line 58
1983–1996	Schedule B, Form 1041, line 9
1997	Schedule B, Form 1041, line 7

For information about throwback years, see the instructions for line 13. For purposes of line 6, in figuring the DNI of the trust for a throwback year, subtract any estate tax deduction for income in respect of a decedent if the income is includible in figuring the DNI of the trust for that year.

Line 7—Distributions Made During Earlier Years

Enter the applicable amounts as follows:

Throwback year(s)	Amount from line
1969–1977	Schedule C, Form 1041, line 8
1978	Form 1041, line 64
1979	Form 1041, line 65
1980	Form 1041, line 64
1981–1982	Form 1041, line 62
1983–1996	Schedule B, Form 1041, line 13
1997	Schedule B, Form 1041, line 11

Line 11—Prior Accumulation Distribution Thrown Back to any Throwback Year

Enter the amount of prior accumulation distributions thrown back to the throwback years. Do not enter distributions excluded under section 663(a)(1) for gifts, bequests, etc.

Line 13—Throwback Years

Allocate the amount on line 5 that is an accumulation distribution to the earliest applicable year first, but do not allocate more than the amount on line 12 for any throwback year. An accumulation distribution is thrown back first to the earliest preceding tax year in which there is undistributed net income (UNI). Then, it is thrown back beginning with the next earliest year to any remaining preceding tax years of the trust. The portion of the accumulation distribution allocated to the earliest preceding tax year is the amount of the UNI for that year. The portion of the accumulation distribution allocated to any remaining preceding tax year is the amount by which the accumulation distribution is larger than the total of the UNI for all earlier preceding tax years.

A tax year of a trust during which the trust was a simple trust for the entire year is not a preceding tax year unless **(a)** during that year the trust received outside income or **(b)** the trustee did not distribute all of the trust's income that was required to be distributed currently for that year. In this case, UNI for that year must not be more than the greater of the outside income or income not distributed during that year.

The term "outside income" means amounts that are included in the DNI of the trust for that year but that are not "income" of the trust as defined in Regulations section 1.643(b)-1. Some examples of outside income are: **(a)** income taxable to the trust under section 691; **(b)** unrealized accounts receivable that were assigned to the trust; and **(c)** distributions from another trust that include the DNI or UNI of the other trust. Enter the applicable year at the top of each column for each throwback year.

Line 16—Tax-Exempt Interest Included on Line 13

For each throwback year, divide line 15 by line 6 and multiply the result by the following:

Throwback year(s)	Amount from line
1969–1977	Schedule C, Form 1041, line 2(a)
1978–1979	Form 1041, line 58(a)
1980	Form 1041, line 57(a)
1981–1982	Form 1041, line 55(a)
1983–1997	Schedule B, Form 1041, line 2

Part III—Taxes Imposed on Undistributed Net Income

For the regular tax computation, if there is a capital gain, complete lines 18 through 25 for each throwback year. If the trustee elected the alternative tax on capital gains, complete lines 26 through 31 instead of lines 18 through 25 for each applicable year. If there is no capital gain for any year, or there is a capital loss for every year, enter on line 9 the amount of the tax for each year identified in the instruction for line 18 and do not complete Part III. If the trust received an accumulation distribution from another trust, see Regulations section 1.665(b)-1A.

Note: *The alternative tax on capital gains was repealed for tax years beginning after December 31, 1978. The maximum rate on net capital gain for 1981, 1987, and 1991 through 1997 is not an alternative tax for this purpose.*

Line 18—Regular Tax

Enter the applicable amounts as follows:

Throwback year(s)	Amount from line
1969–1976	Form 1041, page 1, line 24
1977	Form 1041, page 1, line 26
1978–1979	Form 1041, line 27
1980–1984	Form 1041, line 26c
1985–1986	Form 1041, line 25c
1987	Form 1041, line 22c
1988–1997	Schedule G, Form 1041, line 1a

Line 19—Trust's Share of Net Short-Term Gain

For each throwback year, enter the smaller of the capital gain from the two lines indicated. If there is a capital loss or a zero on either or both of the two lines indicated, enter zero on line 19.

Throwback year(s)	Amount from line
1969–1970	Schedule D, Line 10, column 2, or Schedule D, line 12, column 2
1971–1978	Schedule D, line 14, column 2, or Schedule D, line 16, column 2
1979	Schedule D, line 18, column (b), or Schedule D, line 20, column (b)
1980–1981	Schedule D, line 14, column (b), or Schedule D, line 16, column (b)
1982	Schedule D, line 16, column (b), or Schedule D, line 18, column (b)
1983–1996	Schedule D, line 15, column (b), or Schedule D, line 17, column (b)
1997	Schedule D, line 14, column (2), or Schedule D, line 16, column (2)

Line 20—Trust's Share of Net Long-Term Gain

Enter the applicable amounts as follows:

Throwback year(s)	Amount from line
1969–1970	50% of Schedule D, line 13(e)
1971–1977	50% of Schedule D, line 17(e)
1978	Schedule D, line 17(e), or line 31, whichever is applicable, less Form 1041, line 23
1979	Schedule D, line 25 or line 27, whichever is applicable, less Form 1041, line 23
1980–1981	Schedule D, line 21, less Schedule D, line 22
1982	Schedule D, line 23, less Schedule D, line 24
1983–1986	Schedule D, line 22, less Schedule D, line 23
1987–1996	Schedule D, the smaller of any gain on line 16 or line 17, column (b)
1997	Schedule D, the smaller of any gain on line 15c or line 16, column (2)

Line 22—Taxable Income

Enter the applicable amounts as follows:

Throwback year(s)	Amount from line
1969–1976	Form 1041, page 1, line 23
1977	Form 1041, page 1, line 25
1978–1979	Form 1041, line 26
1980–1984	Form 1041, line 25
1985–1986	Form 1041, line 24
1987	Form 1041, line 21
1988–1996	Form 1041, line 22
1997	Form 1041, line 23

Line 26—Tax on Income Other Than Long-Term Capital Gain

Enter the applicable amounts as follows:

Throwback year(s)	Amount from line
1969	Schedule D, line 20
1970	Schedule D, line 19
1971	Schedule D, line 50
1972–1975	Schedule D, line 48
1976–1978	Schedule D, line 27

Line 27—Trust's Share of Net Short-Term Gain

If there is a loss on any of the following lines, enter zero on line 27 for the applicable throwback year. Otherwise, enter the applicable amounts as follows:

Throwback year(s)	Amount from line
1969–1970	Schedule D, line 10, column 2
1971–1978	Schedule D, line 14, column 2

Line 28—Trust's Share of Taxable Income Less Section 1202 Deduction

Enter the applicable amounts as follows:

Throwback year(s)	Amount from line
1969	Schedule D, line 19
1970	Schedule D, line 18
1971	Schedule D, line 38
1972–1975	Schedule D, line 39
1976–1978	Schedule D, line 21

Part IV—Allocation to Beneficiary

Complete Part IV for each beneficiary. If the accumulation distribution is allocated to more than one beneficiary, attach an additional copy of Schedule J with Part IV completed for each additional beneficiary. Give each beneficiary a copy of his or her respective Part IV information. If more than 5 throwback years are involved, use another Schedule J, completing Parts II and III for each additional throwback year.

If the beneficiary is a nonresident alien individual or a foreign corporation, see section 667(e) about retaining the character of the amounts distributed to determine the amount of the U.S. withholding tax.

The beneficiary uses Form 4970 to figure the tax on the distribution. The beneficiary also uses Form 4970 for the section 667(b)(6) tax adjustment if an accumulation distribution is subject to estate or generation-skipping transfer tax. This is because the trustee may not be the estate or generation-skipping transfer tax return filer.

Schedule K-1 (Form 1041)—Beneficiary's Share of Income, Deductions, Credits, etc.

General Instructions

Use Schedule K-1 (Form 1041) to report the beneficiary's share of income, deductions, and credits from a trust or a decedent's estate.

Who Must File

The fiduciary (or one of the joint fiduciaries) must file Schedule K-1. A copy of each beneficiary's Schedule K-1 is attached to the Form 1041 filed with the IRS and each beneficiary is given a copy of his or her respective Schedule K-1. One copy of each Schedule K-1 must be retained for the fiduciary's records.

Beneficiary's Identifying Number

As a payer of income, you are required under section 6109 to request and provide a proper identifying number for each recipient of income. Enter the beneficiary's number on the respective Schedule K-1 when you file Form 1041. Individuals and business recipients are responsible for giving you their taxpayer identification numbers upon request. You may use **Form W-9**, Request for Taxpayer Identification Number and

Certification, to request the beneficiary's identifying number.

Penalty. Under section 6723, the payer is charged a $50 penalty for each failure to provide a required taxpayer identification number, unless reasonable cause is established for not providing it. Explain any reasonable cause in a signed affidavit and attach it to this return.

Tax Shelter's Identification Number

If the estate or trust is a tax shelter, is involved in a tax shelter, or is considered to be the organizer of a tax shelter, there are reporting requirements under section 6111 for both the fiduciaries and the beneficiaries.

See **Form 8264,** Application for Registration of a Tax Shelter, and **Form 8271,** Investor Reporting of Tax Shelter Registration Number, and their related instructions for information regarding the fiduciary's reporting requirements.

Substitute Forms

You do not need prior IRS approval for a substitute Schedule K-1 (Form 1041) that follows the specifications for filing substitute Schedules K-1 in **Pub. 1167,** Substitute Printed, Computer-Prepared, and Computer-Generated Tax Forms and Schedules, or is an exact copy of an IRS Schedule K-1. You must request IRS approval to use other substitute Schedules K-1. To request approval, write to: Internal Revenue Service, Attention: Substitute Forms Program Coordinator, OP:FS:FP:F:CD, 1111 Constitution Avenue, NW, Washington, DC 20224.

Inclusion of Amounts in Beneficiaries' Income

Simple trust. The beneficiary of a simple trust must include in his or her gross income the amount of the income required to be distributed currently, whether or not distributed, or if the income required to be distributed currently to all beneficiaries exceeds the distributable net income (DNI), his or her proportionate share of the DNI. The determination of whether trust income is required to be distributed currently depends on the terms of the trust instrument and applicable local law. See Regulations section 1.652(c)-4 for a comprehensive example.

Estates and complex trusts. The beneficiary of a decedent's estate or complex trust must include in his or her gross income the sum of:

1. The amount of the income required to be distributed currently, or if the income required to be distributed currently to all beneficiaries exceeds the DNI (figured without taking into account the charitable deduction), his or her proportionate share of the DNI (as so figured); and

2. All other amounts properly paid, credited, or required to be distributed, or if the sum of the income required to be distributed currently and other amounts properly paid, credited, or required to be distributed to all beneficiaries exceeds the DNI, his or her proportionate share of the excess of DNI over the income required to be distributed currently.

See Regulations section 1.662(c)-4 for a comprehensive example.

For complex trusts that have more than one beneficiary, and if different beneficiaries have substantially separate and independent shares, their shares are treated as separate trusts for the sole purpose of determining the amount of DNI allocable to the respective beneficiaries. For the estates of decedents dying after August 5, 1997, a similar rule applies to treat substantially separate and independent shares of different beneficiaries of an estate as separate estates. For examples of the application of the separate share rule, see the regulations under section 663(c).

Character of income. The beneficiary's income is considered to have the same proportion of each class of items entering into the computation of DNI that the total of each class has to the DNI (e.g., half dividends and half interest if the income of the estate or trust is half dividends and half interest).

Allocation of deductions. Generally, items of deduction that enter into the computation of DNI are allocated among the items of income to the extent such allocation is not inconsistent with the rules set out in section 469 and its regulations, relating to passive activity loss limitations, in the following order.

First, all deductions directly attributable to a specific class of income are deducted from that income. For example, rental expenses, to the extent allowable, are deducted from rental income.

Second, deductions that are not directly attributable to a specific class of income generally may be allocated to any class of income, as long as a reasonable portion is allocated to any tax-exempt income. Deductions considered not directly attributable to a specific class of income under this rule include fiduciary fees, safe deposit box rental charges, and state income and personal property taxes. The charitable deduction, however, must be ratably apportioned among each class of income included in DNI.

Finally, any excess deductions that are directly attributable to a class of income may be allocated to another class of income. However, in no case can excess deductions from a passive activity be allocated to income from a nonpassive activity, or to portfolio income earned by the estate or trust. Excess deductions attributable to tax-exempt income cannot offset any other class of income.

In no case can deductions be allocated to an item of income that is not included in the computation of DNI, or attributable to corpus.

Except for the final year, and for depreciation or depletion allocations in excess of income (see Rev. Rul. 74-530, 1974-2 C.B. 188), you may not show any negative amounts for any class of income, because the beneficiary generally may not claim losses or deductions from the estate or trust.

Gifts and bequests. Do not include in the beneficiary's income any gifts or bequests of a specific sum of money or of specific property under the terms of the governing instrument that are paid or credited in three installments or less.

Amounts that can be paid or credited only from income of the estate or trust do not qualify as a gift or bequest of a specific sum of money.

Past years. Do not include in the beneficiary's income any amounts deducted on Form 1041 for an earlier year that were credited or required to be distributed in that earlier year.

Beneficiary's Tax Year

The beneficiary's income from the estate or trust must be included in the beneficiary's tax year during which the tax year of the estate or trust ends. See Pub. 559 for more information, including the effect of the death of a beneficiary during the tax year of the estate or trust.

Specific Instructions

Line 1—Interest

Enter the beneficiary's share of the taxable interest income minus allocable deductions.

Line 2—Ordinary Dividends

Enter the beneficiary's share of ordinary dividends minus allocable deductions.

Line 3—Net Short-Term Capital Gain

Enter the beneficiary's share of the net short-term capital gain from line 14, column (1), Schedule D (Form 1041), minus allocable deductions. Do not enter a loss on line 3. If, for the final year of the estate or trust, there is a capital loss carryover, enter on line 13b the beneficiary's share of short-term capital loss carryover. However, if the beneficiary is a corporation, enter on line 13b the beneficiary's share of all short- and long-term capital loss carryovers as a single item. See section 642(h) and related regulations for more information.

Lines 4a through 4c—Net Long-Term Capital Gain

Enter the beneficiary's share of the net long-term capital gain from lines 15a through 15c, column (1), Schedule D (Form 1041), minus allocable deductions. Do not enter a loss on lines 4a through 4c. If, for the final year of the estate or trust, there is a capital loss carryover, enter on line 13c the beneficiary's share of the long-term capital loss carryover. (If the beneficiary is a corporation, see the instructions for line 3.) See section 642(h) and related regulations for more information.

Gains or losses from the complete or partial disposition of a rental, rental real estate, or trade or business activity that is a passive activity, must be shown on an attachment to Schedule K-1.

Line 5a—Annuities, Royalties, and Other Nonpassive Income

Enter the beneficiary's share of annuities, royalties, or any other income, minus allocable deductions (other than directly apportionable deductions), that is NOT subject to any passive activity loss limitation rules at the beneficiary level. Use line 6a to report income items subject to the passive activity rules at the beneficiary's level.

Lines 5b and 6b—Depreciation

Enter the beneficiary's share of the depreciation deductions attributable to each activity reported on lines 5a and 6a. See the instructions on page 11 for a discussion of how the depreciation deduction is apportioned between the beneficiaries and the estate or trust. Report any AMT adjustment or tax preference item attributable to depreciation separately on line 12a.

Note: *An estate or trust cannot make an election under section 179 to expense certain tangible property.*

Lines 5c and 6c—Depletion

Enter the beneficiary's share of the depletion deduction under section 611 attributable to each activity reported on lines 5a and 6a. See the instructions on page 11 for a discussion of how the depletion deduction is apportioned between the beneficiaries and the estate or trust. Report any tax preference item attributable to depletion separately on line 12b.

Lines 5d and 6d—Amortization

Itemize the beneficiary's share of the amortization deductions attributable to each activity reported on lines 5a and 6a. Apportion the amortization deductions between the estate or trust and the beneficiaries in the same way that the depreciation and depletion deductions are divided. Report any AMT adjustment attributable to amortization separately on line 12c.

Line 6a—Trade or Business, Rental Real Estate, and Other Rental Income

Enter the beneficiary's share of trade or business, rental real estate, and other rental income, minus allocable deductions (other than directly apportionable deductions). To assist the beneficiary in figuring any applicable passive activity loss limitations, also attach a separate schedule showing the beneficiary's share of income derived from each trade or business, rental real estate, and other rental activity.

Lines 6b Through 6d

Caution: *The limitations on passive activity losses and credits under section 469 apply to estates and trusts. Estates and trusts that distribute income to beneficiaries are allowed to apportion depreciation, depletion, and amortization deductions to the beneficiaries. These deductions are referred to as "directly apportionable deductions."*

Rules for treating a beneficiary's income and directly apportionable deductions from an estate or trust and other rules for applying the passive loss and credit limitations to beneficiaries of estates and trusts have not yet been issued.

Any directly apportionable deduction, such as depreciation, is treated by the beneficiary as having been incurred in the same activity as incurred by the estate or trust. However, the character of such deduction may be determined as if the beneficiary incurred the deduction directly.

To assist the beneficiary in figuring any applicable passive activity loss limitations, also attach a separate schedule showing the beneficiary's share of directly apportionable deductions derived from each trade or business, rental real estate, and other rental activity.

Line 7—Income for Minimum Tax Purposes

Enter the beneficiary's share of the income distribution deduction figured on a minimum tax basis from line 27 of Schedule I.

Line 8—Income for Regular Tax Purposes

Enter the beneficiary's share of the income distribution deduction figured on line 15 of Schedule B. This amount should equal the sum of lines 1 through 3, 4c, 5a, and 6a.

Line 10—Estate Tax Deduction (Including Certain Generation-Skipping Transfer Taxes)

If the distribution deduction consists of any income in respect of a decedent, and the estate or trust was allowed a deduction under section 691(c) for the estate tax paid attributable to such income (see the line 19 instructions on page 14), then the beneficiary is allowed an estate tax deduction in proportion to his or her share of the distribution that consists of such income. For an example of the computation, see Regulations section 1.691(c)-2. Figure the computation on a separate sheet and attach it to the return.

Line 11—Foreign Taxes

List on a separate sheet the beneficiary's share of the applicable foreign taxes paid or accrued and the various foreign source figures needed to figure the beneficiary's foreign tax credit. See Pub. 514 and section 901(b)(5) for special rules about foreign taxes.

Lines 12a through 12c

Enter any adjustments or tax preference items attributable to depreciation, depletion, or amortization that were allocated to the beneficiary. For property placed in service before 1987, report separately the accelerated depreciation of real and leased personal property.

Line 12d—Exclusion Items

Enter the beneficiary's share of the adjustment for minimum tax purposes from Schedule K-1, line 9, that is attributable to exclusion items (Schedule I, lines 4a through 4d, 4p, and 4q).

Line 13a—Excess Deductions on Termination

If this is the final return of the estate or trust, and there are excess deductions on termination (see the instructions for line 22 on page 14), enter the beneficiary's share of the excess deductions on line 13a. Figure the deductions on a separate sheet and attach it to the return.

Excess deductions on termination occur only during the last tax year of the trust or decedent's estate when the total deductions (excluding the charitable deduction and exemption) are greater than the gross income during that tax year.

Generally, a deduction based on an NOL carryover is not available to a beneficiary as an excess deduction. However, if the last tax year of the estate or trust is also the last year in which an NOL carryover may be taken (see section 172(b)), the NOL carryover is considered an excess deduction on the termination of the estate or trust to the extent it is not absorbed by the estate or trust during its final tax year. For more information, see Regulations section 1.642(h)-4 for a discussion of the allocation of the carryover among the beneficiaries.

Only the beneficiary of an estate or trust that succeeds to its property is allowed to deduct that entity's excess deductions on termination. A beneficiary who does not have enough income in that year to absorb the entire deduction may not carry the balance over to any succeeding year. An individual beneficiary must be able to itemize deductions in order to claim the excess deductions in determining taxable income.

Lines 13b and 13c—Unused Capital Loss Carryover

Upon termination of the trust or decedent's estate, the beneficiary succeeding to the property is allowed as a deduction any unused capital loss carryover under section 1212. If the estate or trust incurs capital losses in the final year, use the **Capital Loss Carryover Worksheet** on page 27 to figure the amount of capital loss carryover to be allocated to the beneficiary.

Lines 13d and 13e—Net Operating Loss (NOL) Carryover

Upon termination of a trust or decedent's estate, a beneficiary succeeding to its property is allowed to deduct any unused NOL (and any AMT NOL) carryover for regular and AMT purposes if the carryover would be allowable to the estate or trust in a later tax year but for the termination. Enter on lines 13d and 13e the unused carryover amounts.